PENGUIN BOOKS

STOMPIN' TOM: BEFORE THE FAME

Singer/songwriter Stompin' Tom Connors has written hundreds of songs familiar to Canadians from coast to coast. Many of his thirty-nine albums have gone gold, and he has probably appeared in more towns than any other performer in Canadian history.

Tom Connors lives in the countryside of southwestern Ontario with his wife, Lena, and son, Tom.

TO: Bob

FROM: Gwen

"2000"

Stompin' Tom Connors

STOMPIN' TOM
Before the Fame

Penguin Books

PENGUIN BOOKS
Published by the Penguin Group
Penguin Books Canada Ltd, 10 Alcorn Avenue, Toronto, Ontario,
Canada M4V 3B2
Penguin Books Ltd, 27 Wrights Lane, London W8 5TZ, England
Penguin Books USA Inc., 375 Hudson Street, New York,
New York 10014, U.S.A.
Penguin Books Australia Ltd, Ringwood, Victoria, Australia
Penguin Books (NZ) Ltd, 182-190 Wairau Road, Auckland 10,
New Zealand

Penguin Books Ltd, Registered Offices: Harmondsworth,
Middlesex, England

First published in Viking by Penguin Books Canada Limited, 1995

Published in Penguin Books, 1996

1 3 5 7 9 10 8 6 4 2

Manufactured in Canada

Canadian Cataloguing in Publication Data

Connors, Stompin' Tom, 1936-
Stompin' Tom

Contents: v. 1. Before the fame.
Includes discography.
ISBN 0-14-025111-1 (v. 1)

1. Connors, Stompin' Tom, 1936-   . 2. Country musicians -
Canada - Biography. I. Title.

ML420.C743A3 1996   782.42164'2'092   C95-933125-5

*I hereby dedicate this book
to the orphans of the world,
to the struggling artists everywhere,
to all my fans and friends,
and especially to the black-haired lady
with the missing thumb.*

*I would also like to express my
sincere thanks to John Farrington,
whose help and encouragement
provided the incentive for me to go
back and finish the writing of this book:
a project I had begun and abandoned
some fifteen years earlier.*

Contents

Foreword

Stompin' Tom. There isn't a Canadian who doesn't know him. Right?

They know him because he once wrote a song about their home town, or about this beautiful country we live in. They know him as a man who loves Canada as much as any person who has ever lived here. They know him as someone with roots in Skinners Pond, Prince Edward Island. And they know him because he entertains Canadians like no one else has ever done before.

And, of course, you say, they know him as the man who stomps his foot when he's performing and has to carry a piece of three-quarter-inch plywood with him— his own stomping board—to protect the stage from being gouged by his pounding cowboy boots.

But what do Canadians really know about the man they call Stompin' Tom, the Canadian Legend.

Well, surprise! surprise! I've known Tom for thirty years, since his early days in 1964 when he played at the Maple Leaf Hotel in Timmins, Ontario. That is, I thought I knew him, but I didn't. I've since had many surprises, and, I'm sure, you too will be amazed at this marvellous man, who has become nothing short of an inspiration to us all.

This autobiography, long overdue, will support the "Legend" name tag and will give you a true insight into the man who has been a household name for three decades. A man who has given two generations of Canadians a reason to be proud of their country, a reason to stand up and be counted, and a reason to carry on towards success, even in the face of extreme adversity. This autobiography will, at long last, begin to show us just how much we really didn't know about this truly mysterious Canadian who has captured the admiration of so many, while at the same time revealing so little of himself.

While his schooling was sparse, his travels were very

extensive. And in the struggle to survive he tackled many jobs along the way. These were the experiences that so often found their way into the many songs he wrote as he tenaciously clung to the dream of someday becoming a recording star.

This down-but-never-out drifter went on to become the man we all know today as Stompin' Tom, and this book will give you a close look at the heart-breaking early years of Tom Connors, before he ever acquired his stage name.

This volume is like no other autobiography ever written by anyone, anywhere in the world, period. When you read it you'll wonder how anyone could recover psychologically from such a horrible childhood, let alone go on to become a truly great Canadian, even suggested by some as a man who should be appointed prime minister of Canada to clear up the mess governments have managed to get us in.

This book will motivate all of us to better ourselves, our families, and our country. There is never a time to feel sorry for yourself. If Tom had ever had those thoughts he would still be a drifter and a bum, or he might never have awakened from one of those bitter, forty-below nights under a park bench or in a speeding cattle car on a freight train.

That would have been a tragedy.

Reading about Stompin' Tom in *Before the Fame* will put you so close to this guitar-playing drifter that you will feel you have walked every step with him on what seemed to be an impossible journey on his way to becoming one of Canada's greatest living legends.

John A. Farrington
January 1995

Introduction

Hi! I'm Stompin' Tom Connors, and this is my story. Every word is my own, and it's all true. I wouldn't have it any other way.

It's also long. But I've done a lot of things in my life that deserve to be made known, and I sure can't tell you about them in a few pages. If you want to know me, you'll have to take the time to read about me. And if at times you find the going tough, it's because my life has been tough. Nothing ever came easy to me.

Ninety-nine per cent of everything you read here comes from memory. No notes were ever written, and no diaries were ever kept. Consequently, the rare chronological discrepancy may be discovered, but when you consider that the average person cannot remember anything about his own life prior to the age of about five, and then only skimpy flashes of scenes thereafter for the next few years, you may come to the conclusion that either I have a remarkable memory, or I have fabricated the whole damn thing.

Well, before you go any further, let me assure you that the latter is not the case, and the truth is what I intend to tell. My memory started working clearly when I was about nine months old, and it has rarely failed me since.

Consequently, if I should put all the things I want to say in one book, the size would be enormous and the price would be outrageous. Therefore, to conserve space, I have purposely left some topics out. And one of them is my love life.

Some people might say, "Whoa! Now. Just a minute. A story with no 'spice'?" And why would I want to put out a book with none of that "juicy stuff" in it? Something that would really be sure to make the book sell?

Well, I'm not writing this story about my life simply to sell books and make money. I am writing it so people will read and hopefully understand in some way how my years as a boy and a young man have contributed to the principles, outspokenness and sense of fair play that I've tried to bring to Canada's music industry in later life. And to ensure that my reasons are presented with adequate background, I will need all the extra space I can get.

I do have my priorities. And presenting you with a book full of dirt, just to make a buck, would go against everything I stand for. For those who just have to know—yes, I've had lovers in my life, but I've been happily married now for twenty-one years, and I intend to keep it that way.

Suffice it to say that my opinions about love are just as strong as my opinions about life, the government, the music business, the media, religion, philosophy and all the rest of that stuff. And if you care to know me, read on.

In order to get my points across, I have taken pains to explain my inner feelings throughout this work. And, once again, this story is true. I know because I lived it and will probably continue to do so, through memory, for the rest of my life.

I have been a bum. And I could be a bum again. Right now I am comfortable, and if I am careful I may never have to do manual work again. It has not been easy, but I have had some fun along the way.

I believe I have been able to make something of myself because I have principles and persistence. And if the cause were great enough, I would give my life, forsake my friends and I guess even my family for my principles. They are that important to me.

It is difficult for me to sit and write this book, but I have been asked so many times to let people into my private life. The media seem to think I'm some sort of a mystery man because I don't give many interviews. But because so much b.s. has been written about me by now I don't want to waste my time...or theirs...or yours. I just want the opportunity to set the record straight.

One thing I feel I have to state right up front is that I

am not going to tell you anything just for the sake of dressing up a story. And I can promise you that if there's only one thing you're going to find out about me by the time you finish this book, it is that I always strive to be honest in all my dealings. I don't have too many of the airs and graces that a lot of people like to put on when they've made it. In fact, I don't have any.

Because I believe in my country and because I write and sing about it, many people consider me a hero to Canadians and especially to the working class, but to me I'm only doing what I feel each proud citizen of this country should be doing. And that is to try to put in as much as he takes out. I guess it's to the hard knocks of life that I attribute this conclusion.

The mystery that surrounds me is something that has built up over the years. I didn't set out to create a special image. It was created for me, partially by the media. And, to be honest, I have sometimes enjoyed playing along. But now you're going to find out what's under the big black cowboy hat. I know you're going to be surprised. There will be times when you are shocked. And times, I'm sure, you'll be in tears. You'll smile and you'll cry, I can guarantee that.

You'll find out there's a lot more to me than plywood boards, cowboy boots and black cowboy hats. And what you're about to read is the first thirty-one years of my life when there was no STOMPIN' TOM. Just plain Tom. Just ordinary Tom. But sometimes not so "ordinary."

Stompin' Tom
January 1995

First Memories

I was somewhere around the nine-month mark, so it would have been close to Christmas 1936. And though I had seen the light of day only a few months earlier, today would be the first time that anything would be impressed vividly enough on my mind to remain and be stored in my memory forever.

Let me set the stage for you. The scene is a kitchen with an iron stove to my left, a couch to my right and a wooden table straight ahead. I am sitting on the floor and people are walking around.

There are some objects near me on the floor which seem to belong to me: a brown, cuddly teddy bear, a stuffed dog I like to hug, and a few blocks of wood, the kind you would find sawed off the end of boards, or two-by-fours.

There were many more things in this room. Four doors, two windows, a couch, a number of chairs and a solitary, stark, shadeless light bulb hanging in the middle of the ceiling from a long cord.

I seemed to be delighted with my ability to move around, although some times I landed in places I didn't want to go.

I remember being carried from place to place by many people. I didn't know who they were, or what, if any, relationship they had to me.

On this particular day, two or three people made me do something I had never done before. They set up an alarm clock on a chair some distance from me and they knew I wanted it. Oh, how I wanted it.

But I was afraid to go and get it because someone had stood me on my feet, had taken their hands away from supporting me and left me feeling very insecure; I had never walked before.

Still I felt that if I could get my hands on that clock it would be mine. And the amount of coaxing that was going on was distracting me from my fear of falling.

Without realizing what I was doing, I walked over to the chair and put both hands around my wonderful reward, amid loud shouts of laughter and excitement.

It was only after I had walked to the clock that I realized what I had done.

But it wasn't really the walking, so much as the stir I had caused, that filled me with the willingness and desire that made me want to be sure to try that again sometime. So my first steps were completed. I had had an audience, and I liked it. I was a showman back then and I loved it. I still love being a showman today, but usually only on the stage.

When I sit quietly today in my workshop, with a beer in one hand and a cigarette in the other, I can delve deep into my memory and picture this kitchen back in Saint John almost sixty years ago.

It's as clear to me now as it was back then.

Although the people around me appeared as mere shadows or part of the walls or furniture most of the time, they were periodically taking on individual characteristics. It became my greatest preoccupation to summon, disturb or attract these forms in every way I could and whenever the urge prompted me.

As a robust baby, I took great delight in this game because it seemed to please me to no end, just knowing I had acquired this power to move others, as well as moving myself.

As time went on, I seemed to prefer the people who were most likely to be influenced by my little game over those who were more interested in whatever they were doing than what I was doing. I preferred to go for the sure bets—the ones who would take time to play games with me.

I hadn't grasped the meaning or the use of names yet, so I began to know people by their actions.

For instance, Grampy was the one who always scratched his back against the hall door. (For some unknown reason I always wanted to do that, too, though

I suspect it was not so much to obtain relief from an itching back as it was to attract attention.)

Grammy was always cooking, mixing and rattling things in the pantry, on the stove and around the kitchen table, and best of all, giving me things to eat, or to play with, to keep me occupied.

Uncle Aubrey used to sit me on his lap at the table whenever they were playing cards.

Aunt Beattie used to take me and tickle my face with a feather until I would laugh so much that I soon grew tired and sleepy and became oblivious as to how I got to bed.

Then there was Isabel, my mother. She seemed to be nothing more at first than an extension of myself—like my hands, which brought the things I wanted to my mouth.

I didn't consider her as being another person. The feeling could possibly be described better by saying that she was something like a nipple, a sleep or a diaper change. These had always been with me before I became aware of the things around me, and by now had become so commonplace that the only time I was concerned about them was when I needed them...and they weren't there.

I was moving around the house now with much greater mobility and discovering many more things, such as lost pennies, bobby pins, chewing gum stuck under chairs and a rat hole gnawed through the corner of the pantry door.

I remember this hole quite well. I shoved anything I could find through it before pestering the life out of anyone handy to come and open the door so that I could regain my lost possessions.

I woke up one morning a number of months later to find that several torn pieces of cloth and a few clumps of straw were all that was left of my little stuffed dog. Although I didn't quite get the connection at the time, I somehow sensed by the tone of the adult conversation that there was something ominous about the word "rats."

I never did see the rat, but that's probably due to the cat.

And it's funny, as observant as I remember being, I was not aware of the cat in the house until one day I decided to check out the old blanket that was always draped over the couch and hung down to the floor on all sides.

As soon as I was able I did what any curious kid would do—stuck my head under the blanket.

Ahhhhhhhhhhhhhhhhhh!

There were two big green eyes glaring at me from out of the darkness. Half petrified and half bewildered, I soon pulled my head back and sat there not knowing whether to cry, howl or just quietly wait until I got my diaper changed. It scared me all right. Probably the first time I had experienced fear in my life.

It turned out that this was my first encounter with our not-too-sociable cat, who obviously was more familiar with rats than me. Thinking back to it now, and considering all the pestering from me that cat was eventually going to get, it's no wonder he chose to remain anti-social. He was probably psychic and merely trying to postpone the inevitable.

I hated getting my face washed and going to bed. Isabel didn't rank highly in my book of favourite people because she was the one who forced me to do both these things.

She would get everybody to kiss me, hug me and make such a big fuss of me. By the time I was all worked up to the point of wanting to play again, she expected me to quietly lie down and go off to sleep.

It didn't work. How many times I pulled myself up by the iron bars in my crib after she left the room, I don't remember.

It was on one of these occasions, while I was walking back and forth and holding onto the side of the crib, wondering how I would get out, that I heard a commotion in the kitchen.

After some loud talking, I somehow knew we had visitors and before long I heard familiar footsteps coming down the hallway. It was Uncle Aubrey. He peeked into my room and, seeing that I was awake, came in and hugged me.

To this day I don't know whether what he did next was meant to be a prank, but it became the greatest boon to me and the biggest headache for my mother.

He took my hand in his, then ran my fingers over the latches at both ends of the crib. He held my hands and showed me how to push the latches to make the side of the crib come down. Two or three times we did that.

When he made sure I was secure, with the sides of the crib up, he tapped me on the head and left the room. I don't know how long it took me to get that crib side down and crawl out of the bedroom and down the long hallway into the kitchen. But there I was again, the centre of attention, as the look of amazement on everybody's face could only have been matched by the loud howls of laughter coming from Uncle Aubrey.

While I revelled in this first crib escape—which, by the way, gained me many hugs and kisses—the second break-out had different consequences. I don't know whether it was the following night, it doesn't really matter, but there I was crawling down the long hallway, when suddenly a door opened (the bathroom door, I would later learn) and out popped Isabel. She quickly scooped me off the floor, let me have a few whacks across the bottom and quite determinedly tucked me back into the crib.

This was the first time the amount of my crying had been exceeded by the amount of shock received. And while I lay there contemplating the meaning of this new turn of events, it dawned on me that the question as to whether Isabel was an extension of myself, or indeed another person, was now unequivocally answered. I finally went to sleep with the solemn assurance that in spite of whatever reasons there may have been, I not only could not, but would not, have spanked myself.

The few other crib escapes that I can remember are sort of jumbled (a fact which may be due to the one occasion when I fell on my head). Some took place at night and some in the morning. All of them, however, succeeded in attracting one or more adults, who came running to see what had been the most recent occurrence in the long list of phenomena generated by their highly underestimated babe in the crib.

The sound of a broken window, an upset chair or the flapping of a blind around its roller were just a few of the indications that little Tommy was at it again.

The art of climbing up on things now seemed to be mastered simultaneously with the art of getting down from things. Neither chairs, tables, beds nor dressers were out of reach of my unbound curiosity.

You can imagine my amazement one day when one of the adults who had been looking after me at the breakfast table left me alone while going to do a chore (probably hang out some clothes). I clambered from the chair onto the table, leaving behind a dish of bananas floating in milk and coated with sugar. By the time this adult (I can't remember which one) came back, I was sitting on the table after having tasted a number of unknown liquids, chomped away the best part of a bar of laundry soap and devoured a bowl of sugar.

It wasn't until a number of years later, while someone was explaining to me what a hospital was, that I remembered during the sugar bowl incident that I had already been to one, but couldn't remember what they had done to me or how long they took to do it. At any rate the experience must have taught me something because except for a nickel, two buttons and a large piece of gravel, from that time on my desire to swallow things just because of their unusual taste was considerably subdued.

There was one other thing I swallowed. One evening at supper, we were having fish and someone had missed seeing a fair-sized bone in my dinner. I remember gagging, being held upside down and frantically being slapped on the back a number of times until I threw up on the couch.

To everyone's great relief (not to mention my own), the fishbone was dislodged, disgorged and discovered.

I had been born Charles Thomas Connors at the stroke of midnight on February 9, 1936, in the General Hospital at Saint John, New Brunswick. My birth certificate shows my mother's name as Isabel Connors and my father's as "unknown."

We lived with her real mother, Lucy, who was now married to her stepfather, Joe Scribner.

Isabel's mother was born Lucy Raynor at either Pubnico or Tusket Falls, Nova Scotia, near Yarmouth. Lucy's first husband was John Connors, a sea captain from Boston, or some place in Massachusetts, U.S.A. John Connors and Lucy Raynor were the parents of two girls, Beattie and Isabel, so this makes John Connors my true grandfather.

John died some years before I was born and Lucy met and married Joe Scribner from Saint John, New Brunswick, and moved there to live with him. She also brought her two girls, Beattie and Isabel, from Nova Scotia with her.

These few facts are all I know about my mother's family. Much later in life, when I was about fourteen or fifteen, I was able to meet and gather from my real father, for the first time, some of the information pertaining to his side of the family.

My father was born Thomas Joseph Sullivan at Brook Street in Saint John, New Brunswick. He had an older brother Charles (for whom I was also named) and a large number of sisters. His father, Alloysius Sullivan, had apparently come to Canada from Ireland when he was young. He then married Rose Cyr from northern New Brunswick, near the Gaspé. It seems that Rose, or an immediate ancestor, may have been Métis or some combination of French and Micmac. Once again the genealogy trails off, as so often happens when one is orphaned.

My father, before he died, also gave me some details about why he and my mother never married. It seemed that because his family was Catholic and my mother's was Protestant the marriage was prevented by his mother. She gave him a bottle of whisky and five or ten dollars, which was a great deal of money in 1935, and told him to leave town. My young teenage mother was pregnant with me at the time.

My first home was on St. Patrick Street in Saint John. It was a three-storey, flat-roofed, wooden house, with an adjoining alley. We lived on the second storey over Brawley's general store. The only entrance was from the wooden stairs in the back alley. We had a kitchen, living room, two small bedrooms, pantry, bathroom, woodshed and a long narrow hall.

Mr. Brawley and his son Gerald ran a wood and coal yard in the back alley and had a shed attached to the back of the house which served as a machine shop.

St. Patrick Street and all adjoining streets were situated in the poorest and most rundown part of Saint John, about a twenty-minute walk from downtown.

Joe Scribner (Grampy) was good to me. He taught me a lot of things and I had many first experiences with him. He was the opposite of my grandmother. He was always trying to teach me by example as I got out of the crib to the crawling—and then the toddling—stage.

Grandmother was always the disciplinarian.

But in his own way, Grampy knew what he was doing and I would much rather be around him than her.

There was one time though that wasn't very pleasant for him—or for me. He was left to look after me when I still wasn't toilet-trained. I was not quite two years old and diapers were still very much a part of me.

Grammy and Isabel usually took care of emptying me whenever it needed to be done.

But Grampy just hadn't been taught and probably didn't want any instruction in diapering and powdering babies' bottoms, anyway.

He took exception to the smell I had created. Although he cleaned me, it wasn't before he rubbed my nose in it.

I can remember him repeating over and over, "Shame on you...shame on you."

It's hard to describe the full impact these few moments had upon me. But I can say that I fully understood what it was that I had done and firmly resolved never to do again. From that time on, whenever the urge hit me, I would make it known to someone very quickly what I had to do and where I wanted to go. Suddenly, I found that I was being praised for telling others what I wanted to do. It made me feel good. And speaking from experience now, I assume it was a great relief to Isabel and Grammy—as well as Grampy—that diapers could be now put away.

Another strange thing about this dirty diaper incident with Grampy—which may come as a surprise to those who don't believe in any sort of child discipline—I not only gained a healthy respect for Grampy, but it drew me closer to him. I began to study him, trust him and count on his leadership. For, after all, I came to realize, it had been all for my own good.

I felt because of this experience I was a better person—and even more acceptable than before.

It is unfortunate that we cannot learn all there is to know from one or two experiences. And it was unfortunate that I was not able to apply what I had learned from this one experience to other and varied circumstances.

Besides getting me toilet-trained, Grampy taught me my first song. It went like this:

> *I wrote my love a letter,*
> *And I sealed it with a wafer.*
> *The reason why I did?*

So it would go all the safer.
And in this loving letter
I told her all my mind;
That I'd be ridin' donkey
On the Nicker Bunker line.
When the Fredericton branches are open
And the cars are on the track,
I'll be headin' for the Nicker Bunker Line.

I was sitting on his lap, playing with a toy ring when he taught me to sing along with him.

Why this song, I don't know. There certainly isn't much in the lyrics to interest a two-year-old. And the meaning of some of the phrases "ridin' the donkey" and "sealed with a wafer" escapes me to this day. The Nicker Bunker Line, I believe, was an old railroad in New Brunswick.

Going for walks with Grampy was always something else I looked forward to doing. At first it would only be a half block or so where we would pop into a little store for some candy or an ice-cream cone. Then the walks got longer until sometimes we'd even take a small lunch to the old Empire Loyalist Graveyard, in the heart of Saint John, where I could play around in the grass with some other kids while he just sat on the bench feeding the pigeons. I always enjoyed coming here because of the fountain where we would splash and sail little pieces of wood, pretending they were boats. After a couple of hours of this, we would try to guess what Grammy had put in the lunch bag for us to eat, and then we'd head for home.

There was one other place Grampy took me which was my favourite. It was a place which, unknown to me at the time, would somehow continue throughout my life to haunt my mind with great nostalgia. We would start out first by winding our way through the back alleys until we came out on St. David Street. Then turning left we would walk about a block and cross the railroad tracks. This was

Courtenay Bay. Sometimes, if the tide was high, we could only sit on the rocks by the tracks and watch other people fishing, but it was the times when the tide was way out that I mainly remember.

At these times there was usually no one on the beach but me and Grampy: two solitary figures picking their way along the sand, between the moss-covered rocks and the sticks of old driftwood.

It was here that I would listen to the never-ending stories about the long-gone ships, and the valour of men who went to sea and never returned.

Looking across the bay and pointing with his finger, he told these yarns in such a way that he made it seem like he was really there. That all these things were happening right here and now. And for all I knew, maybe they were.

I can't remember the content of these stories today, because I was too young back then to comprehend the meaning of them. But the wistful tone of voice in which they were told still lives in my mind, and often makes me wonder what it is about a small boy that makes an old man want so much to remember back.

Maybe the seagulls knew, and then again, maybe they didn't. However this may be, I seem to recall that at the very least the gulls were not to be criticized for showing any lack of interest. Somehow they were just as curious about us as I was about them.

One fellow, who was perched not too far away, began to squawk as if he too now wanted to tell a story. But Grampy, having no desire to compete with one who seemed to know so much, quietly agreed to concede the contest, giving due acknowledgement, I suspect, to the fact that the gull had as much right to speak as Grampy did. And besides, it was his beach.

At any rate, a fair bargain was struck. And we agreed to listen to the squawk of the gulls in return for the right to examine their sea shells, coloured stones, old bottles and seaweed.

Sometimes we'd come across a nice warm puddle which had been left behind by the receding tide water, and Grampy would take off my shoes and stockings, roll up my pant legs and let me splash around near the edges. Here he could watch me and see that I didn't fall on my face and get a gulp or two of the very salty brine. (This affair was always left till near the last. Mainly, I suppose, in case I got too wet and would have to be taken home prematurely.)

After another study of fishbones, clam shells and corks, which were always scattered here and there on the flats, we'd gradually make our way back to the much higher ground.

Passing by the hulk of an old ship that was stuck in the mud and a broken net tangled with a lost buoy, we at last came to the bank where Grampy would always find his old familiar log to sit down on, light his pipe and enjoy a well-deserved rest.

From this point he was able to scan the whole bay and watch the steady approach of the now-expanding waters.

Taking me on his knee, he would often draw my attention to the direction from which we had just come and try to explain to me how it was that the moss-covered rocks we had just passed had now somehow mysteriously vanished. (Not until this scene came back to me in later years would I realize just what it was that was now happening.)

The beach too had now become considerably smaller, due to the sudden loss of its low-lying flats, and many of its recently familiar characteristics were now missing. It was almost as if a great invisible sea monster had somehow bewitched the entire scene and hungrily swallowed it up. All that seemed to be left was the hulk of an old ship that was itself, even now, caught in a vain struggle, trying to escape from the jaws of these magic waters.

Dousing his pipe and glancing at his old pocket watch, Grampy would now indicate that it was time to shake the sand from our shoes and head for home. Somewhere along the top of the hill before crossing the railroad tracks, Grampy would say, "There she goes," and I'd look back just in time to catch the last scene of another day's memory: to where the old ship's hulk had finally disappeared beneath the rising tides of Courtenay Bay.

While Grampy had been the first to teach me to sing, my mother was my greatest musical influence. Names like Wilf Carter and Hank Snow were household words at our place, and my mother used to know the words to most of the songs. She would sing them around the house all the time.

I can still picture her standing in front of the mirror, wearing one of Grampy's old hats and singing "I'm an Old Cowhand from the Rio Grande." Pausing for a moment to reflect, she turned and went to the kitchen. In no time flat she was back at the mirror—and now there was a more satisfactory performance. She was strumming on the broom!

I'm sure if she could have known that this was all being filmed and recorded, she might have felt a little embarrassed.

But video cameras and tape-recorders were not yet invented. And Isabel had been alone in the house all afternoon. Alone, that is, except for her baby. I was doing the tape-recording and video-taping in my mind.

It was also around this time that I remember going out to my first movie with Grammy and Isabel. It was a western, starring Ken Maynard and Hoot Gibson. But as far as I was concerned, the biggest star of all was Grammy, who, in order to keep me quiet, filled me with chocolate candy.

I mention this, not so much to show that it was recorded in memory, but to show how and why it was able to stay there for so long. A child of two doesn't have any desire to remember a movie or an actor. But everyone knows how even the mention of chocolate candy can create not only the interest, but the desire, in the very same child. In short, this is how I think it works:

Each and every time I was offered chocolate candy after this incident it only served to reinforce the memory of the time I had been given all the chocolate candy I could eat, and more. So every time I think of an abundance of chocolate candy I think, by association, of the movie, and the names Ken Maynard and Hoot Gibson.

I was at the age now where I could say a number of words. I'm not sure how plain they all were, but I am sure they were sufficiently emphasized by a whimper or two, here or there, to get attention. And more importantly, to get my own way.

I also found that some people could say no and mean no while others could say no but change it to a yes with a little arm-twisting, a flash of big blue eyes, the right cry in the right place or just plain old pestering.

Then there was Uncle Aubrey. He was just too good-hearted to ever say no.

I was always glad to see him when he and Aunt Beattie came to visit, which was quite often. No matter what my petty wishes might be, Uncle Aubrey would always find a way to see that they were fulfilled. Letting me crawl all over him...pull his nose...or play with the things he kept in his pockets...there's no doubt he spoiled me rotten. But I sure loved it when someone made a big fuss of me.

I had the feeling he would give me anything and everything I wanted. And for a very good reason. The man was the kind of guy every family needs and most have. He had that way with kids of all ages who knew how to play him for all he was worth when it came to candies or favours.

I mention this about Uncle Aubrey because I often wondered years later which of us had received a lesson from his over-abundance of generosity. While he had unwisely led me to believe that he was capable of giving me anything I wanted, he had not counted on the possibility that even a young child might one day come up with a request that he would not be able to grant.

One evening while I was playing near his feet, I summoned him to the door, making it known in the best baby talk I knew that I wanted to go outside. Putting a sweater on me, he picked me up in his arms and in a jiffy I had again what I wanted, I was outside.

We were on the landing at the top of the steps which led down to the backyard. It was probably late fall or early winter and I remember the night being cool and brisk.

Then it happened.

For the first time in my life I spotted the moon. It was big, round and yellow and certainly not unlike Grammy's big cookies, and here I was with the one person who could give me anything I desired.

I wanted the moon!

I remember Uncle Aubrey laughing and giving me all sorts of explanations, excuses and words of appeasement, but no matter what I was offered in its place, I wanted the moon and nothing but the moon.

"Cookie! Cookie! Want cookie!" I was crying as he took me back in the house, where he quickly provided me with a cookie from the jar. This was not the cookie I wanted, so I hurled it on the floor.

Between howls and screams I could not understand for the life of me why Uncle Aubrey had not given me what I wanted. I was not only hurt, but the shock of Uncle Aubrey not coming through with that big cookie had considerably shaken my trust in him.

As I could not be pacified now with anything short of the moon, I was quickly ushered off to bed. But not before catching a final glimpse of Uncle Aubrey, who was no longer smiling, but had a look on his face which was not to be understood by me for a good number of years.

I finally went sobbing off to sleep, leaving everybody to remain unbothered by the incident. Everybody, that is, except Uncle Aubrey, who I suspect was now pondering how it came to be that while he only meant to bring happiness, he had broken my heart, and in doing so had broken his own.

I was now around two years old and although I knew that Isabel was my mother, I was calling her by her first name. The reason for this was that everyone in the house called my grandmother "Momma" and so I sometimes called her "Momma" too.

Although the winter seemed to pass very slowly, I was picking up words very fast; some of them I heard Grampy say, and later got my mouth washed out with soap for repeating.

These cold winter days had also become a time of great tribulation for our continually pursued cat. The poor thing had only two choices: to freeze outside in peace or to come inside where it was warm—but risky. Her old hiding place under the couch was no longer a refuge. It was more like a meeting place of two opposing factions, the one to play "come here and I'll pull your tail" and the other wanting to play "stay away or I'll scratch you."

The fracas usually began with the cat and me disappearing under the couch. A few moments of silence followed...then bedlam. A great rumble of cats, boots and boys would signal the reappearance, at the opposite end of the couch, of the main players.

I usually looked the worse for wear, with a couple of scratches on my face. The cat, hissing and spitting, was often stuck in an old coat sleeve. And by the time all was untangled and the scratches forgotten, the fracas was once more in progress. Only this time behind the stove.

I don't think either I or the cat ever emerged from these battles a true winner, but when some exasperated adult hit me and threw the cat out the door I am sure that decidedly, we had both become losers.

Between cat fights, and on the days the cat didn't want to come into the house, I would watch Grampy cut hair. One or two of his old buddies would come around in the afternoon for a chat and a haircut. Some of them would also have a shave, mainly the older fellows, who were perhaps less able to do it for themselves.

Although I somehow felt that my presence was not always welcome, I usually succeeded in helping out where possible. Being an expert in the field of getting in the way, playing with the shaving brush and tracking hair around, I felt that my contribution to the entire operation was nothing less than absolutely essential.

One day I even helped by getting my entire face completely lathered, only to back down at the last moment when I saw Grampy coming towards me with a straight razor.

One of Grampy's old buddies was a deaf mute referred to by all, including Grampy, as "The Dummy." And I suppose it was the loud sounds and odd motions that came from him that caused me to quickly scamper each time he showed up to get barbered.

While it's true that on these occasions my presence in the room was always noticeably missing, in my memory today, I still get a very vivid picture of him sitting on the chair and being shaved. As this picture always seems to be set in a round frame, I put it down to the fact that whenever he was being watched, it was always discreetly through the knot-hole in the lower panel of the hall door.

Another time when I quite innocently felt proud to have helped Grampy was on the afternoon he set up a saw-horse and a chair and with his buck-saw proceeded to transform my mother's toboggan into a neat pile of firewood. She was out and didn't find out about this until later on that evening.

I don't remember the full outcome of all this, or the reasons for it happening, but I do remember the atmosphere being one of strained relations for the next couple of days. If I could be permitted to venture a guess, I would say that it had something to do with the fact that Isabel was still a young teenager and already an unwed mother. And because it was thought that she should pay more attention to her obligations at home and not be gallivanting around, this form of punishment was regarded as necessary. After all, Grampy was a very old man and Grammy was always bothered with some sort of malady, the nature of which I never did learn. And probably because of these reasons they weren't always capable of maintaining a firmer control over Isabel's comings and goings.

The winter I turned three years old I was rewarded with my first ride in Gerald Brawley's old truck. As the Brawleys were in the firewood delivery business as well as running the store, I had many occasions to watch Gerald load the old truck from their shed in the back alley and would many times ask him if I could go for a ride. Although he would let me play in the cab and go "Brrrmm brrrmmm" behind the wheel while the truck was being loaded, he would always dodge the issue by saying, "On your birthday, Tommy, you can have a ride on your birthday." Finally my birthday came and with permission from my mother, I was off for a long happy day with Gerald Brawley as he made his many deliveries in that wonderful dilapidated old truck.

I still remember how fascinated I was sitting there beside Gerald and watching his every move. After each delivery he would jump in the truck, put his foot on the clutch pedal, shove her in gear and we were off to the next call while he whistled or sang parts of an old song that had something to do with fishes that "swam and swam all over the dam."

After that first day I think I went on every delivery Gerald made that winter. I even remember how grown-up and important I felt when he would ask me to help him load the truck with the small little pieces of wood that he thought I could handle. Although he would have the whole truck loaded by the time I struggled with one or two little pieces, I felt great satisfaction in believing he really needed my help. And my pride was even swollen to a greater degree the day my mother asked him if he was sure that I wasn't getting in his way. "Oh no," was the reply, "he's no bother at all. He just sits there in the cab keeping me company and watching my every move. I think he's gonna be a truck driver when he grows up by the way he already lets me know whenever I make a mistake. I don't know how I ever did without him."

With my importance thus built up to the nth degree, it is not hard now in retrospect to understand how and why my great bubble of confidence was soon to burst, carrying away with it not only my sense of self-esteem but also my prized position of truck driver's helper.

It happened on a fine spring morning just after we got the truck loaded and parked outside the store on the street that Gerald had to run back in the alley for something he forgot in the shed. It suddenly occurred to me that a person of my "importance" should surely by now be promoted to something better than truck driver's helper. And even a three-year-old knows there can only be one job more important than truck driver's helper, so I immediately promoted myself to the position of truck driver.

With the motor already idling, I got down underneath the wheel and tramped my foot on the clutch. While holding it down I reached over and shoved the floor gear shift into low position and grabbed the wheel to pull myself back up on the seat, thereby releasing the clutch and thrusting the truck forward, landing me against the back of the seat. Quickly turning myself around, I found myself kneeling on the seat with my hands on the wheel and slowly but proudly moving towards the grade that would very conveniently propel me down St. Patrick Street.

My sense of accomplishment now grew to a pitch as I saw all those onlookers dumbfoundedly watching me from the sidewalk as I rolled down St. Patrick Street behind the wheel of a truck loaded down with wood. It occurred to me that all those hours of patiently watching Gerald Brawley's every move had at long last not been in vain. And here I was, amid great flashes of joy and ecstasy, wildly swinging the steering wheel this way and that and thinking to myself, "How proud Gerald would be of me if he could only see me now."

As I neared the bottom of the grade, it seemed like the whole street was now in complete pandemonium. With dogs barking, people hollering and kids laughing at Gerald, who was running to catch up with his load of wood, while my mother, pulling on his shirt-tail in her valiant effort to reach me, was screeching at the top of her lungs for everyone and everything to "Stop, stop, STOP!"

Just then the right front wheel rolled up on the sidewalk in time to meet a telephone pole which hadn't had the sense to get out of the way but instead came crashing through the radiator, causing me and my bright future as a three-year-old truck driver to come to a quick and final end.

After taking me out of the truck and checking me over, I remember Gerald saying how it was all his fault and not mine, and that he should not have left the truck running with me in it in the first place. While this admission spared me from getting a licking from my mother, it could in no way be construed to be a clearance or a clean slate to my next truck ride. The truth of the matter was, I just never got one.

While this was at first hard to take, my disappointment was soon softened by the amount of recognition I received from the other kids, but this too quickly wore off and I somehow retreated into a shell from where I would just idly stand by and watch Gerald loading his truck, coming and going and wishing he would ask me to go for another ride or even just ask me to help him load the truck. Not having a father, I guess, sort of made me miss being with him, and not being able to look forward to the companionship which had been built up over the last few months didn't help much either.

My mother at this time must have also sensed my

growing need for a father because in retrospect it seems now that it was around this time that she was out trying hard to get me one.

While the visit to Canada that year of their Royal Highnesses King George VI and Queen Elizabeth was to somehow signal to Canadians that their lives and their country would never again be the same, it would also stick in my memory as the time of my first great personal upheaval and the foreboding sign of the many uncertain years of insecurity that were soon to follow.

I don't recall who took me to see the great event but I do remember pushing our way through the massive crowds that were lined up in King's Square across from the Admiral Beatty Hotel and waving my little flag as the greatest spectacle I had ever seen came passing before my eyes.

The great array of pipers, drummers and buglers seemed to send their vibrations throughout the whole city. Motorcycles and great long cars covered with ribbons followed by red-coated men riding on the backs of huge horses went by as soldiers, sailors and airmen came proudly marching in time to the wonderful music. Other men who looked like toys with red coats and black fuzzy things on their heads, whom I would later on in life come to know as the Queen's (or King's) Guard, also came by. And then the spectacle of all spectacles came into view as a great and wondrous roar went up from the crowds. A marvellous coach drawn by four to six horses, which looked as if they had just come out of the pages of a story-book, came dancing along the confetti-covered street.

The quaintly designed coach sparkled from the glitter of many fine gems while the great noble horses strode stately in their harness all studded with silver and gold.

On the top of the coach in a great plush seat sat two of the most extravagantly dressed people that I, or anyone else in the crowd for that matter, had ever seen. Here to this old "first incorporated city of Canada," where the once-great "United Empire Loyalists" had come to settle, and where on that day their descendants lined all the streets, came none other than the King and Queen of the whole British Empire. With each smile and gesture of the Royal Couple, flags were vigorously waved as oohs and ahhs went up from the entire throng.

When the parade was finally past, a great hush fell over the crowd as many thousands of people, both young and old, clambered for places in line to follow in the wake of this long-to-be-remembered and so fabulous procession.

I'm not sure but I think it was the following day when the Royal Train made its final departure. Again I don't know who I was with but I remember being at the station proudly performing my patriotic duty along with all the other flag-wavers.

Three-Year-Old Hitch-hiker

It wasn't too long after the Royal Visit that Grammy and Grampy (Lucy and Joe Scribner) passed away.

They died within a few weeks of each other and my mother began to feel she would not be able to cope without the help of her mother and stepfather. She then moved us out of the old flat and into a small two-room apartment where we stayed until her money dwindled and other measures would soon have to be taken.

During this time a Terrence Messer had been coming to the house, bringing his guitar and his friends, and he seemed to like the company of my mother. My mother was also an avid country music fan and loved to sing all the popular cowboy songs of the day.

Terrence also brought Hank Snow around to the house once or twice and they'd just sit around drinking, playing guitars and singing. Later when my mother would hear Hank on the radio, she would excitedly tell her friends how he had once been to our house.

I remember at least one of the nights when Hank was there, but he certainly wouldn't remember me as I was just another toddler in another house among so many he must have visited while just boozing around in those days.

I believe my mother was pregnant again around that time by my father, Tommy Sullivan, who had arrived back in town sometime after I was born. And she probably figured one more mouth to feed was going to be difficult. She may also have been trying to straighten out her own affairs and wondering whether or not she wanted to go and live with Terrence, even though he may have been keen to live with her.

I still can't say whether he knew she was pregnant or not. And maybe she wasn't yet prepared to tell him.

Anyway, she decided to take me to Tusket Falls in Nova Scotia, where she had a lot of relatives.

Although I was only three, this was my first time hitch-hiking.

(Whatever the true reasons for the visit I may never know, but speculation has often led me to consider that she might have wanted to leave me with one of those relatives for a while.)

We got many rides as I started my hitch-hiking career, and we stopped at numerous houses to ask for a bite to eat. Sometimes we stayed overnight, and at one place we stayed two or three days.

At this home they must have had a dozen kids. I recall playing with them around their heavily wooded lot, and it is here that I learned to climb a tree, saw my first turtle and saw a snake for the first time.

And another first for me at this place: after playing in sand one day, it was discovered some of us had lice on our heads. After several washings in a strong solution and a good, fine-tooth combing, we finally got rid of them.

Although I enjoyed seeing the new places and the strange faces of all the different people we met on this hitch-hiking trip, the many hours of walking mile after mile got me down.

Many times when I was tired, we would sit down to rest on the side of the road, and when my mother would say, "It's time to go," I would just sit there and cry. When coaxing and threatening would not get me to move, she would walk off up the road alone and disappear around a bend, or duck into the bushes, and wait for me.

Most times I would eventually catch up to her, still crying my eyes out. Then she would wipe my eyes, blow my nose and often pick me up and carry me for a while.

One time I mistakenly walked in the opposite direction and she had to run back to get me.

It was on this trip that I first noticed a peculiarity about Isabel. As I had never seen anyone hitch-hiking before, it was only natural for me to watch carefully how it was done. As a car would approach, she would take up a certain stance and stick out her arm to let the driver know we were looking for a lift. Nothing peculiar about this, but a closer look at her right hand revealed she only had half-a-thumb.

I suppose I must have noticed this before as she washed and cared for me as a baby, but this is the first time I recall taking special notice of the missing thumb.

I don't think we talked about it then, but she later told me she lost her thumb when she was six years old. She was playing with a brick, pretending it was her doll, her baby. Her family was poor, and they could not afford a few cents even to buy toys for her to play with. She had a dishcloth wrapped around the brick. That was her baby's shawl, or blanket.

She was on the front steps when she set the dishcloth-draped brick on the top step, while continuing to play on a lower step. The brick fell down, hit her thumb and cut it off on the edge of the step.

Though I wondered about this many times, it would be years before I would realize how significant my mother's missing thumb would be in my life.

Upon arriving in Yarmouth, we stepped out of an old truck, thanked the driver and proceeded to a small Chinese restaurant. After satisfying our hunger, I was treated to another experience that would not be soon forgotten, and would often be repeated. Only the places and the faces would change.

As the day was hot and sticky, the door to the restaurant was left open as a huge ceiling fan was vainly trying to cool the air. My mother asked me to go outside and play around the corner. Taking my time, as a kid will do, and stopping to inspect things as I went, I slipped outside completely unnoticed.

But just as I got to the corner of the building my mother came barging out the doorway, scooped me off the sidewalk and ran like hell. Not knowing what was happening I could hear the Chinese restaurant owner hollering and screaming as we ducked into an alley and came out on another street.

After another series of alleys we wound up on the edge

of town, where we soon got a ride to Tusket Falls.

Recalling this incident a number of years later I realized this had been my first free meal in a restaurant. There were also many others.

When we got to Tusket Falls we walked into the countryside, passing a number of farms, and finally arrived at a house which sat on a steep slope near a dirt road.

An older lady with white hair answered our knock. There were hugs and kisses. Isabel kept referring to her as Aunt Hannah, as she was my grandmother's sister.

Later that evening we went to visit other relatives and all through the week we just made the rounds. Each place we visited was much the same as the last, except for one house.

Here I was treated exceptionally well and remember the adults saying how remarkable it was that a three-year-old was able to dress himself, tie his own shoelaces, sit up to the table and make short work of a large breakfast. I felt like some sort of celebrity.

The kids, who were a bit older than me, also treated me well. One gave me a rifle he had carved for himself. My mother tried to stop him, saying I was too small for it, but he wouldn't listen. Later I left it in the back of someone's car while we were hitch-hiking.

We stayed about a week at Tusket Falls. While we were treated well, I somehow got the feeling that for whatever reason we had gone there, it hadn't been fulfilled. For one thing, if we had come for a loan, we left without it.

These were tough times at the end of the Depression, the Dirty '30s.

Arriving back in Saint John we went to live with the Chamberlains, a fairly large and very poor family in the north end. They had been friends of my mother's for a long time.

I don't know how long we stayed, but I think it was from here that my mother went to the hospital to give birth to my sister, Marie. I don't remember the event, mainly, I suppose, because the baby was not brought home from the hospital immediately, due to a large birthmark on the back of her neck which the doctors thought should be surgically removed.

We stayed with the Chamberlains until the fall, when we moved to the corner of Clarence and Erin streets, living in a second-floor apartment with the man who was to be my new father, Terrence Messer. I surmise that Isabel must have had meetings with him several times to make plans to live with him while we were still at the Chamberlains'.

This is when life started to get a little out of whack for us. First we had to take on Messer's name. So I became Tommy Messer, instead of Connors.

The plan had been that Isabel was not going to marry Terrence, but live common-law.

With moral standards so different back in the late '30s, it sure wasn't easy for a single parent. There was no mother's allowance or other welfare for young mothers caught without a husband. And it was difficult to fake marriage, too.

You know how easy it is to get a hotel room today—no questions asked whether or not you are married to each other. Back then, not only were young couples asked if they were married to each other—they also had to produce a marriage licence or a wedding picture. If you couldn't do that you didn't get the room.

It was the same with renting a room or an apartment. You had to prove to the landlord, without a doubt, that you were married.

If anyone found out you were living together (living in sin, as they called it), you were evicted. There was no board to go to, no human rights commission's shoulder to cry on. It was a cut-and-dried matter. If you weren't married then you couldn't share an apartment with someone of the opposite sex—no matter how honourable your intentions.

So right from the start Terrence Messer taught me a scam which would kick into place every time we had to get a new apartment—and there would be lots of times.

The scheme went like this: I would run up and say, "Hey, Daddy, can I have a dime?" just when the landlord was going to show them the room. As long as the kid was calling the man "Dad" the landlord would not usually ask for a wedding picture or a marriage licence. But for all my support, I'd have to give back the dime once we were in the room.

That first flat on the corner of Clarence and Erin streets was in good condition, and no more than a block away from the house on St. Patrick Street where we used to live with Grammy and Grampy. Being so close like this I often felt lonesome for Grammy and Grampy.

Terrence, who had been a lumberjack before coming to Saint John, was now only getting the odd job house painting, driving truck or working at the grain elevators.

On many occasions when my mother would go out to the hospital to visit my baby sister, Terrence was supposed to be minding me. Often he would just go out and leave me locked in a room or free to ramble the empty house, and sometimes I would disappear and roam the streets for a while. His plan was to return just before Isabel arrived home, but quite often she would return home early to find nothing but an empty house.

When I got home they would be fighting. Terrence always claimed that I had somehow sneaked away from him because he had been in the house all the time. Nine times out of ten I would come out of these situations with a good lickin' or a stiff reprimand.

On the days that I left the house it was usually to go back up to St. Patrick Street to try and find Grampy and Grammy. I still did not understand the meaning of death.

On these trips I would stop to visit people I knew on St. Patrick Street and it began to dawn on me that other people always seemed to have more to eat than we did. I therefore began to look forward to eating at other people's houses as often as I could.

Terrence spent most of our grocery money on wine. One day he missed paying the rent altogether, and we got bounced out and had to take a small room on the top floor of a house back on St. Patrick Street, not much more than half a block from where we used to live.

Christmas that year was pretty skimpy, although I do remember eating some chicken while listening to a conversation about what a dirty old son of a so-and-so the pawnbroker, Joe Gilbert, was for only allowing $5 on Terrence's guitar. He said he intended to get it back as soon as the grain boats were loading at the winter port.

A toy airplane was my only present that year and later someone stepped on it and broke it.

As winter set in, Terrence got more steady work and my baby sister, Marie, finally came home from hospital. She was kept in a basket near the door. One time Terrence came home late from work. He had been drinking and threw his big heavy coat on top of the baby. Although it's hard to believe he could have meant it, he touched off one of the biggest fights I had ever seen. It wouldn't be the last.

My mother was only a small woman. Most of the time she took a lot of physical abuse and got pushed around, but when she got mad even Terrence, who was anything but a small man, soon learned to stay out of her way.

She thought nothing of taking pots, pans, stove pokers, broken dishes or even butcher knives to anyone who had foolishly made the mistake of purposely disrupting the sensitive balance of her cool.

A sign there had been a fight at our house was the black eyes. Both Terrence and Isabel often sported them. And on at least one occasion I can remember them both having shiners at the same time.

Terrence had a sense of humour, albeit warped at times. I can remember the time he fed me slice after slice of baloney. The more I ate, the more he laughed. I was so full I eventually was sick to my stomach. I didn't play that game with him again. There was another time he rolled me my own cigarette and with great delight watched me smoke myself sick.

Naturally, I developed a strong distrust of Terrence. I now suspect that even his acts of kindness, which at times appeared to be genuine, were geared more to appeasing his own conscience than they were to obtaining from me any lasting amount of respect.

He found out that my real father's name was Tommy, and because I had been named after my dad, whom he was jealous of, he persistently called me "Tammy." Even as young as I was I think I resented him more for that than for any other reason.

"You still love that bastard, don't you?" he would say to my mother as they repeatedly fought over the same subject, my real father.

"You wouldn't call him a bastard to his face," my mother would reply, and they would be at it again.

On my fourth birthday Terrence served me my first wine. He waited for my mother to leave the house, then he produced a bottle of wine from his black and red checkered bush jacket, and two glasses. He led me to believe that only the privileged few were allowed to drink wine.

When the wine took effect I had trouble standing and I fell and cut open my forehead, just over my left eye. I passed out. I came to long enough to puke all over the coat I was lying on, then slipped back into unconsciousness.

Although I later remember my mother bathing my eye and cleaning me up, I have no recollection of what she said to Terrence when she found out I had been hitting the bottle with him.

If there were arguments, I don't remember, nor did I care.

It was days before my interest in things returned to normal. Even food had lost its appeal. Soup was the only thing my stomach could take.

My sister, Marie, was to go into hospital for another operation. The last thing I remember about her was the two of us lying on the floor, and I was trying to show her how to play with my airplane. I never dreamed that this would be the last time I would see her. All I was told was this second operation to remove the birthmark on her neck had not been successful and she died in hospital shortly after.

One day during this time, I was at the front of the house playing tag with the landlord's kids when I absent-mindedly ran into the path of an oncoming car. Squealing the tires, the driver somehow managed to stop just as my leg was going under the front wheel. The full weight of the car had not gone over my ankle, but I had a bad bruise. As a crowd gathered, someone picked me up and carried me onto the sidewalk. He asked the older kids where I lived and carried me up the three flights of stairs to our room.

But there was no one in at the time so he brought me back down and put me on the sofa in the landlord's living room, where I stayed until Isabel came home. There was no question of me going to hospital. You had to be really ill or badly injured to even think of going to hospital back then. Hospitals were a last resort.

While I was recuperating from my ankle injury I was relegated to the sidelines with Stanley, a boy who had a permanently twisted leg, who always did more watching than playing. Stanley was a couple of years older than me, but because of his leg many of the kids from other alleys in the neighbourhood would come by just to pick on him.

He couldn't run and because he would never fight back he was a soft touch for these kids.

Stanley and I were making our way out of the alley and onto the street when two boys came walking along the sidewalk. "There's the boy who always hits me," said Stanley, as he quickly tried to hobble back in the alley.

As the bigger of the two boys headed straight for

Stanley, overlooking me, he was singing, "Big Suckie Stanley...Big Suckie Stanley...Big Suckie..." Whap! I nailed him right in the kisser.

While he was too stunned to cry or run, I nailed him again. This time his nose began to bleed and he started crying and ran off. I felt good about this. And of course, so did Stanley.

There were many times when I was left home alone. My mother had a job scrubbing floors to supplement what Terrence made, and often the money he made never made it home anyway. Also, Terrence was supposed to be looking after me while Isabel worked, but he usually shirked this responsibility as well. There were also a number of days when they would both be working. When that happened they told me to stay around, play with the other kids and keep out of trouble.

If I was hungry and there was anything to eat in the house I could have it. If not, I had to wait until one of them came home with something.

House on Fire

One day I was sitting at home alone, as usual, when my eyes fell on a box of matches on the floor near the window. I had often lit the odd match when no one was around, and nothing had happened before, so I decided to light a few more now.

How fascinating fire was, I thought, as it began to curl up the wood of the first match. After the second match curled up the same way, I began to think how my mother lit paper in the stove, and how it always curled up quickly as it burned.

Striking the third match, and sitting near the window, I began to wonder if curtains would react in the same way as paper. Suddenly, I found out they did. Quickly remembering how blowing on a match always extinguished the fire, I now began to furiously blow on the curtains. The fire got worse. Beating it with my hands and arms only got me burned, and when I realized the fire was completely out of my control, I panicked and ran from the house.

Luckily, there was a man near the front door as I stepped onto the sidewalk. Upon seeing my singed hair, he called the fire department and then came upstairs to see the fire. He grabbed my mother's water pail and began splashing water on the burning window frame.

After several trips to get water from the hall, when the fire was out, in came the firemen with their axes and hoses.

After looking over the situation and seeing some burnt matches floating across the dirty water on the floor, one fireman asked me if I had been playing with the matches. I told him I hadn't.

"Well, I wonder if a nice big boy like you could tell us how this fire got started?"

"Yes, sir," I said. "I was looking out the window and I saw a big policeman going by and I think he was chasing a bad man. He pulled out his gun, and a spark flew off and came up and caught onto the curtains."

"Well, I guess we are going to have to have a long talk with that policeman, now aren't we? We'll have to tell him to start catching more little boys who play with matches, instead of shooting his old gun around in the wrong places."

Realizing the last statement must have hit home by the look of troubled concern on my face, he nodded to the other two firemen and they all went downstairs, shaking their heads.

After they left I began contemplating my dim future. Would the policeman put me in jail for lighting matches when he found out I blamed him for starting the fire? Or would my mother beat me severely when she got home?

Just when it occurred to me that both of these possibilities might happen at the same time, the landlord showed up to look over the situation.

Seeing I was alone he began to scold me, and just when it looked like he might be on the verge of doing something more, my mother walked in. She could see he was upset at me, but quickly came to my defence and told him, "If I catch you puttin' your filthy hands on Tommy again I'll kill you, you slumpy-looking weasel."

Although he told us to get out that evening, we stayed the night because it was too late to look for another place.

Just as the early spring sunshine began to search for the street over the old wooden housetops, a door slammed, and three solemn figures awkwardly stepped out in the cool morning air.

We were each loaded down with as much as we could carry. Terrence had his guitar, duffel bag and my mother's suitcase. My mother carried her purse, an armload of bed clothes and a bag containing dishes, silverware and what little there was left of the groceries.

Bringing up the rear was me, struggling with two shopping bags, one filled with household odds and ends topped off with my twisted toy airplane, and the other with two or three pots and pans and an old tin kettle perched precariously on the top.

Except for ourselves, and one or two men carrying lunch buckets on their way to work, the street was deserted and quiet.

Then the kettle fell out of one of my shopping bags. It rolled all the way back down the hill. I dropped the shopping bags and ran to pick it up. Curtains were moving, blinds were snapping, and heads began popping out of windows to see what all the clatter was about.

Walking back up the hill I tried not to pay any attention to the threats from this very sensitive audience, until I spotted an old broken broom handle. I picked it up and started banging it like a drumstick on the kettle. Then I dropped it and ran.

I caught up with Isabel and Terrence and figured I would be safer with them, just in case someone decided to chase me.

After resting once or twice along our way, we eventually turned into a side alley which led to a basement flat under a small store.

We stayed there with some friends for a day or so before finding a place on King Street East—our first brick house. It was a basement apartment again, and the only window was in the living room, where you could only see the sky through an iron grate embedded in the sidewalk. The two rooms were very damp, but still a big improvement over St. Patrick Street.

The furniture in the living room consisted of an old wicker chair, a lampstand with no lamp, and a chesterfield which made into a bed. Isabel and Terrence slept there. I had a hard cot in the kitchen, which was a feather bed compared to the many long nights I had previously spent cramped in a cubby-hole. The bathroom was off the furnace room in the very back of the apartment.

As usual we were down to our last few dollars. We needed to buy some wood for the stove. But if we bought fuel we would starve; and if we bought food we would freeze.

Terrence decided to hock his old guitar again at Joe Gilbert's pawn shop.

A few hours later a truck arrived and dropped off a load of firewood which my mother and I carried into the kitchen and neatly piled behind the stove. The wood was wet and very hard to light. We searched in the shopping bags we had brought with us and found a can of lighter fluid. My mother poured the contents over the wood in the fire box, but neither of us saw a small puddle form under the stove.

When the match was struck—pooooof! We had a fire all right. The stove jumped and the covers rattled and in her excitement, my mother dropped the match in the lighter fluid puddle under the stove. Now we had two fires—one in the stove and one underneath.

She filled a large dipper with water and threw it on the fire under the stove. The water mixed with the lighter fluid and the fire spread across the floor. Eventually the water took over and the fire dissipated.

As the last tiny flames flickered and died, my mother, who had been down on her hands and knees, heaved a big sigh and slowly began to straighten up. She looked at the stove which, incidentally, was now going. Then she looked at me and around the room. If she was searching for something that looked in worse shape than she did, she was going to be disappointed.

Her clothes were wet and twisted out of shape. Her face was sweaty and covered with dirt, and if she thought the floor was scorched by the fire, she'd probably scream if she looked at her hair.

Then she said to me, "See what happens when Mommy's not careful? She nearly burned the whole house down."

It was an hour before the kitchen looked presentable again. And just as Isabel was about to clean herself up, in walked Terrence.

"What in the name-a-geezes happened to you?"

Isabel, not in the mood for any jokes, snapped back, "You weren't around today to care what happened to me when I tried to bring in the wood, and you weren't around to care what happened to me when I had to light the fire, so why do you care what's happened to me now?"

That provided an opening for Terrence. "I just thought you were all dolled up like that so you could go out on a big date tonight with Tommy Sullivan."

At the mention of my father's name all hell broke loose. Shoes flew, chairs were overturned and cheap wine spilled as my mother came on with a wild barrage of bare feet and flying knuckles.

"He's ten times the goddamn man you'll ever be," yelled Isabel just before Terrence caught her one, which sent her tumbling into the stove. She burned her arm and went off crying into the other room.

A few minutes later they were sitting together on the chesterfield. They were both sobbing and both taking turns to apologize to each other. Then Terrence said, "Why don't you go out and play, Tammy?"

My mother agreed, but told me to stay near the house because soon she would be calling me in for supper.

"What a strange turn of events," I thought to myself as I walked out the back door, then went around to the front of the house where two older women were having a late afternoon chat. So engrossed were they in conversation that they didn't even notice me as I walked over beside them and laid down on the sidewalk. From here, my previous bewilderment was heightened as I looked down through the grate into our living-room window and watched how Isabel and Terrence brought their strange fight to a climax. And the two older ladies just talked on and on.

Terrence later went to work and Isabel and I went to the corner store to buy groceries. As credit was nearly always the common policy in those days, we only had to pay for half of what we got and the rest was allowed to go "on the cuff." Had we been known to the storekeeper we could have got everything on credit, but as strangers were often a poor risk, we had to be satisfied with what we got.

The next few days were fairly peaceful as Terrence

worked at night and my mother worked in the day. We'd have breakfast together when Terrence came home each morning. Then he would go to bed as my mother left for work, and me—I had strict instructions to stay out of the house so I wouldn't wake up Terrence.

And Terrence could sleep. He usually didn't wake up until my mother arrived home to make supper. If I became really hungry during the day—with the emphasis on really—I was allowed to sneak into the house to get something to eat.

But it sure wasn't easy to get in without waking up Terrence. Once or twice I remember tiptoeing in through the furnace room, then knocking over something and having to run like hell to get back out again.

Eventually hunger took precedence over clumsiness and the rare art of preparing and eating lunch in complete silence was soon mastered.

I was also getting bored playing alone in the backyard day after day, so I began wandering in search of other kids. The old Loyalist Graveyard, where Grampy used to take me for a walk sometimes, was less than half a block away from home, so I began to spend a great deal of time there playing on the grass between the tombstones. When I was tired there were benches to sit on, and on really warm days a fountain to splash in.

I soon met some friends. Tag, hide-and-go-seek and wrestling on the grassy knolls with the boys were great fun. On days when boys didn't show up, it was just as easy for me to play with the girls. Although skipping games, hopscotch, playing house and bouncie, bouncie ballie were not exactly what you'd call a little boy's cup of tea, it was still better than playing alone in my own backyard.

While most of these things were to remain in my mind as merely routine, some experiences naturally stuck out more than others. For example: because I was the youngest of all the unchaperoned kids, I always wound up with the lesser role to play in the games, and was always the fall guy when it came to holding the bag or taking the brunt of a situation.

If we played tag, I was It.

If there was a fight, I'd get the punch in the mouth.

If we played hide-and-go-seek, I would be the one trying to find everybody, even after they all sneaked home.

I remember getting banged on the head one day with a rock. I was knocked out and was unconscious for some time. When I came around all the kids had left.

Another time, when we were playing around a construction site, I was encouraged to jump from a ledge onto a small pile of boards. I landed on a rusty nail, I screamed, and my pals quickly disappeared. It was an old man who heard me crying and helped me out of the construction site and back into the graveyard, where he bathed my foot in the fountain, wrapped it in his handkerchief, and banished all my tears with the rare and wonderful gift of a dime.

Bumps on the head, sore feet and a bleeding nose were not the only things I came home with. There were a number of toys I "picked up" from time to time and hid in the furnace room. Cap guns, rifles, boats, balls, cars, yo-yos were just a few of the things I knew would have to be returned if they were discovered. I was smart enough not to take these toys back to the graveyard, and I couldn't play with them in my own backyard, so I used to take them out only when I was going to some far-off streets and alleyways where I was sure they wouldn't be recognized. But even this wasn't a guarantee that I would be able to play with these toys without having them taken away from me.

It didn't take me very long to learn that when a bigger boy says, "Give me that, or I'll punch you in the mouth," the word no was not the best reply.

Also, when something that is stolen from you happens to be something that you had previously stolen, it's not wise to run home to your mother and cry about it. This gets you in more hot water, as I found out first-hand on more than one occasion.

Searching for Santa Claus

Paul Hashey was one boy I used to chum around with a good deal more than others at the graveyard. His backyard veranda used to jut out into the same alley as the Red Ball Brewery. When we got fed up with playing, we used to ask the men at the brewery if we could help them unload beer bottles.

There were times when Paul's mother would call him in to lunch—and guess what, she used to invite me in for a sandwich, too. Paul and I became very close. We used to sit and discuss many topics of a child-like nature, such as mommies, daddies, toys, the names and habits of other kids in the neighbourhood. One day we got around to talking about Santa Claus. We wanted to know how he made his toys, how he delivered them, who helped him, and how many reindeer did he have?

As Paul's mother listened to us across the kitchen table, she could little suspect where this seemingly harmless discussion was eventually going to lead us.

Outside, after lunch, we had absolutely no inclination to play. We returned to the speculation that if somehow we could ever get to the North Pole, we could help Santa Claus make all those toys, and when he saw what good little boys we were he would undoubtedly give us anything we wanted when it was time to go home.

"I bet Santa Claus would want us to help him, if we told him how much we always help the men at the breweries," said Paul. I agreed, "Yeah, let's go and find the North Pole and tell him."

"But how can we," asked Paul, "when we don't know where the North Pole is?"

"I do," I said, as I thought of a large Santa Claus billboard I had seen the previous winter while passing through Haymarket Square on my way to Aunt Beattie's house. I remembered thinking at the time that Santa probably didn't live too far from where he kept his picture.

So we set off to find Santa.

Leaving the alley and the breweries behind, we walked along Union Street to the corner of St. Patrick Street, where we spotted a bunch of kids playing along the sidewalk. They were about our age, so we stopped to talk.

"Guess where we're going?" I said to one of the boys, who was clunking along with a Carnation Milk can attached to his shoe.

"Where?" he said, as he wiped his nose on his sleeve.

"To see Santa Claus," said Paul. "We know where he lives."

"And we're going to get lots of toys. Does anyone want to come?"

"I do," said one little boy who was holding a hoop in one hand and a stick in the other. As he walked towards us he was followed by two other boys, but the boy with the milk can piped up, "Aw, they don't know where Santa Claus lives..."

"We do so," I said emphatically.

"You don't."

"We do."

After a long string of "we do's" and "you don'ts" we walked away, joined only by Larry, the boy who carried the hoop.

Farther down the street, as we approached Brawley's store, I pointed it out, saying we used to live there with Grampy and Grammy. Next we came to Dick Murphy's house, but after looking in the alley and not seeing him, we continued until we came to Fritz's house, where I lived just a few weeks ago. There were lots of kids around, but because there were some bigger boys we decided not to tell them where we were going.

Nobody, that is, except Stanley, the boy with the twisted leg. At first Paul and Larry were afraid of Stanley because he was so big, but when I told them how even the little boys used to make him cry, they agreed that I could tell him. He said he couldn't come with us, but we promised to tell Santa about everything he wanted and maybe we could bring something back for him.

We crossed over Clarence Street and down Erin towards Haymarket Square. By the time we reached the square we had picked up two other boys and soon everyone began to ask, "Are we at the North Pole yet?"

Although I was just as disappointed as all the rest at not seeing Santa Claus's picture where it was supposed to be on the billboard, I now pointed towards Rothsay Avenue and said determinedly, "This way, Santa must have taken his picture to his house."

This seemed to reassure everybody, at least for a while. But after crossing the Marsh Bridge, the two boys we picked up on Erin Street decided to go back home. We called them sissies for wanting to turn back, and we carried on.

Should we stay on Rothsay or take Thorn Avenue? Even though Larry and Paul wanted to take Thorn, I insisted on staying on Rothsay. After all it was me who had seen Santa Claus's picture in the first place.

As we approached McAvity's Foundry there was only Paul and me left. Larry, who at first began lagging behind, was now so far back that he decided to turn around and go home.

In what would have been less than a moment later, Paul came out with a scream that almost scared me out of my wits. "Santa Claus's house," he hollered. "It's Santa Claus's house."

We shouted to Larry, but he was too far back to hear us.

We looked again. Inside a great iron fence and sitting a good distance from the road, there was a brick house. In front of the house was a large lawn, which seemed to us to be about the size of a small field. And spread all over the lawn was a huge variety of lawn decorations.

Some were carvings of gaily coloured farm animals, which looked like they were pulling little wagons. Some were mechanical, wind-driven devices, such as airplanes and windmills, and some were in the likeness of fairyland-type people.

As neither Paul nor I had ever seen such things before, we mistook them for toys. We tried to climb the iron railing around the property, but it was too high. We rattled the iron gate and made enough noise to wake the dead, but no one came. We shouted, "Santa Claus, Santa Claus, we're here to help you make the toys. Let us in, Santa Claus."

Still no sign of Santa Claus, or anyone else, so we decided Santa must be sleeping. The last thing we wanted to do was wake him up, in case he might get mad and tell us to go home. So we decided to sit down by the fence and wait until Santa woke up.

We would have sat there all night, but a man came by in a car and asked us what we were doing. "We're waiting for Santa Claus," I said, as he got out of the car and came over to us.

"Waiting for Santa Claus," he repeated, as he looked as though he didn't believe what he had heard. "I think you two boys better come and sit with me in the car, and tell me all about it."

Soon the whole story began to unfold, and I remember thinking to myself, "Gee! What a friendly man he must be, because he sure laughs an awful lot."

The man confirmed that Santa was indeed sleeping, adding, "But you better not come here to the North Pole again, for a long, long time because Santa Claus sleeps all summer and he doesn't want anybody to wake him up until Christmas comes. Besides he doesn't give toys at any time to little boys who leave home without telling their mother."

Seeming satisfied now that he had convinced us of the futility of ever returning to the North Pole, he asked us where we lived.

When he realized how far it was, he said he would drive us back to the graveyard. In later years I figured he had been a plain-clothes policeman, but outside the "North Pole" that day he had been a "very nice man."

I escaped a licking when I got home. Isabel and the man shared a few laughs at the door while I was getting ready for bed. She then made me some supper and kissed me goodnight.

I don't know what happened to Paul, but after that he was not allowed to play with me.

There was, however, one more adventure with Paul which finally clapped the lid down on our relationship for good.

It all began when an older boy was authorized to take Paul out to Rockwood Park to see the animals in the zoo.

Just as they were ready to leave I showed up and, of course, wanted to go with them. Along with Paul's help I was able to convince the boy to take me. Soon we were walking along Gilbert Street on our way to the big hill which led to the park.

After seeing a few animals, the boy took us down to the pavilion on the edge of Lily Lake. He went in for a hot dog, candy or a pop and left us outside. We sat too near to the lake and Paul fell in.

In the course of my hollering to draw attention, I don't recall how long he was in there, how deep the water was, or who pulled him out, but he was sure doing some awful crying and panting as he was brought back onto the dock, soaking wet, and covered in gobs of mud and long, stringy reeds.

Again, we had the privilege of being chauffeured up to Paul's house.

I never did get to find out what explanation was given to Paul's mother, but in light of the way we were threatened to stay away from each other, I suspect she was told I pushed him in.

It was unfortunate, but in the days that followed, whenever Paul saw me coming he ran home or went somewhere else to play. While at first he was merely doing what he was told, the restriction soon became a habit and the habit became a dislike, and before I moved away from King Street East, not only he and I, but also his friends and my friends, were often engaged in throwing rocks at each other.

As strange as this may seem, the antagonism eventually got so bad that you had to enter the graveyard with a good deal of caution. If you were caught without your friends by members of the opposing gang, you either had to run like hell or stand and take a beating.

While some people may not believe that this could happen between kids as young as four years old, suffice it to say that I was glad to leave King Street East on the day I learned our rent had lapsed, that Terrence was once again out of work, and we had to move.

Friendly Old Fred

We moved back to Clarence Street, about half a block from where we used to live, and right next door to a bag factory.

It was a two-storey building and we had the front apartment on the ground floor. The one big room had a curtainless window looking out onto the street, an old broken-down bed and a table with one wooden box and one chair to sit on. At the back of the room was a small kitchenette with a one-tap sink and a gas stove which always frightened my mother because every time she would light it, it would always start with a great loud "poof."

Leading off from the kitchenette there was one more very small room with a broken window which looked out onto the back alley. There was nothing in it but the bare walls and the broken plaster which hung down from the ceiling. This was my room.

And when Terrence threw his old heavy winter coat on the floor in one corner, I quickly discovered where my bed was going to be.

The landlord also had one regulation which had to be strictly adhered to: "On account of the gas stove, when you leave the house you'll have to take your kid with you. And under no circumstances must he ever be allowed in the apartment alone."

If I had thought that the living conditions on King Street East were bad, even with my getting chased home by the other kids once in a while, we had now jumped out of the frying pan into the fire.

With food now more scarce than it had ever been, and after a recent fight which demolished most of our dishes, it wasn't at all uncommon to see us eating straight from the can. Isabel and Terrence had seats, so they ate off the table. I didn't have anything to sit on, so I ate off the floor.

This, of course, was not anything to complain about,

because there were some days when there wasn't anything to eat at all.

Waking up every morning in a cold, pissy coat was nothing to complain about, either, because that wasn't half as bad as having to crawl back into it every night.

Even the clothes I wore at this time never came off my back day or night for weeks on end. People must have been able to smell me coming before they could see me—at least until the morning sun had a chance to dry me out. It's a wonder I didn't rot.

On the mornings when Terrence and Isabel had to go out, they put a padlock on the door. If there was anything to eat in the house they would leave something sitting on the sill of my bedroom window. Whenever I got hungry, which was all the time, I would find something to lean against the house so I could climb up to the window in the alley.

When there wasn't anything to use to make the climb, I'd get a boost from some other boy. Then I had to share what little there was to pay for the help.

For some reason, Terrence and Isabel began keeping some very strange hours. It was not uncommon to see them leave very early in the morning and not arrive home until late at night. At first I would come home around suppertime and wait on the doorstep until they arrived.

When it was after dark, I would curl up against the house and fall asleep. If there had been nothing on the sill that day they would sometimes (but not always) bring home some fish and chips and give me some before I went to pissy coat (for some reason, it just isn't right to call it bed).

After a few nights of being left after dark, I discovered there was an elderly night watchman next door at the bag factory. At first he put the run to me, but after asking a few questions he became very sympathetic to my problems and began sitting outside with me on the bag factory steps, where we could watch for Isabel and

Terrence together.

His name was Fred, and although he was fairly old, he was very kind-hearted and provided me with much-needed company. Every hour, on the hour, he would have to go and make his rounds. When he'd come back to the steps, he'd sit down beside me and say, "Well, Tommy, I see you're still here. I'll tell you another little story and maybe by that time they'll be home, okay?"

"Okay, Fred."

And for another hour I'd try my best to listen and stay awake as he'd put his arm around my shoulders and tell me another story.

I don't know how many nights we spent like this. But I know that after the first couple, the "lunch" Fred brought to work kept getting bigger and bigger as he found out what sort of appetite I had.

There were nights when I couldn't stay awake until Isabel and Terrence arrived home. When I nodded off, Fred would take me up to the top floor of the factory and let me sleep there, rolled up in burlap bags. A couple of nights he woke me up when he spotted Terrence and Isabel coming home, but after that he just let me sleep there all night. Although it was dusty and dirty, I must say the memory of it today is far more pleasant than the thoughts of that pissy old coat.

The Ten-Cent Thief

I wasn't on Clarence Street very long before I decided to go back to King Street East and recover some of the toys I had hidden in the furnace room. On the day we moved I realized it would have been too risky to come up with them, and the little thief would have been discovered. Unfortunately, by the time I went back to claim my cache, someone had beaten me to it. The toys were gone.

Another day I went back to our friend Viney's place on St. Patrick Street, where I always knew I could get a cookie or two and a glass of milk. Both the front and back doors were open, but Viney was not home.

As I walked into the kitchen my intentions were to sit on a chair and wait until she came back. But my eyes fell on two dimes sitting side by side on the cupboard. Although I had taken toys before that didn't belong to me, I had never taken money. The thought now entered my head.

Quickly considering all the candy that could be bought for ten cents, I took one of the dimes. Looking out the front door to make sure the coast was clear I darted across the street. I must have been seen coming out of the house by an older boy, but nothing was thought of it until shortly after Viney came home and noticed the dime missing.

The boy then decided to come looking for me.

I had gone up Richmond Street to a store on Prince Edward Street, where I expected to buy a whole dime's worth of candy. But before entering the store I ran into two other bigger boys who had a real con scheme going. Unfortunately, I fell for it and lost my dime.

In approaching the store I was accosted first by one of the boys who threatened to beat me up if I didn't tell him where I was going and how much money I had. Just then the other boy came darting out of nowhere to protect me, and to force the other boy to tell me how much money he had. When it was found that he had a quarter and I had a dime, he was forced to switch with me and apologize.

Now I had a quarter to put down on the counter and buy candy...or so I thought.

It turned out that I didn't have a quarter after all. Someone had taken one of the very large English pennies that were around at the time and covered it with a tinsel-like silver paper to make it look enough like a quarter that it sure fooled an excited four-year-old.

Even the strange clunking sound it made as it hit the counter didn't arouse my suspicions, as I eagerly pointed to the different kinds of candy I wanted to buy.

"You don't think I am going to give you twenty-five cents' worth of candy for this, do you?" said the stern-faced storekeeper, slowly unwrapping the penny and shaking his head rather disgustedly. I realized there would be no point in trying to explain how I'd been taken by the two other boys, and rather than wait for his rebuke, I bolted for the door.

"Don't you ever try that again," I could hear the man shouting as I entered the street, but I wasn't paying much attention because now I spotted a bigger boy running towards me shouting, "You stole Viney's money, kid. I'm gonna get you for it."

As I ran down the alley crying, realizing it was only a matter of time before the bigger boy would catch me, I came to a tall fence which brought the alley to an abrupt dead end. I looked back and saw him quickly closing in. I began to prepare myself for the worst, but just as he was almost on top of me I spotted a small hole in the bottom of the fence that looked like it had been dug by dogs, and I darted through it.

I got through, but as I stood on the other side, the big boy grabbed my foot. I soon got clear by beating him on the arm with a stick and ran through another alley which came out on another street. All the way home I couldn't help thinking what might have happened to me if that big "dough-boy" had been able to get through that little hole.

The Graveyard Beggar

While my reasons now to stay around home were good, they were not to last very long in light of a meeting I had with a group of older boys who had conceived of a way to make money. Each older boy would engage two or three younger boys, around my age, to work with him. To the extent that we were acceptable, we became members of their clubhouse, which was no more than a lean-to against one of the back alley fences.

I was assigned to a boy called Butch and the "work" was to bum people for money. Us little guys were to do the bumming and the older boys got their money by raking off the top of everything we little kids got.

In order to prevent parents finding out what we were doing, it was decided we would work in another neighbourhood. Ironically, Butch's area was the old Loyalist graveyard where soldiers hung out with their girlfriends. This was a lucrative place in the early evening.

We would start out shortly after supper. Upon entering the graveyard Butch would tell us where to go, and which soldiers to bum, and how much money to ask for. If we got hassled by other kids, he'd come and protect us by chasing them away.

We usually got a nickel from soldiers who had girls, and pennies from those who didn't. In the two or three hours we were out, I have no idea how much money we made, but on the way home Butch would stop at a little store to change all the pennies into nickels and dimes.

He usually paid each of us a dime and gave us a bag of candy. That was enough for us little kids. We didn't even think to ask him how much he made. We had been paid. And quite handsomely, we thought. We would even share our bag of candy with him on the way home.

Then things changed a little. Butch found soldiers who were willing to pay him a nickel or a dime—and sometimes even more—to see some girls' legs, or what they might be wearing higher up.

When the price was right, Butch would select one of us to do his dirty work, promising us a bonus at the end of the night. The job was to go over to the girl, and when she least expected it, reach down and pull up her long dress as high as possible, then run towards the soldier, who previously agreed to protect us if the girl decided to get violent.

The scheme worked perfectly for the first couple of times, but when I got caught up under one girl's dress, I was pounded three or four times before I was able to get out. I quickly decided I didn't want to do that job any more.

That's when Butch threatened that he wouldn't pay me, and would ban me from our clubhouse if I didn't do as I was told.

A couple of days later when I went to the clubhouse, everyone was inside and the door was locked. I gave the secret number of knocks and kicks on the door, and Butch yelled, "Okay, Messer, we'll be out in a minute." When the door finally opened, no one was giving orders as they usually did, but everyone wanted to play cowboys and Indians. I was to play the part of a bad Indian who was supposed to be tied up by the cowboys.

After pretending to capture me, they took me down behind an old building near the railroad tracks, and with a piece of cord I later came to know as binder twine, they tied me to a pole, in a sitting position, with my hands behind my back.

I began to think this was great fun and was enjoying all the attention I was getting, and never did I once expect the fearful turn this "game" was soon going to take. After they spread a bunch of newspapers all around the pole at a distance of three or four feet from me, they took a match and lit the newspapers. To say I then became concerned would be the understatement of the century. Especially, because now they all took off and left me.

As I realized by pulling and tugging how hopeless it was to try to free my hands, I began to cry. Soon the newspapers were all aflame, and although they were far enough away that I didn't get burned, I could certainly feel the heat as a light wind blew pieces of smouldering paper towards me.

It was probably the special kind of "dampness" I had in my clothes which prevented them from catching fire, but whatever the reason, I managed to come through it all unscathed.

When the fire died down I began to think again about my hands and as I rolled a piece of binder twine between my fingers I realized it was composed of a large number of very small strands, which, taken one at a time, could be broken with a certain amount of effort. In about fifteen minutes I broke through the thirty to forty strands and finally walked away a free Indian. Needless to say, Butch and his cowboys would not get a chance to capture me again.

As I said before, my mother wasn't home too often when we lived on Clarence Street, but on one of the days she was, she decided to take me to meet my father. We started out early in the morning after Terrence left for the day, and began the long walk to the Armouries at the south end of town.

I remember thinking we'd never get there as we passed street after street that I'd never seen before. Mother kept telling me about what a good soldier my father was. She said she wanted me on my best behaviour, and not to be bold, so he could see "what a great boy he has."

As we came up to a small hut near the gate in a large fence, a soldier with a rifle approached us and asked what we wanted. "I'd like to see Tommy Sullivan," my mother said.

After waiting what seemed to be an awfully long time, another soldier finally appeared and came walking towards us. I felt my mother's hand tighten on mine as she said in a rather subdued manner, "There's your father, Tommy. Be a good boy now and don't forget what I told you."

After they said hello and my mother tried to kiss him and hug him in front of the two guards who were standing in the hut, he appeared to be nervous and not just a little embarrassed.

When she finally let him go, she turned to me and said, "This is our son, Tommy. Come over and say hello to your father, Tommy. That's a good boy."

"Hello," I said rather shyly.

After a great fuss by my mother over how much I looked like my father, the conversation now turned to how she was getting along with Terrence, how he never gave her any money, and would it be possible to get some money from my father to buy clothes for me?

"If I had some I'd give it to you, Isabel," he said. Searching around in his pocket, he took out a quarter and passed it to me, saying, "That's all I've got, honest."

Then he asked Isabel to come back when he got paid.

They both said goodbye and my father walked away. I wouldn't see him again for another ten years.

On the way home my mother asked me if I wanted to go to the show with her. She fumbled in her purse and found the right change and we joined a long line of kids waiting to see the matinée.

Just as the line began to move I noticed something familiar. It was a couple of kids, a boy and a girl, bumming pennies from people as they walked by. With my experience I thought I could do that—and go to the show every day.

From that day on I don't think I missed one show that played at the Mayfair. Some I even went back to see several times. The only problem I ever ran into was with the older boys who insisted on getting their money for a ticket first, before they'd allow us younger kids to bum. But with the cost of a show only twelve cents you could get there before the bigger kids and have your money in hand before they arrived.

I also learned that you could get money if you returned empty pop bottles and beer bottles. These bottles used to bring in two cents apiece; large pop bottles and milk bottles were worth five cents. None were easy to come by.

One day it occurred to me that I had often seen soldiers drinking beer in the graveyard and throwing their bottles in a hole between the graveyard fence and the Golden Ball Garage.

I headed for the graveyard.

After trying several times to reach the bottom of the hole, I was about to give up when a man's voice said, "Hey! What are you looking for down there?"

"Beer bottles," I said as I looked up at a short, stocky soldier, who'd be about thirty-five or so.

"Beer bottles," he said, "and what do you want with beer bottles?"

"I want to sell them and get some money to buy candy," I said, starting to wonder why he was even interested.

"Well, I know where there's lots of beer bottles," he said. "And if I could just get some smart boy to come and help me to get them, I'd give him a whole bag of candy and a quarter besides. Would you like to come?"

"Yeah! But where are they?" I wanted to know.

"Well, you just come along with me and we'll get the candy first," he assured me. "And then we'll go and get the bottles after, okay?"

Before I even said "okay" I was already walking by his side on the way to King's Square and down Charlotte Street.

Stopping at a small store, the soldier bought a fair-sized bag of candy, but instead of giving me the bag, he chose to carry it, and to just dole out one piece at a time as he saw fit.

After another block or so I asked him again where the bottles were.

"Oh, just down here a ways," he said, as I began to notice his grip on my wrist becoming slightly tighter. Soon we turned into an alley, and about half-way down we came to a set of old rickety steps.

"The bottles are up here," he said, giving me another candy and making sure I walked up the steps ahead of him. Coming onto a flat roof, which was sort of wedged between two or three taller buildings, we made our way to a door.

After trying it and seeing that it was locked, the soldier led me over a pile of boards and other debris to one of the inside corners of the roof where an old lean-to had somehow remained rather shoddily attached to one of the taller buildings.

Seeming to be a bit concerned as he looked around, the soldier exclaimed: "The bottles are gone. They were right here in this corner, but someone must have come and taken them."

Showing no remorse whatever, and somehow feeling less tense, I quickly said, "That's okay," and suggested we go back to the graveyard.

"Just a minute," he said, reaching into his pocket and pulling out a quarter. "You still want this, don't you?"

When I told him I did, he said, "Well, you just lay down here and I'll lay down beside you, and after you do a small job for me, I'll give you this one and another one besides, and then when you go back to the graveyard you'll have two quarters."

I quickly changed my mind about wanting any quarters, as he pulled me down alongside of him, and took something from his pants to which I was certain he was physically attached.

"I want to go home," I said, struggling to get away. As he pulled me down the second time his foot must have kicked against a board which was used to prop up the lean-to and the whole thing came down with a crash.

Neither one of us was hurt, but the loud noise attracted a considerable amount of cursing from someone working below, which made the soldier uneasy enough to want to consider another location to carry out his intentions.

"We'll go somewhere else," he said, letting me go for an instant while he buttoned himself up. Seizing upon what I thought might be my only chance to escape, I bolted through a small hole under the lean-to, crawled out from between two rolls of tar-paper and galloped for the steps.

I could hear the clamour of heavy army boots coming over the pile of boards as I ran down the stairs and into the alley, not bothering to look back until I got to the street.

Turning for a short look before rounding the corner, I could see the soldier standing at the bottom of the steps talking to another man. But with no desire to linger further, I ran up the street to King Square, through the graveyard, and ultimately home.

That was the last trip I made to the graveyard for almost a year. And for the longest time, the sight of every soldier I met who even remotely resembled the one who tricked me into going with him would cause me to quickly disappear in the opposite direction.

The experience worried me so much for a while that even little girls found out they could scarc me by merely lifting up their dresses in front of me. On one occasion I was chased down the street and right into my own alley by a girl about a year or so older than me. She had me almost terrified by holding up her dress with one hand and yanking her pants up and down with the other.

Fortunately, as this began to happen more frequently with more little girls trying to get away with it, my fears lessened with familiarity and their little chasing game stopped almost as quickly as it had began.

Goodbye, Old Fred

During our last few days on Clarence Street, I mostly played around home. My mother was home then, and she and Terrence seemed to be getting along a lot better, especially since there was some talk of Terrence's father coming down from McAdam Junction to visit us. His name was Olivar, and I had met him briefly the previous year, but I don't remember any details of that visit, except his wife's name was Mabelene, and his stepdaughter was Doreen.

On one of these last days on Clarence Street, I was searching for beer bottles along the railroad tracks, when a group of kids I had never seen before came down to play on the beach of Courtenay Bay. They made their way out to an old dory which was stuck in the sand upside-down, and they seemed to be having so much fun that I decided to amble out and join them.

There were about a dozen of them. Two or three had bicycles, two or three were babies, and the rest were about my age, or a little older. While the oldest boys and girls were playing with the babies and dunking them from time to time in the shallow pools of water, I made my way over to the kids who were playing around the dory.

It wasn't long before I was accepted and having a whale of a time, chasing the others or being chased myself, and climbing up one side of the dory and sliding down the other.

As the tide began to come in there seemed to be more fun as we slid down and splashed into the water, which was at first no more than two or three inches deep.

But as the tide comes in fast at Courtenay Bay, by the time the kids stopped playing around the dory and headed for the beach, the water was about ten inches high.

Nevertheless, I thought I'd climb up and have one more slide. But as I reached the top and heard one of the older boys calling for me to return to shore with the rest of them, I lost my balance and fell backwards, head-first into the water.

I don't know how long I was there, but it seems my pants leg was caught on a nail in the side of the dory. I remember lots of bubbles. And the fact that I couldn't get my legs down from over my head caused me to remain under water where I couldn't breathe.

After that everything went blank until I woke up on the beach where a boy was picking me up and carrying me towards his bicycle, while someone was saying I was being taken to the hospital.

I remember sitting in the wire basket over the front wheel, as we bumped our way across the railroad tracks and headed up Clarence Street. When we passed the bag factory I was somehow able to indicate where I lived and that I wanted him to stop the bicycle so I could go to see my mother.

As he pulled up to the steps he took me out of the basket and carried me up to the front door where he stood me on my feet long enough to knock and wait for an answer.

"Oh, my God, what happened?" asked my mother, as she opened the door and saw me soaking wet, half propped up against the bigger boy's leg. "He was playing on the old dory down at the bay and he fell in the water, ma'am, and I had to pull him out," said the boy, as they helped me over and put me on my mother's bed.

"When I carried him up on the beach, I thought he was dead," the boy explained. "But when I was about to take him to the hospital, he woke up."

I can still hear my mother thanking him over and over and telling him what a wonderful boy he was for saving me and bringing me home. She gave him a quarter and he thanked her. I remember how my eyes bugged out of my head because I had never seen her give a kid so much money at one time, not even me.

But then again, how could I possibly realize the value

of my life, or the importance of saving it, when I was only four years old?

After the boy left, my mother pampered me for a while and explained how we would be moving to a better place tomorrow or the next day in preparation for Olivar's visit, because she and Terrence didn't want him to see us living in this dump, and that if I was a good boy he might even take me to McAdam Junction for the rest of the summer.

I wasn't too sure about this last part, nor did I even know what was meant by McAdam Junction, but as soon as my clothes were dry I decided to find out.

It would soon be time for old Fred to come on duty at the bag factory, and as he always seemed to be able to comfort me whenever my mind was troubled, I was sure he could clear up this McAdam Junction question. Besides, I had to tell him about falling in the water today.

About an hour or so later I was sitting once more with Fred on the bag factory steps, listening to him tell me what a nice place McAdam Junction was, what nice people lived there, and that my mother had the right idea sending me there, because it was in the country.

He said I'd probably be looked after a lot better, too, in a place where I'd be likely to get lots to eat, and where there would be far less of a chance of my getting drowned.

Just as I was beginning to feel quite happy about going to this place called McAdam Junction, which Fred was making sound so wonderful, I looked up to ask him another question, but stopped when I saw tears coming down his face.

"Whatcha cryin' for, Fred?" I asked, as he now baffled me more by crying and laughing at the same time.

"Oh, I'm not crying," he said, "I'm just glad when I see one of my good friends leaving a dirty old place like this to go to some place better. And when an old man like me is really happy he sometimes looks like he's crying when he's not."

Although I bought this explanation at the time, I know today that he probably came to enjoy my company as much as I enjoyed his, and while he knew that my leaving Clarence Street could only improve my lot, he was very sad to see me go.

"I'm gonna miss you, Tommy," he said, as Terrence came walking down the street towards the house. "But if you ever need a place to sleep again, don't forget your old friend at the bag factory."

As I turned to go, without realizing I would never see him again, I said, "Okay, Fred, goodbye" and was soon running down the street to meet Terrence.

Off to McAdam Junction

The new place we moved into was upstairs in a building just off Coburg Street. Although the entrance was from the back alley, and the house itself looked rather shabby, the inside of the apartment was nice and clean with newly painted walls and adequate furniture.

I don't know where the money came from all of a sudden, but for the first time in a long while the cupboards were stocked with groceries, there was a bowl of fruit on the table, a basket of peaches by the kitchen door, and even some dishes to eat out of. While I now know that all this had been put together just to impress our expected company, and the following week would be back to normal, I wouldn't be around at the time to witness the regression. Instead, I'd be living on a small farm near McAdam Junction.

Although I had lots to eat and a couch to sleep on in the kitchen, I didn't have any friends yet on Coburg Street so I found it pretty dull. The closest thing to excitement for me was taking peaches from the basket by the kitchen door when I wasn't supposed to.

On the afternoon before our company was to arrive, Terrence and Isabel had been in such a pretty good mood that I had already had three peaches without them being missed. I was planning to take a fourth when I was told to go outside and play for a while.

After dawdling around the back steps for ten to fifteen minutes, I thought of going back into the house on the pretext of getting a drink of water. If no one was paying any particular attention to me, I'd just grab another peach and go back outside.

Not seeing any reason why it shouldn't work, I headed for the door and opened it with as little fanfare as possible, not wanting to attract any undue attention. I walked through the living room, past the bedroom—which, incidentally, had no door on it—and into the kitchen. So preoccupied was I with getting a peach, I was having a drink of water before I realized there was no one around.

Thinking this was quite strange, in light of the fact that I had been playing near the back steps—the only entrance—all the time, and no one could have come out without me seeing them, I sauntered back to the kitchen door, grabbed a peach and decided this time to look in the bedroom on my way by, and—wow!

I looked into the bedroom and got myself outside as quickly and as quietly as possible, hoping that I hadn't been discovered standing there watching what was going on.

As I reached the bottom of the steps, I remember thinking about the fight Terrence and Isabel once had when we lived on King Street East, and how I looked down through the grate to watch them make up. Since then I had put two and two together and began to realize that fighting and making up didn't necessarily have to go together, and judging from what I just saw my conclusions were right. Terrence and Isabel hadn't had a fight now for two or three days, but that sure didn't stop them from trying to "make up" for all the fights they were going to have in the future.

The next morning about nine o'clock Terrence went to the train station to meet his folks, and about an hour later they all arrived at the house. As the door opened, the first to step into the living room was Terrence's stepmother, Mabelene, a short, fat woman with short, dark hair, and considerably younger than Terrence's father.

Next came Doreen, a girl of about seven or eight, who was also very plump with long, dark hair done up in pigtails. She resembled her mother very closely, but was only a stepsister to Terrence.

Next came Terrence, with his father, Olivar, whom I recognized right away from our previous meeting. He was a fairly old man of slight build and medium height and had some sort of magnetism about him which attracted me to him right off the bat. While I don't know exactly what his job was, I know he worked a long time with the railroad and carried a free pass to travel on the trains anywhere he wanted to go.

When the usual greetings were over and the fuss was made about Doreen and me finally meeting each other, everyone sat down to talk and have a small drink, while my mother went to the kitchen to prepare dinner.

The conversation was mostly dominated by Terrence, who spoke about getting some kind of a good job in Truro, Nova Scotia, and how he would appreciate it if his father and Mabelene would take "Tammy" up to McAdam for a while, at least until he and Isabel could get better situated. While Mabelene had certain reservations about this proposition, it was Olivar's word which carried, and my trip to McAdam was directly approved.

After dinner there was another drink and more talk about writing letters and sending money over from Truro so that Mabelene could buy me some clothes. Before anyone realized what time it was we all had to hurry down to the station to avoid missing the train.

As my mother kissed me and told me to be a good boy, I got the feeling she wasn't quite as happy about all this as everyone else seemed to be, but when the conductor shouted "all aboard" she helped me up the steps until Mabelene could catch me by the hand, and saying she'd see me soon, she waved goodbye and smiled.

The train ride lasted about three hours and the distance was about a hundred miles.

The first thing which impressed me about the house at McAdam was the great number of cats that greeted us at the door.

When supper was over I was allowed to go out for a little while with Doreen and survey the premises, while Olivar went to the barn to milk the cow. Immediately outside the back door we came to a small building which covered a spring, from where, Doreen was quick to tell me, they got their water.

Next to the building was a handmade swing, and before I had a chance to reach it, Doreen was demonstrating.

From where I was standing my eyes fell on an old black dog who was tied to one of the corners of the house. As I began to walk in his direction I was told by Doreen not to touch him because he might bite.

I was starting to wonder if there was anything around here I could touch, when a small black kitten ran out from under a pile of boards and curled around my legs, acting as if it wanted some petting. As I reached down and began to stroke him on the back, my good friend Doreen was right there to pick him up and show me how to do it correctly.

Thinking I had better get away from her before I got mad, I headed down the path towards the barn. After quickly dropping the kitten she was right behind me with her hand on my shoulder. "No, no, Tommy, you can't go down there, you might get kicked by the cow."

Not being used to this kind of treatment, and having no intention of putting up with it any longer, at the sound of the words "kicked by the cow" I turned around, kicked her in the leg, and went to the barn anyway.

As I arrived Olivar had just put the cow in the field and was coming with the pail of milk, when he asked, "What's Dorie yelling about, Tom?" This was the first time I had ever been called "Tom" and by the way it sounded, coming from Olivar, I really liked it. It also somehow made me want to answer with the truth. "She wouldn't let me pet the kitty, so I kicked her in the leg."

I thought I detected a small grin form around his lips, but he said nothing as we brought the milk into the house.

Mabelene, however, was acting terribly concerned. She asked me why I kicked Doreen in the leg. "Oh, leave the boy alone, Mabe," said Olivar. "Dorie probably deserved what she got. She's always going around thinking she owns everything anyway."

While this took me by complete surprise, because I was not used to having anyone stick up for me, I also felt that some of the same affinity which had developed between me and old Fred was now beginning between me and Olivar—at least to a certain degree. I think Mabelene sensed this, too, and unfortunately allowed it to sink as a wedge between us. And from that moment on she made no attempt whatsoever to hide her favouritism towards Doreen.

While this was of no consequence to me, because even second-best from Mabelene was still far better than I was used to getting, I considered the benefits accruing from this first evening's encounter to far outweigh any disadvantages. Doreen's possessiveness was going to get her nowhere, and within a short period of time she began to treat me like a human being.

But there were other problems ahead, and bed-wetting was going to be one of them. And it would have to happen on the very first night.

"The bed is where Doreen sleeps and the cot is yours" were the last words I remember hearing as I drowsily began to undress. The next sounds were the crowing of the rooster, but he didn't wake up soon enough for me.

It was just my luck that I wet the bed the first night I was there, and if I thought it was going to pass unnoticed I was badly mistaken.

Just as we all got nicely seated at the breakfast table, Doreen said, "Guess what, Mom; Tommy peed his bed last night."

In the middle of trying to swallow my first mouthful of porridge, I crouched down in my chair to make myself as small as possible while Mabelene now asked, "You didn't pee the bed, did you?"

Not being able to raise my voice higher than a mutter, I managed to shyly and meekly say, "Yes," as my red face showed my shame and embarrassment.

As she went to the bedroom and returned with the sheet, she threw it on the floor and glared at Olivar. "See what I'm going to have to put up with? That woman never told me her kid wet the bed. She knew if she had I wouldn't have taken him in the first place. Or at least I would have asked for more money. They probably won't even send the amount they promised anyway.

"If she thinks I'm gonna clean up after her kid..." she said, before Olivar stopped her dead in her tracks.

"Sit down. Eat your breakfast and let the boy eat his. How do you expect any of us to eat with you cluckin' around the kitchen like an old hen? Sit down."

After a few more "shame on you's" and a couple of "see how good I got you that time?" giggles from Doreen, I managed to wolf down the rest of my porridge, leave the table and head for the outside.

As I walked in the woods a little way and sat down on a big rock where I couldn't be seen from the house, I could still hear Mabelene going on about how the mattress was going to be ruined...how clean Doreen was because she didn't wet the bed...and a host of other things which I was going to hear repeatedly for the next several days.

It seemed that no matter what I did, I just kept wetting the bed.

At first I was cut off all liquids after supper. When that didn't work, Olivar would wake me up before he went to bed, take me outside to pee and bring me back to bed.

But before the morning came, the bed was wet again.

I was beginning to hate to sit down at the breakfast table and listen to Mabelene make her comparisons between "good little Doreen" and "bad little Tom."

Nothing Olivar could say or do seemed to be able to keep her quiet.

Then, just as everyone was about to consider me a hopeless case, I awoke one morning feeling very strange. My bed was dry.

Dressing as quickly as I could and feeling extremely proud of myself, I ran into the kitchen to give everybody the good news.

As I sat down at the table I noticed that everyone seemed unnaturally quiet. Thinking there might be something wrong, but still unable to contain myself, I blurted out, "I never wet the bed last night, Mabelene."

Expecting to hear her give me my first compliment, I was somewhat surprised to see both her and Doreen remain strangely silent, while Olivar began to laugh.

"That's wonderful, just wonderful," he roared. "We certainly have a good boy here this morning, now don't we? Ho! Ho! Ho!" he laughed. "And you didn't wet the bed last night? Well, isn't that just wonderful. You didn't wet the bed last night—but Dorie did!"

It was like someone hit me with a sledge hammer.

I immediately looked at Doreen, then at Mabelene, but neither one would look at me or even say a word.

I looked at Olivar, who had just thumped his hand down on the table with another volley of "Ho! Ho! Ho's!" and I finally began to get the joke.

When I started to laugh I purposely tried to sound as much as I could like Olivar, and just as Mabelene said to Doreen, "Come on, dear, let's go to the bedroom," I thumped my hand on the table and said, "Well, isn't that just wonderful" and the house came down with a lot more "Ho! Ho! Ho's!"

I was eventually able to cut down my bed-wetting to about once or twice a week, but after that morning I never had to listen to Doreen or Mabelene ever throw it up to me again.

It was about August 1940 and the weather during the day was exceptionally hot without even the whisper of a breeze being able to penetrate the deeply wooded area.

The little farm itself was situated on what was no more than a dirt lane called the River Road, and consisted of about thirty acres carved out of the bushland in what only could be called a hit-and-miss fashion.

Half-way between the house and the barn was a small chicken coop where the family of hens chased each other around the hay stack, while the presence of a big black rooster ensured their protection against all the snoopy marauding cats.

The only other animals they had were a cow, which

seldom mooed, and a dog which only barked or snarled at night during the occasional visit of a prowling bear.

Surrounded by strangers. Living in virtual isolation. Bears in the backyard. Yet, you know, I was beginning to like it.

And I guess it was my unbounded curiosity, which kept me looking under rocks, peeking into holes and watching squirrels, birds and tadpoles either jump, fly or swim, that prevented any loneliness from creeping into my daily affairs.

I also enjoyed helping Mabelene feed the hens, gather vegetables from the garden and once a week walk the mile to McAdam with her and Doreen to do some shopping.

In the evenings we listened to the radio, played games around the table and sometimes attached long lines of clothespins together and pretended we were driving trains as we pulled them along the floor.

I think we got this last idea from Olivar, who knew everything there was to know about trains and who was always talking about them.

There was also an old gramophone in the living room which Doreen was allowed to play once in a while, as long as she promised to look after it and not break the records.

This was something I really enjoyed listening to and would keep on cranking the handle just as long as Doreen kept replacing the records and playing the music.

One evening as Olivar was sitting down, smoking his pipe, he casually began to hum and sing a few words of a tune which was very familiar to me.

Getting up off the floor, I went over to him and said, "No! No! Don't sing it like that, sing it like this."

And without hesitation I sang him all of the words of the song, "Blue Velvet Band." That left Mabelene and Doreen dumbfounded and Olivar slapping his knee with some more of his "Ho! Ho! Ho's!"

"Can you sing us another one like that, Tom?" he said, clapping his hands in obvious delight.

After hearing me sing two or three more he got up and went to his bedroom and came back with something I had never seen before.

It had strings on it and reminded me of Terrence's guitar.

"What's that, Olivar? What's that?" I impatiently demanded.

"That's my old fiddle, Tom," he said. "And when I get 'er tuned up I want to see if you can dance as good as you can sing."

After making a couple of "ting, ting" sounds and twisting something on the end, he again rubbed this funny-looking stick across the strings and before I knew it the dog began to howl, and the whole house was full of the best kind of music I had ever heard.

Without warning, Doreen grabbed me and swung me around and around, while Mabelene clapped her hands and the whole kitchen began to shake with the tapping of Olivar's feet.

When I finally went to bed that night, it was after helping everybody sing "Buffalo Gal," "She'll Be Coming 'Round the Mountain When She Comes," "Rubber Dolly" and "Turkey in the Straw" so many times I think we wore out the strings. As I went to sleep, it was after having the most wonderful time in my life.

While there were other times that Olivar played the fiddle, there were never any quite as memorable as the first night, but that certainly didn't stop me from asking him to play again whenever I got the chance.

When I look back at it now, I can see the greatest joy I got out of life as a child was singing the old-time country songs. It brought a lot of happiness into what I otherwise considered to be a rather lack-lustre life. I guess if there was anything constantly positive during my first few years on this planet, it had to be country and western music. Terrence had a guitar and played it, my mother loved it and sang it, and so did I. And given this background, it should come as no surprise that I could sing literally hundreds of songs all the way through before I was even ten years old. I even suspect that Olivar would have had me playing the fiddle had circumstances allowed me to live longer with him in McAdam.

Besides visiting some of the neighbouring farmhouses and occasionally playing some of the usual games with the kids, Doreen and I would sometimes be allowed to walk into town, buy some candy and take in a "picture-show."

The trouble was, they always seemed to have love movies instead of cowboy pictures. While I was never exactly what you could call thrilled, Doreen would always come away absolutely ecstatic. I guess she felt the same way about love stories as I was later to feel about adventure movies.

One evening after supper, as we played around the hay stack and Doreen was still talking about the movie we had seen that day, she decided we should play house the way we often did, only this time there would be a slight difference. She would continue to be the mama, but instead of me being the little boy as I usually was, I was now supposed to take on the responsibilities of being the daddy.

Soon we began to play the roles of certain movie characters, which naturally involved a lot of hugging and kissing, and before long, in imitation of all good lovers, we were expected to go to bed.

Crawling in between the chicken coop and the hay stack and finding a small, concealed niche in which to lie down, the stage was now set and the players were ready for Act Two.

"This is the part they don't show in the movies," said Doreen, as she pulled her big blue bloomers down to her ankles and kicked them off.

"Now you have to take down your pants," she said, "and lay on top of me."

As a certain picture of Terrence and Isabel now

flashed through my mind, I said, "Oh! I know. You just want me to play 'making up.'"

"No," she said. "This is not making up. This is making babies. Now press your diddy bird into the minny bird, like this, and kiss me."

After several unsuccessful and completely awkward attempts, I finally said, "I can't, Doreen, your belly's too big, and when it gets in the way I can't reach."

"Well, you get on the bottom," she said as she rolled me over, "and I'll get on the top."

Soon she was rubbing herself so tightly against my body that my poor little diddy bird was getting extremely sore from the chafing. As I tried to squirm around a little to get some relief, I was told in no uncertain terms that I wasn't doing it right and "you can't make babies if you are going to move around so much."

"But you're hurting my diddy bird. And besides, I don't like playing this game any more."

"Well, I don't like playing with you any more, either," she said, "because you don't know how to play right."

And with that she jumped up and started pulling on her bloomers, just as Mabelene began to call from the back door, "Doreen, it's time to come in now, and bring Tommy with you."

As we crawled out from behind the stack, Doreen answered that we were coming, and after stopping long enough to give me the kind of look that could only mean she thought I was the world's greatest failure, at least the world's worst lover, she stomped away and headed for the house.

She spent the rest of the evening listening to the radio and watching Mabelene mix dough for the next day's bread.

During the next day or so, Olivar had decided the north side of the house was in such a bad state of repair that he called another man in to help him do some shingling. As I was always ready to lend help whenever I could, I naturally wound up breaking the man's ruler one morning when I accidentally hit it with his hammer.

I guess he figured this action on my part was now reason enough to put the run to me. But as he chased me around the corner of the house, the old black dog, who hadn't made a move for the last three weeks, didn't like being disturbed and quickly grabbed him by the leg. After three or four yanks and a couple of rips, the tug o' war was over and the man went back to shingling, apparently satisfied that he had come away a winner, of at least a small part of the battle and a small part of his pants.

I would have liked to look back around the corner a couple of times to see what Olivar was doing all the ho! ho! hoing about, but decided to stay where it was safe and watch the old dog as he proudly chewed away on his half of the man's overalls.

Later that morning Mabelene got a letter from my mother in Truro and immediately decided to take me to McAdam to buy some clothes.

I presumed the letter contained money, although I wasn't told it did. I mention this because after subsequent letters I was told they contained no money and that anything I received was bought by Mabelene herself. While the truth of this may never be positively substantiated, I choose to believe that at least some of the letters contained money, and that in some cases at least a portion, if not all, got spent on Doreen.

However, that day I certainly had a good time in McAdam. I got a pair of shoes, two pairs of pants, two shirts and a warm coat for fall. And while Mabelene tucked them all into a big bag, I felt like a pauper ready to become a king as Doreen and I chomped away on a couple of big suckers.

After the shopping was over, the day was still by no means complete. The word was out that a troop train was coming through later on that afternoon and a lot of people were planning to go up to the station house to wish the soldiers good luck on their way to World War II.

As the train came chugging to a stop, all the windows

were open and the soldiers began to cheer as great shouts went up from all of the people.

As Doreen and I and Mabelene found ourselves situated right up at the front of the crowd, a great idea now entered my head. Breaking away from Mabelene's hand, I walked out on the platform in front of everybody and looked up at one of the soldiers on the train.

In the middle of a hush that now fell over the people I spoke in a loud voice, "Hey! Big soldier…can you give a dime to a little poor kid?"

After about three seconds of silence, during which Mabelene tried to dash out and grab me, the soldier said, "Just a minute, lady."

Then looking at me and speaking a bit louder, he added, "Of course I've got a dime for a poor kid. As a matter of fact, Sonny, where I'm going I can't spend my dimes anyway."

He then tossed a handful of change onto the platform and a great roar went up from the rest of the soldiers, who now began doing the same thing with their loose change. In less than half a minute the entire platform was covered with pennies, dimes and nickels, and the kids began to scramble for them.

As the crowd went back to cheering, the old steam engine gave a toot-toot and slowly chugged away from the station, leaving some with a tearful eye and the kids with a surprise fortune.

When Mabelene spoke of the incident later, I noticed that it was always to mention the embarrassment I had caused—and never to tell that Doreen had picked up about three times as much of the change as I had. But the account was always good for a chuckle or two nevertheless.

Being centre stage there at the train station didn't bother me a bit. I wasn't shy. I guess I really didn't know what being shy was all about.

Besides, to lead the kind of life that I was leading you had to learn to fend for yourself.

The School Christmas Concert

My first appearance on an actual stage brought me a standing ovation—maybe I should have been an actor, not a singer. All that fall I had been attending school with Doreen in the town of McAdam. I just followed her to school one day, found her Grade 2 classroom and plunked myself down in a seat behind her. Her teacher, Miss Hawes, allowed me to sit there with a colouring book and thereafter to attend school each day with Doreen any time I felt like it, even though I was only four years old.

It's funny how I just couldn't wait to get to school when I wasn't supposed to be there. But later, when I was supposed to be there I just didn't want to go.

There was even one day when Doreen was sick and she couldn't go to school—but I still went anyway. I soon became such a part of the class that they even found a part for me in the school concert.

The teacher, principal and kids thought I was too young for a big part, so they planned to have me walk onto the stage when the Grade 2s had performed their show, say, "Thank you and Merry Christmas everybody," and return to my place at the end of the line. Then we would all walk off the stage softly singing "The First Noel." At least, that was the way it was supposed to have worked. That was the plan, but there was always the unforeseen, especially whenever a boy named Tommy Messer was involved.

The concert hall was packed with adults, and the confidence that most of the kids had displayed while rehearsing in the classroom had all but disappeared as they began to contemplate the possibility of making mistakes in front of so many people.

As the Grade 1 class came off the stage to a round of applause, it was now Grade 2's turn to go on. I was to be the one to lead everyone onto the stage, because I had to be at the tail end of the line and the last one to leave when our act was finished. Doreen was to follow close behind me and take up a position next to me to keep me company and to remind me, if necessary, what my line was when it was time for me to end our part of the show. After Doreen came the rest of the class in single file.

As I took my first two steps on the stage, I just had time to look towards the audience and smile as I went flat on my face, tripping over one of my shoe-laces. Some of the people must have felt embarrassed for me. Not too many laughed. But when big fat Doreen, who should have been watching where she was going, tripped and fell right on top of me, the whole house began to roar.

As I came quickly to my feet and stood rigidly with my shoulders back and faced the audience, Doreen got up, placed her hands on her hips with a "humph" that could be heard by everyone in the school and in a tone that could only mean it was all my fault, she said in a whisper that sounded very much like a low growl "We're not supposed to stand here, Tommy, now keep on walking."

In what must have begun to appear like a scene from a Laurel and Hardy movie, I turned to my left and started walking, and walking, and walking, and walking, until I was about ten feet past the spot on which we were supposed to stand. Turning around to see if Doreen was still behind me I found myself alone, and the audience falling off their chairs from laughter as the class, looking very concerned, watched Doreen trying to attract my attention by flapping her wings, clucking and doing everything but lay an egg.

As I hurried back to my place, determined not to make any more mistakes, I again resumed a rigid stance with my chest out and my hands at my sides, while the audience began applauding as though they assumed that everything that had taken place until now had all been planned.

The applause continued, although somewhat subdued, as each of the kids now stepped forward to perform their individual parts. Everything was going smoothly until

Doreen's turn came to recite the poem "'Twas the Night Before Christmas." Everyone in the class had agreed that this was the hardest poem to remember, but since Doreen had learned it in what seemed no time at all, the teacher considered it only right that she be allowed to recite it on the night of the concert.

As she stepped forward to the front of the stage and curtsied to the audience, she began:

> 'Twas the night before Christmas
> and all through the house,
> not a creature was stirring…
> not a creature was…stirring

After she repeated the word "stirring" a number of times she stopped and began to shift her weight from one foot to the other, becoming stage-struck and bobbing up and down like a pop bottle in a bathtub. A hush now fell over the audience as she started into a long, low hum, interrupted only by a few snickers from kids in other classes.

Just when it seemed that our teacher, or someone, was about to come and take her off the stage, I began to sense the graveness of her predicament and without thinking what the consequences might be concerning the possibility of making another mistake, I quickly hastened to her side, took her by the hand, and in the same confident way I had often heard Doreen herself deliver the poem, I began to proclaim in a loud, clear voice:

> 'Twas the night before Christmas
> and all through the house,
> not a creature was stirring,
> not even a mouse.
> And the stockings were hung
> by the chimney with care,
> In hopes that St. Nicholas
> soon would be there.

Doreen still seemed to remain oblivious to what was going on as I continued:

> *The children were nestled*
> *all snug in their beds,*
> *while visions of sugarplums*
> *danced in their heads.*
> *And mom, with her kerchief,*
> *and I in my cap,*
> *had just settled down*
> *for a long winter's nap.*

You could hear a pin drop now as Doreen stopped humming and began to clutch my hand so hard it was hurting me. Trying not to let it show, I proceeded:

> *When out on the lawn*
> *there arose such a clatter,*
> *I sprang from my bed*
> *to see what was the matter.*

Doreen now started to mumble as if she was searching for the proper words, while an old lady in the front row began wiping her eyes with a handkerchief as though she were crying.

> *Away to the window,*
> *I flew like a flash,*
> *tore open the shutters*
> *and threw up the sash.*
> *Where the bright pale moon*
> *on the new-fallen snow,*
> *gave lustre of day*
> *to the objects below.*

Here Doreen began to say the words a little more clearly.

> *When what to my wondering eyes should appear,*

> *but a miniature sleigh and eight tiny reindeer,*
> *With a little old driver so lively and quick,*
> *I knew in a moment it must be St. Nick.*

At this point Doreen regained her full composure and as the audience showed how pleased they were by gently applauding, together we both continued to recite in unison and with much greater enthusiasm.

> *More rapid than eagles*
> *his reindeer they came,*
> *as he whistled and shouted*
> *and called them by name.*
> *"Now Dasher! Now Dancer!*
> *Now Prancer! and Vixen!*
> *On Comet! On Cupid!*
> *On Donner and Blitzen!*
> *To the top of the porch!*
> *To the top of the wall!*
> *Now, dash away! Dash away! Dash away, all!"*

In what seemed like only a moment or so we were saying the last line:

> *And I heard him exclaim*
> *as he drove out of sight,*
> *"Merry Christmas to all*
> *and to all a good night."*

Doreen was now smiling broadly, as indeed she had every right to do, for those in the audience who weren't wiping their eyes were giving us a standing ovation.

The class was now getting ready to sing "The First Noel" and as Doreen and I walked back to join them, Doreen remembered I had a line to say before the class could leave the stage.

I got to my place at the end of the row just as the crowd was sitting down from the standing ovation for

Doreen and me. The people in the front had begun to sit down first and that left a clear view for me to see some of the people who were still standing at the back.

That's when I spotted my mother.

I found out later she had come on the train to surprise us. Terrence was with her. When we were not to be found at home they came to the concert.

The Grade 2 choir was now singing "The First Noel" and I was beside myself with excitement. Instead of saying "Thank you and Merry Christmas, everybody" I shouted, "Happy thank you" and "Hi, there, Isabel" as I climbed off the stage like I was jumping over a backyard fence and scrambled up the centre aisle to my mother's arms.

During the next few minutes I am not sure what the reaction from the audience was, or how the class managed to get off the stage without me. But neither did I care too much as I listened to my mother tell me how happy she was to see me, and what wonderful things she had brought to give me as soon as we got back to Olivar's.

As time went by and the concert drew to a close, everyone's attention was drawn to a grey-haired man wearing glasses and a light-coloured blue suit, who came out on the stage to thank everybody for coming, and to say a few words on behalf of the teachers and students who were responsible for what he called "a really wonderful evening of superb entertainment."

After pausing a moment to allow for the applause to subside, he now hit the audience with a few special words that went something like this: "And now, ladies and gentlemen, as most of you know, it's been nearly twenty years since I became principal of the elementary school in McAdam. And for twenty years before that, as a teacher, I taught in a great many schools in this area.

"In all of this time, as you can well imagine, I have seen a great many boys and girls come and go, but tonight on this stage, I saw something happen, the like of which I never saw before in all my forty years of teaching experience."

He now told the audience how the teachers behind the curtains were just about to interrupt the concert by bringing Doreen off the stage when she was in trouble, and how utterly amazed they were to see a mere four-year-old boy step forward and not only help Doreen out of her difficulty, but recite word for word a very long poem which he had never been taught, and one which would have been very hard to learn, even by a child of over twice the age.

He also explained how I came to be going to school in the first place, and while my attendance record had been perfect so far, I was not enrolled officially on the school register because of my age.

"But ladies and gentlemen," he said, "on behalf of all the teachers and all the students of McAdam Elementary, who wish to honour this boy for the extraordinary qualities which were displayed here tonight, it is indeed my pleasure to recall to the stage, for the purpose of receiving our crest and our school pin, the boy we are all proud to name as our honorary student of the year, Tommy Messer."

I think my mother almost fell off her seat as Olivar, who now seemed to appear from nowhere, grabbed me by the hand, hoisted me up on his shoulders and quickly headed for the stage. I don't suppose there was anyone in all of McAdam who was better known at that time than Olivar Messer, and as he came down the centre aisle with me on his shoulders, all you could hear was "Yay, Olivar, yay, Olivar!" over the sounds of whistling and the clapping of hands.

As I stepped on the stage, the principal called for silence and after attaching the school pin to my sweater and handing me the crest, he ruffled my hair a little and said, "Tommy, you're a remarkable boy. And when your visit to McAdam is over, I hope you'll come back to see us again sometime. But if you can't," he said, pointing to the pin, "you'll always have this to remember us by."

As he shook my hand he made a gesture to the audience which now reacted in a way that could only be described as deafening. Before I could say thank you or anything, Miss Hawes ran out from behind the curtain and gave me a big hug and hoisted me back on Olivar's shoulders, and I was taken back to my mother at the rear of the hall.

It had certainly been an exciting evening, full of wonderful surprises. And as the people left the hall they made a point of coming over to me and Isabel and Terrence to shake our hands and wish us a Merry Christmas.

As soon as Mabelene and Doreen were able to join us, we left the hall and headed for home in a large sleigh which had been provided earlier by one of the local River Road residents. He was sort of a rural route taxi driver, and he had a full load both ways on the sleigh. What payment he expected I don't know. But most people in those days did a lot of things for others "just to be neighbourly" so I suppose there may have been no payment involved this night.

When we got back to the house I spotted some Christmas gifts that Isabel had bought. After much pestering she allowed Doreen and me to each open one gift. Dorie had a pen and pencil set, and I got a toy revolver.

Then Mabelene called us for lunch, and before we knew it we were ushered off to bed where the fatigue of a long and eventful day soon overcame any desire to stay awake.

There were still a couple of days to go before Christmas. Terrence and Isabel were staying for the holiday, so Terrence and Olivar went into the woods and brought back a small Christmas tree which they set up in the living room. Mabelene and Isabel soon started to decorate it, with the help of Doreen and me, but after breaking a couple of ornaments I was told to go and busy myself elsewhere.

I didn't really mind the mild rejection, because the tree was beginning to take on a rather fascinating appearance—even without my expert assistance.

I had never experienced this Christmas-like atmosphere in a house before, so it is not too difficult to understand why I had certain longings for McAdam during the years that followed.

Christmas Day itself started with a bang as Doreen and I were up at daybreak creating an unholy mess of papers and boxes as we opened our presents. We got mostly clothes. While this seemed to delight Doreen very much, I didn't really feel the same enthusiasm.

I suppose this naturally comes from being a boy, but there was one item, a blue snowsuit, which I hoped Isabel would never insist on me wearing. It was bright blue, and while I had often seen other kids wearing them, I already considered myself much too old for that sort of thing. I guess because I had been wearing overalls for so long—and because we couldn't afford any better—I just automatically became quite content to wear exactly what Terrence wore. I began to fear that if Isabel insisted that I wear it, I would lose my "big boy" status which I was always trying to attain. I was also sure that no "big boy" would be caught in that infantile get-up.

It even crossed my mind that there had been a mistake and that it was meant for Doreen, but I couldn't see her in it either.

As kids do, Doreen and I had a couple of fights over our new Christmas gifts. She went so far as to step on and break one of my toy soldiers and I got in a little hair-pulling.

Isabel came along and slapped me across the side of the head, but Mabelene talked sweetly to Doreen. When Doreen started smirking because I got hit and she didn't, my mother and her mother were heading towards a dust-up which I'm sure my mother would have won hands down. Mabelene was no match for one of Isabel's stinging attacks.

But it didn't come to that—Olivar walked in and wished everyone a Merry Christmas and things calmed after that.

In a short while it began to look like adults had a lot more fun at Christmas than the kids. They opened their gifts and Olivar shared a liquid gift with the rest of the adults. No one seemed to notice when the music lost its rhythm and became slurred that my arms had grown weak and I couldn't keep the gramophone turntable cranked enough.

Because of a late breakfast we didn't have any dinner, but all day I could smell turkey cooking.

When supper arrived, it was a feast. What dishes couldn't be placed on the table were placed on the cupboard.

There was everything you'd expect at a turkey dinner with all the trimmings. I don't know what bugged out more: my eyes before I started eating, or my belly after I was done. But I can honestly say that never in my life—before or since—have I sat down to a Christmas dinner where so few people had so much and so great a variety. In my estimation there was five times too much for us. We were eating leftovers until New Year's. There have been many days since that I have looked back and longed for one of Mabelene's big meals. But it never happened again.

We danced and sang that night, and I showed my mother how Olivar had taught me to dance to the "St. Anne's Reel." (Somewhere along the line I lost this dancing ability, probably due to the lack of practice over the years.)

As I lay in bed that Christmas night I remember thinking how nice it felt to be part of such a warm, close family. I had never felt this way before.

While I don't mean to imply in any way that I would have chosen or preferred this over being with my mother, I simply mean that I was thinking how wonderful it would be if I were living with my mother and Terrence and they could always be as happy as they were that Christmas.

There was another round of singing and dancing for

New Year's Eve, and this time a few neighbours joined us. During the party Olivar played the fiddle and Terrence accompanied his father with the guitar. That is, until the stove pipe fell down. And while Terrence and another man were busy putting it back up, Olivar just kept on fiddling an old tune he called "The Crooked Stove Pipe." Needless to say, this kept everybody laughing and having a good time until everything was back to normal.

Doreen and I were allowed to see the old year out and the new year in, but before everybody started singing "Auld Lang Syne," I was curled up in the corner counting sheep.

On the second day of 1941 Terrence left for Saint John. He had to get back for work at the winter port, and he was going to find a place for Isabel and me. We were to stay on with Olivar and Mabelene for a couple of days. Olivar didn't like the idea of me going back with my mother, though. He wanted me to at least spend the winter at McAdam.

Fireworks were also close on a number of occasions during the next couple of days between Mabelene and Isabel. But nothing really came of it all. To this day I still think that if Mabelene had shown any signs of wanting me to stay with her and Olivar my mother would have probably allowed me to stay.

Things were so tense between the two of them that on the day we were leaving, Mabelene said she wasn't coming to the station to see us off. Eventually, when Doreen insisted she wanted to go, Mabelene changed her mind and came with us. After a fifteen-minute sleigh ride to the station, she and Doreen stayed in the sleigh while Olivar came right on to the train to help us get settled.

After patting me on the head and telling me to come back and see him sometime, he left the coach. As we pulled away I was waving goodbye to Doreen and Mabelene through the steamy window as they sat in the sleigh waiting for Olivar, but I don't know if they saw me or not.

First-Time Run-Away

At Union Station in Saint John, Terrence was there to pick us up and we went by streetcar to our new place at 110 Charlotte Street. It was two rooms in the basement, and we shared an upstairs bathroom with another tenant.

There were no groceries when we arrived, and when Isabel found out that Terrence couldn't account for the money he had when he left McAdam just a few days ago, that rang the bell for round one in a long series of fights that would eventually lead to their first separation.

My mother suspected Terrence of having another woman. He never confessed that night, but he wasn't a good liar and gave a number of lame reasons for where the money went—loaning the money to a good buddy, losing it at poker, being rolled by a woman, etc. But he promised to reform, and to show good intentions he actually gave me a quarter before going to work that night.

While he was gone my mother tucked me into bed and left me with these comforting words, "Have a nice sleep, and when you wake up tomorrow you'll be able to play outside, and for the first time you'll be wearing your nice, new, blue snowsuit."

I almost had a heart attack. I thought she had forgotten about that damn thing.

Next morning I went out to play before breakfast and before Terrence came home from work, so I could avoid having to put on the snowsuit. Though I later got hungry, I just didn't bother to return.

It worked that day, but the next day I was forced by Isabel to wear the snowsuit and out I went into the backyard. I stood outside for about an hour before mustering up enough courage to go out onto the sidewalk.

As soon as I got outside I noticed a few boys playing soldiers. I went towards them and asked to play, and when one answered I couldn't believe my ears: "Hey Freddy, whatcha tink of da stupid lookin' goil here, she

86

wants to play 'soldiers.'"

Before I could pull myself together Freddy finished me off with "Naw, we don't play wit goils. Send 'er home to 'er mama and tell 'er to play wit 'er dolls."

I lashed back: "I'm not a goil, I'm a boy." And I showed them the boy's cap I was wearing under the parka that was attached to the snowsuit.

One said, "Well you sure look like a goil to us, don't she, gang?"

Then another piped in, "Yeah, what d'ya tink of dat, Freddy, a goil wit a cap on? Ha! Ha!Ha!"

I began to realize that just by standing there I was making things worse. So I headed for home. I didn't want to tell my mother what had happened. She might have thought it was just an excuse and decided to make me wear the suit all the time.

But I hit on a plan that worked for a while. I went into the house, changed into my overalls in the upstairs bathroom, and put the snowsuit under the bathtub. Then I went outside to play.

Although the boys now let me join in their games they continued to call me "goil" for the two or three months that I lived on Charlotte Street.

My mother soon caught on to my quick-change Superman trick, however, and as I sat down for supper one night she asked where my clothes were, and when I lied she whacked me. She said it wasn't for changing my clothes, but for lying.

I sure paid the penalty that night for lying. She hit me about ten times with a leather belt. My arms and legs tingled from the pain and I carried the marks for days.

"If you ever lie to me again, I'll kill you," she told me. "Do you understand?"

I understood that all right, but what I couldn't fathom was why she made such a big deal of me lying to her, while every time Terrence and she went looking for a place to stay, I was to lie about their marital status.

She eventually permitted me to go outside without the

snowsuit however, after Freddy came to the door one day and asked if "goil" could come out to play. She realized then the torment I had been through for a few days wearing that sissy suit.

It was some time later, on a certain pay day for Terrence, that we all went out with him to cash his cheque and get some groceries. My mother and I came straight home, but Terrence had to make a detour to "pay some money he owed to a buddy." Then he'd pay the rent when he got home.

When he didn't come home for supper it was fight time again. And when he finally showed up, staggering in from the apartment upstairs with a wine bottle in each coat pocket, the row went on until Terrence fell asleep at the table.

Next morning the battle resumed. Terrence was hit with a frying pan full of fresh hamburgers and a kitchen window was smashed by a flying can of beans.

This was the end for us at Charlotte Street. It hadn't been a pleasant time. In the course of the fight it came out that there was a strong indication that Terrence had been sleeping with the woman upstairs.

The landlord kicked us out after the police had to be called to simmer things down. Again, we were allowed to spend the night packing our stuff if we promised to be quiet. The next day we wound up getting a place on Sewell Street.

There was only one room, with kitchen facilities. They used to put the dresser between the place where I slept and where they slept. We were in the same room. The dresser, even with a blanket over it, didn't stop me from peeking at them from time to time.

Everything was fairly quiet on the home front on Sewell Street. I think this was partially due to the fact both of them now had a job. I think my mother was house cleaning somewhere.

We only stayed there a couple of months before moving to a bigger place just around the corner and down the hill at 98 Dorchester Street. That would be around early fall of 1941.

People in another apartment had a record player and played a lot of cowboy and country and western music. I used to spend a lot of time up there listening to the songs of Gene Autry and Wilf Carter. Their record player was electric and I had never seen one before.

When Christmas came that year, both Terrence and Isabel were out of a job and again it was very sad. We didn't have a Christmas tree, while everyone else was getting Christmas trees. But I found a discarded bough and a few strands of tinsel in the backyard. On Christmas Eve I decorated the bough and prayed to Santa Claus that he would bring me something. Then with my arms around my special tree I went to sleep in my usual place on the floor in the closet. But when Christmas morning came, there was nothing on it, and I sure got awful lonesome for McAdam Junction all of a sudden.

Later that winter I had a terrible experience across the street from our house where there was a long embankment. Along the sidewalk at the top of this embankment was a long steel pole railing that ran the full length of the street. I was kneeling in front of the railing watching a wrecking ball working at the bottom of the hill. The day was fiercely cold and I stuck my tongue on the bottom rail. I began to yell and scream because it got stuck to the rail and I was pulling a lot of skin off my tongue as I tried to get free. It was sore for a week.

(Not too long after this incident I learned of an excellent way to prevent most, if not all the damage one can do to his tongue, should he ever be so unfortunate as to find himself in the same predicament that I've just described. Children in particular could often make good use of this advice: If you happen to get your tongue stuck on cold metal, whatever you do, don't panic. And don't be in a hurry to pull it off. Just stay there breathing slowly and deeply until your warm breath raises the temperature of the metal surrounding your tongue. In a moment or two the metal will thaw and your tongue will slide off quite easily, sustaining no damage. It really works, and it saves a lot of pain.)

Another time I was sporting a big black shiner for a couple of weeks. Terrence was lying in the bed one day and I still don't know whether he meant it or not, but his boot came up and he kicked me in the eye. Each time I looked in the mirror I wondered if I was going to turn totally black, like the little kid I always played with who lived downstairs.

In the spring of 1942 my mother, who must have been pregnant at the time, stole a baby carriage. She was sent to jail for about a week.

The carriage had been a very light colour and Terrence painted it dark brown so it couldn't be recognized. But the police caught up with it anyway and my mother had to do the time.

While she was in jail, Terrence brought another woman to the house. Her name was Jenny Haynes. I resented her taking the place of my mother, but what could I say, or what could I do? I didn't want to live with them any more, so I decided to run away. I knew we had gone to Olivar's by train, so I thought if I followed the railroad tracks I could find him at McAdam Junction.

The next day I left Saint John, heading west, walking the rails, not realizing that Olivar lived more than a hundred miles away.

As the hours went by I kept walking the tracks and eventually I was walking through the bush. I stuck to the tracks all the time and it was late that evening when I came to a field where a kid was playing with a dog.

I talked to him—he was about my age—and I said I was going to McAdam. He asked me if I wanted to stay at his house for the night. As I didn't want his father and mother to know about me being there, I asked him if I could sleep in his little tent which was not too far distant from where we were. He said I could and then I asked him not to tell anybody.

He kept it a secret. The next morning when I woke up I didn't see him around, so I continued on up the tracks.

Some hours later, as I was walking the tracks beside a river I saw a house that looked very much like Olivar's. It was quite a distance from me on the other side of the river. It may have been because I wanted to see Olivar so much that I was certain the people I saw in the yard were Doreen, Olivar and Mabelene.

I started shouting Doreen's name. The girl heard me, but showed no recognition. I hollered her name several more times and would have gone up to her had I been able to cross the river. As I eventually had to pass by this farmhouse, I began to realize I was wrong and this was not Olivar's place at all.

I walked the whole second day, and didn't have anything to eat. I was afraid of being discovered and taken back to Dorchester Street. It was in the evening of the second day, just as I had walked past a railway crossing, when a car pulled up. The driver was a Mountie. He called me back to the road from where I was on the tracks and he asked me where I was going. I told him to McAdam Junction to see Olivar. By then I was twenty-five or thirty miles out of town.

After he got me to explain who I was and where I lived, he drove me right back to Saint John. At first he took me to the police station and gave me something to eat. Then he and another Mountie took me home.

While I waited with the other Mountie in the cruiser, he went in the house and spoke to Terrence. What was said I don't know, but when he came out Terrence was behind him and he told me that I could go in. I was so tired I went to sleep almost immediately.

About two days later Isabel came home and when she found out that I had run away she wanted to know why. When I told her about Jenny Haynes she hit the roof and another big fight with Terrence began.

This fight wound up with her leaving Terrence altogether.

We moved in with a couple of her friends on Prince Edward Street and after a little while we left Saint John for Montreal. Somehow, she came into some money. I don't even want to speculate how that may have happened, although I suppose she could have run off with Terrence's paycheque from his work as a longshoreman, or somehow got her friends to loan her some money.

Anyhow, she bought a train ticket and we ended up in Montreal. I was six years old, and travelling with us was a new baby girl. Her name was Nancy. Isabel was the mother, but again, the father, like mine, was probably marked "unknown" on the birth certificate. Whatever the case, I am quite certain that Terrence was the father.

The Montreal Farmhouse

THE FIRST PLACE we stayed in Montreal was at a hotel in Outremont, just across the street from a very large billboard displaying a poster for Black Horse Ale. We lived in one room and every time we looked out our window all we could see was this horse.

On the second day there, Isabel took the baby and me uptown on the streetcar to do some shopping, and I got lost. It was the first time I had seen huge department stores and I was really fascinated by the escalators.

Well, my curiosity got the better of me. I stopped to stare and gawk at various things and got separated from Isabel. I wound up finding my own way home by streetcar. I just walked on with a crowd of people and I guess the conductor thought I belonged to somebody. The streetcar was going back the other way and I got off at the right place and went up to our hotel room and waited for Isabel outside the door. She came home about three hours later and proceeded to bash the living daylights out of me. She said the next time I'd better stay around her.

I believe she had floor walkers and cops on the search for me throughout the store and up and down the streets. When they couldn't find me anywhere, they told her to go home and wait till they came up with some news.

I took my stripes. But Isabel must have also realized that if Tom could find his way back to a hotel room in the big city, then why not use me to babysit while she went out to work.

I don't know what she did, but she would leave me to fend for myself and look after the little baby. Now there wasn't any television to keep us both occupied, so we either slept, played or cried. Food was scarce, as always.

I had also become quite jealous of the baby. I had been the main recipient of Isabel's affection for so long and now this baby was getting all the attention. I didn't have much use for her, but I was smart enough to look after her when left alone.

Just after we moved from the hotel to a cheaper room, I started making the baby cry and Isabel gave me a lecture. This was a different type of a lecture. This time when she talked to me she really hurt my feelings. She didn't beat me, she kept on talking to me. And I was hurt for the first time in a new way. I was being hurt emotionally. I felt ashamed of my actions and it smartened me up considerably.

Whatever her job was, it didn't last too long—enough to get us some groceries and a couple of little things for Christmas. And then we moved out of there and she started getting help from some organization down on St. Antoine Street. I remember going with her several times when she went for help. In those days she had to do an awful lot of walking from one end of town to the other.

I assume it was some kind of welfare she was getting— she would have to walk, dragging us two little kids, all over Montreal. She hardly ever had carfare.

She seemed to be collecting a little money from here, there and everywhere. We would walk to some office and we'd be just bedraggled from walking. She'd be exhausted from carrying the baby everywhere she went. And so she'd get something there—either a cheque or some money or some kind of a handout and then we'd walk all the way back to our little room. One evening she arranged to have Nancy and me baptized in the Catholic Church, and before we left she successfully hit the priest up for a handout. And presto, we're eating again.

I developed impetigo around this time in my right hand. I have some scars from it, in between my fingers, to this day. Impetigo is a kind of skin disease. My hand puffed up and Isabel didn't know what it was. It kept getting worse and worse. So finally she got me to an outpatient's ward in a hospital where they looked at it and had to make an incision. Then they put cloths and gauze in between my fingers, up under the skin inside my hand.

They put my arm in a sling and I had to hold it up. I wandered around like that for a month or so until it healed up.

Then Isabel moved us again. We were like gypsies, moving all the time. I was about six years old now and she wanted to put me in a school. We moved out to Rosemount, but my first few days in school there were a disaster. I don't know what it was, but I got into so many fights, and lost them all, that she took me out of school.

Moving was a way of life for me. In fact, I moved more times in my first five years than most people do in a lifetime. But now here was something new—Isabel took on a job as a housekeeper with no rent to pay. Stability at last? Well, maybe?

The home was way out in the country and the master of the house, Mr. Wood, had just lost his wife. The house was dirty, the son didn't seem to care about it, and there were two dogs living there. And Mr. Wood turned out to be a cheap old bastard, anyway.

He'd allow us only so much food and kept the rest locked away in one end of the house. When he remembered, he gave us enough food for a meal or two a day. But half the time he forgot to give us the rations that were supposedly part of the deal, so we didn't have anything to eat at all. That wasn't anything new for me and my mom. We knew that every time we ate we'd enjoy it because we didn't know when the next meal was going to come. Now, even with a deal that included meals, we were losing out again. That always seemed to be our luck.

Then one day Mr. Wood's son showed my mother how to pick the old man's door lock and after that she would get some food, even if he forgot to put some out. Still, there wasn't a day that went by that I could say we had three squares. And even to this day I am not a big eater. I eat to live, not live to eat.

I had a little bit of fun around there because I could play with the dogs. However, I wasn't going to school, and I wanted to go really badly. Other kids my age were going but I wasn't.

Our closest neighbour was a Lithuanian immigrant family who lived on a farm about a mile away from the Woods' house. Charlie Ezekius was his name, and I never did know his wife's name. I just called her Mrs. Ezekius.

I used to take out the Woods' dog, Prince, and get him on the leash and try to run behind him all the way to Charlie's house. I'd let Prince run like hell and I'd just be hanging on to the rope. I used to have a great time doing that. Soon my mother got to know the woman—and we'd go to visit and even eat there sometimes. My mother and Mrs. Ezekius became great friends. The Ezekiuses had had a hard time in the old country so they really seemed to understand my mother's plight. Mrs. Ezekius would talk about her days as a refugee and Isabel would tell her about everything, from how she lost her thumb as a little girl to the long string of circumstances which led up to her present misfortunes.

The Ezekiuses had two children with whom I often played in the fields or along the brook. Tony and Mary were both a year or two older than I was, but we always got along very well. I also enjoyed the haying and other farm chores.

In spring I'll never forget walking across the ploughed fields to go grocery shopping with my mother. The food-supplying deal with Mr. Wood by now had been changed and we had to go into Montreal to the nearest place where we could buy our own. If we went by road it would take forever, so we often took the short cut across the farmers' fields. And we were way the hell out in the middle of nowhere and had to walk at least four or five miles across ploughed fields. If you can imagine that in the springtime.

This would usually occur on Saturdays when Mr. Wood's son was available to mind Nancy, who was usually asleep with a fresh bottle before we left.

I remember my mother losing her shoes and other things as we lugged groceries across these many miles of mud. Even some grocery articles often got left right where they dropped.

My first experience with a horse happened one afternoon when old Charlie Ezekius had me on the wagon where I soon learned how he made the horse go by saying, "*Tlick, Tlick,* git up." Old Charlie got off the wagon to do something and I said to the horse, "Git up" and the horse took off out of the gate and down the road and kept on going.

We went about half a mile down the road with Charlie running behind the wagon. I didn't know how to say whoa or stop.

Finally, the horse stopped trotting and started to walk. That's when Charlie caught up to us. He was all puffed out.

He got up on the wagon, stopped the horse and turned him around.

It was a good thing it was a docile horse because he probably would have knocked me right off the wagon. Although Charlie gave me a lecture, I could see a bit of a grin on his face as we drove back to the farm.

When I met him again, years later, one of the first things he talked about was the day the horse bolted out of the farmyard—with me at the reins.

In a Halifax Hospital

When my mother and my sister and I eventually made our way back to Saint John, we hitch-hiked. It was a long, old road and we spent a lot of nights in a lot of houses which were owned by French people, and my mother would try to talk with her hands all the time. Even though the people couldn't understand us very well, they were usually very kind.

In Saint John again we visited some people and then we took off all the way around to Nova Scotia. She must have got some money somehow in Saint John because we went by train. There was no hitch-hiking.

We got off the train somewhere around Amherst or Truro, Nova Scotia, and here we ran into Terrence Messer again. I don't know whether Isabel knew he was there, or whether it was a stroke of luck, fate or whatever. Anyway, he was working in Truro so we lived with him again for a while, maybe a couple of months.

But, true to my mother's love life, it didn't work out again. So she took off. Or he took off—I don't know which. But, whatever the truth of the matter, we were back on the road again, this time heading for Halifax.

Free lunches (and dinners and breakfasts) were common when my mother and I and Nancy were hitch-hiking. All our restaurant scams were similar. Sometimes we'd sit by the door and just walk out when our plates had been licked clean, but not before the waitress's back was turned. If we didn't sit by the door we would wait for the cashier or the waitress to go into the kitchen to get someone a plate of food. We'd bolt for the door and that was it. We'd run like hell, down the alley or up the street.

If we didn't do this, we wouldn't eat. The Depression was still fresh in everyone's mind, and World War II was still raging. Times were tough for everyone. And for us they just seemed a little tougher.

Isabel was only sixteen or seventeen when she had me. She was just a kid—a poor kid at that. The hand-to-mouth existence was not new to her. And when you couldn't provide the necessities of life legitimately, then there were other means.

Isabel had a friend or relative named Sybil in Halifax. She might have been a cousin. When you live a life like mine, pretty well devoid of family ties, and running from one friend or relative to the next, seeing them only once or twice and never keeping in touch, you can't always remember the family relationships, even when you're told.

And I can't imagine that I was ever formally introduced to all these people anyway. My mother was never one for pomp and ceremony. She did what she had to do to be civil and friendly for the time it took to get a meal or a bed and that was that. There was often little or no time for pleasantries.

Sybil and her husband lived in a hovel in a rundown part of Halifax.

Although she gave us some money, she wouldn't let us stay at her place, and wouldn't feed us. So we went to another lady's place, in the same rough and rundown ghetto-like area of Halifax. This lady must have had more than a dozen kids.

We wound up staying there—the three of us (me, Isabel and the baby). But I wasn't there very long before I developed a disease which almost killed me.

We were out playing in a little alley behind the house between the buildings in a small yard that was used as a dump. Neighbours threw their cans and other garbage out the door into this little area. It was one of those great places that kids love to play in and explore. It was filthy, but there was always excitement there, and perhaps even a little mystery.

We'd been playing hard for a long time and had worked up a sweat and a thirst. We drank out of some rusty cans and within a short time I got terribly sick. They wound up rushing me to the hospital where they found out I had diphtheria. By this time I was unconscious.

They tell me I was about nine days in a coma before I eventually came out of it.

I remember the day I came around. When I woke up an attending nurse hollered down the hall and a whole bunch of people came in. There were nurses in the room and even some doctors. Finally, the place became packed to standing room only with health care experts who had been trying their damnedest to keep me alive.

I guess they'd worked on me for nine days with no response and no sign that I was ever going to come out of it.

Crowded though it was in that room, these medics began to have a big celebration, although I was the only one who didn't know what the celebration was about. I hadn't been awake any more than five minutes when I started singing some songs that my mother had taught me and I guess because I seemed to be having such a ball they were all happy and smiling.

One of the songs I sang was, of all things, "The Star Spangled Banner." It's a country and western version of the U.S. national anthem and was popular at the time.

It went like this:

> *There's a star-spangled banner waving somewhere.*
> *In a distant land so many miles away.*
> *Only Uncle Sam's great heroes get to go there.*
> *That is where I'd like to live also some day...*

(Now that just goes to show you how much Canadians were influenced, even way back then, by American songs and music.)

Another song I was singing was Hank Snow's "Blue Velvet Band," which I still sing today every once in a while.

During the time I was in the hospital Isabel had obtained some assistance and moved us into a tiny two-room apartment, not too far from where we had been staying. She also made arrangements to enroll me in a

Halifax school.

After I was home for a few days I started to go to school at St. Mary's and they put me in what they called "high grade one." By now I should have been in school a year or more, but because of all our travelling, I wasn't.

I enjoyed the school all right, but I didn't enjoy the kids because they wanted to pound me. They used to chase me home every day and they'd wait to get me when I was going to school in the mornings.

I had to find out where all the back alleys were—my escape routes—because the kids would gang up on me.

I looked for all the short cuts and all the little boards in the fences that were loose, and hoped that nobody else knew they were there. I would scamper through a different yard every day. It may not have been a short cut to school, but it was a much safer route than walking the streets with the rest of the kids.

Before long I didn't care too much about going to school, although I enjoyed the actual sitting in the classroom and learning things. But even that didn't last a hell of a long time. I complained to my mother so often about being beaten up every time I went to school that she eventually took me out.

I don't know what it was about me that attracted others to want to beat the tar out of me. It could be that I was a stranger. A loner. Not by choice, I might add, but by circumstance.

I wanted to fit in. I really did. I wasn't the kind of kid to mope around. But I was different enough back then that kids noticed and picked on me as an easy target to tease and have some fun with because I had no friends.

Kids can be cruel when they want to be, and I know all about that. I had more than my fair share of battling prejudices before I really knew what the words meant, and I'm sure those youngsters who were taunting me were also unaware of what psychological damage they could do to another kid, barraging him with all the negativity of their ways, their put-downs and threats.

But I was a survivor. It was this rough introduction to the real world that made me tough. I knew I was not enjoying the standard of living of the majority of people I bumped into, but I had to make the most of it. And I did.

And now we did the thing that Isabel knew best. We moved again.

This time we moved right down near the Halifax waterfront. And it wasn't long before I started playing around the wharf. It was here, on a certain Sunday afternoon, that I was playing "Follow the leader" with a couple of other kids, when my attention was drawn to a plank which served as a walkway from the dock to one of the smaller boats.

We Land in Jail

"Follow me," I shouted, as I stepped on the plank and proceeded to walk across.

I only got about half-way when the plank tilted and I fell in the water. I couldn't swim, and everything was blue and bubbly. There were flashes of some sort of light, and I thought I was going to die. Or that maybe I was already dead.

I was drowning. And I guess one of the kids had been smart enough to holler to one of the men who were working up around the dock. He quickly came down the wharf ladder and reached out, and I guess he grabbed me by the hair of the head and pulled me out.

I don't know how many times I had gone down or up during the ordeal because I lost consciousness. But he pulled me out and carried me up the ladder to the top of the dock where he laid me down on my stomach. I don't know what he did, but it worked and I was catching my breath again.

After saving my life he wanted to know where I lived, and then he took me home. When we got there, I was still dripping from head to toe. My mother didn't give me a lickin' but she told me I'd have to stay in bed for a couple of days. I guess I was in pretty rough shape but, as always, I was soon back on my feet looking for more adventure.

We moved one more time, then we pulled out of Halifax altogether. We hitch-hiked down somewhere towards the Annapolis Valley. It was just about twilight one evening when we passed this little town in a bit of a valley with a river running through it.

It was just a quiet little place with one store and maybe four or five houses. The store was just before a bridge and I remember saying to my mother, "Well, let's go in and buy something," and she said, "We can't, I've got no money." This would be in the very early spring of 1944, perhaps the middle of March.

There was no snow on the highway itself but there was lots in the fields and on the side roads. There were also a lot of woods around these parts. As we walked past the store and across the bridge we went up a little hill till we came to a bend in the road. Just as we made the turn, the village went out of sight.

Just ahead of us was a cabin in a field, hidden among the trees. It was vacant and looked like somebody's summer cottage. So now, as we were out of view of the community, we made our way up through the snow and Isabel broke into the cabin through the screen door. She smashed a pane of glass in the door itself and reached around somehow, got the door open, and in we went. There was some wood in the wood box so she started a fire, and got things warmed up.

As the three of us were pretty hungry, she told me we were going to eat after it got dark. We waited until midnight or one o'clock. Then, after telling me to stay with the baby, she went out. I guess she was gone about an hour or an hour and a half. When she came back she had all kinds of groceries. So we ate, filled our bellies and went to sleep in the beds. Warm and contented.

There were few nights I went to bed like that when I was a young kid.

But the ecstasy of a full belly and a warm bed didn't last very long. Early in the morning we heard a rat-a-tat-tat! Rat-a-tat-tat! We were still in bed, sleeping soundly when we were awakened by the knock on the front door.

It was a cop.

Isabel wanted to put me out the back door while she and Nancy were going to go out the front and meet up with me later. I'm not sure what her plan was, but it didn't work.

The policeman had hold of her, so where could I go alone? She was trapped and so was I.

The cop said, "You're going to have to come with me"—the usual lines—and, naturally, I had to go, too. He put us in the cruiser and drove immediately to the store. There was some talk there. I didn't understand half of what was going on, but he was saying something about having some of the evidence and that there were groceries back in the cabin.

The cop thought it was pretty obvious that Isabel was the one who had taken the groceries. So after the talk, he turned the car around and drove us into a bigger town. I think it was Annapolis Royal, but I couldn't say for sure. It was one of those towns in Annapolis Valley.

I was taken to a house and left there with the baby. This was only temporary while Isabel had to go to answer to some charge. It didn't take very long anyway—we wound up that very same night in jail. This was a big square building in an alley which was adjacent to a small farm.

You could see hens, geese and cows from where we were, so it wasn't that big a town.

Just inside the door was an office with a desk, and over to the left was a large staircase. Straight ahead there was a hall where you could see cells with big iron bars. Then over on the right side was an enormous kitchen with a big wooden table and lots of cupboards. This building was actually being used as the living quarters for the police as well as the jail.

We were immediately taken upstairs and locked into a room on the right-hand side of the hall, about half-way down. There were several other rooms along this hall with bars on all the windows. There was a big lock on every door and a mattress on the floor of each room. They came back later and threw in some blankets. There was me, my baby sister and my mother, and that's where we stayed for about a month. I remember how we could hear the mice running around the floor at night and we were scratching all the time from the lice and bedbugs.

After about a week or so, they allowed Isabel to come down to the kitchen for a couple of hours each day to help out with making meals for the prisoners. This was while my sister would be having her nap.

In the meantime, they had me tied in the backyard to a small chain. I guess they didn't want me wandering off anywhere.

Then one day I got beaten up pretty badly by a goose, or a gander, that had wandered over quite near to where I was and because of my chain I couldn't get away from him.

Unaware of the danger, I decided I was going to have a little fun and started playing with him. He didn't quite take a liking to it and flew at me and picked at me pretty good, while beating me with his wings and lunging at me with his body until somebody heard me screaming and they came out and put the run to the bloody thing.

Other than that little bit of scary excitement, it was pretty dull being in jail. They did let me wander around inside a little bit, but they wouldn't let me down the halls where the men prisoners were in the cells.

I could go down into the kitchen. And when nobody was looking from time to time I used to steal cookies and other small items of food and trot it upstairs to my mother and slide them under the door, or try to hide them some place so I could take them to the room with me later.

Here I was stealing from a jail and raiding the kitchen operated by the police. I had no sense of what was important to my mother and what wasn't. I could only hope she was quite proud of me learning the tricks she had taught me. When I think about it now, it was a wonder she didn't send me for the bloody key or something, so we could have gotten the hell out of there.

We all stayed in jail until Isabel had done her time. They treated her quite nicely the day they let her go. The woman who had been cooking the meals, with a little bit of help from Isabel, had become quite friendly. I think she was a cop's wife. She waved us goodbye and we were back out on the street again.

We then made our way through town and onto the highway where we started hitch-hiking.

Next stop was Digby, just a little further along the Annapolis Valley. There Isabel worked in a hotel where they also gave her a room. She waited on tables, scrubbed floors and worked in the kitchen. When she finally saved enough money, we took the ferry boat from Digby back to Saint John, New Brunswick. This would be about May 1944. And had she known what was going to happen within the next couple of days, she would never have taken us on this trip.

My sister Nancy was about a year and a half old and I was eight. And this is where my life with my mother was about to end.

Upon our arrival in Saint John, Isabel began looking for a place for us to stay. She went to the YWCA and took us along. That's where she made her big mistake.

She didn't know at the time, but there was an APB (All Points Bulletin) out on her. The authorities were on the alert. They must have heard she was back in the Saint John area. We had just come in off the road and I guess they knew that she was out there somewhere with a couple of kids.

When she went to the Y to get some milk for the baby and try to get me fed, and see if we could stay the night, someone secretly phoned the law, and they came to get us.

As the lady and my mother went through the hall into the kitchen with the baby I was told to wait in the office, which also doubled as a large sitting room. While she was in the back, somebody brought me a glass of milk and a couple of cookies to eat while I was waiting for my mother to get food for the baby.

With a certain feeling of anxiety in the air my mother, who was always very leery, began to suspect something was up. She probably thought someone had called the authorities. She had to, because as soon as she got the milk warmed up for the baby she decided not to wait for any further hospitality. She quickly prodded me to finish my milk and we immediately headed for the door.

Just at that moment the door opened and in came a Mrs. Corbett from the Children's Aid Society, and with her were a couple of plain-clothed policemen. My mother almost knocked Mrs. Corbett off her feet as she bolted for the door and tried to get by them, but one of them grabbed hold of her and the other one tried to catch hold of me.

For the first five minutes or so he wasn't very successful. I was up on the tables, kicking over lamps, pulling down curtains and screaming to high heaven as I narrowly escaped his grasp nearly a dozen times. At one point, the bulb exploded in one of the floor lamps as it went crashing to the floor. The policeman had gotten his feet all tangled up in the electric cord and fell on his ass in the corner.

By this time Mrs. Corbett had snatched the baby from my mother, who was now acting like a wildcat. As she bit, scratched, kicked and screamed at the other policeman, the whole place was beginning to look like a hurricane zone.

I tried to get into the hallway which led to the kitchen but two of the YWCA women blocked my way. This is where the policeman grabbed me and pulled me away from them, little knowing what a firm grasp I had on one woman's blouse. As he yanked me away from her, he took blouse and all.

By this time another cruiser with two more policemen had pulled up and as I was dragged from the building I could see them forcing my mother and Nancy into a car and driving off. That's when my world caved in, and I started to cry. As all the fight went out of me, they put me in another car and drove me to the Children's Aid Shelter at the foot of Garden Street. Here they put me in a small detention room with the door locked, and that's where I stayed and cried for the rest of the night. I just knew I was never going to see my mother again.

Some Commentary

AT THIS WRITING, in 1995, over fifty years have come and gone, but I can still remember that ferry ride and the last few days with my mother and my sister as though it only happened yesterday. It was a very traumatic experience. And even though some people may criticize my mother for what she did and how she lived, and will even say that taking her kids away from her was the right thing to do, I can only say I strongly disagree. And even when rehabilitation is found to be necessary, there has to be a more humane way of doing it than to wrench a mother's children away from her as if she were some sow with a litter of pigs. This method of treating human beings is nothing short of barbaric.

Indeed, as my story progresses, the reader will see that even after the authorities took me into custody, my lot in life was in no way improved. And neither was the lot of my mother and my sister, as I was to find out a great many years later. (They had both been taken into custody and separated from each other at this time, as well.)

It seems to me that only when a mother doesn't want her children should they be taken away from her. In that case, the authorities may be justified in their actions because the children, by this time, will no doubt have sensed the rejection by themselves and be a lot more likely to adjust to a new environment. But as long as a mother shows love and a willingness to protect her kids she should be allowed to do so, and nobody should have the right to take them away from her. Even if she has to beg, borrow and steal to feed and clothe her children, it should be obvious that what she needs is help. And that help should come by way of understanding and concern for the welfare of the family as a unit. The mother should be encouraged and given the opportunity to get back on her feet, where she can once again provide her love and care with confidence.

Having said this, I know it is difficult for some people,

especially those who take the security of a good home with respectable parents for granted, to understand or identify with the fears and uncertainties experienced by those who are born in abject poverty. And it is to help bridge this gap and create a better understanding that I have chosen to relate most of these harrowing experiences which took place during the first years of my life.

In the first place, the odds for our chances to survive as a family were very slim. It was during the Great Depression when even the rich began to struggle to survive. The middle class had become the poor and the poor became the beggars, the thieves and the outcasts.

My mother, as a mere child herself, was thrust upon this scene through no fault of her own. Her father died when she was young and her sickly mother, in search of support, went to live with a man who was already quite elderly. Along with a state of poverty, a lack of discipline probably contributed to her lack of education, and when she found herself pregnant in 1935, at the age of sixteen, she was certainly unprepared to cope with the dog-eat-dog world of the Hungry Thirties.

While it is true that World War II resulted in the birth of many thousands of illegitimate children, thereby causing society to more readily accept these abnormal occurrences, if you became an unwed mother in the thirties, both you and your child were considered to be the scum of the earth. You were not only disowned by members of your own family but you were shunned even by those you considered to be your most intimate friends.

The realization of these cold, hard facts must have been devastating to Isabel when her mother and stepfather died within three years after I was born, and except for the mere pittance with which she was able to rent us a room for a month or so, she was left to face her shame alone on the streets of destitution.

When she found that even her second pregnancy by my father was not going to secure him as a husband, her predicament just went from bad to worse. And as desperation set in, along came Terrence Messer.

Although this union was doomed from the start, my mother must have concluded that living with Terrence was the only way she could provide a home for me and the baby who was yet to be born.

The fights that went on between Terrence and Isabel usually always took the form of personal attacks on the other's self-worth. She hounded him about his drinking, not having a job, not looking hard enough for work and for "running around" on her, while he hounded her about being a "slut" for bringing those two little bastards into the world and for still being "in love with that no-account son-of-a-bitch from the North End."

These fights usually resulted in Terrence taking off for days at a time and then returning without a cent to pay the rent. This of course meant we had to constantly move.

Because of all this, I no sooner got acquainted with the kids of one neighbourhood when I quickly found myself a stranger in another. What I'm trying to say is that no matter what happens, you're always an outsider. Always unwanted. You're told to go out in the backyard and play with the rest of the kids, but you're very stand-offish. You haven't been introduced to anyone or made to feel welcome by anybody. You have no toys of your own and you only get to play with the other kids' toys if they let you. So you stand over there and watch, and hope the ball they're playing with will roll over towards you. If it does, you quickly pick it up, put on your best smile and throw it back to one of the kids, hoping they will invite you to play.

You hope that your smile, through the hidden tears and your feeling of low importance, will bring a comment like, "Hey, kid, you wanna come and play ball with us?" Your answer of course is, "Yeah, can I?" So you play ball for a little while, but you remain stiff and self-conscious and always very careful that you don't make a mistake. If you do, you're out, and again you'll hear those words, "Get away, kid." It's always okay for anyone in the group to make a mistake because they know each other, but if something goes wrong they don't look too far for a scapegoat.

Even adults who should know better, quite often take this easy way out. Sometimes a father will come out when the kids are in trouble, and guess who gets the kick in the ass? You. The other kids will merely be told to get in the house. And though you may not have had any part in the mischief, you're told to "get the hell home where you belong and don't come back any more." In this case, just being a stranger has made you guilty.

Besides the constant moving, there was also the problem of food. You could often find yourself playing in the backyard with some kids when a door would open and a mother would call, "Joey, get in here and wash your hands—it's suppertime. Come and get your soup and your sandwich." Another mother would then raise a window and holler, "Is little Mary over there with the kids?" When the answer was, "Yeah," then you'd hear, "Mary, it's time to come in for supper." So right on schedule, each and every kid was called in to get something to eat. That is, all except for little Tommy, who sits on the steps and waits for them all to come back out again, with their hands and faces clean and their bellies full.

There was no suppertime for Tommy. But this was something he was already used to. He didn't have any supper last night, and if he gets something to eat tonight, it will be his first today.

After Terrence and Isabel separated I began to feel more and more how much my mother needed my help as well as my co-operation. Seeing her walk sometimes for miles with a baby in her arms, to knock on somebody's door, and then be told by some friend or relative to "get the f——— away from here and don't ever come back," and then see the tears she cried, caused me to want to be good to her and to help her whenever and however I could. This created a special bond between us, one that today, though, try as I may, I can no longer describe.

One of the many tricks I would help her pull on landlords so she could get out without paying the bill was that I would first go out in the alley and untie our suitcase and any other luggage she may have lowered down from our window in the bedsheets, and haul them off and hide them until she arrived. She would then take the baby and walk past the landlord as if she was going for a stroll. If she was asked for the rent, she would merely say she was going to pick up her cheque or that she would have it first thing in the morning. The fact that she was going out without her luggage would always allay any further suspicions. She would then meet me in the alley and—zippo—we disappeared.

Another thing that's important to note is that every place we went it was always the lowest of the low who would help us. Families who had ten or twelve kids themselves, with hardly enough food to go around, would take us in and feed us. We were begging from the paupers and sharing crumbs with other beggars. But these were the only people who seemed to understand our predicament, and probably because they weren't much better off themselves.

And once again, it is this understanding of the plight of others that we need so much to acquire, before we proclaim judgement upon whether or not another person is in need of "rehabilitation."

There is one thing I know, and I know it for sure: if my mother had been given the opportunity to bring up her kids in a different way, she certainly would have taken it. Had she been given some other choice to better herself, without the fear of losing her children, she would never have been running the roads, begging and stealing and making a nuisance of herself in the first place. I also believe the decision of the authorities to separate her from her children for the sake of "protecting" us and "rehabilitating" her was not only a mistake, it was a crime. They not only broke her heart, but they broke her spirit, and they killed a certain something inside. The only thing she ever had that was hers in life was her kids, and even this they took away.

Thus far, the reader has seen just how difficult it was during the first eight years of my life. But most of these hardships were of a physical nature and due mainly to the lack of money, food, housing, clothing and other basic human necessities. These are the kinds of problems that will cause dissension even among the best of families. But through all this I always knew I had my mother. And even though I seldom received her undivided attention, I still knew she was there. If not at this very moment, then as soon as circumstances would allow. This gave me a sense of being a part of someone and a sense of belonging. And in my estimation it's the most important feeling a child can have. I even began to feel that Isabel needed me almost as much as I needed her.

But, alas! As the reader will find out in the pages ahead, that feeling of being a part of and belonging to someone was torn from my heart on so many occasions by appointed guardians with no sensitivity and little understanding, that I still have great difficulty sometimes relaying these qualities to my own family even to this very day.

If there is one consolation, however, it is this: from the spring of 1944 onward, the authorities and their appointees never once failed to indelibly impress upon my young and developing mind one very important piece of information, although I'm sure it was unintentional.

To wit: all the beds, food, clothing and regimentation in the world can never again replace even the smallest piece of a broken heart.

Becoming an Orphan

At the Children's Aid shelter there were a bunch of kids. They had a girls' dormitory and a boys' dormitory in this building and a backyard with a high fence around it, a big industrial type of fence that reminded me of a fence around a jail.

I was probably there for a couple of months. It was a Protestant orphanage and my being Catholic (since my trip to Montreal), I guess they were waiting to make a transfer. I tried to mind my own business, but I was curious about what was happening. I hadn't heard from my mother, and no one would tell me what had happened to her and Nancy.

Though there were umpteen incidents in the shelter, one or two here will suffice. Once I got hit in the head with a milk bottle thrown by a kid named Harold Vaughn. He was standing with his back turned to the toilet talking to another kid as I decided to go over and have a leak. As I was standing there peeing he quickly decided to have a bowel movement and without even looking behind him, he sat right down in the line of fire. When he felt the pee all over him he grabbed a quart milk bottle that was sitting on the back of the toilet and let me have it across the forehead.

The bottle broke and there was blood everywhere. Tears, too.

It bled so bad that I wound up in the hospital for a couple of days with my head bandaged like an Egyptian mummy, and I still carry the scar to this day.

While I was in the hospital I had hoped to hear from my mother, but no such luck.

After returning to the Children's Aid shelter, me and a couple of other kids planned running away. It didn't actually materialize because I felt I wasn't there long enough to know them or to be able to trust them.

When you are in a place like this, you just don't do things that could make things worse than they are.

115

You've heard the saying that there is honour among thieves. Well, that's a truism. When you're contemplating doing something you've got to make sure that everyone's on side, and that no one will squeal. You don't take chances, whether you are five or fifty-five.

I went to the Protestant Sunday school for a while, but because I was Catholic they eventually moved me. Besides me, there were two other Catholic kids, two brothers, Billy and Lloyd Veniot, who were also slated to be transferred.

They took the three of us to an all-boys Catholic orphanage in Silver Falls, New Brunswick, which was about five or six miles out of Saint John.

St. Patrick's Orphanage was a big brick building out on Loch Lomond Road. There were about 150 kids there, and the first thing I noticed was that they were not dressed nearly as well as in the Protestant place we had just left. Everybody at St. Pat's wore the same drab overalls and a shirt.

It was right out on a farm. I suppose that was the reason for the overalls. Outside and around the barns everybody had their chores to do. They worked at milking cows, hauling in hay, feeding livestock, cleaning out stables, etc.

In the building itself they had a room where the bread was made. It smelled good in there, but you didn't get any more food, unless you stole it.

The work in the laundry room was hard and very hot, and making dairy products in the milk room was also exhausting at times when butter was being churned, or cheese was being made.

They had an old covered milk wagon, pulled by a horse, which the older boys drove into Saint John to deliver milk and other dairy products while the younger kids did the rest of the work.

There were boys here from the age of one to twenty-one, and everybody from the age of four or five years old had sinks and toilets to clean, floors to scrub or dishes to wash. There were jobs for everybody.

It didn't take me and the Veniot boys long to size up the situation. The very first day we got there we decided to run away. We took off and made it all the way back to Saint John, where they went looking for their mother.

It was no use for me to look for Isabel because I didn't know where she was.

When we finally found their house their mother wasn't home. I think it was their aunt who answered the door, and the man inside said, "You kids better get your asses back to the orphanage."

I remember how dejected the boys felt. The man had given the oldest, Billy, a few cents, so we got on a streetcar with a plan to go some place even further away, but it didn't work. We drove all around Saint John a couple of times and came back to the same place where we were told to get off by the conductor. We were pretty down and getting kind of hungry, so we decided to walk back to the orphanage.

It was twilight by the time we got there and they were still out searching for us, so we decided to hide out in the gravel pit across the road from the orphanage until it got a bit darker.

After a while we decided, "Okay, let's go up and maybe get something to eat and find out if we get a bed or maybe just a lickin' for running away on day one."

Well, we didn't eat. They put us straight to bed in a dormitory with about fifty other boys. I guess they didn't tear into us because we hadn't even gotten established, and it was after all only our first day there.

I ran away a couple of times after that, and each time I received the big, heavy lickin' that accompanied every return, or capture, of "little urchins" like me who were looking for their mom or dad or maybe just a better way to live than this.

We didn't have any chores assigned to us for the first full day at the orphanage. We went to school, which was right in the building, and my life—rather existence—at

St. Patrick's Orphanage now began.

One day I was out in the so-called ball field where everybody else was. We were playing and running and trying to forget who we were and why we were there. I suppose we were just trying to be little children, even though we all had big problems.

There was always a nun watching from one end of the field and another nun watching from somewhere else. It was like a prisoner-of-war camp, except there were no guns and no watchtowers.

I was up near the woods when one of the kids who had been playing closer to the woods than I was came over to me and said, "There's a woman over there in the bushes and she says she's your mother—she wants to talk to you. So we'll cover for you. Looks like she's got a big bag of stuff, too."

While trying not to create suspicion, I began skipping and sort of dancing around until I disappeared into the woods. Sure enough it was my mother and she had a bag of stuff. I don't know whether she stole it or where she got it, but there was candy in it…there was cake…a piece of pie…and a whole mishmash of other things.

She hugged me and told me the cops were after her, and she might not be able to see me again for a long time. (Today, I know this visit took place during a brief escape from her incarceration.)

On the very day I had hopes that she would come to get me and take me with her, away from this bloody hell—that was the day she was telling me it was over.

She tried to explain to me as best she could that I'd have to stay at the orphanage. She would be back to see me one day, but right now we were not going to be together for a while.

In the event that we might be separated for a long time she told me to always remember to show her that I had a distinguishing birthmark on my neck, just a tiny thing, shaped like a hotdog, and I would always be able to identify her by her missing thumb.

Even with her talking like that, it never occurred to me at the time just how long it would be—six or seven years—before I would get to see her again.

So the parting was nothing special. No big hugs and kisses. Just sadness and disappointment.

As soon as I brought the bag out from the woods, Isabel had disappeared. The bigger kids grabbed the bag and I got a couple of candies out of it before it spilled all over. By the time everybody grabbed something, the goodies were gone.

And so was my mother.

Life at the Orphanage

St. Pat's was a rough school, but when you rule with the kind of iron fist—iron rod that most of these nuns ruled with, it's no wonder their violence bred violence among their young wards.

The circle of life for most kids revolved around the so-called rec room—and there was fighting there continuously. When there wasn't a fight in this corner, there was a fight in that corner. If there wasn't a fight in that corner, there was a fight in another corner.

The older guys would always get the younger ones picking fights with each other.

"He said this against you. You're not going to take that, are you?"

Then they'd go to the other guy: "He said this against you. You're not going to take that, are you? You're not going to be chickenshit. You're not going to be a coward."

Then they got you together so they could watch the two of you pound the living daylights out of each other. Each battle had to be decisive. If you just gave up, the other kid was taunted to batter you until you were really hurt and bleeding. Then he was expected to pick on you every day thereafter. He was to be your master and you had to do his bidding or take another pounding.

I must have been extremely unlucky because I was in these fights every day, every day, every day. And when it wasn't real fights it was wrestling, which always led to a fight anyway. It was continuous competition day in, day out.

The food wasn't good there, either. And there wasn't enough of it. So everybody had to find ways of snitching food, and many got quite adept at it.

While my job was mainly scrubbing floors, I didn't get a chance to steal any food. So those who worked in the bread room or the kitchen would steal some for me in exchange for stories I'd tell them and songs I'd sing to entertain them.

Even at that young age I had a knack for telling stories. They'd get me in a corner and I'd tell stories that I'd just make up as I went along, and before I knew it I'd have quite a few kids gathered around.

Sometimes I'd owe so many guys so many stories they'd push me around if I didn't tell their story first. So the biggest guy I owed a story to always got his story told first. I had to protect my interests; especially my neck.

Everybody had some kind of a nickname at the orphanage and mine was Cowboy. I sang a lot of cowboy songs and the kids just kept asking me to sing another and another while feeding me pieces of stolen bread. A hunk of bread for a song wasn't a bad price, and it sure kept me from going hungry. In turn, I guess they figured a yodel or two was a welcome change from the daily drone of the Latin hymns. I have to credit my mother for my knowledge of cowboy music. As I said before, Isabel was a real country and western fan, and when she used to sing all those songs I just naturally picked them up from her.

I can also credit her for the stories, too.

Even though I was only eight years old, I had been subjected to so much through hitch-hiking and moving around that I had a good background from which to cull ideas and put stories together. I had also seen a great number of movies which had story lines I could remember and stretch, while some of the orphans had never seen movies before.

Hitch-hiking was also an experience that these other kids never had. So, as often as not, I would exaggerate these hitch-hiking stories and place my mother right in the centre where she was built into such a hero that she was beating up cops, taking great risks and overcoming insurmountable problems.

Before long, the name "Isabel" was like that of Wonder Woman in the comics. She was known by all. And I am sure all the kids who sat around with mouths wide open often wished they had a mom as brave as mine.

Searching for food was a constant activity at St. Pat's. For instance, everybody had a little bottle that they either found somewhere or just picked up at the dump. This they would fill up with milk right from the cow or steal it from the milk room.

Once the cream came to the top and the rest was discarded, it was allowed to sit in the sun until it was ready to churn. We'd then sit and shake it to make a little butter. And with a stick or your finger you'd put the butter on your bread. I'd like to say it was yummy. It wasn't. But it was better than eating the bread without anything on it.

We would steal turnips, potatoes, carrots and other stuff from the garden, by sneaking through the fence when the nuns weren't watching.

We'd get these raw vegetables and cut them up with sections of the haycutter scythe, which we would keep sharpened with a rock. Turnips and raw potatoes were a regular treat. No potato chips and chocolate bars and peanuts for us. If you wanted a snack, you had to be creative.

Everybody had what they called a secret compartment under a rock, or in a tree, or under a tree stump. You didn't tell anyone where you stashed your cache. And that's how we managed to supplement the skimpy portions of food we were served at the table.

The older boys used to enjoy playing pranks on us young kids—pranks that were sadistic and often bordering on torture. Not always did I have enough stories in the bank to be able to pay off some big brute. Often I had to face the music like everyone else. They would get the "babies" to chase you, for instance. The "babies" were all those under five or six years old and anyone who could crawl, toddle or run. There would be about twenty-five or thirty of them running after you and if you touched one, then the older kids would beat the shit out of you.

The babies would kick you, bite you, scratch you, do anything they could to you, so you had to run from them. You couldn't get out of the rec room because all the doors were locked. You just ran and ran and ran till you were tired, then they came at you from all angles, like an army of ants. If you survived this ordeal, there was still nothing to be happy about. There was more to come tomorrow. No matter what game you played you always had to be suspicious of the other kids' motives. You just never knew when that punch in the face was coming.

It may all seem a bit remote now, but when you're there, and you haven't got anyone to turn to, there's just no refuge. You can't go to a nun and tell her because if you do that, then they'd really get you later. Nobody is to squeal on anybody. So it's an impossible situation. You can't get out of it.

Now the nuns themselves, of course, believed in discipline. Their artillery was a number of sticks, including knotty bamboo sticks, as well as thick leather straps which were cut from horse harness in the barn.

Each nun carried one or the other around with her all the time. So if you did anything in school that was a little childish, daring or a little silly, they gave it to you.

And there were always kids up for stealing this or stealing that and the nuns would line them up for their punishment. They would then be asked how they had stolen something and who had helped them, but the kids would never say boo. This got the nuns so mad that they would then take it out on the whole class—everyone got the strap or the stick, the innocent along with the guilty.

One of the nuns' favourite tricks was to stick your head between the rungs of your bedstead, then twist your head so you couldn't get away. Then they'd hit you. And usually more than one of them attacked you at the same time.

If you ran away from the orphanage, then you really got it. The nuns would come into the dormitory about midnight or one o'clock in the morning, lash your arms and legs to the bed posts and then come at you with their straps, all over your back.

There was no second chance with the nuns. If your work wasn't done in school, or if you were caught doing what a lot of kids might do, but should not be doing, there were no second chances.

There were no warnings either. We all learned the hard way from the nuns. They wouldn't say, "Next time you do that, this is going to happen." The punishment was swift. You lined up and got it now—and regularly.

Wetting the bed was one of the big things. Every morning there were thirty to forty kids lined up to get their "medicine," which could be anything from five to ten cracks of the strap or the stick on each hand.

You couldn't move, you couldn't take your hand away, and you couldn't cry. If you did try to protect yourself, you got more "medicine."

Although I was ashamed and hated myself for it, I was still wetting the bed. In fact, it was a common problem at the orphanage. All of us who wet the bed were housed in the same dormitory, known as St. Vincent's.

We were made to sleep on rubber sheets with the windows open and no blankets. Even on some of the coldest winter nights we had to leave the windows open.

It was freezing in that room. When we fell asleep and nature took its course, the urine would often freeze to the rubber sheets and we, in turn, would often freeze to the urine.

Blankets were allowed, but only if you were able to go three nights without wetting the bed.

We did figure out ways to beat the system—and get a blanket for three days with a clean sheet. We slept on our towels. Then we would wring out the towels before daybreak and our beds would be dry when the nuns came around in the morning.

It was never pleasant using those towels afterwards for their real purpose, however.

Sometimes if you woke up in the middle of the night and found your bed wet you'd go and steal someone else's towel, dry your rubber sheet with it and then put the towel back. This may not have been fair, but then again, nothing else was fair either.

Every morning there was a bed inspection. This was done by Sister Anne-Marie. She was built like a tank, and when you saw her coming with her big bamboo stick you stayed out of her way. She would have put the fear of God into the bravest of men, to say nothing about how she terrified us little kids. Another nun who was just as bad was Sister Bernardo. And of all the nuns to be feared, these two were feared the most.

Even with the minimum penalty of five cracks on each hand with that horrible bamboo stick, your hands would often bleed, so you can imagine what the extra blows to the hands and other parts of the body would do.

If you tried to run away from your punishment, two nuns would grab you and shove your head between two rungs at the foot of the bed. Then they would come at you any way they could hit you. It wasn't always just two nuns who would hit you when you were trapped like this, either. And the "medicine" often went on until the nuns got tired, or they just couldn't take any more. Then they'd leave you hanging there with your head between the bars, often too weak to free yourself without help from some of the other kids. And I can't ever forget the one kid who was brave enough, stupid enough, or just fed up, frustrated or scared enough, that he tried to run away for the third time.

He had his head shaved as well as getting the beating.

We are talking Canada in the mid-1940s. The war was coming to an end, but in some sectors the atrocities were still going on. As children with weak kidneys we could no more help wetting the bed than a Jewish kid could help being Semitic. But in both cases, the attitude of the overseers was somewhat similar.

We are not talking about murder here. We are talking about humiliating a defenceless human being; one who had neither family nor friends to turn to; one too young to know how or to whom he might complain; a young boy not more than eight years old, who was being severely beaten merely because he had a medical condition that made him pee in his bed.

Two beds over from me there was another boy so disturbed that he incessantly banged the back of his head against the wall all night long in the dark, continually whimpering, "I want momma, I want momma." This went on every night, and it sure didn't do anything to promote any wholesome thoughts in the minds of the rest of us.

And the really disgusting part of all this was the lack of sympathy displayed by these nuns who were supposed to be serving their Lord and Master Jesus Christ.

When you see this sort of callous treatment of any human being, never mind a child, it leaves a lasting impression. It's the kind of thing that nightmares are made of.

It's the kind of thing that moulds a life. These nuns had every opportunity to be mother and father to us, but they treated us like cattle. Probably, in some cases, worse than cattle because the cattle would have kicked back.

Today, my heart goes out to all those poor young people who were unlucky enough to be incarcerated in any similar religious boarding school or orphanage.

In all too many cases, as soon as the door to the outside world closes behind you, you may very well find yourself at the mercy of a depraved mind.

Perhaps the celibacy vows which these nuns and priests take have something to do with the way they treat fellow human beings when there is an opportunity for them to show power. I don't know this for sure, because I'm no expert, but I do feel that the trust they command because of their devotion to their Saviour is lost when this type of behaviour is uncovered. I also know that you can't always judge everyone by the actions of a few. But there were certainly a lot of times in years gone by that I'd give wide berth to any sister in a habit when I saw her coming, even if she wasn't built like "Attila the Nun."

One good thing about the orphanage was that we all learned how to be self-sufficient. We learned to work together to get the job done, knowing that if we didn't, we'd certainly pay the consequences. But this also led to an underground industry which the nuns weren't always aware of. When the opportunity would allow, we would make frequent trips to the public dump, which was not too far away.

We were always picking through the dump to find an old wheel or something, and maybe a couple of boards and some old rusty nails to make a sloven, which was our word for a makeshift cart.

As we had no hammers, the nails were just banged in with rocks. A sloven was two boards with a couple of cross-pieces on them with wheels. You'd get a number of spikes and you'd put them through these crooked old wheels that usually didn't have rubber on them, then pull them around on a piece of rope. It was quite a sight to see what different inventions the kids would come up with. They'd carve guns, bows and arrows, and many other things with the crudest kind of knives. And of course everything had to be kept out of sight.

Sometimes we'd find food at the dump and if it wasn't too far gone we'd eat it. Once we got into a big load of maggoty dates that were thrown out by some company, and before anyone realized what we were eating, we all got a belly full and were quite sick.

Some kids were also able to sneak away through the woods to steal cigarettes from a store on the back road, while others just burnt their lips from smoking rolled-up newspapers and magazines. Fire was usually obtained from any piece of glass which would magnify the sun.

Other than the priest, the only man we ever got to see was old Bill McNulty, who came to visit us from time to time. We were always glad to see him because he always brought a bag or two of assorted candies and licorice. He would often take us swimming in the river and show us how to do sports and play games. The winners of each event would always be rewarded with a candy. He was a very fair man, but if you crossed him he would subject you to the "hot oven." That was when you had to crawl on your hands and knees between the legs of all the other boys as they whacked your backside. By the time you got through the legs of sixty or seventy boys, your arse was pretty sore. Bill, however, was always looked up to by the kids, and I think it had a lot to do with the fact that he had also been an orphan in St. Pat's.

My first job at the orphanage was making the beds. I then went to scrubbing floors on my hands and knees. After that I worked in the milk room, the laundry room and the bread room.

Just before I left there I was washing pots and pans in the kitchen. Each job had to be done to perfection or you paid the consequences. One bed not made right could result in having to make them all again. One spot on the floor not scrubbed enough could result in having to redo the whole floor.

The first day I worked in the laundry room, Sister Anne-Marie, the nun who loved to beat the kids with the big bamboo stick, dumped me into one of the large washing machines while it was still running on account of some mistake I made. I nearly drowned in the hot soapy water and when she finally pulled me out, all soaking wet, she was laughing.

As this was my first time in the laundry room I had absolutely no idea what had to be done. You were just expected to pick things up as you went along and hope you didn't make a mistake.

In fact, there was no training. It was all trial and error. And when I say trial, there was no justice. The nuns were judge and jury and as soon as even the tiniest thing went wrong, penalties were handed out. There was no defence. This was a dictatorship.

To this day I don't know why I was put in the washing machine. Maybe it was some kind of cruel initiation or maybe it was just Sister Anne-Marie experiencing some kind of strange delight at my expense. Who knows.

I'm only sure that on a scale where kindness is rated as a 5 and cruelty rated as a 1, Sister Anne-Marie and Sister Bernardo would rank as a 0. All the other nuns would rank as a 1 or a 2 and maybe a questionable 3. The only exception to this rule was Sister Bernardine, and for her kindness, her understanding and the quiet little favours she would often secrete from the larder of the rest of the nuns to give the boys who helped her, she would rank as a strong 5 plus.

As her duties were to look after the chapel and keep it clean, everybody wanted to work for her. In fact, we would fight to work for her. Whenever she wanted a couple of boys or even three or four boys to do a job for her, there was never any shortage of volunteers.

She wouldn't make us work hard and then afterwards in the corner of the chapel some place, where none of the other nuns could see, she'd give us all a piece of cake. Or she might have a couple of peppermints and give us each a peppermint or some little thing like that that she'd hidden away. She was quite old and not very big, and for some reason she always reminded me of a little candle flickering somewhere in a cave.

When I used to scrub the dormitory floors for another nun, it would take a couple of days on my hands and knees. There was no mop. I had a big bar of soap and a big scrubbing brush and a couple of cloths. And, of course, the floors were not like they are today, flat and usually linoleum.

They were wooden floors with grooves an eighth of an inch thick and those boards were—damned if I know how old. But when you were done scrubbing you almost had to see your face in it. In between the cracks there could be no dirt. So you stayed on your hands and knees and made sure everything was spotless.

If the floor wasn't clean and didn't meet with the nun's expectations, you had to do it over again. And just to make life a little more difficult, she would sometimes spill the dirty water all over it, dregs and all. It was like being in the army.

Making beds was the same thing. I had about ten beds to look after. If one of them didn't meet the specifications they were all torn apart and you started from scratch. They helped you get started by ripping apart every single bed. Later on in life, when I was about thirty-five years old, I wrote a song having to do with this very subject. It's called "Orphan's Christmas" and it's on my Christmas album. (Due to a slight memory discrepancy while writing this song I stated that my age was seven years old when in fact I was eight. Everything else in the song is true.) Printed here is that account.

It was coming on Christmas and the talk in the classrooms was that the Sister Superior had announced that Santa Claus would pay us a visit this year.

The kids were excited about this because in an orphanage you never got anything other than an apple or an orange at Christmas. But the word was out that Santa was going to bring all the kids—every boy in the orphanage—a sled.

On Christmas morning, after the chores were done, Santa Claus arrived in the big rec room and all the kids were lined up. But someone had given a wrong head count and there was one less sled than there were boys. No one realized it at the time, except me. I realized it because I was the only one who didn't get a sled.

Wouldn't you know it, this was one of the days when I didn't do my beds properly and I had to do them all over again.

By the time I got them made right and got down to the rec room, three-quarters of the kids had already lined up, had shaken Santa Claus's hand and received the usual apple, orange, a little handful of nuts—and a sled.

Because I was late I was at the tail end of the line. The pile of sleds was getting low and I said to myself, "There's only four sleds left and it looks like there's five boys."

I thought maybe he had one hidden someplace, and for all I knew Santa Claus was a miracle worker. He'd probably come up with one from somewhere.

Finally Santa shakes my hand, gives me the handful of nuts and an apple and an orange, and after I look at him for a moment, he looks around and starts shaking my hand again and patting me on the back. Then rather nervously he says, "Well, Merry Christmas."

You could see that there was something wrong and there was certainly something wrong with me, too. Because by that time I realized I wasn't going to get a sled, and I was pretty heart-broken over the whole affair.

Everybody in the orphanage got a sled, except me. So I went away by myself and cried and went through what any normal kid would experience in a similar situation. I just couldn't seem to stop asking, "Why me?" and "What did I do wrong?"

Another thing in the orphanage was the diseases. There were mumps, measles, whooping cough, chicken pox and a host of ringworm, hives and rashes, along with lice and other irritations.

When one kid caught something, everyone would catch it. And I guess I had them all.

Once when someone higher up got the brainy idea that all the boys should have their tonsils removed, they sent a weekly busload of us to the general hospital in town and there we were de-tonsilled, en masse.

After that episode the next thing we were all to receive was an appendectomy. Thankfully, I left the orphanage before my turn came up for that one. But a lot of the other boys were not so lucky.

And speaking of luck, I remember how unlucky I thought I was the time I got transferred from my job in the bread room to washing dishes in the kitchen. By the time we had the breakfast dishes washed it was time for dinner, and when that was over we started washing again in preparation for supper. After supper we washed till chapel time and then it was time to go to bed. It seemed like wash, wash, wash was all I ever did. Then I heard the news.

One of the boys who had replaced me in the bread room had just lost a couple of his fingers in the slicer and had to be rushed to the hospital. That sure made me wash dishes a little harder and not consider myself to be so unlucky after all.

Another work-related accident that eventually took a young boy's life happened just a day or two before I left St. Pat's. My best friend at the orphanage was Gerry Marks (one of my hitch-hiking buddies of later years), and it was his younger brother, Arnold, who was involved.

It was the time for taking hay up into the barn and Arnold was "pulling slack" on the hay-fork cable back at the far end of the loft. It seems that someone forgot to give the signal and as the cable snapped tight from the force of the tension, it caught Arnold by the arm and ripped it off. He was then rushed to the hospital and later died.

Though I wasn't there for the funeral, Gerry told me about the sad event when I met him a number of years later. And if there's one small postscript that I could add to this by-gone tragedy it would be this: Let no one forget that his death was "work-related," and that Arnold was only seven years old.

Today when I think of all the things that went on at that orphanage I can't help but wonder how so many people could live their lives practising so many contradictions and still feel so righteous. How could so many people preach and teach children the catechism and the gospels, force them every day to attend mass and to serve the priests as an altar boy, such as I was, all in the name of a loving Jesus, and at the same time pound the bodies and torture the minds of innocent babes whose only crime was stepping out of line once in a while or uncontrollably peeing the bed?

It seems to me the reason there was so much violence between the boys was because that was the only reaction they learned from the nuns. If someone irritated you, just give him a good pounding. That's what was being done by those who were supposed to be showing you an example. All through the week our catechism and other instruction taught us what thoughts and actions were considered to be sins and which ones were not.

Then on Saturday evening we all had to line up to confess our sins to the priest and to God and to ask that we may be forgiven. As if it wasn't enough to be extremely fearful of the beatings you took from the nuns and the bigger boys each day of the week, you became extra fearful on Saturdays. You might forget or miss a mortal sin that you should have told the priest and if you should happen to die with a mortal sin on your soul you could go straight to Hell and burn for ever.

When those poor nuns went to confession I sure hope they didn't miss telling anything.

Hope for Adoption

Once or twice a month we would all get cleaned up and dressed up for what I would call the parade of the orphans.

It was like a cattle auction. The children would have to take part in a line-up—and a person would select which child they wanted to take from the orphanage.

It happened so many times at St. Patrick's that you didn't get upset when you weren't chosen. You knew that your time would come—or you hoped it would—sooner or later. I remember my hope of getting selected was based on the thought that if I got adopted I could run away from a foster home much more easily than I could from the orphanage and probably be punished much less if I were caught and brought back. This would enhance my chances of finding and seeing my mother once again. I had run away from the orphanage a couple of times before and was tied to my bed and strapped for it when I was brought back. I was hoping the consequences for this in a foster home would be less drastic.

I don't know what sort of deals were made between the orphanage and the families that took the children away. We didn't understand what the terms were, but in those days we thought we were being adopted, although there were different forms of adoption. I forget now how it went: I think if they couldn't get the signature of your mother, then no one could adopt you, but you could be sent out on a guardianship deal to work on a farm or something of a similar nature.

I believe that's how I got to go to Skinners Pond, Prince Edward Island.

Cora Aylward had been one of the women who came to look the boys over a couple of times before and on this particular day I happened to be one of the boys in the line-up.

After talking to several boys she picked me out of the crowd.

When you were selected, you'd be taken to another room where the prospective child-rearer would look you over more closely.

I'd got this far before in other line-ups, but they'd always taken some other kid.

This day, however, was going to be different. It was my turn to be selected to leave the orphanage. I guess Cora must have liked my looks or the answers I gave her. I didn't know what she did and I wasn't told anything about her or her family—or even where they lived. I just knew that one day soon I would be leaving.

About two or three weeks later I was called out of the rec room and told to go down to the reception room to meet a woman from the Children's Aid. They dressed me and cleaned me up and they even had a suitcase packed for me. I went with this woman in a car being driven by a man to Saint John, where we boarded a bus and travelled to Apohaqui, New Brunswick.

That was the home of Cora Aylward's family. She was originally from New Brunswick, but I found out she had married Russell Aylward from Skinners Pond, Prince Edward Island, when he was over in New Brunswick a number of years earlier. Cora was visiting her mother in the old homestead at the time this woman from the Children's Aid took me there and dropped me off with my suitcase. It was then I found out I was going to be leaving with Cora for Skinners Pond, in a couple of days.

I don't know if the Aylwards paid anything for me or not.

A number of years later I was told by some of the kids who were adopted out of there that that's what was happening, but I can't really say whether or not it happened in my case

There was a lot of doubt cast on the operation and maybe there was some kind of a scam, but I just don't know.

During my first day in Apohaqui I met my new "sister," Marlene. She was adopted by the Aylwards in the same way as I was, but she was only two years old. I'm not sure what went on there either, but they got her as a baby from Saint John a year or so before they got me. It was now 1945 and I was nine.

Thanks to old Bill McNulty I was a pretty good swimmer by this time, too. And when Marion, Cora's sister, decided to take me and a group of other kids out swimming on the Kennebecasis River, I couldn't wait to show off my stuff. We were only supposed to be swimming around the edge, but I decided to dive in and swim across to the other side.

Well, the panic was something incredible. I couldn't believe that anyone could have such concern about my life as Marion did. She said that the year before a couple of kids had been drowned out there from the undertow and that I shouldn't be so daring. She appeared a bit shaken and immediately took us home again.

I guess this was something that no one was expecting of me. I might have had a nice little innocent face on me, but when I met other kids I just had to show them up.

And when it came to feats of daring I had very little fear.

After my stint in the orphanage I think I also had the golden rule a little screwed up. I believed I should do unto others what they would do unto me, only do it first. It was going to take me a little while but I eventually got it straight.

I guess Cora realized upon hearing of the swimming incident that this new little boy she got was certainly no wimp. She began to see that she was getting a little more than she bargained for. And I certainly didn't expect the future to turn out the way it did either.

At any rate we got on the train and headed out for Prince Edward Island. We stayed on the train as it drove on the ferry and soon we were across the Northumberland Strait and heading for my new home.

My New Home on P.E.I.

I was in a land I had never even heard of and already I was beginning to feel out of place. One of the problems was the orphanage had sent me off in a pair of knickerbockers and I felt really stupid when I looked around and found that nobody else was wearing them. In fact, I thought I was better dressed than King George VI when I saw him in a grandiose parade in Saint John. Everyone else must have thought so too, by the way they just kept staring at me. Instead of a little orphan boy going to Skinners Pond, I looked more like little Lord Fauntleroy on his way to Buckingham Palace.

It was late at night when we pulled into the Tignish train station. Anthony and Freda Keefe were there in their car with their two boys, Bennett, who was a year older than me, and Earle, a year younger.

They had the only car in Skinners Pond at the time. It was a '39 or '40 Plymouth and was really packed when we drove from the station to Skinners Pond, about six or seven miles on an old dirt road. (At the time there was no pavement around that part of the Island.)

It took us about half an hour or so to get to Skinners Pond under the star-filled sky. There was no electricity there either, so when the stars and moon were covered by cloud it was really dark.

There wasn't much of a ceremony when we got to the Aylwards' farm. Cora introduced me to her husband, Russell, and then to his mother and father. After that I met Russell's sister, Betty, who was only home for the summer convalescing, after hurting her leg in Boston, where many of Russell's relatives had moved over the years.

As soon as the Keefes left to go home, Cora showed me where my bed was. It was in the hall at the head of the stairs, and it didn't take me long to get in it. When I woke in the morning, the first thing I wanted to do was look out the window to see what kind of a place I had moved to.

I could see the Knoxes' house across the way and I saw a couple of kids over there. Other than that it looked pretty remote.

Right after breakfast Russell had to go to the Keefes'. He and Anthony owned a potato sprayer between them—and I had arrived just in time to spray potatoes.

We walked up the road together, just behind the team of horses. And as we went past one of the houses (James Doyle's), I noticed lots of kids out at the gate who were gawking at me. The Doyle family ended up having about twelve kids, but at that time they had around ten—and it seemed they were all out there that first morning at Skinners Pond to look me over.

One of the main things I was about to learn in Skinners Pond was that everyone lived on the barter system. That is, everyone traded their goods and services back and forth without the use of money. Everywhere I had been up to now, if you had no money you didn't eat and you could be thrown right out of your home for not paying your rent. If you had no money you didn't even have clothes. In Skinners Pond it was different. Only in the fall when there was a surplus of goods would anyone have some money, and when they did, it was usually sent away to Eaton's or Simpson's in return for something you needed to buy from their catalogues, such as winter boots and heavy coats and things you couldn't make yourself.

For the rest of the year a day's work at planting potatoes or hauling in hay by one man might be exchanged for a day's work of threshing grain or cutting down firewood from another. A fisherman might trade a quantity of fish to a farmer for enough wood to last him the winter or he might help the farmer to cut, saw and split his wood in exchange for a winter's supply of meat or potatoes.

Socks, mitts and sweaters were all made from the wool of your sheep. Leather for harness, heavy work mitts and belts came from the hides of other animals. Lard and wax for candles came from pigs. Pillows and mattresses came from poultry or just plain old straw. Everybody's bed clothing and underwear was usually made from flour bags. Rags and potato bags were used for making carpets, and one year, there was even a kid who came to our one-room schoolhouse wearing a bull's bag over his head for a winter cap.

Since there was no electricity, knitting, sewing and reading had to be done by kerosene lamp or candlelight.

Water came from the well, or the pump, and was heated on the woodstove for washing or bathing. Under every bed there was a chamber pot for emergencies, but for the rest of the time you had to walk (or sometimes run) to the outhouse, which was usually situated somewhere near the barn.

There was only one telephone in Skinners Pond in those days and that was in our house. It was fastened to the wall and operated with a crank. Anyone who had business or health problems or just needed to say Merry Christmas to a loved one would come to our house and stand in line.

As I said, Anthony Keefe had the only car in the district. He would only run it in the summertime, however, as all the roads were blocked with snow by the middle of November. Everyone else travelled by horse and light wagon, or by horse and sleigh in the winter.

Those who could buy a battery from the catalogue in the fall could listen to the radio that winter until the juice ran out. The radio was, therefore, only used to listen to the news, the weather forecast, a few special programs in the evening and, of course, Don Messer and His Islanders. If you were caught tuning in to anything else you were quickly admonished to "get away from there, and turn that thing off before you run down the battery."

This then, in essence, was the mode of life upon my arrival in Skinners Pond.

Everything from washing the clothes to milking the cows was done by hand. Even in the orphanage we had had electricity. So here I was, in a totally different world.

I also noticed the schoolhouse only had one room and I was later to find out that only one teacher taught all the grades from one to eight. And wouldn't you just know it; on my very first day of attendance, Cora made me wear those frumpty dumpty knickerbockers.

I had a feeling that they weren't going to go over too well, and I was right. At the first recess some kid teased me about the get-up and we were into a fight.

So while the start to my life in P.E.I. was rather unfavourable, little did anyone know that the people of Skinners Pond would one day be well known across the country because of me, and that the premier of the province would make me an honoured citizen by holding a special day in Charlottetown during the Island's Centennial year, when I would be named P.E.I.'s goodwill ambassador.

But there was certainly no parade for me in those early days on P.E.I.

Pretty soon Cora began shoving it down my throat that I should be grateful to her because she had taken me away from the orphanage.

Well, that didn't wash too well with me. She began treating me meanly, and instead of being happy my life at Skinners Pond was becoming a drag—even though they had "saved" me from the orphanage.

I just didn't seem to see eye to eye with Cora and that caused all sorts of rows. She couldn't stand to see me idle. Now, I want to tell you that I did a lot of work, both in the house and out in the fields at Skinners Pond, which a lot of people still living can attest to. But I don't know, even to this day, why my new-found mother belittled me so.

She constantly reminded me that I was just an orphan who was also a bastard and that I should be grateful because she had rescued me.

It was then I began to feel that Cora really wished she had gotten another girl, instead of me, and I still feel the same way today.

But, like it or not, I was a boy all right, even though the short pants and knickerbockers may have made me look a lot different from the other boys who were wearing jeans or overalls. It wasn't long though before I made sure I was wearing the same. I merely had a couple of "accidents" while climbing over a barbed wire fence.

Because of my tough upbringing I also didn't like taking orders. I was opposed to all kinds of authority. I would buck it simply to buck it, especially if it came from anyone with an attitude that in any way resembled that of the nuns in the orphanage.

This could get me into an awful lot of trouble. But at the time it seemed to be my only way of fighting back.

Though it wasn't by choice, I was slowly becoming a misfit and many nights I would cry myself to sleep, pining for my real mother who was now far across the Northumberland Strait in New Brunswick. Even if times had been tough when I lived with her, she was still my mother and I wanted to see her again.

I suppose it would be about seven or eight times that I tried to run away from the Aylwards in Skinners Pond, with the sole purpose of getting off the Island to look for my mother, and I used to think of her every day.

Had Cora been even half as decent to me as Russell was I often wonder if I would ever have tried to run away at all. Russell always knew I gave 100 per cent in everything I did and that I would stop at nothing in order to excel. I guess I needed so much to be wanted that I was always trying to prove that I was worthy of other people's confidence.

Every time someone hinted that I was in any way inferior to the other kids, which was most of the time, I'd silently take an "I'll show you" attitude and go out of my way to bust my ass to gain a more favourable status in that person's opinion. Ninety per cent of the time it didn't seem to work, and with Cora it was 100 per cent of the time. No matter what I did there was never even the slightest hint of praise from anyone.

As time went on I was hopelessly heading for a burnout, but through it all I always liked Russell, and each time I ran away it really wasn't because of him.

I often tried to figure out why Cora always had it in for me. There was something. We didn't click from the first day. And from what I could discern, she didn't care too much for other boys, either.

I noticed in later life, when I'd go "home" for a visit, if young girls came in the house, she couldn't do enough for them. But when younger boys came in, she treated them like barn animals. They should always be kept outside in the barn, whereas girls were more "civilized" and should stay in the house and be treated with kindness.

I could see myself in some of these boys' positions, except I was worse off when I was young. I had to live in the same house with her.

I was told right off the bat that the clothes that I wore outside had to come off in the porch and when I came into the house, I was to sit on a chair and shut up. I couldn't get up and walk around the house. I had to wash in the porch, come into the house, sit on the chair and wait until I was called to supper. No talk, nothing, It was impossible to feel welcome in this family. I was always being treated like a servant.

My adopted sister, Marlene, on the other hand, always reminded me of one of those babies from the orphanage. She could kick me, punch me, pinch me, spit on me, anything her little heart desired, and that was okay.

She was a spoiled little brat. I'd even seen her get up and crawl across the table at mealtime, and not a thing happened.

But if I reached for an extra piece of bread without asking politely, I got my fingers cracked. So I had to sit at the table, shut up and say nothing. Just eat. And if I ever stayed at the table longer than Russell, I would certainly hear about it. So when I was really hungry I had to wolf my food down to get enough before Russell decided to get up. It was better to be chastised for eating too fast

than it was to be accused of "overeating like a little pig."
And so there was always that tension.

It's hard today to describe. But what eventually happened was that I had to use my wits with Cora. What I mean by that is the only way I was accepted by her was when I appeared to be retarded or stupid. I found out that the best way to get around her was to be an idiot. The more idiotic I acted, the better she liked me. So when something was said, like "Bring in a couple of armloads of wood and put them in the box," I'd say "Ya-yeah, ok-kay." And I'd stutter and stammer and get such stupid looks on my face that she would smile in a way that told me she was pleased and that now I was on the good side of her. In her good books, so to speak.

This pretence eventually got so bad (or good) that Marlene used to go around imitating and making fun of me because she really thought I was stupid. And I used to think how odd it was that Cora never suspected my playacting and just seemed to be very contented with the fact that this bright-looking boy she got from the orphanage was gradually becoming more retarded every day.

And when I made a good mark or did something well at school, Cora just seemed to hate it. She always gave me that displeased look of hers, which told me she didn't approve of me doing well at anything. Without even bothering to take a look at my good marks she'd push the papers back across the table at me with a comment like, "Go and get your work done." After this happened a couple of times I didn't bother showing her anything any more. This appeared to suit her just fine, because half the time she didn't even know what grade I was in, nor did she enquire. To this day I can't understand why any woman would not want a child to succeed, but that was Cora. She was strange. She had this mean streak.

Now Russell's mother was different. But then she and Cora never got along, either. Cora made the old people sit in the living room all the time. That's where they had to stay. Once they came out and had their meals, they went back in the living room and that was that. But I used to hear them saying some odd things now and again out of her earshot. Things like "Why is she so mean, like this?" and "Why does she do these things?" This was like an echo coming from inside my own head, an accurate reflection of my own sentiments.

Some of the things I learned to do in the orphanage, like carving and making my own toys, were also a no-no with Cora.

Every time she found anything that I had made—or if she suspected that I was making something—she'd send me to do something else, and while I was gone she'd bust it. I had to hide everything that I'd make—everything. She was ruthless. Things would be smashed to smithereens. We're not talking about her just bumping into them, or knocking them over—she would take a hammer, or whatever she could lay her hands on, and completely destroy things beyond repair.

The workbench was in an outbuilding we called the little house. We kept the hammer there, and the pliers and the wrenches for fixing the machinery.

Every time Cora saw the little house door open she'd be over there to see what I was doing. There was a little window in the place and I was constantly keeping watch to see if she was coming. When I saw her I'd quickly dart outside where I had a chance to run because I couldn't trust her.

Each time she caught me in there—and it wasn't that I wasn't supposed to be in there—she'd beat the living daylights out of me with a long switch as I scrambled back and forth over the coal in the coal bin trying to stay out of her reach.

The saying "raking someone over the coals" could have been attributed to Cora. I've seen me get black and blue and not know what it was about until later.

Then when Russell came around, I'd ask her in his presence why she beat me. Then the answer would be something like: I hadn't fed the chickens on time or some other minor infraction. While I was not allowed to argue back or defend myself against these charges, this was my way of letting Russell know the beating took place. She'd hit me first, and find an excuse for it later. This made Skinners Pond anything but the home sweet home it could have been.

Whenever my outside work schedule wasn't all that demanding, especially in bad weather, I'd take some time to whittle away at something. I used to love making things to play with. The Aylwards were not big on providing toys for me, so I had to make my own. There were toys in the house, but they were mainly Marlene's, and a boy like me didn't want to play with girls' toys, no matter how hard up I was. So I would try to make my own. I was just very careful that I wouldn't be caught either creating it, or playing with it. Cora figured that if I could find the time to make toys then I'd also take some time out to play with them. I had to work and if I had a few minutes to myself then I was expected to look for work to do to help the Aylwards, rather than have a little bit of pleasure myself.

On the occasional Sunday morning when I was left at home to feed the stock while everyone else had gone to church, I would sometimes find the time, perhaps an hour or so, to pursue some activity that I might not otherwise be allowed to do. It might be carving a knife or a gun out of wood, or shooting my slingshot or bow and arrow, or just playing around with the dog or one of the cats.

On one of these Sundays in the spring of the year while there was still quite a bit of ice on the ground, I spotted the black lamb that one of our sheep had had some time during the winter. As all our sheep were white, for one of them to have a black lamb was extremely rare. I had let the sheep out of the shed to roam around the barnyard for some recreation and the black lamb had wandered off a little by himself.

Seizing the opportunity to sneak up and catch him, so

I could pet him, I did so. But just as I caught him, from the corner of my eye I could see the ram coming on the dead run. And he was mad.

Our ram was usually fairly docile, but he could be a terror if he was provoked.

I quickly let go of the black lamb and started to run, but I fell on the ice, just as the ram went sliding by me. Although he missed me, he kept circling around and around and wouldn't let me get up to run to safety.

I just had to keep lying on my back on the ice with my feet always pointed towards him as he kept circling. He must have kept me there for over an hour till everyone got home from church and Russell was finally able to get him back in the shed.

When it was all over the ram had worn a perfect circle in the ice from going around and around and I, with my continuous turning, had worn a big hole in the centre. For about a week thereafter, Russell would have to explain to the visiting neighbours how the bull's eye and target came to be drawn in the middle of the yard. Everyone of course had a great laugh out of this, except me.

I had learned a great lesson, and didn't find the whole thing very amusing. I also never bothered to try to catch any of the lambs again, especially the black one.

Another Sunday in the summertime when they were all at church I went in the barn to get a big basin full of grain to feed all the geese, ducks and chickens we always had around the place. At one part of the granary there was a small pile of barley with which Russell had made some barley beer.

Not realizing the significance of what I was doing, I scooped up a big basin of this barley and scattered it around the barnyard for all the fowl to eat. After this I just went ahead feeding the pigs and doing up some more of my chores in the barn.

When the folks coming home from church drove in the yard, Russell let out one hell of a bellow. "Tommy, what in the hell did you feed them chickens?"

As I came running out of the barn saying, "I don't know, why?" all I could see were hens, ducks and geese flapping their wings in the craziest way that I had ever seen, and squawking and staggering and just toppling all over each other.

The whole damn lot of them were drunk as a skunk.

As I started to run with a little help from Russell's boot, Russell's father, Bill, was practically doubled over in the yard from laughing while Cora and the old lady just walked to the house, pretending they hadn't seen a thing.

One fall after all our own crops were in I was allowed to go working for some of the neighbours threshing grain and picking potatoes. The work was hard and the going rate for a kid at the time was around fifty or sixty cents a day even though you did as much as an adult. After all was said and done I had amassed the great sum of $10.

Now with the $10 burning a hole in my pocket, and knowing a kid down the road had an old bicycle for sale, I decided I would very much like to have my own transportation.

I asked Russell, who said it was okay to buy it as long as I didn't ride it when Cora didn't want me to. So that evening, around dark, he gave me permission to walk the two miles down to Adrian Leclair's place. When I got there I discovered the bike was in pieces. He shone a flashlight on the numerous parts that made up this once-beautiful bicycle. It now looked like a pile of junk.

But that didn't scare me off. I still wanted it. I knew I could fix it—especially if I kept it out of sight of Cora. If she found out the condition it was in, and the time I would have to take to fix it, I knew she would tell me to take it back. So I gave Adrian the $10 and he gave me the bicycle in parts. In place of one pedal there was a great big wooden block with a bolt through it. And the head of the bolt, every time it came around, it hit against the frame. Click. Click. Click.

He helped me to put the bicycle together quickly so I

could ride it home. It was a hard ride. Bumpy ride. I found out there were no inner tubes in the wheels. There was rope on the rims and the tires were over the rope—and the tires were shot. They wouldn't hold the tubes anyway.

There were other things missing, too. For instance, there was no bolt down through the gooseneck of the handlebars, and on the way home I was riding down the hill going into Skinners Pond when the front wheel got stuck in a rut on the road.

I tried to hold my balance by turning the wheel. The handlebars turned, but the wheel didn't, so I went ass-over-tea-kettle into the ditch—and landed on a skunk!

The skunk took off one way and I took off the other, but he pissed on me before he left. So there I am wheeling the bike home in the dark, walking alongside of it, with the handlebars in one hand and trying to push the bike and keep the front wheel straight with the other.

I was stinking to high heaven. And anyone who knows anything about skunk spray knows that the only thing to get rid of it is tomato juice, and that we couldn't afford. We were lucky to have just a few tomatoes growing in the garden for a short time in the summer, never mind having tomato juice this late in the fall.

When I finally got home and put the bike away and headed for the house they wouldn't let me in. I can't say that I blame them. After an argument took place between Russell and Cora and his father and mother as to what method of getting me back to normal should be used, I was instructed to go to the barn, take off all my clothes and rub myself with some good fresh cow manure.

After this was done I had to wait for about half an hour and then go and jump in the brook. There Russell was waiting with a big bar of floor-scrubbing soap which I had to use to thoroughly wash myself. Then I had to put on a clean set of overalls and shirt and present myself to Cora to see if she would let me in the house. As it was, she did-n't and I was told to sleep in the barn. The next day I had to wash my clothes in the brook, but as I wasn't able to get the stink out I was later told to burn them.

When I took a good look at my new bike the next day I realized that I shouldn't have spent the ten bucks on it. I think there were about ten spokes in one wheel and maybe just seven spokes holding the other together. It's a wonder it held me at all. By the time I got it all bound together with haywire it looked and sounded more like a contraption than it did a bicycle. But due to all the work I had to do, I didn't get much time to ride it anyway. When there wasn't anything to do in the barn I was in the fields. I was either taking in the hay, taking in grain, picking potatoes, ploughing the fields, or harrowing.

And when my work was done in the fields, it was home to bring in the wood, feed the stock, do the barn chores.

And when all that was done I would go into the house, get my supper, scrub the floors, wash the walls, wash the clothes. You name it. I did it. Cora always, always, had something for me to do.

And I couldn't go anywhere except on Sundays when they'd let me away for an hour or two, to go up the road or across to the Knoxes' to play with the kids.

I don't know why Cora didn't want me mixing with other people, especially other kids. That was always a mystery. She seemed to have a streak through her. She was not bad when Russell was around. But when he'd be up in the field, she'd be after me. If he went to Tignish—look out. It really got bad. The minute his back was turned she zeroed right in.

I'd try to talk to him about it and his answer would be, "Oh, that's women. You can't do anything about it. They have to have the last word, so don't say anything to them."

I'd say, "What can I do? Everything I do is wrong. What can I do to please her?"

The only time he'd talk about it was when we were out milking the cows. I knew he'd be stationary long enough to talk to me about this delicate subject of his wife, who obviously wore the pants in the family most of the time.

I'd have to pick my words carefully because I didn't want to rile him. Cora wasn't a subject he liked to talk about too much. Maybe it was too painful for him to talk about her. Maybe he realized he'd made a mistake and had resigned himself to the fact that he had to stay with her "till death do us part."

Whatever few words I managed to get in with Russell about his wife's treatment of me, there was absolutely no talking to her.

Every chance she got, she kept mentioning to me that "you will never get this farm—you will never be an Aylward."

I wasn't at school very long when I wrote my name Tommy Aylward in one of my books and Cora found it. From that time on it was murder. She said I was getting strange ideas to be calling myself Tommy Aylward, and she never wanted to see that again. Ever. On any books. Anywhere. "Got it?"

That hurt me. And, of course, with me using the name Messer and living with the Aylwards, that always left open for discussion my ancestry, the fact that I didn't have a mom or dad, and that I was just a bastard.

It would have been less hurtful and harmful to me if I could have been known as Tommy Aylward. You know how kids can forget some things after a while. If I'd been allowed to call myself an Aylward I think it would have prevented a lot of hard feelings, a lot of scraps and a lot of tears on my pillow. After all, all I ever dreamed of was to feel that I was wanted and to feel that I was part of something.

But the Aylwards weren't really adopting a son, or even wanting to make me feel at home—that wasn't the name of the game. The name of the game was simply cheap labour.

They wanted to get every ounce out of me that they could, and didn't want to give anything back. Food, clothing and shelter; I got the basic necessities. But love, care and consideration were totally absent.

There was even one day out of the clear blue sky that she told me in no uncertain terms that if I had any ideas about ever owning this farm when I grew up I'd better get them out of my head now, because this place would never be left to such a no-account as me. Being only ten or eleven years old at the time, this thought of ever inheriting the Aylward farm had never occurred to me until she mentioned it.

So, in so many ways I was being made to realize that the only reason I was with the Aylwards was to work.

I could see love in other houses. Even though I saw the kids get a slap on the ass once in a while, I also saw their mom give them a welcome home kiss, or their dad talk to them about how well they were doing with their chores, or at school, or at keeping their room tidy.

Usually, the slaps on the ass or the scolding that I saw other kids get from their parents were for legitimate reasons. They didn't get the tar pasted out of them with some blunt instrument just because they didn't feed the chickens at the exact time. They were getting a slap to teach them that they had done something wrong.

So amid all this constant negativity it became impossible for me to entertain even the slightest hope that one day there might be a future for me in Skinners Pond.

I tried to talk, but when that didn't help, I did the only thing a young boy could think of to get out of that hellish life with the Aylwards—I started running away.

At first I'd just go out into the woods—and cry. I'd stay there for hours, lying by a pole fence and just cry and sob and think of my mother and wonder where she was. Then as I began to wander farther away, the Mounties would pick me up and take me home again. On these first few trips I never got any farther than Elmsdale or Bloomfield, and within twenty-four hours they'd have me back in Skinners Pond.

One spring day when the smelts were running up the brooks, I didn't come home from school and left everybody to believe I had run away again.

They looked for me everywhere. The Mounties had given up hope of finding me and thought that I had somehow eluded them and got off the Island altogether. For five or six days and nights I was at the shore hiding in the brush near the waters of the large pond that the district of Skinners Pond was named after. I had built a small lean-to and that's where I stayed. I didn't venture out in the daytime where I could be seen, but would wait until the evening around dark when the smelts were running and go and catch a bunch by hand and put them in a potato bag.

Around midnight when I was sure everyone was in bed and absolutely no one would be at the shore, I would light a little fire with some matches that I stole from the house and some of the little pieces of driftwood that were lying around everywhere.

Now with my lean-to situated between my little fire and the view from all the houses I would cook up all my smelts on the end of a piece of wire, much the same as you would do today with a marshmallow or a wiener, and there I would gorge myself with my one big meal of the day.

After that I would just look at the stars and think of my mother before going to sleep. Sometimes I'd even wake with a start after dreaming I could see my mother's hand, the one with only half a thumb.

After six days and nights of boredom from the same diet and loneliness I sauntered on home to a major lecture and a swift kick in the arse from Russell, which only gave me more determination and resolve to find a way to leave Prince Edward Island some day for good.

Not so long after this week of eating so many smelts, one of our neighbours, Leslie Knox, gave me my first chew of tobacco. I had been over to their place while they were picking the dirt out of their Irish moss when my curiosity got the best of me. I asked Leslie what he was chewing and he told me it was licorice. When I asked him if I could have some, he obliged by cutting me off a fair-sized piece of tobacco, which at that time was known as Twist.

I popped it in my mouth and began to chew. "Wow," I thought, "this licorice tastes terrible." But watching Leslie chew his with a pleasant smile on his face, and me never wanting to be outdone by anyone, I tried to smile, too, and just kept on chewing. After swallowing a few mouthfuls of tobacco juice, my stomach started feeling awful, the farm yard began to swirl around, and I fell backwards over the fence I was sitting on and landed in the bushes.

Amid the great peals of laughter coming from Leslie, along with everyone else, I tried to get to my feet, but I couldn't. All I could do was crawl to the road and head for home across the field on my hands and knees. I was coughing and sputtering and wondering what had happened to the ground. It just wouldn't stop moving. When I got home I threw up and fell asleep in the burdocks and rhubarb which grew beside the house. Needless to say, I certainly didn't get any sympathy from Russell and Cora when they later found me. There was no more going to Knox's for awhile. And of course, no more licorice tobacco.

Through the winter my bed time was always seven or seven-thirty and the same in the summertime if it was raining and no more work could be done outside. As it wouldn't get dark in the summertime until nine o'clock, I would often lay and read comic books which I smuggled in the house and hid inside the attic hatch situated on the ceiling just over my bed. As comic books were also taboo, I had to be very careful. If Cora ever caught me with them, I'd be dead.

This was always hard to understand because all the other kids in the district were allowed to read them, and that's how I was able to obtain comic books in the first place. I would trade some of the toys I made for them.

Another difficulty I had was trying to get anyone to

believe that Cora was anything but the nice friendly person she always presented herself to be when she came in contact with other people. When neighbours came to our house or we went to theirs, Cora was always so sweet that butter wouldn't melt in her mouth. She wouldn't even disagree with anyone let alone show the slightest sign that she might be unhappy with something. That is, until she got home and there was no one else around. That's when it all came out.

For a while I tried to tell people what was really going on and just how bad she was treating me at home but no one would listen, and what was even worse, they thought I was making it all up. They liked me and appreciated the excellent work I would do for them on many occasions but then they started to think I was a liar. After this I stopped telling anybody because I knew it was no use. Now I was getting along fine with everyone as long as I confided in no one.

No one, that is, except Billy Ellsworth, who lived down the road. He'd be about twenty or twenty-one at the time, and when I'd open my heart to him about Cora he understood. He'd listen to my stories, my complaints and frustrations and with a sympathetic word, he'd tell me "not to worry, Tom, sometimes life's like that. Just take things day by day and something good is bound to turn up sooner or later." On the day I ran away and got as far as Bloomfield before being caught, it was Billy with his horse and wagon who gave me my first ride for about five miles. But he'd never go so far as to openly support my claims in front of other adults in Skinners Pond. He also didn't want me to tell anyone that he gave me the ride.

The Spirit of Adventure

When I look back on those days now, I guess I was the real Huckleberry Finn of Skinners Pond. Most of the time I wore a pair of overalls and nothing else. No shirt, no socks and no shoes. That was my style in Skinners Pond.

And I was just as adventurous as Huck. I'd think nothing of getting up on a barn roof and running across the saddle board from one end to the other, when I got the chance, just to show off to the kids.

This wasn't anything new to me. In the orphanage you had to do an awful lot of things to prove yourself to the other boys. You didn't worry about hurting yourself. You showed no fear and took your own life into your hands with a devil-may-care attitude.

All the things I had done in the orphanage I had done when adults weren't around, so now here I was in Skinners Pond doing variations of these daredevil tricks—always making sure that adults were not close by.

I would climb up to the roof of the barn on the inside and away up near the rafters I would hang by my heels on the hayfork rope. I was just like a trapeze artist in a circus.

The kids would stand in awe. We'd all be around ten years old at the time. I never encouraged anyone else to try these things. I really didn't want them to try. I wanted to be the centre of attention—the main attraction. I wanted to be known as the daredevil. I wanted them to come to see me. I really needed the attention badly, probably because I was not getting any positive strokes from my folks at home.

When I arrived at Skinners Pond the games the other kids were playing were pretty dull as far as I was concerned. I wasn't used to such tame activities and I guess I appeared to them to be a show-off most of the time.

It wasn't enough for me to do anything in the normal way. If I was riding on a horse's back I would often stand

155

up on the horse just to show it could be done. When it came to work I had to plant or pick potatoes faster than anyone else, do more ploughing and harrowing than anyone else, coil more hay and stook more grain than anyone else, and just altogether make it very plain that no matter what anyone else could do, I could do it better. And I usually did.

Although I would never brag about my accomplishments and always let the actions speak for themselves, the pace at which I drove myself to surpass the deeds of others often drew only resentment. (Incidentally, this habit stayed with me for a long time and I still have to watch myself and keep myself in check. For no matter how sincere the effort, people most often think of you as some kind of a show-off if you're always doing more than they do, and even though it may not be your intention, they won't want to work with you if they think you are always trying to make them feel inferior.)

I would tell the kids all kinds of stories, similar to the tales I told to get extra food at the orphanage.

By the time I was telling them in Skinners Pond they were becoming more elaborate. I also knew I had a more gullible audience so the embellishments got a little bigger and bigger all the time.

As for singing, I didn't do too much of that around the barn while doing the chores. I was afraid of creating unnecessary problems with Cora.

But as soon as I got away from our buildings I would sing. And I don't mean just sing to myself. I would be singing at the top of my lungs. Twice a day I would have to go three-quarters of a mile to bring in the cows for milking. And they didn't seem to mind my singing; the milk was always plentiful.

In Skinners Pond, the social life was something that most often took place at the neighbours' houses. At the Aylwards' we always seemed to be going to bed as soon as the work was finished. And on the occasions when Russell and Cora did go out to a party, Cora always proved to be the wallflower-type and could never seem to fit in to the spirit of things.

The entire district was made up of people who were either French or Irish, two groups that are traditionally well known for their love of party-making. But in Skinners Pond, the French were the ones who seemed to have the edge. The fiddle, of course, was by far the most popular instrument. A party was never really a party without it.

Russell's father, Bill, who lived with us, played the fiddle. But he was quite old when I arrived in Skinners Pond, so I only heard him play once or twice. Apparently, when he was young, he was the life and soul of the party, and always the man of the hour when he showed up with his fiddle.

This was the era I often wished I had lived in, the time of home-grown, home-made entertainment, back when there was no TV, little radio, no videos, and the only records owned by anyone had to be cranked up on a wind-up gramophone.

I found that most of the old folks all seemed to have that great fun-loving spirit that I would like to have seen among some more of the younger generation. But a lot of them seemed to be losing it.

At first I didn't know just how popular Russell's father really was among the French people, because all I ever saw him do was sit in the living room. It wasn't until I began to visit some of the French families down the road that I realized they weren't talking so much about Russell Aylward as they were about Billy Sa Pitt. (The strong accent here should be on the word "Pitt." Old Bill's father's name had been Peter or Pete, and as the custom among the French was to follow a man's first name with that of his father, Billy Sa Pitt meant "Billy, of Pete" even though his last name was Aylward.)

When I first heard about this "Billy Sa Pitt" I thought I would like to meet him. He seemed like my kind of a guy. He had a reputation among the French as being the best damn fiddle player on the Island.

Nobody could beat Billy Sa Pitt, they would tell me.

Every time he played the fiddle, he would be step-dancing at the same time. And when he wasn't step-dancing, he would be singing. He was a real entertainer, and in his day, everybody was after him to come to their parties.

It took me the longest time to realize that the old fellow sitting in our living room at home was actually the famous "Billy Sa Pitt" that everyone talked about. He had always been so out-going when he was among the villagers, they had a hard time believing that I had lived with him for so long and the stories about his great early days as the "fiddle king" had never once been discussed.

Again, perhaps, the subduing of his colourful reputation around the house may have had something to do with Cora, who was very stuffy about such things.

(Incidentally, Russell's brother, Charlie, who was Bill's youngest son, went on to win fiddling contests around Charlottetown and other parts of the Island after he moved away from Skinners Pond.)

As time went on, and I began to hear a lot more stories being told by the old-timers, I could see that life in the community had been a lot more interesting in their day than it was now. For one thing, I could see that each of them was an individual character unto himself. Each had a rich history of doing things in his own way. Each seemed to have an independent, undying spirit. And each seemed to have that special something that I was looking for.

I wanted to find that same love for life among the young people. I knew I had it to a certain degree, despite the problems and restrictions I had to overcome in my daily life, and I did want to reach out to all the other kids and somehow tell them there was a lot more to life if they'd only use their imaginations once in a while.

It seemed to me that they had lost that rich vitality that I could still see in the twinkle of their grandparents' eyes. I suggested they should be singing, instead of poking fun at those who do. I felt they should be laughing, be daring, taking a few chances and having a good time.

I told them they should try whittling something once in a while, especially as they didn't have nearly as many restrictions to face at home as I did. But even with the restrictions, I was making toys for the whole neighbourhood every time I got the opportunity.

I was whittling knives, guns, windmills, bows and arrows, slingshots, and many things they had never seen before. The answer I mostly got when I asked the kids why they didn't want to make these things, even after I offered to show them how, was, "I can't."

Well, Tommy Messer could, and he did. But I often wondered if the others ever realized just how free they were to do these things for themselves if they really wanted to. Could they imagine how lucky they were, living in such a beautiful place as Skinners Pond, with the love and encouragement of a good mom and dad, brothers and sisters, aunts and uncles, and grandpas and grandmas?

I couldn't seem to understand what was going wrong with this particular generation. To me, they seemed to have lost their creative abilities, or at least the desire to be creative. I guess that's why I loved being around the older folks rather than the kids. When the older folks talked, they talked with spirit. They spoke with verve. They spoke of making things out of nothing, creating farms out of woods and swamps, and even making the very tools that made the lumber that went into the dwellings that still stand today as memorials. These were the real people; the pioneers.

One of these old lads that I was especially drawn to, and became very fond of, was old Josey Jerome. His real name was Josey Arsenault, but as I believe his father's first name was Jerome, that's why he was often called Josey Jerome. (I mention Josey in one of my songs, entitled "Home on the Island," and again in a poem, entitled "My Tribute to Josey Arsenault." The latter is included in this work.)

When I arrived in Skinners Pond, Josey was over sixty, and though he was about ten years younger than Russell's father, Bill, they used to chum around a lot together.

You'd always see Josey at most of the parties where he would sing lots of songs, play the mouth-organ, step-dance and tell stories. A song that he sang most often was a very funny one called "The Man Behind."

Though Josey had been a fisherman in his younger years, during the time I was there he owned the only store in Skinners Pond. It was situated about a mile away from our place, and about once a week old Bill would send me there to get him some pipe tobacco.

Josey was always somewhat of a character, and I would just love hanging around the store with some of the other kids to listen to him tell a few of his great stories.

In his later years we became great friends, and we often sat for hours talking together. During these talks, he never failed to amaze me with how much he knew about almost every subject, and I would dare say he was a lot more on the ball than a lot of other people around Skinners Pond, even today.

He was as honest a man as you could ever find, and throughout his life he wouldn't steal a thing from anyone. He was a fun-lovin' guy, full of wit, full of great stories and interesting as hell.

He always had a smile on his face, and yet he was never afraid to show the trace of a sad tear. He was tough, but sensitive. A real gentleman. A real friend.

Through all the years of his eighties and nineties he always kept a twinkle in his eye. He eventually became the oldest man who had ever lived in Skinner's Pond. And though he always referred to himself as "The Kid," he finally passed away at the ripe old age of 106.

I wrote the following poem for Josey in 1985 for his hundredth birthday. It eventually got printed in a couple of the Prince Edward Island newspapers. The words in quotations throughout the poem are phrases that were very often used by Josey himself.

His favourite swear word, in place of saying "Jesus Christ," was "Cheese and Crackers."

My tribute to Josey Arsenault of Skinners Pond on his hundredth birthday, October 30, 1885, to October 30, 1985.

To my friend Josey Arsenault, 100 years young
And to all the great "times" and great songs that he sung
To the dances he danced on yesterday's floor
To the fiddles that played till they couldn't play more.

To his friends now living and his friends now gone
He's "The Man Behind" and he still carries on
He's a grand old man and a master of wit
And "you can't pull it over this young fella yet"

For in each long day he packs a year
And in every smile he drops a tear
He enjoys his life, his pipe and his "nip"
And he'll quite often trade you a song for a sip

From the years that he fished till he ran the old store
Till he gathered up moss on the Skinners Pond shore
For the 100 years that he walked this sod
I truly believe that he walked with God.

You say "a 100 years old?"; no! "a 100 years young"
And there's songs in his heart that he still hasn't sung
And when he ain't got you laughin' he's makin' you cry
And by "old cheese and crackers" how I love the old guy

And I'm sure that one day up on high somewhere
I'll again meet "the Kid" with the silvery hair
And when I get "home" at the end of the line
I'll be hand in hand with "The Man Behind."

Stompin' Tom Connors
Crown-Vetch Music

As a kid, I was always a great romantic in terms of envisioning all kinds of adventures. As well as running with pirates on the high seas, I wanted to be Robin Hood, Jesse James, Wilf Carter, Hiawatha and Samuel Champlain all at the same time. And with the exception of the old folks who always extended me an understanding glance, most people saw me as some kind of an incorrigible aberration from the acceptable norm.

The idea that an orphan who had been shunned by his own kind could possibly contribute anything worthwhile to the community other than good old-fashioned hard labour was considered to be ridiculous. New ideas and creativity were things that could only come from good breeding and notable pedigree. Just one example to bear this out came on the day that I asked if I could try to play an instrument, maybe the fiddle, or even a mouth-organ. (I knew there would be no use asking to play a guitar as there wasn't one in the house and they would be too expensive to buy.)

Well, you should have heard the comments and the laughter. "What? You play music? Do you think you have talent or something? Ha! Ha! Ha! Don't you know that people with a 'tin ear' can never learn to play music? Ha! Ha! Ha! The only way you will ever be able to carry a tune is in a basket. Now go out and get your work done and don't be so foolish." (To this day I can still hear the neighbours laughing each time Cora would tell and retell them the story about the day I wanted to play music.)

With music shot down and ridiculed, so was my chance to be Wilf Carter. Well, maybe I could be a pirate or Samuel Champlain? But for that I would need a boat, and I'd better not ask for one. "I'll just have to find a way to make my own."

There was a long deep hollow on our farm with a brook running through it which emptied into Skinners Pond. The hollow was densely covered with willows and alders to such an extent that an ancient cedar pole fence in the midst of this jungle had now been rendered use-less. These poles gave me a brilliant idea. "I'll build a big raft and sail it on Skinners Pond."

For the next two or three weeks, every chance I got to slip away I was down in the hollow pulling and tugging on poles like a little beaver. Each pole had to be dragged for a quarter of a mile through the thickest of brush, floated through a culvert at the road and assembled in a well-hidden spot where the brook entered the pond.

Although today the pond is much smaller than it used to be, due to the harbour they built, at one time it was a lovely piece of water about a mile long and an eighth of a mile at its widest. The depth would range from about two feet to fifteen feet. And this was to be my "ocean."

It took a few more days to bind the poles together with cross-pieces that were either nailed down with rusty spikes or tied with rope, and the whole project was completed in about a month.

Then came the day my "ship" was ready to sail. I finished it on a Saturday, and Sunday was going to be the maiden voyage. There was a long pole in the centre for a mast and an old shirt was nailed to it for the sail. I had another pole to push me away from shore, like the big oars used to guide the gondolas in Venice. I now decided I was Robinson Crusoe. I'm going to sail around the world. And away I go.

No one knew I had been working on the raft. Secrets were something I had learned to keep to myself at a very early age. I knew that as soon as I set sail there would be a lot of kids on shore to see what I was doing. The pond ran along the bottom of all the farms and when I set off I could see there were kids playing in their fields. And it wouldn't be too long before they spotted me.

I figured, oh boy, this is going to be spectacular—another coup for Tommy Messer.

Nice guy that I am, I started offering boat rides to the kids. "Oh no—Mommy wouldn't let me do that," and "Daddy might kick me in the rear if I went there."

"Ah, come on—nobody is going to see you," I tried to assure them. There were some little hills between the pond and the houses, and if we stayed in near the shore and didn't venture to the far side of the pond the parents would not be able to see us. After pointing this out, and doing a little more coaxing, about two or three kids became brave enough to join me on the raft, and away we went for a sail.

All that Sunday afternoon we were up and down the pond and everyone had a hell of a time. The following Sunday—the same thing. The kids, especially the boys, were beginning to argue about whose turn it would be to get the next ride. If the kids had had some pennies I could have made a small fortune. But at any rate, and as all good things must come to an end, it wasn't long before the adults began to wonder what the attraction was, all of a sudden, for all the kids around the pond capes.

The kids had been saying they were going to pick berries. So I suppose it occurred to the adults that maybe they had better go down and check things out. After all, nobody was coming home with any berries.

It was Billy Doyle who was on the raft with me the day we made our final voyage. I think we were poling along the shores of Tahiti, on our way to Easter Island, when Billy's father, James, came over the top of the bluff. We could see his cap coming over the top of the grass as I desperately tried to get in close to the shore so he might not be able to see us.

Too late. He lets out a whoop: "Billy, get your ass in here as fast as you can so I can kick it up to the house."

Billy started to cry and I had to get the raft in. I had the pole ready, so as soon as Billy jumped off the raft I gave myself a good shove. Though James couldn't reach me, he said, "I'm letting Russell know about this." And he kept his word.

I got another kick in the ass and the raft got busted up. But we had a hell of a time there for a few weeks sailing the "high seas" of Skinners Pond and creating future memories.

In my dreams that raft went all over the world. Docking at certain European ports, picking coconuts in Hawaii, and trading for treasures in China. These were only some of the voyages that were taken. As a passenger, you were also treated to a very scary story about escaping from cannibals or meeting zombies on the Island of Death.

It was just after the raft scene that a big plan to go digging for treasure was cooked up. And by who this time? Why, Blackbeard, the pirate, of course (another one of the imaginary roles I would assume when the occasion called for it).

I was always telling the kids—and so were the old fellows—about people who had found treasure. Sometimes, it was only a few coins on the shore and sometimes a whole trunk full.

I had heard of some guys who were going around with mineral rods and every once in a while there was somebody up or down the shore using coat-hangers and other kinds of wire—sort of divining—to find treasure. So I used to go around when I had the chance and rig up things like witch hazels, to try to find water, but you had to have something made of iron to find minerals. I tried all kinds of gimmicks, but nothing would ever work. I never found any treasure.

Then it occurred to me. Why don't I arrange for someone to "find" some treasure? Wow! What a scheme. If I only had some treasure to find and a map to find it with, the scheme might just work. Especially if nobody knows about it, except me.

But, how can I make the whole thing appear real to the other kids? I worked out a plan.

I got an old piece of some kind of cloth paper that I found sticking out from underneath some shingles at the barn. It may have been some ancient form of insulation or tar-paper, and it was all yellowed and sort of water-marked by the rain.

I then took an old rusty nail—as rusty as I could find—and drew myself a treasure map.

Now, I had to decide where I was going to bury the treasure, what the treasure was going to be, and whether it would be believable or not.

Also I had to plant the map so that somebody else would find it, or at least its discovery would look like an accident. This involved quite an intricate plan on my part. So I went away up in our field to where there were two old elm trees growing together against the line fence. There were some other trees around and a brook close by, and the spot couldn't be seen from any of the houses.

Twin elm trees—two elms growing out of the same root—this just had to be the spot.

So I got the map drawn, sneaked up an old shovel and a pick, and started digging a hole about the size of a grave. Every second day or so I'd get to sneak back and dig a bit more dirt.

When I cut the sods out I made sure I cut them perfectly so I could put them back again in perfect position.

I finished digging the hole and then found some old scrap metal from pieces of ancient machinery—nothing of any value. I then buried these pieces of iron and put a big flat slate rock on top of them. Then I filled in the hole and put the sods over nice and neat, patting down the grass and making sure everything looked undisturbed.

I went out in the field and got a couple of cow flaps that were dry enough to pick up and carry—much like the cow-dung clock I wrote about in my song "Margo's Cargo"—and placed a couple of these patties in such a way as to make it look as though the cows had been there a few weeks ago, and thereby avert the suspicion of anyone digging there.

At last I had my treasure buried. Now, where was I going to hide the map? It needed to be in a place where it couldn't be seen, but could easily be stumbled upon if someone happened to be wandering in the right place.

There was a part of the swamp where we used to play a game I used to call Robin Hood and Little John. I had read about it in school and I'd got the kids to play it. I'd make staffs for them and we'd cross the brook on a big log in a part of the hollow we cleared out. This was so Little John and Robin could have a staff fight on the river during which one guy would get knocked in the water.

When time would allow, we'd meet on Sunday afternoons to play these games.

Near that spot there was a huge, half-rotten old tree stump. There were no trees that size any more in the hollow, but you could tell by the stump that there had been some big trees growing there at one time. This old stump must have been a hundred years old. It was so big around I don't think a man could put his arms around it.

You could rock it back and forth a bit, so I took an old rusty tobacco can that I found in the dump, put the map inside it, made a little alcove under the stump and placed it in there. Not too deep, but just enough that it was sticking out a little bit.

Now I had everything ready.

It had taken me about three weeks to get all this stuff together and by that time the sods had also knitted themselves together quite nicely.

Along came the Sunday afternoon that I had everything planned for—we were all going to meet in the hollow to play Robin Hood and Little John. I had the hatchet with me as we just walked around talking and making plans for the day.

As we decided which kid was going to play the role of Robin Hood, Little John, Friar Tuck, etc., I casually led everyone over near the big stump. In the course of the conversation I began striking it with the hatchet a few times.

With each whack I'd strike it just a little bit lower until finally the axe clunked against the tin can, the sound of metal against metal. When somebody said, "What's that?" I said, "What's what?" and I hit the stump again.

"No. Hit the stump lower. There's something made of iron or tin down there." So I hit it again and, of course, I knew just where to hit it.

"Yeah, that's it," said one, as the other kids began digging with their hands until they pulled out the rusty tin box. They got it open and what do they find, but this treasure map. So we get looking at it, and holy mackerel! There was a route drawn out on it with so many steps to here and so many steps to there. And there was a big X at the end of the line where it says something about "twin elms." The kids said there were no twin elms around Skinners Pond that they knew of. I said, "Well, I don't know what they call the trees, but there's something like that up in our pasture. Let's check the direction and see if it works out." So we started following the map, first along the brook, then into a small swamp.

After this we came to a line fence and just on the other side, near a group of other trees, were the twin elms. I said, "It looks like this is the end of the trail. This must be where it stops. Holy cripes—let's go get some shovels and some picks and let's dig. Maybe we'll find all kinds of treasure."

I told them all to go home and sort of play around a little bit first, then sneak away with the picks and shovels and meet me back at the treasure site in about twenty minutes. This way no one would get suspicious and start asking a lot of questions.

Soon they all arrived back and we started to dig. We had to take it on shiftwork, of course, so one guy would start digging and then another would take over.

While they were digging I started telling them a story about ghost ships and Captain Kidd and how, when he buried treasure, he always buried a dead man with it. I told them I had just thought of this danger, and maybe we shouldn't be digging here. The dead man may come back to haunt us or the ghost ship may come back and fire its phantom cannons.

Then I told them about a couple of guys who were

digging for treasure when a ghost ship arrived from the sky, dropped an anchor in the hole they were digging, and killed them. "So we'll have to be careful," I said. "The guy down the hole won't be able to see, so we'll have to keep our eyes open. And if anyone sees a ghost ship coming, holler. That way the guy can get out of the hole in time and we'll all run for cover."

"Yeah, okay," a few of them said as they started looking in all directions. This also made the guy down the hole dig faster so we could find the treasure and get the hell out of there.

Soon the hole was about four feet deep and I made sure I wasn't in the hole when they hit the rock. I forget who was down there, I think it was Earl. His shovel hit something that went clunk. "I found it! I found it!"

So I said, "Let me go down and see." He jumped out and I went down and took the shovel and I exclaimed, "Oh geez, it's just a big rock. Give me a hand somebody, we've got to see if we can lift this thing up."

It was a lot easier to drop it into the hole, I'll tell you, than it was to pull it out.

I had put another little layer of soil between the rock and the stuff I had hidden and also an old piece of wood, so when the shovels hit it they'd think they hit a treasure chest. And that's exactly what happened. It worked out perfectly.

The next guy to dig hit this piece of wood. "There's wood down here," he said.

"That's a good sign," said another.

"That's the sign that the treasure chest must be handy now. And we're in the right spot. The rock we found doesn't mean anything, but wood down there means we must be close to it."

He pulled out this piece of wood and everyone wanted to know if he saw anything else.

"No."

"Well, keep digging."

Soon we heard the sound of his shovel hit against

metal, and you should have seen the look on his face. He jumped right out of the hole and said, "I'm going home."

I said, "What's the matter?"

"There's something down here."

"Let's dig it out."

"No, no, no. I'm going home."

"Don't be a baby," I said, "stay here. It must be the treasure."

Next thing you know he was gone and a couple of others were looking a little scared. Finally, one of the others was coaxed to go down and start digging.

"Yeah, I hit something here."

"Well, see if you can pull it out."

After he tossed up a piece of junk, I said, "There must be more there."

He said, "I think there is. But did you see any ghost ships yet?"

"No, it's all clear up here."

So they started hauling pieces of metal out and everybody was down there helping to bring the treasure to the surface.

But before we could get it all, it was time to go. We planned to return the next Sunday to finish the job and to get the treasure but we never did go back. I had to return myself and cover up the hole before someone found it, or even worse, fell into it.

I didn't want a calf or Russell—or even Cora—to fall into it so I eventually filled up the hole and then told the other kids how I had dug down a little deeper, but I didn't find anything. I said I still thought there was treasure there and that we should all go back and get it some day when we got bigger.

From that day to this I've only told a couple of them what really happened with that treasure hunt. Some of them live in the Toronto area where they'd see me at a concert or meet me at a party and ask if I remembered the time we went digging for treasure. I'd kid them for a while, but after we had a beer or two I'd tell them the whole story. They'd usually laugh and call me a few choice names, but they all liked the story—and especially the fact they had all had a part in it.

As I said before, the only car in Skinners Pond was Anthony Keefe's, and that's the only car most kids ever saw.

When I first started school in Skinners Pond, the school would take a break and everyone would go outside when a car was passing by.

If some kid was half-way to the outside toilet and he happened to look up the road and see dust flying and thought there was a car coming, he'd run back in the school and let the teacher know. The teacher would then ring the bell and everybody would go outside and stand by the road. As the car went by everybody would wave while getting completely covered with dust. But as long as we saw the rare spectacle, it was wonderful.

On days when there was no school, every time the grader went by to smooth out the bumps in the road, there were always a number of kids running behind it, just to watch. By the time one group of kids got tired out, the kids from the next farm would be out waiting at the gate. Old Jack Nelligan was the operator, and on this account he was considered to be a hero.

While cars were scarce in Skinners Pond, car wheels were not. The farmers would often buy them from outside and use them to replace the steel-rimmed wooden wheels on their heavy wagons. This meant the kids could often come by an old discarded tire or two to play with.

What we used to do was nail a board across the inside of an old tire. Then you drilled a hole in the centre of the board and put a bolt through and attached two pieces of slab-wood to the bolt. Now you had two long shafts for handles protruding from the tire.

If you can picture this—the two shafts came to the point at the centre of the board that was nailed inside the tire. Your bolt became an axle from which the tire could turn around and, of course, you're pushing on the shafts so you can propel the tire anywhere and steer it at the same time. When you close the shafts together they act as a brake on the sides of the tire to slow it down. This came in very handy if you were going down a hill. Otherwise it would only go as fast as you could run. This contraption was very popular and most kids had one, pretending it was their car or truck.

There was only one thing wrong with it, or at least something the parents didn't like—every time you went through a puddle you had mud splashed up on you because there was no fender.

The kids just loved to go through the puddles and they'd go home with mud all over their clothes and faces. Many of them always wore their oldest pair of tattered overalls when they used this tire toy, so the flak they got from their parents wouldn't be as great as when they were wearing their Sunday best.

There were also two kids from down the road at Skinners Pond who could play the guitar, Franklin Perry and Dorothy Doucet. I used to love it when they brought their guitars to school and would often try to sing with them.

At an amateur show in Tignish, shortly before I ran away the last time, Franklin played guitar for me, sitting in a chair on the stage. I stood up behind him singing "Thinking Tonight of My Blue Eyes," but we didn't win anything.

When I first went to P.E.I. most of the kids didn't think I could sing, or didn't like the way I sang. Maybe they thought I was too show-offy. They just wouldn't listen to me, let alone want to sing with me. The first year we had a Christmas concert at school, the kids got together and told the teacher that if I was allowed to sing they wouldn't sing with me. So I suppose the teacher had to make a choice here. In order to get all the kids singing together or singing for the parents, my voice would have to be excluded.

This didn't make me feel too good, but it certainly didn't stop me from singing while going for the cows. They could hear me all over the place, singing my cowboy songs and testing the tonsils I didn't have with some yodelling. Everyone always knew when I was out around, either ploughing the fields, or going for the cows, or picking berries. When they couldn't hear me singing they knew I must be up to something.

When I first started running away it was really only for a short distance. I'd go up in the field and have a good cry, or go to the capes and look across the sea and dream about my mother.

But now I was getting to an age—twelve or thirteen—when I felt I could look after myself if I had to. So running away for real was a natural progression.

The first few times I did it to attract attention at home and hope that it might change things. Then how far could I get before the Mounties caught me? How much effort would they put in to tracking me?

And would anyone care? Would anyone even notice that I was missing from the supper table?

Cousin Danny

One Sunday morning as we left Palmer Road Church for home, I was in my usual place, standing on the back of the light wagon and hanging on to the back of the seat. As Russell and Cora were going to stop off for a few moments at Frank's place in Waterford (Frank was Russell's brother, and Waterford was the next district to Skinners Pond), I asked if I could stay at Frank's for a while and visit with my "cousin" Danny, and then walk the two miles home later that evening in time for milking the cows.

Permission was granted on condition that Danny and I would go picking wild blueberries back in the fields near Frank's woods. About an hour later we had each picked about a quarter of a bucketful of blueberries, when I suggested to Danny that we run away. Danny and I were the same age and as we always got along so well, he soon agreed. After eating all the blueberries we picked, we hung the buckets on a tree limb and took off through the woods. We came out of the woods up on the Palmer Road near the church, and then, so we wouldn't be caught, we took all the back roads towards Elmsdale and then on to Summerside, a distance of about fifty miles.

Every time we saw a car coming we hid in the ditch for fear it might be the Mounties. And because we only asked for rides from farmers who came by with horses and wagons, it took us two days to get to Summerside. And we walked practically all the way. All we ate was blueberries from along the side of the road. And although they were often very dusty, we ate them anyway. As we had left on a Sunday we were both wearing our Sunday shoes. Mine were a pretty good fit, but Danny's were about two sizes too large for him and before we had walked even twenty miles he was carrying his shoes in his hands and limping because both his heels were full of blisters.

He also wore these big thick glasses with one lens

cracked down the middle. They were now covered with blueberry stains and he was having a hard time seeing through them. He took them off once in a while but when he did he couldn't see anything at all. We slept out every night, and one of those nights we slept in a blueberry patch. After lots of tossing and turning to stay comfortable, we woke in the morning to find ourselves covered with stains from so many crushed blueberries.

Poor Danny still had his white shirt on that he always wore to church. It looked a lot more blue now than it did white.

Just before noon on Tuesday, we came walking into Summerside. By now Danny was talking about going home. He was limping and hungry and covered with blueberries from one end to the other. I told him we were only fifteen or twenty miles from the ferry, but no amount of coaxing was going to get him to go any further.

Although I was getting mad at him, I also felt sorry for him because we were such good friends and I didn't want to leave him alone. Besides, every time I looked at him I had to laugh. He looked like he had been dragged for about twenty miles behind a team of horses through a blueberry patch. I probably looked the same.

Just about then I thought, Maybe if I could get him something to eat he might feel better and be more willing to continue our journey. So I said, "Let's go into a restaurant and get something to eat. We have no money, but we'll pull an old trick my mother once showed me."

He wanted to know what kind of a trick, but I said, "I'll tell you after we eat."

Just as we were about to walk in the door of the restaurant, who came walking out but the town constable. Although he smiled, I could see he had a very discerning eye. "Hi there," he said. "I haven't seen you boys around here before. Where do you live?"

Before I had a chance to say "Just up the street," Danny spilled the beans. "He's from Skinners Pond, and I'm from Waterford." We were trapped and I knew it, but I couldn't do anything as Danny just kept blabbing.

After hearing our story about running away, he said, "Well, you boys just better turn around and start back home again, or I'm going to have to lock the both of you up in jail. But first," he said, "are you hungry?"

"Yes sir," we said.

And he took us in the restaurant. After showing us where to sit, he went over to the waitress and very quietly asked her to bring us something to eat. With our mouths hanging open, we could hardly wait till we saw her coming to our table.

She plunked down two large glasses of milk and two very big pieces of, what else? Blueberry pie. Danny and I looked at each other and back at the waitress a couple of times and after a short pause, the constable says, "What's the matter, boys, don't you like blueberry pie?" "Oh! Yes sir," we said, as we began to eat very rapidly. "This is our favourite kind of pie, ain't it, Danny?" I said.

But Danny didn't answer. He was having too hard a time to swallow. About ten minutes later, the constable escorted us out the door and, pointing towards the way we came into Summerside, he said, "Now that's the way back home, boys, and see that you take it. And remember, I'll be watching."

When we finally got back on the highway, poor Danny's feet were so sore he couldn't limp another step. All he kept muttering was how much he never again wanted to see another blueberry. I made some kind of a crack about how he'd have to keep on seeing blueberries because his glasses were covered with them. He didn't appreciate the humour and just grunted. "Let's start hitch-hiking cars, Tom, I can't walk any more."

In a matter of minutes we had a ride which took us back as far as Portage, which was about half-way home. After walking and thumbing for another couple of hours, Danny was getting pretty weary, and when we saw a Mountie car coming we just decided to flag him down. "Where have you fellows been?" he asked, when he found out who we were. "We have been looking all over for you."

"We went to Summerside," Danny said, and proceeded to tell him the whole story. After calling in to the Alberton detachment to make his report, he drove us home. First he dropped Danny off in Waterford and then he drove me to Skinners Pond.

It was about 10 o'clock at night when we arrived. As he went into the house, he told me to wait in the car. He had a little talk for about ten minutes with Cora and Russell, probably allowing Cora to vent her spleen on what a "snakes and snails" kind of a kid I turned out to be. And then he came out to the car and told me to go into the house.

When I went in I was told to go straight to bed, without being offered a bite to eat or a glass of milk. And, like every other time I got into bed, there was again no one to console me or offer any kind of encouragement. I was just left to sob myself to sleep, only thankful I didn't receive a lickin'.

The next day when I got up absolutely nothing had changed. And this further deepened my resolve that one day I'd be leaving Skinners Pond for good.

(At this point, I might add that just a few years ago, before Danny Aylward died of lung cancer, he told me that he met and chatted with the policeman we had met in Summerside and that he still remembered the day he fed us and sent us home. I believe Danny said his name was Elmer MacKay.)

Escape to Saint John

Finally, one day, I succeeded in running away from Skinners Pond for good. The time was right.

I had temporarily left Russell and Cora and had gone to work for another couple of farmers, helping them bring in the harvest and other things that labourers do on farms. Their names were Andrew Doucette and Joe Ellsworth. When I got a little money together I bought a train ticket with another guy from the village of St. Louis, who had also been out working with other farmers that fall.

His name was Bud Fitzgerald and he was a couple of years older than I was. When the work was done we both had the same idea—let's get off the Island.

We bought our tickets to Cape Tormentine, New Brunswick, so that our ferry passage would be included. And when the train drove aboard the boat I could see a Mountie car parked right at the wharf.

You could see they were looking for somebody. And as I watched them from the train window, I kept ducking down as we passed by. They never once suspected I was on the train now boarding the boat.

Every time I had run away before they had picked me up walking, so they thought it was going to be the same this time. I knew they were looking for me, and I felt really good inside that I had finally been able to fool them. This was one time the Mounties didn't "get their man (or boy)."

I had finally made it across the Northumberland Strait and immediately Bud and I started hitch-hiking towards Saint John.

So at thirteen years old I was on the road again.

It took us about three or four days to get from the ferry at Cape Tormentine to Saint John, a distance of about two hundred miles over roads which were nothing like they are today.

It was a hot afternoon that first day walking around

Saint John, neither of us knowing where to go. Even though Saint John was my home town, I didn't know a soul there—at least no one that I could track down in a few minutes.

It had been about four years since I left the orphanage to go to Prince Edward Island, and if I could help it, I certainly wasn't going to head back there. This living on the edge must have been too much for Bud because after only a few days on the road, sleeping outside and having very little to eat, he wanted me to go back with him to the land of the bright red mud.

With prospects for the future looking rather gloomy, he lost his love for hitch-hiking right then and there. He said he'd had enough of the hobo life. He tried to convince me to go back to P.E.I., but there was no way I wanted to return. I suppose it was fine for him, he had a loving family at home to go back to. But for me, if I didn't see Cora again that would be just fine.

So Bud left for the Island and I never saw him again. (A number of years later his sister told me he had been killed in a truck accident some time after he went home.)

As I now began to wander the streets alone, I was getting pretty hungry, and soon decided that if I was going to stay in Saint John, I'd have to find a job. I went down around the waterfront and soon I ran into an old rubby. He was hanging around drinking rubbing alcohol when I met him. I asked him how I could get a job loading boats. " Ah," he said, "I got a friend of mine. I work for him once in a while here and there and he's a real good guy. If you really want to work he'll get you on. Are you a good worker?"

I said, "Yeah." So he said, "You wait here."

He went into the shed and he brought out the guy, who looked me over and simply said, "I hear you want a job."

When I said I did, he said, "Well, you're kind of young, ain't you? Can you work?"

I said, "You're damn right I can work."

So he says, "Well, obviously you're not in the union or anything, but we're busy and I'll try to fit you in somehow."

He asked me how old I was and I said I was sixteen.

There was no interview. No job application to fill out. Just being recommended by the rubby was good enough for this guy. And I had a job, just like that.

I started the next afternoon loading skids. I was grateful for the job, but there was no way I could wait a week for my first paycheque. I had no money. No place to stay. No food.

For a couple of nights I'd slept in the Loyalist Graveyard, under one of the flat tombstones. This was the same graveyard I had played in many years before, and it wasn't uncommon to see the odd derelict spending the night there.

I didn't have any problem getting paid for the first day before I started work on the second day. I felt a lot better. And while I worked on the skids, my mouth was watering just thinking of the food I'd get after work. I had not had anything to eat in four or five days.

As soon as I was off work I went to a restaurant and bought two or three hamburger steaks and about six pieces of pie. They must have thought I hadn't eaten for a month. I forget what the bill came to, probably five or six bucks, which is quite amazing when you consider a full-course meal back then was about seventy-five cents.

Anyway, that night I was still leery about trying to get a room. I still hadn't figured out how I was going to get a place without someone asking too many questions. And if they didn't get the right answers, the Children's Aid Society, the orphanage or the cops might be called in to take away my freedom once again.

So I went to look for a cardboard house for the night. I found an alley where there was a lot of garbage lying around and got a couple of boxes together for a mattress. Then I lay down and covered myself up with some other pieces of cardboard. I had a reasonable night's sleep, enough rest that I was able to go back to work the next day. And with the few dollars I had left I planned on eating regularly again for a change.

After working about two hours I saw a strange car pull up at the end of the dock and a couple of men got out. They looked like detectives to me. I'd seen enough of them in my day. And sure enough, my hunch turned out to be right. Then another car pulled up behind and there was another man and a woman in the car. I thought, oh, oh. Somebody squealed, and the authorities are after me again.

What to do? I am not going to stand here and be taken prisoner again by these people—just because I don't have a mother. What kind of crime is that? It's not my fault. Why don't they leave me alone?

All these thoughts ran through my mind in just a split second. But the main concern now was not feeling sorry for myself, but how was I going to get out of there, safe and sound. I liked my freedom too much and I wanted to keep it, but my only escape route was now blocked.

I took a quick look around and spotted a dory down in the water. When I saw them heading towards me, I darted for the dory. The tide was low and there was a ladder leading down to the boat.

I figured I'd be able to get across to the other side of the harbour where I could duck out of sight, hide for a while and later leave town.

So I was down the ladder and trying to get the boat launched. I didn't take time to untie the rope at the top of the wharf because I thought I'd get it untied on the dory.

Now I was fighting with it. I couldn't get it free.

Soon, one of the detectives is down the ladder, pulling on the rope as I'm trying to get out. He wins the tug o' war and pulls me in where he puts his hands on me.

I couldn't get away. By this time his buddy was there helping him to get me back on the dock. I felt like diving in the water, but there was a lot of sewage, oil and grease, and even a couple of dead seagulls. Plus, I didn't think I could swim well enough to get all the way across the Saint John Harbour.

I was desperate to be free, but I wasn't stupid. I was smart enough to know that while I may have lost this battle, I hadn't yet lost the war.

Every time they caught me I learned something from it. I knew what not to do the next time. And I knew that no matter where they put me, I would always try to escape. I was getting to an age and size, now, where they wouldn't be able to keep me locked up forever.

I was thirteen going on thirty, and already had a lifetime of worry, work and adventure packed into my few years. But here I was again, being taken into custody by the same people whose control, authority and regimentation I had only come to fear, mistrust and resent.

I was supposed to have another five years of schooling and five years at home. But what home? Where? I had already decided that school was not for me. I had to get out and work—and look after myself.

The detectives now took me over to the second car that I saw pull in behind them. And, sure enough, this guy and this woman are from the Children's Aid and they start putting me through the same third degree they give all runaways or orphans—"Who are you? What's your name? Where are you from? What are you doing? Who's looking after you?"

I started to lie to them at first and tell them a big cock-and-bull story, but the guy didn't buy it. So he said, "Well, you're too young to be working here. You're coming with us until we find out who you really are."

When I saw my first tactic wasn't going to work I said, "Well, okay." I spilled the beans and told them who I was, how I came to be there, and the whole thing. They then took me to a place, got me a room and they said, "Now it's better for you if you stay here until we clear this mess up. And you'd better be here tomorrow when we get back or it could go really bad for you." Thinking the alternative might be jail if they had to go looking for me again, I decided to stay put.

Next day the man from the Children's Aid came back by himself and told me he had talked to Skinners Pond to corroborate everything I had said.

He said I was too young to be working at the docks, but he gave me a choice—I could go back to Skinners Pond and live with Cora and Russell, or I could stay in Saint John and go to school if I abided by all the rules of the Children's Aid.

But, no matter what, I had to go to school until I was sixteen. Then, afterwards, I could be on my own for the rest of my life.

This meant I'd have to go to school for almost three more years before I was free from the Children's Aid.

As far as I was concerned that wasn't really a choice. I made my mind up right then and there. I was staying in Saint John.

They promised to get me a "softer job" in a bowling alley or as an usher. The job was to be part-time, so I could pay part of my room and board. And the Children's Aid offered to outfit me for school—books, pens, the whole bit. Plus some clothing.

I was quick to put in the stipulation that there were to be no knickerbockers, or the whole deal was off. He laughed a little about that one, when I told him how those damn knickerbockers had caused me a few bumps and a swollen knuckle or two fighting with those kids who used to laugh and give me a hard time in my early days at Skinners Pond.

Gooding's Boarding House

My first boarding house belonged to a Mrs. Gooding who boarded men with a variety of occupations—some worked on the waterfront, others at the fertilizer plant, and one guy was a bus driver. Mrs. Gooding's house was at 38 Cliff Street, and though her boarders were mainly men, she had a couple of tiny rooms in which she could not expect a full-paying working man to sleep, so she always kept three or four boys who were in the care of the Children's Aid. One of them happened to be Lloyd Veniot, whom I had run away with on my first day at St. Patrick's orphanage about six years earlier. The other Children's Aid guys at Mrs. Gooding's were Billy Steele and Kenny Fallon, also from St. Pat's.

As the four of us boys were homeless and wards of the Children's Aid Society, she charged less to put us up, but at the same time she expected us to help out with the chores, which included keeping the street clean, taking away the garbage, tidying up the rooms and many other odds and ends, from helping in the kitchen to picking up the groceries before and after school.

Though shovelling snow was one of my jobs I'd often be thinking, "What a soft touch this is compared to my past thirteen years."

The people at the Children's Aid Society told me, "All you have to do is continue going to school and get yourself a part-time job to help pay for your clothes and a few school necessities and we will look after the rest until you're sixteen"—but that was the catch. It was the "going to school until you're sixteen" that bothered me.

Besides, I had a purpose for running away from the farm on Prince Edward Island and coming to Saint John, and neither the Children's Aid nor anyone else was going to know what that real purpose was.

As I shovelled away, I wondered where my mother was and how difficult it was going to be to find her. In the last month or so I'd been looking up old contacts every chance I got, but the inquiries were leading nowhere. As usual my mother was keeping her tracks covered.

My first Christmas away from Skinners Pond was rather uneventful. I had Christmas dinner with the other boarders and the Children's Aid sent me and the other boys a box of clothes, mostly gloves, shirts, sweaters and other things for the winter.

It was half-past six according to my $2 pawnshop watch—which sometimes ran and sometimes didn't—as I put the snow shovel in the shed and walked out the now snow-free alley towards the street. Mrs. Gooding was at the front door and as I went by she said she was watching me through the window and that she knew she could always count on me doing a good job. I thanked her and said I was going up town and that I would be back home at the appointed time, while in the back of my mind I was thinking, "I'm glad she liked the job I did because now she'll be less likely to say anything if I come home late."

It started snowing again as I turned the corner from Cliff Street on to Waterloo Street, where I was just in time to see a man with a big bag of groceries slip on the ice and fall on his ass without spilling anything.

I couldn't help chuckling to myself over the surprised look on his face as I continued on my way towards Union Street.

The lights grew brighter as I walked towards the main part of town. The store windows were still sporting their "January Sale" signs. As I came to Ben Goldstein's music store I stopped to look at the guitars in the window.

This was something I couldn't resist doing ever since I arrived in Saint John. Whether I was going up town for a couple of hours or returning home, I'd always make sure the route I chose would take me by this window. And there I'd stand for ten or fifteen minutes at a time dreaming of the day when I could own my own guitar.

My First Guitar

As I looked at the guitars in Ben Goldstein's window I usually thought of Gerry Cormier, one of Mrs. Gooding's boarders, who worked at the fertilizer plant.

Gerry had an old guitar that he would strum and sing along to in the room he shared with me and Billy Steele, and although he often had a hard time pronouncing the English words in the songs he would sing with his French accent, I would sit and listen to him by the hour, watching with envy and admiration the way he manipulated his fingers on the strings.

I told him once that I had written a couple of songs, but when I sang them to him he was unable to chord to them. I naturally took this to mean that the songs were no good, not knowing at the time, of course, that just because he was able to play three or four chords which sounded beautiful to my ear, and was a maestro in my eyes, this did not mean that the chords for my songs could not be found by a more qualified player.

All this notwithstanding, my every hope was that I could save up my dimes and nickels until I had $19, which was the exact amount on the price tag of that small, shiny guitar I was always looking at in Ben Goldstein's window.

However, the more I thought about saving up $19, the more I realized that it wasn't going to be that easy.

One day when I was at the peak of my yearning for a guitar I plucked up enough courage to ask Gerry if he'd ever thought of parting with his, and if he did, how much would he sell it to me for.

I was surprised when he let me have it for $2. Even then, I had to work hard for that two bucks, but I knew I was in for the time of my life now that I had a guitar. Gerry was nice enough to show me how to make my first couple of chords, but the guitar, itself, was so beaten up you couldn't do much with it.

The frets were worn down smooth, the neck was bowed

and there were a bunch of other things wrong with it.

I had admired the guitar, and the way Gerry played it, as we sat on the bed in our room at the boarding house and sang our hearts out. But when I tried to play some new chords on it, I discovered the faults couldn't be corrected and realized I should have saved up to buy a new guitar after all.

Nineteen bucks was a lot of money back then, but I did everything I could to save it. I shovelled snow, swept sidewalks, set up pins at the bowling alley and walked three miles to school every day just to save bus fare in order to buy the guitar sooner.

There were no such things as credit cards in those days and it took me about a month to save the $19.

What I also did, just to give me the impetus I needed to save for it, was ask Ben to put the guitar on the "lay-away plan." This way, it got taken out of stock, my name was placed on it and I was given so many weeks to pay for it. But I couldn't take it home until it was paid for in full.

I used to go to visit it quite regularly. If I said I was in that store every day for a month, I don't think I would be exaggerating. I might leave him a buck, or a few dimes, every time I went in. I think the biggest amount I ever placed on it at one time was $4.

Then came the big day. I finally raised the $19 to get the guitar out of the store. It was now officially mine, but I realized I had a lot to learn. I only knew two or three chords, just what I had picked up from watching Gerry and the little bit he taught me.

I didn't know how to tune a guitar, and when Gerry wasn't around to tune it for me, it sounded awful.

But I played it a lot more than I had played Gerry's. And I was getting used to it. At first I had some problems with hand positions, mainly because Gerry's guitar didn't have good frets, which meant I was doing a lot of guessing.

And because I didn't know how to tune a guitar the other boarders used to pound on the door and threaten to break my neck, or the guitar—or both. Especially the guys who worked at night and slept in the daytime.

I had to watch whenever I left the room that there wasn't anyone lurking on the stairs, because they had promised me on more than one occasion that if I didn't stop that "goddamned banging" they were going to kick the shit out of me.

I lived for that guitar. I just couldn't put it down. I'd fall asleep playing it at night and I'd wake up the next morning and it would be close to me, ready to be played. My bed partner, Billy Steele, never complained about the guitar spoiling his night's sleep, so I figured he must have either enjoyed it, or was just able to ignore it. Billy didn't talk a lot, so I never really knew for sure.

One friend who never complained about my guitar playing, though, even in those early learning years, was Steve Foote.

When I wanted a change of pace from sitting in my room, playing the guitar, I'd go to the Silver Rail Restaurant and hook up with Steve and some of his friends. The Silver Rail was an all-night restaurant and just one of those many greasy spoons that could be found at that time in almost any section of any waterfront town. The customers ranged from sailors and longshoremen to loose women and winos.

I was supposed to meet Steve there again on that night, and as I walked in I made a sign to the youngest waitress that I wanted coffee and that I would be sitting in the last booth near the jukebox. As there was no one in the place right then who I knew, or cared to know, I slumped myself down awkwardly in the vacant seat with a slouch and an "I don't give a damn" glance, which I was always sure would let the others know that I was not to be easily reckoned with.

As I mentioned before, I was used to hard work on the farm, doing as much as any full-grown man and for the same number of hours a day. Having worked with men I learned how to have older interests, and now—even though I had just turned fourteen—I was not above taking advantage of my older looks and somewhat keener sense of judging character. I was tall and wiry, I looked to be over sixteen, and when I spoke with people they always took me to be much older.

I couldn't afford to buy cigarettes very often, but Steve would be here with lots, any minute now.

The grocery store where he worked "wouldn't miss them anyway." So while I was waiting for him I lit up a two-day-old butt, which I knew would help my act, especially while being studied by a guy who didn't like the way his girlfriend was looking at me from the other side of the restaurant.

Just then, the waitress came to the table—and right behind her was Steve, throwing down a pack of cigarettes and walking towards the jukebox with a quarter in his hand, saying, "What'll it be, Tom, Hank Snow?" I said, "Yeah" and dumped a couple of lumps of sugar in my coffee.

Steve knew I liked Hank's music because of the great acoustic guitar runs he always played throughout his songs. Runs which I was trying desperately to learn on my own guitar (but with very slow progress, I must admit). As we sat there talking I began to realize just what good friends we were becoming. We seemed to have a lot in common. Steve told me about his younger life, and although he had always lived in the city, his father was often cruel to him and his home life had been quite miserable as a result.

I don't know whether it was because of some of the parallels I saw between us or just my need to at last confide in someone, but that night I decided to tell Steve everything about my life. I guess I felt I had finally found someone whom I could trust.

As he sat opposite me in the back booth I began to recount the first thirteen years of my life, pausing only to cream and sugar each new cup of coffee or to light up another cigarette. As each hour went by, Steve seemed to display even more interest, sometimes asking questions and shaking his head at some of the incredible answers.

I told him the reasons why some people still called me Tommy Messer, why my name was really Tom Connors, the life with my mother, the orphanage days, the farm on P.E.I., the reason for coming to Saint John, and my mysterious quest for the woman with the missing thumb.

Searching for My Mother

I always had this dream in the back of my mind that one day I was going to be reunited with my mother.

No matter what I did, no matter where I worked, no matter how hard things got—she was the only hope I had.

I can't begin to tell you how many times it went through my head over those long and ever so lonely years. I often wondered what would have happened if we hadn't kept going back to Saint John. Perhaps I would never have been taken from her, and all those years of mental anguish may have been mercifully avoided.

But my mother was a creature of habit. And, obviously, her habits were predictable enough that the authorities, on occasion, were able to catch up with her.

I was always on the lookout for a black-haired woman. I'd see a black-haired woman two blocks away and I'd have to go and check her out.

I'd follow her up the street and get as close to her as I could until I could see her hands. I only needed to look at the one hand—the right hand. If the thumb was off I figured it would have to be her. How many women with black hair were going to be missing a thumb on the right hand?

I would have had great difficulty picking Isabel out in a police line—except for her thumb, or the lack of it. You see, I couldn't remember what she actually looked like. And I didn't have any pictures that were taken when we were together. Again, this is one of the many drawbacks of being brought up without a mom and dad—no one chronicles your development from childhood to adulthood. There are no birthday pictures. No first-day-of-school pictures. No Christmas pictures—a tough situation when you're looking for somebody.

Anyone could have shown me a woman and said it was my mother, and I would have probably picked the prettiest woman out of a crowd and claimed her for my own.

That's how I saw my mother. The many years of my yearning imagination working overtime to will her back to me had quite often produced some striking women.

The reality of it all, though, was that my mother had had the foresight when we last saw each other back near the woods at St. Patrick's Orphanage, to remind me about that one significant feature that set her apart from all other women. With the exception of my good friend, Steve, who offered to keep his eyes open for this strange woman, most of my other friends thought I was weird. They questioned what they thought were my strange antics, following pretty, black-haired women. Actually, I followed all black-haired women around. They didn't know I wasn't interested in whether they were pretty or not. I was just interested in whether they had a thumb missing from their right hand.

Sometimes I'd just take off right in the middle of a conversation. "What the hell is the matter with you?" they would ask. Especially the guys who got to know me more. They saw me do it every once in a while. They began to think I was really odd. Probably thought I was a nut case. Maybe a crackpot.

I didn't want to involve anyone in my story. It was too personal. I didn't want the whole town of Saint John asking me stupid questions. And besides, though I didn't like to think of it very often, I had considered the possibility that Isabel might be dead. And if this were the case, so was my link to the past, and all those years of longing for my real mother would now have been in vain.

Return to Skinners Pond

When the real possibility of never finding my mother again finally hit me, I was even prepared to let bygones be bygones with Cora.

I hadn't given up looking for my own mother, but after so many years my chances of ever seeing her again were growing slim. No contact. No news. No pictures. No leads. Little hope. It was going to take a miracle for Isabel and me to be ever reunited.

If there was only some way that there could be a reconciliation between me and Cora, or just even an understanding between us, it might help to fill the void. I began to ask myself if maybe Cora could have a change of heart. Would the time that I'd been gone make any difference or would she be just as cold and aloof to me as always? After thinking on it for a while, I decided there was only one way to find out.

So a year after running away from Skinners Pond I decided to go back during the summer vacation to see if I could patch things up with Cora.

I planned to tell her, "Look, I'm not such a bad guy after all—I don't know why you have to hate me so, or despise me, but can't we just put away our differences and learn to get along as other people do?" Big words for a young teenager to be saying to a woman in her forties who was never known to show any remorse or compassion, but I was willing to give it a try.

As much as I had hated the years I had spent with Cora, I was desperate for some love, someone who cared about me, and someone I could care about in return.

I hoped that maybe she might have learned a lesson of some kind—that maybe she would be better to me—and then, if that were the case, I might not even go back to Saint John. I might stay in P.E.I. and continue living there if things were all right. Besides, I missed Russell quite a bit, and I somehow felt it wasn't his fault that he was probably in bad need of somebody to help him on the farm.

But, alas, it didn't work out that way. I was there for only about twenty-four hours when Cora went right back into her old routine. For Russell's sake she pretended she was glad to see me for the first day or so and then without warning, she was quickly back to the silent treatment. Though I tried several times to engage her in conversation she acted either disturbed or too busy and dismissed the whole thing by asking me if I didn't have something better to do.

I knew quite a few chords now on the guitar and I could strum to all the songs I had written. I now had about twenty-five or thirty songs and I had just written one about the men who were building the Skinners Pond harbour. Everyone liked it, and my playing and singing was now being enjoyed by more and more people. All except Cora, that is. What on earth was she going to do now? The hopeless kid with the "tin ear" was not only becoming a singer and a musician, he was also writing his own songs. And even worse, a lot of people were making favourable note of it, including Russell. "Drats!" The same Tommy Messer she always tried to control was now "out of control." People were now asking me to sing at their wedding receptions, and even paying me to do it. It may have only been a dollar or two, but it was still money.

I also got paid a couple of dollars the night they held a dance in the Skinners Pond school. Andrew Jones was the fiddler. And when his guitar player didn't show up, he asked me to provide the rhythm. This was the first time I had ever accompanied a fiddle player. And when we both sat down to play, Andrew said I was doing great, but I needed to learn one more thing: "When you're playing without electricity," he said, "you'll have to bang your feet in order to be heard." I guess that's where I got into the habit, and I've been banging my foot ever since.

There was another night in the Tignish Legion Hall, when the local people wanted me to get up on stage and sing a song with a band from New Brunswick. After I sang one song, the crowd kept applauding for more, but the leader of the band told me to go back down to my seat. When I started to leave, the crowd stood up and shouted for one more. But as I walked back to the mike and started to sing, the leader again told me to get off the stage and gave me a shove. I turned around and gave him a punch in the mouth. He took his guitar off, I took mine off, and we both went at it.

When one of his band members tried to help him, some of my friends came to help me. Soon everybody was into it. My guitar somehow remained unscathed, but practically every other instrument on the stage got smashed and the wires were hanging from everywhere. That was one time when I didn't get the blame for what had happened. Everyone said I gave the guy what he deserved.

The following day, however, when the word began to spread throughout the countryside, I wasn't too popular around the house. According to Cora, I shouldn't have been there causing trouble in the first place. This was just the excuse she'd been waiting for, and she harped on it every day thereafter.

I think she also sensed that I might be starting to enjoy my new-found popularity throughout the area, and that I might even be toying with the idea of staying around for a while. At every opportunity, she kept hinting there was no way she wanted this to happen.

I'm sure Russell did though, because the day I was leaving he drove me out to Elmsdale in his pick-up truck. Elmsdale was where I could get on the main highway and start hitch-hiking back to Saint John. This was something he had never done before and on the way out he was saying things like, "It's too bad you couldn't have stayed around, just when I needed you the most."

I told Russell I didn't want to hurt him, or for that matter Cora. But I said the trouble all this time had been Cora, and right from day one it had been Cora all the way through. I said I would love to have stayed, in fact the plans in my mind were to have stayed and helped him to make the farm what he always wanted it to be.

I told him, "I would like to be a son to you" and discussed that kind of thing. "But," I said, "I just can't. It's impossible for me to live in the same house with Cora for very long. You have to know that. I don't care if you take me outside the truck and pound the piss out of me. I won't run from you this time. I won't run away. But I'm telling you the truth."

Well, he had a few tears in his eyes and so did I. He gave me a couple of bucks which he could ill afford, and said, "Well, I guess that's how it is."

When we got to the main highway I got out on the road and watched Russell leave. The truck bounced along the dusty road and eventually out of sight. All you could see were the dust clouds that followed it.

I don't think I ever felt quite like that before. Here I was losing a friend. To me, Russell was the closest thing I had ever had to a father. I genuinely believe he cared about me, as much as he dared show in front of Cora.

And I think he knew I cared about him, too.

The Reaching Hand

Now I was more determined than ever to find my mother.

I thought long and hard as I travelled back to Saint John about how hopeless it had been trying to get Cora to accept me. And if my real mother was still alive somewhere I knew I just had to find her, that's all there was to it.

My summer holiday visit to Skinners Pond had been largely disappointing, with the only benefit being that I had lost any feeling of guilt that I may have previously felt for having run away from there in the first place. It also effectively eliminated any lingering thoughts of a possible return.

In September I was back attending the Saint John Vocational School by day and working as an usher at the Capitol Theater in the evenings.

Not too long after settling into this routine I started hanging around with some teenagers who lived around Haymarket Square. And it was here, on a Sunday afternoon, while a group of us guys and girls were chatting in the doorway of a small soda fountain, that a very strange thing began to take place.

The conversation had become rather boring and my thoughts became withdrawn. I was day-dreaming a bit and I started thinking about my mother.

Just then a black-haired woman came walking past us with two little girls in tow. I couldn't get a good look at her because she had one child in each hand and the girls each had an ice-cream cone in their free hand. The little girl on the right-hand side of her wasn't any more than three steps past me when she dropped her ice cream on the sidewalk. The mother let go of the little hand to reach down to pick up the ice cream.

And there, in plain view, was the hand with the missing thumb.

I checked the hair. Sure enough, it was black. Now what to do?

I waited until she got up the street and turned the corner where the railroad tracks which ran through Haymarket Square went between some houses and then up towards Christie's lumber factory. As she disappeared from sight I quickly told my friends I just remembered something I had to do at home and then took off like a shot.

When I turned the corner the woman was following the railroad tracks with the two little girls.

So I walked a little faster and caught up to her. I said, "Excuse me, ma'am, your name wouldn't happen to be Isabel, would it?"

Of course, I was looking down now at this little woman—she wasn't very tall. She looked around and looked up at me—I was very tall for my age. She then looked at me rather fiercely and said, "What's it to you?"

Well, when I heard her speak, I knew that it was Isabel. So I immediately thought of the little birthmark on my throat and tore my shirt open and said—"If your name is Isabel, I'm Tommy—do you remember this?"

Immediately she got weak at the knees and I had to grab her. She fainted in my arms.

Now the kids began to panic. They started hollering and screaming, kicking me in the legs and biting me, while I'm trying to hold up and comfort their mother— my mother!

While I tried to gently shake her and tell the kids it's all right, and not to worry, they kept on screaming, "Get away from us" and "Leave my mother alone."

As young as they were, they were feisty kids. I guess if they were living with Isabel they had to be.

My mother came to after a couple of minutes, but those two minutes seemed like two forevers. As she gained her breath, she started talking to me like I was one of the kids at her feet.

I had been a little boy when I last saw her, and even with that imagination she had as a kid which enabled her to fancy a brick as being her doll, she just couldn't see me as anything but a little boy.

She had a bag of candy that she was dishing out to the little girls, and every time she gave them one she wanted to give me some. I didn't know what to do. I was feeling extremely uneasy.

Then she asked me to come with her to visit some friends of hers. So we went up the railroad tracks, in through an old broken-down gate and into a little alley, then along a pathway which led up to an old set of stairs that were badly in need of repair.

Outside, it looked like the house that Jack built. It was crooked, with tar-paper hanging from everywhere.

I followed my mother through a door hanging by one hinge and into a kitchen. I guess one end of the house had almost sunk out of sight. The stove was sitting way down in one corner and the entire floor was on a slant. The difference in height from one end of the room to the other had to be about ten or twelve inches. And this in a room that was no more than twelve feet by twelve feet.

Isabel was excited and she started telling everybody— "This is Tommy! This is Tommy! Do you remember Tommy? I used to bring Tommy."

They said, "Yeah, we remember Tommy."

And I remembered them, too.

As soon as I saw the kitchen I knew I'd been in there before, but I didn't know who they were. I couldn't remember my way back to the place or I probably would have been to visit them to ask them about my mother's whereabouts since I'd been back in Saint John.

Soon Isabel was saying she was on her way to Montreal.

"I've got to go and catch a train," she announced to me and everyone else. Whether it was the truth or not, I don't know. It seemed like she didn't want me to know exactly what she was doing. But she gave me a phone number of a woman in Montreal who would always know how to get in touch with her. Then after telling me to be a "good little boy," and that it would be better for me to remain with the Children's Aid, she and the two girls were gone. Although the search was now over, I somehow couldn't help but feel the meeting had not meant quite as much to her as it had meant to me. I felt really uncomfortable and totally mixed up.

I had spent so many years wondering what I was going to say to my mother when I met her. Then when it happened it took me by complete surprise.

I was speechless. My mind went blank. I didn't know what to say. I couldn't take my eyes off her. She couldn't take her eyes off me, looking me up and down and studying me.

For so many years while I took beatings at the orphanage, stood on the capes at Skinners Pond, searched the streets of Saint John, or simply day-dreamed, I always thought of the black-haired woman with the missing thumb as my mother. But I never thought of her as anything other than being bigger than me. And she couldn't imagine that I was not a baby any more, and that I had become a young man.

As the days passed after this short meeting, a strong feeling began to come over me that the dream I had always had of some day being reunited with my mother had quickly come to an end.

For the first time in my life I began to doubt. The years without her had been long and the separation had been costly. I began to realize we were two different people living in two different worlds. The dream I had dreamed for so long was of a son meeting his mother and they live happily ever after. But the reality felt more like we had become complete strangers to one another.

I found myself feeling sorry for her and at the same time feeling hurt that I was in no position to help her. I was in no position to even help myself. Maybe the trouble with this meeting was that she also felt the same way and there was nothing either one of us could do about it.

I had achieved my goal of finding my real mother, but

now I realized my hope of ever finding the mother I once knew was gone and without it I felt more alone than I ever had before. The ties had become more permanently severed than I had ever dreamed. There were no pieces to pick up, no compensation for the loss and no joy to replace the grief. The victory was hollow and empty.

"Sally" Was a Tailor

My life changed after meeting my mother. No longer did I have to chase after black-haired ladies to see if they had a missing thumb.

My outlook on life changed, too. My hopes of getting a mother to give me some guidance and love were dashed. There wasn't going to be any home life for me. I was on my own and completely alone. That's what life promised me, unless I tried to change things by myself. I was determined I was going to do the best for me. I couldn't let my spirits sink. There was no sense in being down in the dumps or feeling sorry for myself. No one cared anyway.

I was determined to make the best of what I had.

Shortly after my mother left for Montreal, one of my enquiries led to finding my real father. I had always known his name was Tommy Sullivan (my mother always called him "Tommy"), but my search for a Tommy Sullivan had always come to a dead end. Then one day while asking after him around the docks a guy said to me, "Tommy Sullivan?

"Yeah, I know him. But nobody calls him Tommy. Everybody knows him as Sally. He used to work as a long-shoreman, but now he runs a small tailor's shop over on Main Street." (Apparently, "Sally" was the nickname he came to be known by over the years because his last name was Sullivan.)

Well, this turned out to be just the lead I was looking for, and the following day after school I walked down Main Street, found the little tailor shop, took a big breath and walked in. In front of a sewing machine, behind a small counter, sat a man in his early thirties. And pasted on the wall behind him was a sign that read, "We mend everything but a broken heart."

As he looked up from his work I said, "Sir, would your name happen to be Tommy Sullivan?" "I believe it is," he said. "And who wants to know?" I said, "My name is Tom

Connors. And if you knew my mother Isabel at one time, I have good reason to believe that you are my father."

He immediately dropped the pair of pants he was holding and with a look of complete disbelief he hollered through the open door to the small apartment in back of the store. "Lil, for Christ's sake, Lil, come here."

As a short, stocky, blonde lady came rushing into the shop he said excitedly, "Lil, do you have any idea who this is?" As she shook her head rather questioningly, he said, "This is my son, Tommy. Isabel's boy." He then put his arm around my shoulder and said, "And what a fine lad he is too. Come on in the back."

Very soon we were seated in the kitchen where a long series of questions and answers ensued. He wanted to know what had happened over all the years and how my mother was.

By the time I had told him the whole story and how I had just recently found Isabel, several hours had passed and I now had to get back to the boarding house.

He asked me to come back and see him again as soon as I could, and we said goodbye.

While I was there I also met his two other sons, Tommy and Bobby, half-brothers of mine, who were both younger than me by two or three years. These boys were by his wife, from whom he was separated. He was now living common-law with Lil.

During the next few weeks I went to visit them quite often. But as the novelty began to wear off and a certain jealousy began to develop towards me in the mind of the oldest of the other two boys, my visits were increasingly discouraged and soon they stopped altogether. Not too long after that my father and Lil broke up and I heard later that the youngest boy had drowned. The whereabouts of the oldest boy was unknown to me until many years later when I heard he had died in Toronto. In the meantime, fate came between me and my promise to go to school until age sixteen.

Coal Boat to Newfoundland

I was just turning fifteen and I couldn't resist an opportunity one day to buy a guy's identification in a restaurant. I hadn't planned to leave school, but I was getting itchy feet.

The guy was looking to buy a bottle of whisky. I gave him the five bucks I had for all the papers in his wallet. Although he was just about to turn nineteen, he didn't look much older than me.

The next morning he was supposed to join a merchant ship, a coal boat. His name joined the ship, but he didn't. And that's how I went to sea.

Nobody knew where I was and I didn't tell anyone— either at Mrs. Gooding's or the Children's Aid Society. I suspect they may have all been quite proud of me when they later found out that I had just won the New Brunswick High School Drama Trophy for my role as Prospero in Shakespeare's *The Tempest*. But I really didn't care. I was fifteen now and really anxious to get out of their clutches, and I wasn't going to pass up this opportunity to be a free man at last. Come hell or high water, I was going to sea, where nobody would ever find me again. And they never did.

There are a lot of stories to tell from my days on the coal boats, and the fact that I could sing and play the guitar always went over well with the crew.

I got my ideas for the "Coal Boat Song" while I worked on the boats that ran from Cape Breton to Newfoundland. Although I didn't write the song at that time, I did write a number of other songs and poems while on board.

I still do that today. Experiences once had are always there, so lots of times when I'm writing a song the experiences that go into it are not always current, but could be something that was done a number of years ago.

That is my resource. Having travelled all over and done a lot of jobs, I have this pool from which to draw when I'm writing.

I was crazy when I was fifteen. I had no fear. I'd seen too much and lived too much to ever worry about myself. No one was going to miss me anyway, so why should I even care.

The work aboard ship usually consisted of splicing ropes and cables, battening down hatches and chipping and painting. This latter is very dangerous at the water's edge when the ship is moving. Then there were the storms.

I remember one night when I was helmsman of the *Irvingwood*. I was walking across the top of the hatches during a North Atlantic gale, with no lifeline attached, just to get a coffee for the second mate (the galley and the mess was "back aft" and the wheelhouse was "midships"). You wrap a lifeline, like a clothesline, around your waist so you can move around the deck in heavy seas without fear of being washed overboard.

Well, that night I decided to challenge the storm without a care in the world, and not even bothering with the lifeline.

Big waves were rolling over the hatches of the boat, and when they'd subside I would run like a son-of-a-gun. Well, I got about half to three-quarters of the way across the hatches when I saw this wave coming. I was on a dead run, but I didn't make it.

The wave caught me and washed me right across the ship and into the sunken walkway which ran along by the side of the hatches. This walkway was about three feet below the top of the hatches and had two cables which acted as a railing along the side of the ship. Just over the railing, of course, was the deep blue sea.

I was wearing a big, heavy coat and a big sailor's scarf. When the wave hit me, it dragged me and washed me over the hatches down onto the deck of the walkway on the other side of the ship. I was headed overboard when my leg got caught in between the two cables that acted as the railing.

If you can picture a wrestler hanging out over the ring by one foot that is twisted up in the ropes, you'll know my position.

Now I was hanging over the side of the ship, by the foot. There was a storm howling and no one could hear me hollering, even when I tried.

It was 2:30 in the morning. The second mate didn't know where the hell I was. There was a storm outside, and every wave that came smashed over me, because the sea was on the other side of the ship. So I was on the downside (that's what they call it when the waves are coming from the far side of the ship). Every time a wave came over the top I got another wash. And I don't know where my coat went. The coat came off me. The scarf was gone, too.

There I was trying to unhook myself, dangling there like a bungee jumper, reaching up to get my foot free from the cable and get back upright on the ship. Meanwhile, I was getting half-drowned every time a wave washed over. Good thing one of those real big ones didn't come while I was trying to free myself. It didn't go calm, but for a few minutes I wasn't bashed by a wave and was able to untangle myself from the cable, pull myself on to the deck and head back to the wheelhouse.

After all I'd been through, alone, for those past few minutes, as I staggered into the wheelhouse, exhausted and soaking wet, the second mate said, "Where's my coffee?"

"I'm afraid, sir, you'll have to go get it yourself."

I said, "Take a look," and proceeded to show him the marks I had on my leg from the cables as I hung over the side.

He then gave me shit for not using the lifeline and told me to "take the wheel and get dried off and forget about the coffee until the storm died down." Hell, he didn't get his coffee that night.

Then there was another night in a worse storm.

The second mate again sent me back aft for something.

It was even a worse night than the one before. When they get a storm over the Grand Banks those seas out there can often produce some of the roughest waters in the world. And on this night we were being tossed all over the place like a piece of paper.

I was on what they called the 12 to 4 watch—that was 12 noon to 4 in the afternoon and 12 midnight to 4 in the morning. The time now was about 3 A.M. I left the wheelhouse and went down the closed-in stairs and tried to open the steel door, which led to the outside deck.

Just as I opened it a wave hit it, and the water started pouring in. It immediately put about six feet of water in the five-by-five cubicle at the bottom of the stairs, and with the force of the water in there the door slammed shut.

I couldn't get the door open while I was in the water. But as long as I stayed afloat I was safe enough because I couldn't go anywhere. It took a while before the water finally seeped out through the crack underneath the door. I was swimming in there, hanging onto the stair rail waiting for the water to recede.

I felt safe enough as long as the door stayed closed, but if it opened again I could have been flushed out into the sea with the escaping water. After the water seeped out on its own I was about to go back to the wheelhouse when I remembered the beads I always carried around in my pocket. Having been brought up a Catholic, I recalled having read a story about a group of Christians whose lives were in peril aboard a ship during a terrible storm. There was a saint aboard who took out his prayer beads and threw them into the sea and the sea calmed and everyone was saved. So I thought, "What the hell, what have I got to lose? Let's see if the same thing will work for me."

Now that the water had seeped out of the cubicle I opened the door and blessed myself, tossed the beads out and commanded the sea to calm. Before I could get the door closed another wave came up and hit me and I went sailing half-way back up the stairs. I said, "Oh well, that's my answer, thank you very much."

Now when I think about it, it's funny. The things you'll do when you're a kid of fifteen.

There was a lot of drinking, smoking and gambling on those ships, but we never had any women on board. And definitely not any stowaways.

You've heard that sailors have a girl in every port. Well, you don't need a blue serge uniform and a smart white sailor hat to have a girl in every port.

Even us coal boat men had a girl in every port, or plenty of opportunity to get one. Of course, K.C. Irving didn't pay a hell of a lot of money, but you spent what you made. And usually there were plenty of girls wanting to share a laugh and a few drinks.

Later on I joined the *Irvingdale* with Gerry Marks, a fellow orphan from St. Pat's.

Just in from the Caribbean, we took the ship from Saint John up to Rimouski for repairs, and while we were there a bunch of us got out one night and got all corned up. On the way back, one of the guys had done something and the cops were after him, so we figured the best, safest place to be would be aboard ship.

When we got back, we got out of a couple of cabs and I walked up the gangplank. I was already up above, almost right on to the deck when a paddy-wagon pulled up. Then a couple of cop cars. The cops jumped out and while they were looking for this guy, he went to hide underneath the gangplank.

I was standing on deck watching this. A couple of cops spotted him and went underneath the gangplank to arrest him and put the cuffs on him. Well, when that happened I jumped from the top of the gangplank down on top of the cops.

Then there was a free-for-all. It was us guys against the cops. The cops won. I wound up in jail.

A couple of other guys were locked up with me but were let out the next day. I was there for a couple of days, and when they let me out the ship was gone, and Gerry was gone with it.

I knew they were going back to Saint John to hire more crew, so when I got out of jail, I took off for Saint John hitch-hiking. I thought I'd get back aboard, but no such luck. I told the captain I was sorry and that I was only trying to protect a friend, but he didn't see it that way and gave me a black mark on his report to the company. I later sailed again, however, under another shipper.

Though my total experience at sea was brief compared to a lot of other Maritimers, I've gained a deep respect for all the waters and all the ships that sail them. I salute every sailor in the country, whether they be merchant, commercial or armed forces. And a very special salute goes out to our fishermen, as well. The sea is unpredictable. You can't imagine how cruel it can be until you experience one of those North Atlantic storms.

I admire all those who make a living on the sea, and even though I am a Maritimer myself, I am glad I have found another way to make a living. The people of the sea, both men and women, are among the bravest in the world.

Hitch-hiking with Gerry Marks

By the time Gerry got back from his trip on the Irvingdale, I was getting itchy feet again and asked him if he wanted to hitch-hike out west. Gerry had heard about the oil fields, and as he was always more anxious to work than I was, we headed for Alberta.

With all the hard work that I had done up to now as a kid, all I wanted to do was see the country. The more, the better. And work began to have no appeal to me at all. I had already asked my friend Steve Foote if he wanted to go, but he wasn't interested, so Gerry and I just took off.

We each had a little satchel with a few personal belongings, like socks, safety razor, my guitar, and away we went.

So my first trip west was with Gerry Marks and little did I know that from then on I would be on the road for the next eleven years hitch-hiking back and forth across Canada and the United States in all kinds of weather, in all seasons.

Right now it was spring, but we hit about two weeks of some desperately cold weather, especially in northern New Brunswick, through Rivière-du-Loup and down through Quebec on the St. Lawrence shoreline.

When we couldn't get a ride we'd go into different houses and knock on the door. Sometimes they took us in. Sometimes they just gave us a cup of warm tea, and we'd stand by the stove and get warm and then out we'd go again.

We'd walk for a mile or two and then go into another house. Sometimes they'd feed us and sometimes they'd keep us for the night.

I remember one house where there were two sisters about our age, and naturally we took a shine to each other. They tried to teach us French and we tried to teach them English. Their parents and their grandparents were there and we all had a pleasant evening.

It was funny for them to hear us try to say French words and sentences and vice versa, and we spent a hell of a good time laughing like a bunch of young kids. Gerry and I could both play the guitar and sing, so we also played songs all evening.

Then they put Gerry and me in a bed up in the attic. That was great. They gave us a nice breakfast the next morning and we left and talked most of the day about what we thought the possibilities of coming back and seeing the girls would be. I forget their names now.

We went on like that. When we got to a big enough town, we'd go into a restaurant and offer to scrub the floor or wash dishes to get a meal.

When we got to Ontario we got into an argument about something on the road, and as the days went by it began to fester. On our way out west somewhere, we decided to split up for a while. Then Gerry got a ride and I didn't. And when I finally got a ride, I couldn't find him. We both wound up going west, but we got separated and after that I didn't see him again for a couple of years.

I later learned he had gotten a job near the border of Alberta and Saskatchewan, while I continued on to British Columbia. I'll never forget my first impressions when I spotted the Rockies. They were just spectacular and breath-taking. I couldn't keep my eyes off them.

I hitch-hiked out to the coast before coming back to Calgary. And from there I decided to go to Red Deer, Edmonton and Saskatoon before heading back east.

Now in certain places, hitch-hiking wasn't allowed. When I got to Red Deer, for instance, I found that somebody in their great wisdom had made it illegal to hitch-hike on the highway from there to Edmonton. It was by no means a major highway back then, as it is now. It was just a regular two-lane road with one lane going each way.

It was my first time along this route, and as I stood there with my thumb sticking out a cop drove by. He pulled the cruiser over, backed up, and said, "You're not allowed to hitch-hike here."

I said, "Well, thanks for letting me know, officer, but I'm stuck. I haven't got a cent and I'm trying to get to Edmonton."

I told the cop there was a truck driver in Edmonton I had met in Winnipeg who told me if I looked him up when I was in the area he could get me a job. Of course, this was a cock-and-bull story because I wasn't fussy about working anyway.

"So I'm trying to get to Edmonton," I told him, "and this is the last leg of my trip. I have no money, so how else am I supposed to get there?"

He said, "I don't know how you're going to get there, but you're not hitch-hiking on this road. You'll have to take a bus."

I said, "Well, you know as well as I do that you've got to have money to get on a bus. I haven't even got money in my pocket to eat or stay anywhere, let alone get on a bus."

"Well," he said, "I don't care, but if I catch you here again hitch-hiking, I'm going to lock you up."

"Well, in that case, sir," I said, "because I have no other alternative, I request that you lock me up now. I happen to be very hungry and I guess if you lock me up the least you'll have to do is feed me. And as I have no place to stay, I figure the jail is just as good a place as any to stay in, out of the cold. So there you have it, sir, I'm ready and available."

"Don't give me that shit," he said, "and don't be hitch-hiking on this road. 'Cause if I catch you here again I'm locking you up." He then started the car up, wheeled around and went back to town. No sooner had he done this when the next car came along, and I stuck out my thumb.

He must have seen me in the rear-view mirror for I saw him turn the cruiser around and start coming towards me again. When I saw that he was getting close, I stuck out my thumb. He pulled up and said, "I told you, you're not allowed to hitch-hike on this road, didn't I?"

I said, "Yes sir, you did."

"Well, get in the car."

I got in the car, and the cop wheeled around and took me back to town where he dropped me off on one of the street corners. "Now," he said, "there's the bus depot. If you can't get on the bus, then don't let me catch you on that road again."

I went into the bus depot and talked to a bus driver about getting a free ride. No way. I told him what the cop said, but still, no way.

So I left the terminal and walked out to the road again to start hitch-hiking. By this time it was almost dark. And, naturally, along came the cop. When I saw him coming I stuck out my thumb. He slowed down, took a long look at me and just kept on going up the road.

Soon after that I got a ride part way and then a second ride which took me into Edmonton. It didn't matter to me whether it was illegal or not because if the cop did put me in jail for a month, so what? I was going to eat and have a roof over my head, so what the hell did I give a damn about?

It's not a federal offence or anything—I mean they are not going to lock you up for ever—so what's he going to do? Put me in jail for a couple of days and feed me. What's so bad about that? I could probably use the rest anyway. Good times are here again and thanks a lot for the favour.

The guy who gave me the ride into Edmonton was a truck driver who owned his own transport truck. I wound up staying at his house for about a week, and I worked for a couple of days with his brother on a construction job. Of course, my heart wasn't in it, and though they were very friendly to me, I just had to see more of the country.

I got to play on the local radio station and do a couple of amateur shows when I was there, but one morning, bright and early, I was off to Saskatoon and all points east. By about the middle of June I was back in New Brunswick and heading for Saint John.

The Tobacco Fields

I no sooner arrived in Saint John when I met a couple of guys my age, Art Coles and Calvin Taylor, whose nickname was Sonny. They were working at the Golden Ball Garage. They were pumping gas and got talking about going to Ontario. Somebody's relatives were going. I think it was Art Coles' aunt. She had several kids and they were going to Toronto to live. I think her husband had got a job there and sent money for them to take the train and join him.

Art wanted to know if Sonny Taylor wanted to go to Toronto, and Taylor said he thought he might be able to get a job in southern Ontario. He said his sister Lillian lived near Port Burwell with her husband, who was a tobacco farmer, and they quite often hired help to pick the tobacco.

The fact that I had already been to Ontario impressed them and when I said I'd like to go back with them but didn't have enough money, they each spotted me half the price of the fare to Toronto, and a day or so later we were on the train.

Also on the train was Art's aunt, Pearl and her kids. Pearl's husband came to pick us up at the Toronto train station, but as his car would not hold us all, Art and Sonny and I followed them home by cab. The first night me and the boys stayed at the YMCA to allow Pearl and her husband to get settled, then we stayed at their house for a few days before we set out hitch-hiking to Port Burwell.

Art Coles still had a few bucks, which he shared with us by buying us the odd hamburger over the next couple of days, but by the time we got to Tillsonburg, about twenty-five miles from our destination, we were all broke.

As Sonny and Art were now a bit weary, Sonny called his sister, and soon her husband, Adam Resch, came out in his truck to pick us up. We stayed with them for about a week and then we all took jobs working separately for some dairy farmers up towards Kitchener until the tobacco harvest started.

When we went back to Adam's place, we found out he would only have jobs for two of us. He took Sonny and Art on and I went to work for another tobacco farmer at Colten Corners on the other side of Tillsonburg. I only primed there a few days when I heard that Art Coles didn't care much for the work and took off back to Nova Scotia, where he was originally from.

As Adam was now short of a man I quit the guy I was working for and joined Sonny and the crew down at Port Burwell. That was my first year in tobacco. Although the work was hard, we often found time to get out in the evenings or on a Sunday and play guitar and sing in the old bandstand in Port Burwell. We used to attract quite a crowd. We also got quite popular with the girls.

Once the harvest was over, I bought a 1941 Chevy panel truck. The body was a little beaten, but the motor was running good.

I got my first licence to drive at a service station in Aylmer. I told them my name and that I was sixteen and they didn't ask me for any further identification.

In no time I was heading back to New Brunswick, driving my first vehicle from Tillsonburg to Hamilton along the old Highway 2. In those days the highway went right through the bloody cities—through Hamilton and through Toronto, and you know, there was a red light at every block.

Highway 2 was right down along Queen Street, Toronto. I got through there and kept on driving. I don't know what was on my mind. I guess I was saying to myself, I've got to make the trip all in one night, I was so anxious.

I guess I just couldn't wait to show everyone on the east coast how well I had done to acquire myself a vehicle. There was hardly anyone down there who had a car at my age at that time. And was I going to be popular or what?

At last I was going to get some respect. I drove through Toronto and Kingston, then to Gananoque before falling asleep at the wheel around 5 or 6 o'clock in the morning. I was really lucky I didn't do any damage to myself because the truck went down an embankment and broke off a telephone pole.

A transport truck came along about five seconds later, hit the wire and took the pole and flung it away. It landed about thirty yards farther up in the field. All you could see and hear was sparks and the truck driver didn't even stop.

Now it was daybreak and who should come along but a cop. I was just coming out of the ditch and taking a good look at myself.

All I had was a little wee cut on the knuckle of my little finger, but as for the truck, the radiator was shot, the water was all out on the ground and the front was all dinged in.

I had some money on me, approximately $80, that was supposed to be for gas and oil.

The cop took me into Gananoque to visit the magistrate in town, who worked in a service station. I didn't have to go to trial or anything.

The cop said he'd have to charge me for careless driving and I paid my fine to the magistrate right there in the gas station. I think it was $60, and they charged me $15 for the pole. All I had left was some $4 and change. And, of course, I didn't have a truck.

The neck was broken off my guitar and there I was hitch-hiking down to Saint John—after all that hard work. All I had was the receipt for the truck. When I arrived in Saint John, I'll never forget the reaction from Steve when I told him about owning a truck and losing it in the accident.

"Bullshit."

I said, "Oh, yeah? Look," and I opened my wallet and showed him the receipt.

"Ah, you can get a receipt like that from anybody."

Nobody would believe me.

So there I was again, back to normal.

All except one thing, that is. I had no guitar. But I ran into a guy I knew who was working at Pope's machine shop down on Paradise Row, and he said he could get me a job there. I didn't normally want to work, but buying a guitar was an emergency. After crashing for about three months in a flop house and saving every penny by practically starving myself, I quit my job and walked into Joe Gilbert's pawn shop one day and slapped down $40 on a second-hand guitar. I think it was an old Harmony.

All equipped for the road again, I went to see Steve to ask him if he wanted to go with me.

Hitch-hiking with Steve Foote

Meanwhile, Steve and a couple of other guys had been talking about going to Montreal. They had come into some quick money as a result of breaking into a store or something. I don't know which one of them pulled the job, whether they all did, or some of them, but they were all talking tough and acting as though they were heavy-duty gangsters in a big hurry to get out of town.

They thought it was smart to pull some kind of a "job" and then head for Montreal to hide out. They were going by train.

I didn't have any money, but I wanted to go along for the trip. So Steve got the other guys to chip in and they paid my way.

When we got to Montreal, the four of us had a falling out after we were there for about a week or so. It's no wonder we were scrapping. We all rented one room with only two beds. The other guys slept in the beds and I slept on the floor.

One day when we were walking down a street, to my great surprise I ran into my father, Tommy Sullivan, who had come up from Saint John and was now down on his luck. He asked me for a loan of five bucks. As I didn't have it, I asked Steve if he would give me five bucks to give to him. Steve said, "No problem" and after I introduced them my father left. I would not see him again for a number of years.

After a couple of weeks when the other two guys wanted to go back to Saint John, Steve wasn't sure whether he wanted to go back or not. So I said to him, "Why don't we take off hitch-hiking?"

"Well, geez!" he said. "I never hitch-hiked before, but the money is running out." We'd lived pretty high for a couple of weeks there—going around eating big in fancy restaurants and drinking lots of fancy booze, and everyone except me was dressed in what I could only call a hood suit, complete with fedora.

They really looked like members of some mob right out of the movies. I used to laugh at them, and in the end I think that's what broke it up. They didn't like me poking fun at them. I used to say, "If you guys could only have a look at yourselves…"

They were all growing moustaches, glancing from side to side and looking really shady. Two of the guys were about three years older than me and Steve and they didn't like me hanging around because I was sort of laughing at them and saying, "Who do you guys think you are anyway? You're all going to wind up in the penitentiary somewhere if you don't smarten up. And if the cops wanted to nab somebody you'd be the first guys they'd come looking for."

Though they tried to get back sometimes by saying that life in the pen would probably be preferable to bumming around banging on a "starvation box" (meaning my guitar), I usually got the best of them. When they finally saw that I couldn't be lured into their petty schemes, they decided they didn't want any more to do with me.

So one day when Steve and I were out drinking at one of the bars we decided to draw up some plans of our own. Incidentally, neither Steve nor I ever had any problem getting into bars when we were young, even though you had to be twenty-one to drink. As long as you looked the part and minded your own business, you were never bothered. I always had the height, and my actions were definitely not those of a kid. And Steve at that time was sprouting a moustache, and with his stocky, muscular build he looked pretty rough.

At any rate, Steve and I talked, and the more I kept building the merits of hitch-hiking up in his mind, the more interested he became.

Before too long he decided to go with me, and the very next morning, bright and early, we were on the highway. First time out on the road we spent the night in jail in Cornwall, Ontario. We hadn't done anything wrong, in fact we checked ourselves in.

From Montreal to Cornwall I had already briefed Steve on some of the "rules of the road." One of the main ones was: In the event that a person finds himself destitute and requests that a policeman help him by providing shelter from the elements for the night, the policeman is obliged to do so. I assume the reason for this is that if a person, through desperation, breaks into some place causing damage, the policeman is considered partly responsible if he refused to lend the assistance which might have prevented the crime. Then on the other hand: If a policeman were first to discover that you are destitute, he would have the right to book you on a vagrancy charge and lock you up for the night. Then in the morning, after you faced the magistrate, you might remain locked up for a month.

What all this really means is that if you're broke and have no place to stay, and you see a policeman approaching, make sure you ask him for his assistance, first, before he discovers your predicament by demanding to know who you are, what you're doing, and your financial status. In short, everything depends on who asks first.

So this night in the Cornwall jail, the officer at the desk just took our names and showed us to an open cell. We were free to go at any time we wished.

Now back in Montreal, Steve had bought us both a pair of cowboy boots for the journey out west. And before this night was over, these boots were to become the focus of another major rule which all drifters must never ignore.

As we sat on our cell bunks, Steve, who had never spent the night in jail before, began asking a whole lot of questions. In going over some of the rules of the road, I happened to mention that the first guy out in the morning is the best dressed.

"Well, what do you mean by that, Tom?"

"Well, if you don't damn well watch your clothes and if you have anything good, if you've got a wristwatch or a new pair of boots, such as we've got, you'd better watch, because when you're sleeping in these places somebody will grab them. And if they're the first one out in the morning, they got your boots and you're left with theirs."

"Oh! Well, nobody will get my boots. And, besides, I don't sleep soundly enough for that to happen."

"Well, you can't be too careful," I said, "you can't trust anybody, nowadays."

So while Steve tried not to let his worry show, I told him I usually put my boots together and I made a pillow of them. Then if anybody tried to take them they'd have to move my head and wake me up. And if that happened, they'd really get the boots. Steve thought that was a great idea.

He then put his boots under his head and we just talked for a while. Pretty soon our "crowbar hotel" started filling up. First a couple of drunks got locked in. Then there were two or three other drifters, much like ourselves, who came wandering in just by their own choice (and also free to go when they pleased).

I waited for an hour or so for Steve and all the rest to fall into a deep sleep and I moved very quietly to take his boots from underneath his head. He didn't even feel it. In a few seconds it was over, smoothly done. I stuffed them down behind the radiator outside the cell. There was also an old bag of shoes that I found in one of the corners of another room and I picked out the worst pair I could find with the soles hanging off, and about seventeen sizes too big, and I put them under his bunk.

Knowing Steve slept like a log, and figuring he was good for the night, I crawled into my bunk and went to sleep. If he didn't wake up when I was trying to get the boots, I thought, he'd probably be good there till the morning.

I woke up first, and, of course, I had to wait for him.

Meanwhile, the other guys woke up, and left. Finally, Steve woke up and the first thing he said was not "Good morning," or "Where's breakfast," but "Tom, Tom, wake up. Where's my f——— boots?"

Pretending to be startled, I said, "What's the matter, Steve?"

"Somebody stole my f——— boots, Tom," he said, and he was now pulling me out of the top bunk.

I said slowly, in a long, disbelieving kind of drawl, "N-o-o."

"Yeah—my f——— boots are gone. It had to be those guys that came in here last night. They looked pretty shifty. I'm telling the cops."

I said I thought that would be a good idea, as I sort of kicked the shoes under the bed, as if it had happened by accident. Then I said, "Oh, are those your boots down there?"

He picked up the old shoes and said, "That dirty f——— rotten prick. If I ever find him, I'll kill him."

And then, with nothing else to wear, he put the old shoes on. You could hear him all over the place with this clump clack, clump clack. No laces in them. They had to be 150 years old. The leather wasn't even soft any more. They were as hard as wood.

I can still hear him telling the policeman, "Officer, somebody stole my boots. I had a brand new pair of cowboy boots—somebody stole my boots and look what they left me."

The cop looked and laughed. Like me, he must have had visions of Steve clompety-clackin' down the highway in those horrible-looking shoes.

The cop said, "I think I saw a guy walking out of here with a brand new pair of cowboy boots." The cop didn't know what happened and he didn't give a shit anyways, but when he said that, Steve's last hope vanished.

As he clomped back to the cell he was almost at the point of tears when I pulled the boots out from behind the radiator and I said, "I'm only trying to teach you a goddamned lesson, Steve. Always make sure that nobody can steal anything from you."

As he brightened up with a mixture of surprise and relief, he said, "Oh, you bastard, Tom, what did you do that for? I felt terrible."

I said, "Yeah, well, remember: when you go to sleep in jail or anywhere else make sure that everything is safe, and you won't have to feel terrible. If I could steal your boots from you, and you didn't know about it, so could somebody else. Now that you've got your boots, you can throw those stupid looking things away."

When the cop saw what was really going on, he started laughing like hell. And he was still smiling and shaking his head as we went out the door.

The next thing I learned after a couple of days was that Steve couldn't go nearly as long as I could without eating.

His continuous grumbling and bellyaching about food and how long it was going to be before we ate again inspired me to come up with a good name for him: "Starvin' Steve, the Highway Grieve." I think it bothered him a little at the time, but as soon as he got his belly full he took it in good humour.

In Southwestern Ontario

When we got to Paris, in southwestern Ontario, we again tried to check in to the local jail for the night. As we went in, a cop was sitting at the desk reading a book. When I asked him if he would put us up in a cell for the night, he said, "No, now, beat it."

"Well, we have no money, officer, and we're just looking to get in out of the weather," I said.

Again he said, "No. I'm not going to put you up. So scram."

I said, "Look, we have no place to go and it's getting cold out and I don't think it's decent for a couple of fellows to be walking around in the middle of the night with no place to go, except to sleep on a bench."

"Well, I don't give a damn," he said, "now, get lost."

"In that case," I said, "it's going to be cold for us out there, and maybe it's going to be cold for you, too."

"And what do you mean by that?" he said.

"Well, I think I'll go out and find a brick and throw it through your window so you can be cold all night, too. Then you'll have to put us up by arresting us."

"All right, you arsehole," he said. "In there."

So we ended up spending a quiet night in the cell at Paris. In the odd place, the police would give you a meal ticket, a little chit with which you could get a bite to eat at a greasy spoon somewhere in the morning. You might get a bowl of soup and a piece of toast or at least a cup of coffee. But in this place we got nothing.

Upon leaving the jail I told the cop I couldn't believe how disappointed I was after spending "an evening in Paris." And half-way out the door, Steve shouted back, "Yeah, and the meals were no hell, either."

By getting Steve to southwestern Ontario I was trying to kill two birds with one stone. First I wanted him to see the places Sonny Taylor, Art Coles and I had travelled to the year before and show him where I had primed tobacco. But my main reason for bringing him down this way was that I wanted to introduce him to some of the people who knew that I had actually bought and paid for my own Chevy panel truck.

Till now he still thought it was bullshit.

When we got to Port Burwell we of course stopped in to see Adam Resch. "How are you doing, Tom? Don't tell me you're back to hitch-hiking again. What happened to your old truck?"

Bingo!

That was all I needed. Steve said, "So it's really true then, that Tom actually had a truck. I didn't believe him."

After I told Adam about losing the truck in an accident, he soon brought the conversation around to a subject that was always a lot more interesting to Steve: food. "I guess the boys must be pretty hungry, Lilly," he said to his wife. "Maybe you'd better get a good meal cooked up for them."

Soon Steve was in his glory. He hadn't had a good meal like this since he left home. Don't get me wrong, I was enjoying it too. But Steve always had a more obvious and more elaborate way of showing it.

After supper, we talked about tobacco and the approaching harvest. Steve showed a great deal of interest and said he wanted to give it a try, now that he knew how much money there was to be made. (And of course, if Tom had bought a vehicle the year before, why couldn't *he*?)

After asking about Sonny Taylor, Lillian's brother, we were informed that he was now working up near Tillsonburg and that he would be glad to see us. Soon we were off to bed and after a big, healthy breakfast and some more chit-chat in the morning we were again heading for Tillsonburg.

Sometime that afternoon we met Sonny, who took us to a restaurant and bought us a hamburger. He said his job wasn't paying all that well and he was just holding onto it until tobacco harvest and then he was going back to work for Adam and Lillian.

I told him we were on our way out west and asked him if he wanted to come. He wasn't interested, so we just said, "Okay, good luck and we'll see you."

After Sonny left, Steve again brought the subject around to working in tobacco. "Why don't we forget about going out west for now, Tom? Let's just see if we can get a job around here for a while, work the tobacco harvest, get a good vehicle and then go out west."

I wasn't prepared for this. I wasn't really interested in working, but I needed time to think my way through this.

"Okay," I said, "we'll enquire around and if something turns up in a couple of days we'll take it. If not, we'll head out west."

The words had no sooner fallen from my lips when a voice behind me on the street says, "Tom! How the hell are you? You're kind of early for the harvest, aren't you?"

It was a guy I had met while playing the guitar the year before on the Port Burwell bandstand.

I said, "Yeah, me and my buddy Steve, we're just looking for a little work between now and then."

"Oh!" he said. "I know a guy on a farm down here near Eden, Val Tisdale. He needs a couple of guys to help him cut some wood and he also gives room and board; as a matter of fact, he's sitting over in the hotel right now, looking for someone to hire."

Steve said, "That's just great, Tom. Let's go."

My heart sank.

Here I was hoping I had two days to steer Steve everywhere except to a place where we could find a job, and out of the clear blue sky this bird appeared. What could I do now but tag along? Over to the hotel we went and before you could say your own name, the guy bought us a couple of beers and hired us.

In no time we were in the back of the truck and out to the farm.

He fed us really well, which for Steve was a big plus, and it took me two weeks or more to find some excuse to get Steve to leave. One day when we were having a hard time cutting and splitting some very gnarly and stubborn tree stumps, the boss came along. He wasn't in a very good mood that day, and neither was I. He wanted to know why more work hadn't been done and I just seized on the opportunity. "If you want more work to be done, as far as we're concerned you can do it yourself!"

That was it.

"You can both come to the house then, and get your pay."

Soon Steve and I were walking down the road, but not without a great deal of tension between us. We argued about why I said what I did and why I got us both fired. Though I agreed it wasn't Val Tisdale's fault, Steve suggested we split up. As it was only a couple of weeks now till the harvest, he would get his own job somewhere and I could get mine. We agreed to meet again by contacting Adam Resch.

Upon seeing Steve's determination to work the harvest, I decided I'd work it, too. But with a few bucks in my pocket, I had no intention of working somewhere else between now and then.

I hitch-hiked around Ontario for a couple of weeks and then headed back to see Adam Resch in Port Burwell to find out if Steve had made a contact.

Arriving in Tillsonburg, I walked through town and then caught a ride with three guys in a pick-up truck who were going as far as Vienna. As the cab was full, I climbed in the back. While passing through Straffordville I was standing up in the back, leaning against the cab, when I heard a familiar voice calling my name.

"Tom, Tom, stop! It's me, Steve." I thumped on the top of the cab and the guys stopped the pick-up and let me off. I ran back to where Steve was and after greeting each other excitedly, we walked back to the service station where he said he was now working.

I asked him about the prospects of getting a job priming tobacco, but he informed me that the weather had been ideal and the harvest had started almost a week early. My chances of getting on somewhere now might be slim. Most of the farmers had hired their help almost a week ago.

"Well, what about you?" I said. "How come you're not working in tobacco?"

"Well," he said, "Howie here, the owner of the station, is giving me a chance to own a car if I work here and I almost have it all paid for."

"Wow," I said. "That's fantastic. A car paid off in less than a month. Where is it?"

"Right over there," he said, as he pointed to an old, dilapidated, Model T Ford.

"Does it run?" I asked.

"Run?" he said. "C'mon, jump in and I'll take you for a ride."

As we headed for the passenger side of the car he said, "I'll have to get in on this side right now. The door don't open on the driver's side."

As he opened the door I could see there was only one seat and that was for the driver. There was no floor and when you looked down you could see the ground under the car as well as the frame, the drive shaft and the transmission.

Where the passenger's seat and the back seat should be, there were three or four planks that supported a piece of foam rubber and a couple of shabby-looking blankets that were supposed to act as a bed.

After he got in behind the wheel I jumped in and squatted down. When he started the motor the planks began to rattle as if we were having a major earthquake. And after he sounded the horn with a long o-o-o-g-a-a we bounced across the lot and headed down the highway.

As we bumped along, I couldn't help but think to myself, "Well, if neither one of us is going to be able to work the tobacco harvest, and if it's only going to take Steve another week or so to pay for this jalopy, I might as well stick around and encourage him a little bit and maybe by then he'll finally be ready to hit the road with me and head out west."

By the time we got back to the service station my plan was pretty well formulated. Although I figured the old Model T wouldn't make it for fifty miles, never mind out west, I said, "By God, Steve. Now we've got the right rig. In a week or so you'll have the car paid off and we won't have to hitch-hike out west at all. We'll just take it easy. Work a few days here and a few days there to buy gas and oil and we can sleep in the back of the car. That's what I call 'living the life of Reilly'."

Steve appeared to be interested as we entered the little restaurant in the service station, so I figured I'd pursue this line of thought for the next few days. "Hey, Howie," Steve said. "I want you to meet my buddy I was telling you about, Tom Connors."

"Oh yeah," said Howie, as he looked me over. "You got to be the guy that plays the guitar and sings. How about giving us a song?"

It turned out that Howie and his wife were real big country music fans and before I got the second song out of me, his wife was cooking me a couple of her famous hamburgers (I say "famous" because I never tasted a hamburger as good as the ones she made, either before that day or after).

I liked the burgers and they liked the songs. And for the next few days I found a way to earn my grub. I would just sit there and sing and as long as the customers enjoyed it, I ate.

I really can't say I liked the sleeping quarters, though. Being cramped up in the back of that old Model T with Steve every night wasn't exactly the "life of Reilly" that I had previously envisioned.

All through the week I had Steve pretty well convinced to go back on the road with the car.

Then one night I almost lost it. About the second night before we were supposed to leave I wound up getting the runs. Steve always parked the old jalopy just under the bright yard-light in the middle of the front parking lot. The location was exactly half-way between the road and the gas pumps.

It was about 2 or 3 o'clock in the morning and I got these awful cramps. As I woke up and looked out the car window and saw the place all lit up, I knew it would be impossible to run the distance it would take to find the amount of shadows I would need to do the amount of what I wanted to do. There was no doubt about it, I had to go. And I had to go *now*!

As Steve snored away, I rummaged around and found an old rubber boot. And just in time, too. I was only able to get the door open, sit the rubber boot on the running board, stick my arse out and let 'er go. As I filled the boot about three-quarters full and placed it beside the car, I promised myself that I would wake up before anyone else in the morning, empty the boot, wash it out and nobody would be any the wiser.

I was feeling much better now, so I soon fell asleep. As I didn't wake up as early as I thought I would, I also didn't hear Steve getting up. He apparently got dressed without waking me...slid on the only rubber boot he could find, and as he drowsily spotted his other rubber boot outside the door, he just automatically...well, to use an old cliché...he put his foot in it.

Well, as you can imagine, all hell broke loose. And no words can describe the language he was using to tell me what kind of a human being I was, as he pounded on me to wake me up. I instinctively knew what must have happened and was about to profoundly apologize, but when I looked out the door and saw the state he was in, all I could do was laugh. He was standing there glaring at me with a red face that looked like a steam boiler just ready to explode.

He had put his foot right down into the boot and the liquid had squished up on his pants and was running over on the ground to form a puddle under where he was standing.

He was cursing and swearing.

His arms were moving everywhere.

The pressure had far exceeded the boiling point.

And he was raving mad.

And while I can't say as I blame him, I just couldn't resist asking him, "What's the matter, Steve. Shit yourself?"

"You son-of-a-bitch, Connors, that's the last goddamn trick you'll ever play on me."

"But Steve," I was saying between belly-laughs, "it wasn't a trick."

I was trying to explain to him what had really happened, but he wouldn't have any of it. The more I tried to be serious, the more I laughed. And the more I laughed, the madder he got.

Finally, he just stomped away towards the service station to clean himself up in the washroom. I could tell by the obvious trail he was leaving every time he put his right foot down that Howie would no doubt be asking him a few questions.

And every time I thought of what one of those questions might be, the belly-laughs started all over again.

He didn't speak to me all that day and all that night. It wasn't until the next afternoon that he'd even look at me. And finally, by suppertime, we were back on speaking terms.

As we talked that night about leaving, the direction of the conversation began to take another unusual twist. Somehow Steve had got wind of the sugar beet harvest about 150 miles farther down in southwestern Ontario and the word was that they would soon be looking for help.

Because we had missed getting on for tobacco Steve now suggested we go working in the sugar beets before going out west. While I wasn't too pleased with this option, I really had very little choice in the matter, especially in light of the last two days' events. So not wanting to rock the boat too much (or was it the jalopy?), I just agreed.

The next day Steve got paid. And after making his last

car payment, he was left with a grand total of $15. (To give the reader some perspective on value at the time: a dollar could buy you three or four gallons of gas.)

Soon we had the Model T packed, said goodbye to Howie and his wife, and with Steve behind the wheel and me sitting on a pop case, we headed out for sugar beet country.

Pretty soon we were chugging up one hill and very cautiously rolling down the next (there was about 180 degrees of play in the steering wheel and the old jalopy damned near got away from us a couple of times).

After we had been driving for about forty or fifty miles I noticed the "old girl" (as Steve called her) wasn't chugging up the hills as easily as she had before.

About ten miles later, when she finally chugged up to the top of a really long grade, she coughed, sputtered, jumped and finally conked.

We were stopped in the middle of nowhere.

To be on the safe side, we had taken all the back highways and this one was really out of the way. To our right and about a quarter of a mile down, there stretched a long valley with a river running through it. Between us and the river there was a series of open fields with what looked like a swamp and a few trees at the very bottom. To our left was just a high hill covered with forest.

After getting out and looking under the bonnet we found there was nothing we could do to get the "old girl" started. We thought if we pushed her a ways we might eventually come to a down-grade where we could just get in and let her roll down the hill and maybe come to a service station somewhere at the bottom.

As the day was very hot, and with no down-grade in sight, we soon gave up our plan and decided to leave her there till we could find someone to fix 'er.

At this stage, and always being of a "practical" mind, I suggested she wasn't worth fixing. Why spend the $12 or $13 we had left on a car which might conk out again before we drove another fifty miles? Besides, depending on how far we were away from anything, it might cost us $4 or $5 just for towing.

Steve was beginning to see the light of day. "Well, what do you think we should do, Tom?"

Without hesitation and pointing towards the deep valley, I said, "Why don't we have a little fun? Let's just push 'er off the road, down over those fields and watch 'er sail into the swamp?"

As I watched Steve's eyes I could tell he was thinking of what an unholy fate my suggestion was about to bring to his very first and well-loved automobile, so I quickly added, "Did you ever see one of those movies where a car goes careening off some mountain road and tumbles into a gorge somewhere? I bet the guys who have the job of setting those scenes up really enjoy seeing the results of their work."

That did it. Two minutes later we shoved the old jalopy off the road, which had no ditch, and just watched the "old girl" go.

She went pretty straight for a little ways till she started to pick up speed. Then she started to zig-zag.

About three-quarters of the way down she hit a rock and went arse over tea-kettle. She landed on 'er side, rolled three or four times, came back on 'er wheels and disappeared somewhere in the swamp.

After laughing like a couple of fools, I shook Steve's hand and said, "Well, that takes care of that. Now let's get the hell out of here and go and see if we can find them sugar beets."

For the next two or three miles we just laughed and joked until we came to a service station with a little lunch counter. We went in and ordered a couple of hot-dogs. As usual, Steve just wolfed his down, got up and went to the washroom. As I was finishing mine I noticed Steve talking to some guy who looked like he worked at the station and they seemed to be discussing some kind of a deal.

It wasn't long till Steve came back, paid the waitress

and we were on our way.

I wanted to ask Steve what his little meeting was all about, but as soon as we stuck our thumbs out on the road a car stopped and gave us a ride.

About ten or fifteen miles later when the guy let us out, I wanted to know what happened. It seems that Steve was telling the guy about his Model T breaking down about two or three miles back, and because we were in a hurry and didn't want to bother with it, we just pushed it off the road. The guy interrupted and said, "Well, hell, if you don't want it and you are just going to leave it there, why don't you sell it to me? How does five dollars sound?"

Steve, never being one to pass up a good offer, shook the guy's hand and took the $5. The only thing was, he didn't tell the guy just how far off the road we pushed it.

Even today, we often get a chuckle out of wondering whether or not the guy ever found the car he bought. He may be still searching.

Incidentally, after hitch-hiking all over southern Ontario that summer and fall, we eventually missed the sugar beet harvest (I have no idea how that could have possibly happened), and finally we headed out west.

Winter in Northern Ontario

It was snowing by the time we got to North Bay, and as the rides weren't going too good we decided to go down to the railroad yards and hop a westbound freight. We couldn't find a boxcar, so we had to settle for a cattle car.

If you know northern Ontario in the winter, you'll know how cold it was with the raw wind blowing through the cattle car slats as we rolled on through the night.

We got on the damn thing about 1 o'clock in the morning in the North Bay yards. We had to wait for about two hours or so until the engine hooked our car up to the train and was ready to roll. When you have experience you know what cars are going to move, and what cars are not, and besides you talk to the yardman, the guy who pulls the switches for the engine.

If he's a good guy, fine, he'll suggest what car to get into or what train is moving, and where it's going—east or west. If he's a bad guy, he may just put the run to you.

Well, if you think it was cold waiting in this cattle car when it was standing still, it sure was a lot colder when we finally got rolling. We covered ourselves up with a bunch of fertilizer bags that were piled up at one end of the car and wished to God we were still back in North Bay.

We didn't feel like jumping off the train in the middle of nowhere in a snowbank, so when the cold started to get really unbearable we tried running back and forth from one end of the car to the other beating our arms against our bodies to generate some warmth, but it wasn't working and we were getting tired.

We now decided to set fire to some of the fertilizer bags, and if we could get the attention of the engineer he might slow down the train to see what the hell was going on and maybe we'd get a chance to hop off. Right now the train was going too fast for us to see where we'd be jumping in the middle of the night. It was possible we could be going over a trestle and jump in the river.

We finally had quite a fire going, and with the wind blowing through, all the boards were singed on one side of the car. Still, the train didn't stop, so obviously no one saw anything. Although we had all the bags burned by the time the train pulled into Sudbury, we were damn near frozen.

It was just about daybreak and altogether we had been in that cattle car for about five hours. Jumping off the train just before it got into the Sudbury marshalling yards, we found a restaurant and asked to mop the floor or wash the dishes for something to eat. They gave us a meal and a chance to warm up and soon we were on the road again, hitch-hiking to Sault Ste. Marie.

By the time we got as far as Espanola the weather was becoming quite fierce and after enduring a couple of big snowstorms we decided to knock on a lot of doors.

The people along that way were very kind to us and many of them kept us overnight. Some of them kept us for two or three nights, and some wouldn't let us go while it was still storming. This meant we would often be there for the better part of a week.

As a matter of fact, it took us over two months to go from Espanola to Sault Ste. Marie that winter, mainly because of the bad weather and the great hospitality we were shown.

The guitar and the singing also had a great bearing on the situation and I am sure in some places we might have been lost without it.

There was even one stretch there, between Blind River and St. Joseph's Island, when I was singing and playing at so many parties every night, that I sometimes wished I had slept out in the snowbank. With the amount of free booze I was consuming, I wouldn't have felt a thing.

Many times today when I am driving over some of those same roads—not just along that stretch but everywhere in Canada—I often think of those old days and the many houses where we used to be given a meal, sing some songs, play some cards or checkers, or just tell some long stories before going off to bed.

While I can't be sure which houses they were any more, especially after so many years, and maybe the same people don't even live there any more, I still can't help but wonder where they may have gone, or what they may now be doing.

Sometimes I wish I could thank each and every one of them again for all their individual kindnesses, but when I realize it is impossible, I just drive by. And I guess I hope in my own little way that the songs of Stompin' Tom may somehow serve to remind them that each and every precious little piece of the Canadian heart they once so graciously entrusted to me is now slowly, but surely, being gratefully returned.

Going back to my story, we now started hitch-hiking from Sault Ste. Marie to Port Arthur/Fort William (now known as Thunder Bay) until we found out the road was under construction and there was no possible way to get through.

As I had travelled out west before by taking the road from North Bay to Cochrane, I soon realized that from where we were now the railroad was once again our best option. We'd have to take another freight.

But first Steve had to be convinced. After all, it was still wintertime and visions of nearly freezing to death in that cattle car from North Bay to Sudbury were still fresh in his mind. After obtaining a road map and showing him the distance we would have to travel by road, first back to North Bay, then to Cochrane and Hearst, he began to see the advantage of going directly to Hearst by way of the Algoma Central.

Arriving back at the "Soo," we headed straight for the railyards where an engine was now making up a train. The yardman was quite co-operative and said there was one boxcar sitting by itself. He told us to get in there and make sure we put a little stick or something in the door so that we didn't get locked in during the shunting.

He said he was supposed to go around putting seals on

these cars, but he'd purposely miss that one.

Before we knew it we were rolling north through open country and as the weather had turned considerably milder and we seemed to be having a thaw, we opened the boxcar door to view the scenery.

We were smoking string and anything we could find on ourselves and in the boxcar. We even dug the lint out of our pockets to fill our pipes. Whenever you were stuck for cigarettes you just filled your pipe with whatever you could get, and smoke away.

When the train slowed down at one spot we figured we must be coming into Hearst. So we jumped off and decided to walk into town. But there was no town. There was only a railroad gang there—mainly Métis or Cree—and only one building where they all ate and slept.

As we approached one of the guys who was working on the tracks, we told him what had happened and asked him where we were. We also wanted to know when the next train was coming through and if we could get a bite to eat somewhere while we were waiting.

He told us we had made a big mistake. This wasn't Hearst at all, it was Franz. And we were still out in the middle of the bush. Even worse, the train only came through there about once every three days. As another couple of guys joined the conversation, one of them said they could flag the train down when it came through, but in the meantime, he'd go and talk to the foreman and see if he could get us some work for a couple of days to earn some money, or just work for food.

Unfortunately, when the foreman was called, we could see right away that he didn't like us. He looked like a big bear, and before he even heard half of our story, he said, "The best thing you guys can do is leave right now. There's the way to Hearst, now take it."

He then started up the tracks after us with a big shovel in his hand, hollering, "Get the f——— out of here before I cut your heads off with this spade."

At first we ran for a little ways and then we walked.

And we walked, and we walked. As a matter of fact, we walked for four and a half days—that's how long it took us to get from Franz to Hearst along that railroad track. It had to be over a hundred miles.

The train went by once, but she was going too fast for us to jump on.

Once we thought we saw a bear or two, and another time we saw a couple of moose. There were all kinds of animals out there in the middle of nowhere. It was still wintertime, but sort of mild now and coming onto spring. If it had been just a couple of weeks before, we could have been caught in a real bad blizzard and probably would have perished.

Steve had a package of Freshie, an unsweetened soft drink powder, in one of his pockets. He'd probably lifted it from some store we had been in. And when we found a little place where the snow was melting, Steve poured half of the Freshie into a little puddle upstream while I drank the water as it came trickling down over the rocks. Then I went up and poured in the rest of the Freshie and Steve had a drink. It may not have been too nourishing, but that's all we had in the four and a half days.

When we got to Hearst we were pretty lean and bedraggled. We went into a restaurant and asked to work for a meal, but we looked in such bad shape we must have scared them. They put the run to us.

We bumped into a cop and he told us to leave town. We were not wanted. He told us they had enough bums around Hearst now and they didn't want any more.

So we headed out towards Long Lac, another hundred miles or so west of Hearst. At that time there wasn't even a service station between Hearst and Long Lac. And from where we stood, there were only three more houses between us and a hundred miles of woods.

We thought we'd better try each of them in hopes of getting a meal. At the first one—no way. But at the the second one, this great big guy came out and when I told him we needed food, he just grabbed Steve by the back of the neck and gave him a haul, saying, "Get in here, you guys." Steve went face down on the floor and just lay there for a few minutes. He was that tired and bedraggled. I sauntered in and sat down.

Then the guy hollered at his wife, "Maggie, get these boys something to eat. These guys look awful hungry."

He was a nice guy, but really gruff. He asked us where we'd been, how we got so dirty, and "Where in hell do you think you're going, anyway?" While Steve was just too hungry to say anything, I told the guy about Franz, the long walk into Hearst, and how we were trying to make our way out west.

"Well, there's a long road between here and Long Lac," he says. "The best thing for you to do after we feed you is stand out in front of the house and hitch-hike. If you don't get a lift before nightfall, come on back in and we'll try to scrounge up a place for you to sleep for the night." He then gave us a couple of bucks each and said, "I wouldn't go any further than that, if I were you."

We stood there on the road for about an hour after we got fed and cleaned up. And now we felt much better. Soon a guy came along in a truck, and as he pulled over and said he was going down about half-way, we jumped in. He said there was a logging road about fifty miles away, and that he'd take us into the camp, where we could meet another guy who was going into Long Lac the following morning.

In the logging camp, I sang some songs for a few of the boys and the next day the other guy took us down to Long Lac, bought us a couple of beers in the hotel and put us on the road to Geraldton.

It was almost a year now since Steve and I had left Montreal to go out west, and here we were only as far as Geraldton, Ontario. As the crow flies, this was still four hundred miles from the Manitoba border.

Although Steve had started out with me as a greenhorn, he had now become a lot more seasoned, especially by the experiences of the last few months.

I guess he was beginning to realize the road couldn't get much harder than what we had just been through, and with summer just around the corner he was finally looking forward to his first trip out west.

As an encouragement, I kept telling him how beautiful it was out there and of all the jobs that were available (if anybody had a mind to work). I told him about the trip Gerry Marks and I had made the previous year and how Gerry liked the west so much that he'd stayed out there and got a job as soon as we arrived in Alberta. I said I had a pretty good idea where I could find him. And because he was probably pretty well fixed by now, he would be in a good position to help us out.

All this kind of talk just made the road look a little brighter. And after a few more rides we were soon sailing through Beardmore and Nipigon and on to Thunder Bay.

From Port Arthur to Winnipeg

Even back in those early days I would sometimes try to get radio stations to let me sing a couple of songs over the air, so that was the first place I made for when Steve and I hit Port Arthur. The station's call letters in those days were CFPA, and as we walked in I reminded the guy that he had let me sing over the radio the last time I came through and I wondered if he might let me do the same thing this time.

He remembered me very well and said he often wondered where I went to afterwards, as a number of people who had been listening at the time had asked him the same question. (After all, it wasn't very common for people listening to the radio to have their normal music program interrupted by the voice of a fifteen-year-old drifter singing his own songs.)

About fifteen minutes later, he had me set up in their little studio and at the signal I was ready to go. After he gave me a nice build-up and introduction, the first two songs I sang were "My Reversing Falls Darling" and "My Home Cradled out in the Waves." The announcer then explained that these were two of the songs that I had written and that I had also sung them over the station about a year and a half before.

He also told the listeners that I was born in Saint John, New Brunswick, that my home was now in Prince Edward Island and the two songs I just sang were about both these places. After mentioning I had a buddy by the name of Steve hitch-hiking with me this time, and that we were both only seventeen, he asked me if I had written any more songs lately. When I said, "Yes, I have," he asked me to sing a couple more.

I then sang "Bonnie Belinda," which was a story about a girl in northern Ontario, and one called "I'll Be Gone with the Wind."

When I finished the last two songs, the announcer thanked me and wished me well, expressing the hope that I might come back some time. After I thanked him and all his listeners, the station again resumed its regular programming.

While Steve and I were being informed of all the complimentary phone calls that had just come in, the door opened and who should be standing there but an Italian guy whom I had briefly met on my last trip through town. He had heard me on the radio and rushed right over to see if he could catch me before I left the station.

He now wanted me to come home and meet the family and hear some of his accordion playing. I thanked the radio announcer (whose name has escaped me after all these years) for being so obliging. I then introduced my friend to Steve, and away we went.

At this point, I might like to add that there were many local radio stations in those days that were just as obliging as the one in Port Arthur. Every station was equipped with a studio, and live music and entertainment were always welcome.

Today, it's all recordings. And as a result of the performers now being one step further removed from their audience, radio has become a lot less friendly.

Although it's a long time ago, I think my Italian friend's name was Mario. He and his father had given me a lift the last time I was through and I had stayed at their house for a couple of days. Mario was about a year older than me and he was learning to read and write music.

As he had learned the melody of "Reversing Falls Darling" from hearing me sing it so often, he had written it down in music sheet form since he last saw me, and he now wanted me to have it. He had brought it right to the radio station with him.

When we got to his house, Mario wanted to play music right away, but his mother said to come and eat as supper was already on the table. Of course, that was good news to me and Steve. Mario's father was also glad to see me and decided to bring out a special bottle of his wine.

There were about four more kids in Mario's family, all younger than him. And after they all took their places at the table, his father said the grace and we all had some wine with spaghetti and meatballs.

Mario's poor mother couldn't get over how much spaghetti Steve could put away, but she just kept right on feeding him. Two big plates was all I could handle, and I sure knew it when I was asked to sing right after supper. Mario had a big piano accordion and most of the music he had learned to play was Italian. But you could see he really loved to hear the country and western songs.

That evening they invited a few of their friends over who had also heard me on the radio, and of course, they wanted to hear me sing.

They also noticed, the more wine they got into me the better I sang. Before the night was over, they even had me and Steve and Mario all singing together. And what made it even funnier, we were all singing in Italian. Later, as the guests were leaving, one man said he was going to Dryden on the following day, and if we liked, we could ride along with him.

Next morning, while Steve and I were still nursing a "big head," we piled into the guy's car, thanked everybody, said goodbye to Mario, and that evening we found ourselves in Dryden.

At the Dryden police station that night the cops put us up in a very cold basement where we huddled around an old furnace to try to keep warm. But when we were leaving in the morning the officer asked us if we had any money, and upon hearing we didn't, he wrote us out a note to take to a small restaurant where they gave us some toast and coffee.

Arriving once more on the outskirts of town, we began hitch-hiking and walking to keep warm. Although it must have been April or May, the nights and the mornings in that neck of the woods could still be cold.

It must have taken us a week or more just to get from Dryden to the Manitoba border. The rides were bad and the road was long and very twisty. I think we walked most of the way, 'cause all the rides we got didn't take us more than five or ten miles at a time. We knocked on a few doors, got a few handouts and stayed in a number of houses, and after what seemed like forever, we finally arrived in Manitoba. The driver let us out in a small town that I forget the name of, and after a couple more rides, we landed in Beausejour.

As it was very late at night, Steve still hadn't seen much of the landscape. But as we left the town lock-up the following morning, Steve said, "Wow! This is magnificent! Now I know what you've been talking about."

As we progressed along the road towards Selkirk and Winnipeg, all he did was talk about the contrast between the great forested hills of Ontario and the ocean-like flatness of the Prairies.

He kept taking big, deep breaths and puffing them out, and saying how "refreshing" it all was. "We haven't eaten much in the last few days, but geez, Tom, after looking at all this I don't even feel hungry."

I gave him one of my "Yeah, sure Steve" looks, and said, "Yeah, sure Steve. But I'm sure you'll get over it by the time we hit Winnipeg."

"Aw! What's the matter with you, Tom? You don't always have to look on the gloomy side, you know."

While that remark immediately brought back a few thousand memories of the not-too-distant past when I had to use every convincing ploy in the book to encourage him to even come this far, I just gave a shrug and stuck out my thumb to the oncoming traffic.

About 10 o'clock that morning we were dropped off on the north side of Winnipeg. All the way down Main Street on our way to the centre of town, all I could hear was "When are we going to get something to eat, Tom? We should have stopped into a farmhouse in the country. We'll never get something to eat around here." I wanted to say, "I see you're at it again" or "I told you so" but I just kept on walking.

All of a sudden Steve starts into sniffing, and he says, "Hey, Tom. What's that smell?"

"What smell?" I ask.

"Them frosting-covered cinnamon buns," he said. "For Christ's sake, can't you smell anything?"

For the next half a block he must have been walking four or five steps ahead of me. And before I knew it he had his nose up against the glass of a bakery shop window. "There they are, Tom. Look, I told you. There they are, frosting-covered cinnamon buns. And cookies, and doughnuts, and everything."

"Okay, okay…" I said.

> *Starvin' Steve, the highway grieve,*
> *Don't be crying on your sleeve;*
> *We shall eat before we leave.*

"Let's go around to the back and see if they'll give us some day-old bread, or something."

"Now you're talkin', Tom. That's a lot more like it," he said. I had to run to catch up to him. He was already half-way down the alley. A moment later, we put on our saddest faces and knocked at the back door. A big guy dressed in white with a tall chef's hat answered. "What can I do for you boys?" he asked, as if one look at Steve licking his lips couldn't tell him.

"Well, we're just hitch-hiking through…" I began. "We haven't eaten in two days…blah! blah! blah…and more blah! blah! blah!…and we were wondering if you might be able to spare us some day-old bread or buns or something."

"Well," he said, pointing to seven or eight bags and a couple of boxes of garbage, "if you boys would like to take this stuff and throw it all on that truck over there, I'll scrounge around and see what I can come up with."

In five minutes flat the job was done and we were back standing at the door. When he came out he had two big see-through bags of day-old bread, buns, cakes, cookies and doughnuts of all description. There had to be at least twenty-five pounds of stuff jammed in each bag.

"Here you go, boys," he said. "Maybe that'll hold you for a little while?"

"Oh! Thank you very much, sir," we said, as Steve grabbed the biggest bag and we headed out the alley. It wasn't any time before we were into the goodies and marching down the street with our hands full of cinnamon buns and our faces covered with sticky frosting.

We must have been quite the sight as we turned the corner of Portage and Main with everybody stopping to gawk at us. They must have wondered, "Who in the hell are those two odd-looking birds?" with big red-plaid lumber jackets on, one with a satchel, the other carrying a guitar and both awkwardly trying to eat from bags of cakes and doughnuts large enough to feed an army.

Every time we met a bum on the street, we stopped and gave him a handful of cookies.

By the time we got to the west end of Winnipeg, where we could now start hitch-hiking again, we had finally eaten enough out of the bags to be able to stuff them into the large pockets that extended all the way across the backs of our lumber jackets. We finally polished them off that night in the jail at Portage la Prairie.

From Brandon to Banff

One place we could often pick up a dollar or two was at the residence of a priest. Though Steve had been brought up in the Pentecostal faith, I had been a Catholic and it was therefore up to me to do all the talking. Sometimes the priest would buy your story and sometimes he wouldn't.

Well, on this particular day in Brandon, Manitoba, we were not only going to find a priest who wouldn't, but the manner in which he refused should be noted.

As usual, the residence was beside the church. There were three or four steps leading up to a small veranda with no railing, in front of the side door. Steve stood about half-way up the steps as I went up to the door and knocked. In no time the priest was standing at the door and I began to tell my story.

As I got to the part where I wondered if he might be able to help us in some way, he just drew off with a punch that was meant for my chin but glanced and hit me in the neck and knocked me backwards off the veranda.

"No!" he shouted. "Now get the hell out of here, the both of you, or I'll call the police," He then slammed the door with a force that almost took it off the hinges. As I picked myself up off the ground, a lot more surprised than I was hurt, Steve, with a half a grin on his face, came out with this gem: "Well, Tom, that's the first time I've seen a Catholic priest 'convert' a guy into a holy-roller."

The reference, of course, was to the way in which I rolled when I hit the ground. "Yeah, yeah," I said. "Now we're both Pentecostals. Let's get out of here before I go back and 'convert' that bastard into a moron.'"

Two or three days later, on a fairly warm afternoon, we landed in downtown Regina. As was our custom sometimes when we hit a large enough town, we headed for the Sally Ann (Salvation Army hostel) in hopes of getting a bed for the night and a couple of meal tickets.

As we waited in the line-up to see the captain, we got friendly with the guy standing ahead of us. His name was Harry Demers, "but you can call me 'Flowers' like everybody else does," he said, as he pointed to the two small roses that were tattooed one on each side of his forehead near the temples.

"How did you get them?" I asked.

"Oh, I got drunk one night a number of years ago with a bunch of buddies down in northern New Brunswick," he said, "and a couple of the boys decided to play a trick on me when I was sleeping and now they have been calling me 'Flowers' ever since. By the way, where do you guys hail from?"

When I told him we had just landed in from the east coast he asked us if we wanted to work. I said, "Maybe. Why, what's the deal?"

"Well," he said, "the CCF government out here has set up an office downtown and if you want to work they'll put you up in a small hotel room till they find you a job. There's lots of construction going on around here now, and the pay is not bad."

Steve and I looked at each other and asked him how to get to the office. We arrived there about five minutes to four, just as they were closing up for the day, but the guy decided to give us an interview anyway.

After we put on our best "we want work" faces, and gave him our story, I couldn't believe my ears. He was giving us a voucher to take to one of the little hotels just off the main drag where he said they'd put us up for a week and give us a couple of meals a day and then pack us a lunch starting from the day they had a job for us. If they couldn't find a job within the week, we were to go back to the office and have another chat with him.

Well, all we could talk about as we walked down the street towards the hotel was what a great government the people of Saskatchewan had. There wasn't one other place in Canada, to my knowledge, that would afford that kind of opportunity for someone who was down and out to get back on his feet. Even though I had no intention of working when I came to Regina, this voucher in my hand was certainly an incentive to do so. And though it was breaking my heart, I intended to honour it.

We spent about three days in the hotel before we got word about a job, during which time the old guitar was making us enough money to do some drinking, meet some people and have some fun.

The morning we were supposed to go to work, I was hoping it had somehow been all a mistake, but sure enough, there was the guy at the door ready with his truck to take us to the job. We drove out to the suburbs where they were putting in a new subdivision, and after driving by their big sign which read "Gilhorn Construction" we got out and were assigned to our duties.

They took us over to where a backhoe was digging and while Steve was given a job fitting waterpipes together down in the trench, I was given a wheelbarrow and told to move a pile of sand from one location to another. In about an hour and a half when I had this fair-sized pile nearly all moved, along came a guy wearing a white shirt and a beautiful white cowboy hat. "Hey you!" he says to me. "What do you think you're doing? I've got a machine that's going to be working here in a little while and that pile of sand is going to be right in the way. Now turn that wheelbarrow around and put that sand right back where you got it."

"Yes, sir," I said, and proceeded to do as he told me.

As on any construction site there is always a lot of water and mud, and this one was no different. And as you can imagine, pushing a wheelbarrow full of sand through the mud is no easy task.

By the time I had the sand almost all put back, the guy who had originally told me to move it showed up again on the scene. He looked at me for a moment, scratched his head and said, "I thought I told you to move that sand over there? Now, what the hell are you doing bringing the damn stuff back for?"

"Well, that guy over there near the shack, with the white cowboy hat on, told me to," I said.

"Never mind what that guy tells you. He only pushes a pencil. I'm the foreman on this job and that sand is in my way. Now start movin' the goddamn stuff back there."

"But, what if he comes over and tells me to move it back again?" I said.

"Well, you just tell him that I told you it's got to stay there, because over here it's in the road of the backhoe trying to dig this trench."

"Okay," I said, and started taking the sand back. While this was damn hard work and I was feeling like a fool going back and forth for nothing, I could see that my pants and boots were so caked with mud I was going to need new ones, and staying with the job was the only way I was going to get the money to buy them.

Sure enough, not a half an hour went by and here comes Mr. White Cowboy Hat. I could see him fuming as he left the shack. He was still twenty feet or so from me when his jaw began to flap. "Are you stupid or something? Don't you know the difference between 'over there' and 'over here'? Now what the f——— are you doin' bringin' that sand back here for?"

I said, "Because the guy over there told me to. He said it was in the road of the backhoe and he wanted it moved because he would be digging a trench there."

"Well, you go and tell that asshole the plans have been changed and we're going to start digging over here. And you, you stupid bastard, if I see you coming back this way with one more load of sand, you'll be on your way downtown to pick up your time."

Well, that was it. I said, "Look buddy, I'm not a stupid bastard. And I'm not stupid enough to carry your f——— — messages back and forth. If you assholes can't get your goddamn plans together, don't expect me to. I'm not your f——— flunky."

With that, I cracked him right in the chops. He fell on his arse in the mud and his big, beautiful, white cowboy hat went flying in the middle of a big puddle of muddy water.

I hollered down in the trench to Steve, "C'mon! We're gettin' the f——— out of here."

Steve jumped out just in time to see the guy getting up out of the mud as I marched over to the middle of the puddle and started jumping on the guy's white hat. "And furthermore," I was shouting, "I hope you never find your fancy f——— lid."

"Wha-what's going on, Tom?" Steve was asking as we hurriedly walked off the construction site. When I told him what had happened he started to laugh. "Well, you sure made a nice mess of that guy's beautiful white cowboy hat," he said. "Geezes, Tom, I don't think I ever saw you so mad. Anyway, what the hell are we going to do about our clothes? We got no money to buy new ones."

"I don't know," I said. "But let's just get the hell out of here and maybe I'll think of something."

By the time we had walked all the way back to the hotel there was a message at the desk for us from the guy at the government office. He had already heard what happened and wanted us to come down and tell our side of the story.

After seeing the mess we were in and finding out that these were the only clothes we had, he told us to go back to the hotel and wait while he tried to get us the money we had earned.

The following day we got the message to go down to Gilhorn's office and they would pay us. In the meantime, we could just stay in the hotel till he found us another job. Little did he know that for me there wasn't going to be another job.

When we got to Gilhorn's we thought it might be best that I didn't go in, just in case there might be trouble. When Steve came out with our cheques he said everything was cool.

We then went back to our hotel, got them cashed and headed for the war surplus store where we got all decked out again, right down to the western boots and two black cowboy hats.

It was now Friday evening and our room didn't run out till the following Monday. That was when we were supposed to go back and have another chat at the government office, but we never made it.

We hung around and drank on Friday and Saturday nights, of course, and knowing there was no way they were going to get us a job till after the weekend, we pulled out on Sunday. I'm sure Steve would have liked to stay around for a while, but when I told him I'd already had enough of this "work business" and that I was hitting the road, he reluctantly tagged along.

We'd been on the road together now for over a year and almost knew each other's jokes off by heart. And to pass the time we started telling some of them over again. Only this time, to beef them up a little, we'd pretend we had a harelip while telling them. While this kept the jokes from getting stale for a short time, our new-found ability to imitate the people with this impediment was soon to come to a dramatic end.

Though some of my readers may find this story humorous, as did I on the day it happened, others may see no humour in it whatever and realize, as I do today, that its ending could have turned out to be more tragic than it did. I only ask my readers to remember that this was the prank of a couple of seventeen-year-olds and I certainly don't recommend that anyone try it today.

We came walking into this little town way out on the prairies, and as we had about a dollar between us we decided to go into the town's only restaurant for a piece of pie and a bottle of pop. Before we went in, we decided that one of us was going to pretend he had a harelip, and if anyone couldn't understand what he was saying, the other fellow would act as his interpreter.

We flipped a coin and the lot of acting as the harelip fell to Steve. He was also supposed to initiate all the conversations. As we entered the restaurant, there was a counter with a number of stools and a long row of booths along one side. We made our way to one of these booths and sat there smirking until the waitress came to take our order.

When she asked what we would like, Steve, of course, spoke first in his imitative voice. "We'll have a nithe peeth of raithin pie, pleeth, and a thmall bonnle of Pepthe."

"Excuse me," she said. "What was that again?"

Interpreting for Steve, I said, "We'll have a nice piece of raisin pie, please, and a small bottle of Pepsi."

When she went away we broke into a bout of wild snickering.

As the order was being served, Steve asked the waitress several more questions. And each time she'd look at me and nervously ask what it was he had said. I'd no sooner tell her when he'd be asking her something else. When she could no longer stand the frustration, she made some excuse to get back to the kitchen, and the look on her face told us she had no intention of coming back to our table if she could possibly avoid it. This only gave us more great delight, and by now you could hear Steve talking like a harelip all over the restaurant. And I, of course, was prodding him on.

While all this was going on, and quite unnoticed by us, a guy had come into the restaurant and sat on one of the stools up at the counter. After listening to us talk for a while, he came over to our table and introduced himself, first to Steve.

"I wath jutht lithening to you thpeak, an' it lookth like we both have the thame problem. My name ithe Lethlie, what'th yourth?"

Upon hearing this guy speak with a real harelip, Steve almost shit himself. I'd never seen Steve ever get such a stupid look on his face in all the time I had known him. You could see the wheels turning as he looked to me for help and gobbled down the rest of his Pepsi, just to buy another second of time.

After trying to hide himself behind a handful of napkins while wiping his lips, he finally composed himself long enough to say, "My name ith Thteve, and thith ith Tom."

"Oh, hi Tom an' hi Thteve. You don't mind if I thit down with you guyth, do ya?"

Now, me, never being one to miss the golden opportunity to see someone squirm, just as Steve was trying to get out of his predicament by saying, "We thure would like to, Lethlie, but we mutht be going," I spoke up and said, "Sure Leslie, you and Steve just sit there and talk for a while till I get back. I think I've got to go to the washroom." As I got up to go, that "you son-of-a-bitch" look in Steve's eyes bored a hole right through me.

I couldn't keep from laughing all the way to the washroom and for five more minutes after I got in there.

When I finally figured Steve had had enough, I tried to pull myself together as best I could and started back to our table. I got there just in time to hear Leslie finish explaining the nature of his own cleft palate and was now asking Steve to describe his. Well, when that got just too much for me to handle, I grabbed my guitar and said to Steve, "I'll see you outside, Steve. I think I'll get a little fresh air. It's gettin' kinda stuffy in here."

I don't know exactly how Steve finally got away from Leslie, but when he eventually walked out the door I just howled. Steve called me all the names under the sun, but I couldn't hear a thing he said. I knew he was telling me off. I could see his lips moving, but the laughing was uncontrollable. Every time I caught my breath it was only long enough to say, "Jeeteth, I'm thorry, Thteve. Now what wath that you were thayin'?"

And then there was more laughter.

Pretty soon Steve began to see there was no use staying mad at me and when a snicker or two finally escaped from the side of his lips, he said, "It could have been you instead of me, you son-of-a-bitch. And if it had, I guess I would have laughed my arse off at you, too. But you sure had me in a tight spot there for a while."

Now we were both laughing.

We agreed that in the end, there had really been no harm done after all. And poor Leslie had not been hurt in any way. So with a final resolve to never pull that kind of a stunt again, we set out walking down the long prairie highway.

A day or so later we got a ride into Medicine Hat, Alberta, with a guy who put us up for the night. I'd been playing and singing in the back seat of his car and that night he was having a party with a few friends. One of the latecomers to the party was a guy who worked at the radio station. He invited me to come down and sing a couple of songs over the air the next day.

After that we struck out for Lethbridge. And then to Fort Macleod. It was here we had to decide whether or not to head for Vancouver through the Crowsnest Pass or go up to Calgary first and then go by way of Banff and Lake Louise.

As we knew the Stampede was only a month away, we began to have some romantic notions that we might get a job or at least take some part in the rodeo. So the Calgary route was confirmed.

In the meantime, we met a guy in Fort Macleod who had the contract for digging all the local graves. He asked us if we wanted a job for a couple of days and I don't know why, but we took it. The next thing we knew we were standing with a couple of picks and shovels in the cemetery, looking at each other, and wondering what in hell we were doing here. "I've got five graves to dig in this cemetery," the guy said, "and two in another one. I'll go over to the other one, and you guys can stay here."

"Well," I said, "seeing how business is really boomin' around here, we'd like to get paid as we go. We don't have any money for grub."

"I'll pay you at the end of each day," he said. "I'll put you up for the night. And I'll be around in a couple of hours to bring you a lunch." We had one grave dug by the time the lunch came and it gave us a kind of a morbid feeling sitting there eating lunch while he was busy putting down cloth and preparing the hole we had just dug to receive someone's dead body.

We dug two more graves that day and by the time he came to pick us up we had callouses on our callouses. He paid us that night and we ate in the local restaurant. When we got back to his place, he showed us to an old broken-down bed in his garage. And after wrestling, fighting and pushing each other out of bed all night as we slept, we were feeling pretty grumpy in the morning.

After breakfast in the restaurant, we were back in the graveyard digging. About a half hour later I said to Steve, "Look, I'm not sure whether I want to hang around here for another day. My goddamned hands are all full of blisters and my back is damn near killing me." I had no sooner got the words out when we saw the guy's truck coming back in the cemetery.

"Hey, you guys. Hide over there behind those tombstones and stay out of sight," he said. "We've got a burial coming." As soon as it was all over and all the mourners left, he called us over to the grave where they put the body and said, "Okay! Take your shovels now and cover this guy up."

"Just a minute," I said, "you hired us to dig graves, you didn't say anything about covering some guy up."

"Yeah, that's right," Steve said, "and besides, how do we know he's even dead? I heard about a guy they buried by mistake one time and when they dug him up he was still alive."

"Well, that can't happen around here," the guy said. "We always make sure they're dead before we bury them."

"And how do you do that?" I said. "Hit them over the head?"

"Listen," he said, as he kicked a couple of good-sized stones down on top of the box, "are you fellas going to cover this guy up or not?"

"Well, not if he's still alive," Steve said.

By this time the guy was shaking his head. "What in the hell do you guys want me to do, anyway, open the goddamned box to see if he's dead or not?"

Steve said, "Not while I'm around here. C'mon Tom, let's go."

With that, we threw the shovels on the ground and headed for the road. I'm still not sure what the guy in the coffin thought of the conversation, but the last time we looked back, the guy that hired us was still scratching his head.

We arrived in Calgary a couple of days later and "flopped" in the Sally Ann. The next day we ran into a couple of bronc riders who were going to be ridin' in the Stampede and one of them played the guitar. We went up to their room, sang some Wilf Carter songs and just chatted about what kind of preparations they had to make before entering the rodeo.

After listening to these guys talk for a while and seeing how much gear they had to have, we were convinced that entering into any part of the Stampede required a lot more experience than we had.

Before leaving Calgary for Banff, I went down to one of the radio stations and sang a couple of songs. Stu Davis, a very popular country singer at the time, was there. I believe he might have been taping one of his shows. We spoke briefly and I left. On the road to Banff the rides were very poor and the going was slow, and most of our conversation focused on the scenery as we approached the lofty snow caps of the Rocky Mountains.

Steve had also told me about one of his sisters whom I had never met. Her name was Nedris, and she and her husband were now living in Vancouver. His plan was to go and visit her when we got there. Unfortunately, fate had other ideas and his plan was not to be realized, at least not the way we expected.

Steve had started to grow a moustache again, much the same as he had worn over a year ago in Montreal.

I told him he was starting to look like a hood and with rides being as slow as they were around here, I suggested we might have more luck if he shaved it off. Steve didn't like this suggestion at all and somehow over the next two or three days the issue cropped up several times. We finally got to Banff, spent the night in the lock-up, and hardly walked a couple of miles out of town the following morning when the issue flared up again.

I expressed the view that drivers going through the mountains were more apt to pick up younger-looking people, and because he was wearing a moustache they thought he was an older man and were therefore more leery about picking us up.

Although in later years Steve admitted that he had really been overly stubborn about the matter and probably should have shaved it off, on that day it was just not to be. As the argument grew hotter, we decided to separate and cool off. I was to walk ahead a little ways, and if he got a ride by himself he would speak to the driver and ask him to pick me up on the way by.

After I'd walked around a bend in the road I began to think it all over, and in half an hour or so I decided to go back and see if we could possibly straighten this matter out in a more friendly way. I carefully watched every car that came by to see if Steve had got a ride and I didn't dare thumb any cars for fear that if they bypassed him and then picked me up, we would get separated for sure. I walked back around the bend and there was no Steve. I kept right on walking back into Banff, but still no Steve. By that time I finally figured out what must have happened. Instead of hitch-hiking towards me to pick me up, he had gone to the other side of the road and hitch-hiked the other way.

I began to feel that it had all been my fault. I wanted to find him and apologize, but I reasoned that if he'd got a ride there was no way of telling where he would be right now. I therefore went down to the railyards and hopped a west-bound freight.

To Vancouver Island and Back

That day the train went through the Kicking Horse Pass and on through to Revelstoke, British Columbia.

Some time later that night it stopped in Kamloops. When I heard someone friggin' around with the door, I thought it might be the railway police so I ducked down in one corner at the back end of the boxcar. Soon a shadowy figure hopped in, closed the door and made his way to the end of the car where I was crouching.

As I knew I had the advantage of the darkness because he had just come in from outside, I decided to make my move first. I stood up and banged my fist on the side of the boxcar to draw his attention in that direction and quickly moved around behind him. With a choke hold from the back I threw him to the floor and hung on. "Who the f——— are you," I said, "and what are you doing here? And you'd better tell me the truth or I'll drive this knife right through you."

I didn't have a knife, of course, but he didn't know that. "Don't, don't, don't," he yelled, as he told me his name and what he was doing there. It turned out he was just a hobo like me and was only taking the freight down as far as Hope.

The train by this time was rolling again and I told him, "I'm gonna let you go. Now crawl over there in that corner and sit down and stay there."

I sat in the other corner, and as it was pitch black in there I decided not to speak too much to him in case he took it as a sign to be less afraid of me and start to move closer. Besides, he still thought I had a knife.

I figured he must have made this run before, because he seemed to know exactly when the train was pulling into Hope. It was almost daybreak and when we began to slow down he said, "This is where I'll be getting off."

"Okay," I said. "But keep scratching the side of the wall there till you get to the door so I'll know where you're at. And if you stop scratching, I'll be right behind you."

It only took him about two seconds flat to get to the door, open it and scram. And judging by the speed with which he did the scratching I dare say he took a cord of wood under his fingernails with him as he left.

I don't remember his name and I never told him mine. But I bet if he's still around today to read this, he'll have one hell of a surprise when he finds out that the mystery man he rode the freight with that night was none other than Stompin' Tom.

A few miles later, somewhere near Chilliwack, I jumped off the train myself and thumbed the rest of the way into Vancouver. For two or three days the Sally Ann gave me a bed in the men's dormitory and four or five meal tickets. All beds and meal tickets that I might need after that were to cost $1 per bed and thirty-five cents for a meal ticket.

If you used the ticket in the morning you would get one egg with a few potatoes and toast and coffee. The rest of the day you would get a coffee with a bowl of soup and a sandwich. This bed and meal ticket practice was pretty well standard with the Salvation Army across the country at that time. But to obtain the initial "freebie," you had to line up at a certain time of the day to see the captain and tell him your story. If he bought it, you got the freebie. If he didn't, you got nothing and had to pay right away. That is, if you had the money.

After three days when I still had no money, I had to resort to bumming on the streets like so many others were doing.

You'd just walk up to someone and say, "Excuse me, sir, I just got into town from the east. I have no place to stay, and I'm hungry. Could you spare me a dime or so for a bowl of soup? I'd greatly appreciate it."

If you got it, you'd go on to stop another and another until you had enough for a bed and a couple of meal tickets for that day. And of course, the following day found you back doing the same thing. The people who gave were sometimes generous and sometimes not. About seven out of ten would just tell you to get lost.

Whenever I had my meal tickets and bed secured for the day, which was usually by noon, I would go back to the Sally Ann where they had a large room for the men to sit around and chat or to play chess or checkers. I'd always loved checkers since I was a kid and here was an opportunity to play with some of the best.

There were several old men, whose names I now forget, who had won Canadian chess and checker championships in the past, and it became my sheer delight to not only watch them play together but to actually get to play some games with them once in a while.

Practically every afternoon for the next month and a half you could see me with these old fellows engaged in a game of either chess or checkers.

In checkers alone I played and lost seventy-six games with one old fellow before winning one.

Then I began to win one out of a dozen and before I left I was winning two out of five. I also played a lot of chess, but in that game I didn't become nearly so proficient.

Because you always had to be in the Sally Ann by 7 P.M. to ensure they wouldn't give your bed to someone else, sometimes I didn't get to sleep there. When that happened I was usually down around Hastings Street, sometimes known as "Gastown," trying to sing and play in some of the little bars and restaurants for a few bucks.

When I made some money I'd flop in a $2 room in one of the rundown hotels, and when I didn't, I'd just go and sleep in the park.

There was no use going back to the Sally Ann once the doors were closed.

The cigarettes I usually smoked in those days were OPBs (other people's butts). You could always find them in the ashtrays of bus depots, hotel lobbies, or just pick them up along the street. I always carried a tobacco pouch in my shirt pocket for depositing the contents of each butt. And for just a nickel, you could always buy a package of cigarette papers for rolling your own.

In order for my readers to gain a full understanding of the circumstances at that time, I should add at this point that it was virtually impossible for a young unmarried man to obtain welfare of any kind in those days. This was still 1953 and the hippie era had not as yet even been dreamed of. It would be another nine or ten years before governments and other organizations would begin to provide hostels for young men and women hitch-hiking across the country.

It was early one afternoon when I was walking along one of Vancouver's busy downtown streets. I was just picking up a few cigarette butts on my way to the Sally Ann when I had what could only be described as a psychic experience. With absolutely no reason to do so, I just stood up after picking up a couple of butts, glanced across the busy street, and spotted a man and a woman walking among the crowd on the other side.

With no hesitation whatever, I began shouting over the hustle and bustle at the woman across the street. Although I had never met her I was absolutely positive that I knew her name. "Nedris! Hey, Nedris!" I called, as I immediately headed across the street, dodging in and out between the line-up of cars.

"You're Steve Foote's sister aren't you?" I insisted. And with a complete look of surprise on the face of the man walking beside her, she began shouting, "Hi! How are you? You're Steve's best buddy, aren't you?" Between car horns blowing their annoyance at me, I acknowledged I was.

After asking questions like "What are you doing out here? Where's Steve? And how long have you been in town?" she introduced me to her husband and asked, "How did you ever know it was me on this busy street? Did Steve tell you what I looked like?"

"No, he didn't," I said. "All he told me was that you were living in Vancouver. And I have no idea what made me look over at you when I did. All I know is, in that one brief instant, I was deadly certain it was you."

"That's funny," she said, "because when you called out my name, I knew you right away, even though Steve had only mentioned you to me once. It's funny how I even remembered your name."

After having a good laugh at all this, they invited me home to supper. What a great supper it was, too. I hadn't had a home-cooked meal in a long time. After supper we chatted for an hour or so and then I had to get back to the Salvation Army before they gave my bed away.

Shortly after meeting Nedris and her husband, a guy who had been staying at the Sally Ann had an offer to go to Victoria with a guy who owned a car. He told me if I wanted to come along and play my guitar, the driver would pay my passage on the ferry. And besides, he'd enjoy the company.

The next day, after singing to the passengers on the ferry, I arrived in Victoria. I said thank you and goodbye to my friend and the driver and headed out for Nanaimo.

The first car that stopped was going right through to Port Alberni. I sang songs for the driver practically all the way and he took me into a restaurant and bought me a meal. When we got to Port Alberni he put me up for the night, gave me a good breakfast and a couple of dollars and I then headed out for Campbell River.

When the rides weren't going too good around Courtenay, I started hitch-hiking on both sides of the road, depending on which way the cars were coming. It just so happened that a guy who was going back to Nanaimo picked me up and I never made it to Campbell River on that trip. After spending the night in jail at Nanaimo, singing to the cops, one of them took me down to the ferry the next day and after speaking to one of the operators he got me aboard, passage-free.

In a couple of hours I was on the mainland and later on that day I arrived back at the Sally Ann in Vancouver.

In the next day or so I ran into a German fellow by the

name of Karl who had just recently come to Canada. It seems he had some relatives in the Okanagan Valley that he wanted to visit and as he had run out of money, he was wondering what his prospects would be should he decide to hitch-hike. As I figured I had already been in one neck of the woods long enough by now, I told him there would be no problem and that I would go with him. The next morning Karl and I were heading east.

By the time I got him to Osoyoos he felt confident enough to hitch-hike by himself and headed north towards Penticton. We said goodbye, and I proceeded east to Midway, Grand Forks and Trail.

As it was still early evening when I got to Trail, I walked to the other side of town to try the rides before deciding to look for a place to flop for the night.

About an hour and a half later, I was just about ready to give up and walk back into town, when an RCMP car pulled over and the Mountie asked me where I was going. He then asked me if I could play the guitar. And when I told him I could, he said to jump in the back seat and sing him a few songs.

It turned out that he was a real country music lover and knew the words to a lot of songs himself. He also said he fooled around with the guitar a bit and started requesting a lot of Hank Snow and Hank Williams songs.

He said he was going as far as Creston, a distance of about eighty miles, and then he'd be turning around and driving back. He said he wasn't supposed to be doing this sort of thing, but because it was getting so late at night and he enjoyed the music so well, he figured he'd take the chance. He drove fairly slowly all the way, just so he'd get to hear a few more songs. And when we got to Creston he gave me a couple of bucks, wished me well and let me out. As he turned around and drove the other way, I thought to myself what a great guy he was and how it was too bad there wasn't a hell of a lot more like him.

I couldn't find the town lock-up that night, so I just walked to the other side of town and went to sleep along the side of the road. When daybreak came, a couple more rides took me to a cut-off on the highway. Here the driver said he was going south to the United States and let me off so I could continue going east.

There was another hitch-hiker standing here on the corner and after making his acquaintance, the two of us walked along together for three or four miles until we came to a service station in a place called Yahk. It was a hot day for walking so we decided to go in for a cold bottle of pop.

As we sat down, the owner, whose last name was Thring, spotted my guitar and asked me to play something. Soon his wife came out of the kitchen and started to listen along with a few other customers. Before we knew it, we were invited to the owner's home where we eventually spent a couple of days. On one of the nights we were there, a dance was being held about ten miles away, down in Eastport, Idaho, in the U.S.A. And, of course, we were invited.

There was quite a bit of drinking that night. And after I got up and sang a few songs with the band, I was asked to dance by one of the American girls. Although I couldn't dance very well, I was having a good time until one of the American guys decided he didn't like a Canadian dancing with someone he considered to be his girl. When she told him she was no longer "his girl," he began rounding up some of his buddies, and before long they decided they were going to kick the Canadians out. When the fight started I couldn't find my new hitch-hiking friend anywhere. He just vanished.

After getting in as many licks as I could (and also taking a few), I finally got shoved out the door with several other Canadians, while the fight was still going on inside. One of the guys who had come to the dance with us somehow managed to grab my guitar, which I had left on the stage, and brought it out to me through another door.

By the time the gang we came with were all assembled and ready to take off again across the border, my new "friend" appeared from nowhere and jumped into one of the other cars. When we got back to Yahk, B.C. I didn't want to upset our very considerate hosts by lighting into him, but I sure told him the next day when we struck out for the highway. As a matter of fact, I sent him up the road. And when I got a ride I just left him there.

Incidentally, it was about thirty-five or more years later when I was playing a concert in one of the towns in British Columbia that Mrs. Thring came up to me while I was signing autographs after the show. She reminded me of who she was and asked me if I remembered the time, so long ago, when I spent a couple of nights at her place. When I told her I did, she said she often wondered what had happened to me, and that she had no idea until she came to the concert that night that Stompin' Tom and the drifter who had stayed at her house so long ago were one and the same person.

After chatting a while and wishing each other well, I thought to myself how nice it was for people to come up to me after so many years and tell me they still remembered that "half-starved" kid with the guitar.

Anyway, after leaving Yahk I got a ride with an older couple who were going up to Radium Hot Springs. And the day after that, I was back in Banff where Steve and I got separated. And now, once again, I was headed back to Calgary.

My very last ride going into town was with two guys sitting in the front of the car while I sang them a few songs in the back. Before I got out, one of the guys gave me a couple of western-style shirts and a few other odds and ends he had in a shopping bag. He said he had lots more, and if I could make use of anything in the bag, I could take it. So there I was walking down the street towards the centre of Calgary with my guitar in one hand and my newly acquired shopping bag in the other.

At this point in time I could never have guessed what kind of surprise I had in store for me within the hour.

Meeting in Calgary

It seems that after Steve and I separated in Banff, he went back and hitch-hiked around Alberta for a while. And one night as he went into a railroad station in a small town to ask if he could sleep on one of the benches, as was our custom to do from time to time, who should he meet in the station but Gerry Marks.

Gerry, who'd been working at odd jobs from Osage, Saskatchewan, to Taber, Alberta, had just bought a ticket for the train back to New Brunswick. As Gerry had a guitar and a nice new buckskin jacket, Steve could see he had some money, and so he decided to start a conversation with him. Remember, they had never met each other before. "Hi, how are you doing?" Steve said. "You wouldn't have a cigarette on you, would you? Where 'bouts are ya goin'?"

Gerry said, "I'm going back to New Brunswick. Saint John. I'm waiting for the train to come through."

"Saint John? I'm from Saint John."

"You are?" Gerry said, showing a lot more interest.

"Yeah," Steve said. "Maybe we know some of the same people. Did you ever run into a guy named Tom Connors?"

"Tom Connors? Geezes, I left Saint John with Tom Connors and hitch-hiked out here, but we lost each other on the road and I've been here for the last two years."

"Well, whadaya know? I hitch-hiked out here with Tom Connors, too. Tom is my best buddy."

"Well, what's your name?"

After they introduced themselves to each other, Gerry decided he didn't want to go back east after all and he cashed in his railway ticket.

He and Steve then went to Calgary.

They got themselves a room, spent Gerry's money, hocked the guitar and even hocked the jacket. They still had another week left before the time ran out on their room and decided if they couldn't land a job between now and then, they'd hitch-hike back to Toronto where Gerry's brother, Harold, was living. Just as they were walking along the street, planning all this, who should be coming down the street the opposite way but me, with a shopping bag in one hand and my guitar in the other. I spotted them first but I couldn't believe it.

"Hey! What the hell are you guys doing here? What a coincidence! There's a million and one places in North America where any one of us could be and here we are bumping into each other on a busy street in Calgary. What's the odds of that?"

Well, needless to say, there was quite a reunion in Calgary that night, although nobody had any money. I wound up sleeping in the room with these guys. We'd take turns in the bed. Then we'd go out to the Harbour Light hostel and listen to their religious sermons so we could qualify for a meal. If you sat in there and listened to the sermon, they'd line you up after and give you a couple of sandwiches and a spoonful of beans.

We stayed there a few more days until the rent ran out on the room. And believe me, that bed was precious. We had a rule. The first guy to get sitting on the bed was the guy who got to lie in it. However, if he got up to go to the washroom, the others could pounce on the bed and claim it as their own.

When you are sleeping in a chair you don't sleep very soundly, so whenever someone did go to the washroom there was no chance they would be able to get back into the bed. Now it was their turn to sleep in the chair.

One day Steve and I were out some place and when we got back in again Gerry was lying down on the bed pretending he was sleeping. So we started talking rather quietly.

Then I said, "Come on, Gerry, you're not sleeping. Besides, you've been in that bed long enough."

Not a sound. I then made a sign to Steve to pass me over a cup of the tea he was making. We couldn't afford any milk for it, but we had some sugar left over.

As I went near the table to get the bowl I looked at Steve, gave him a big wink, and in a voice hardly above a whisper, I said, "Steve, look at the maggots in this sugar."

Gerry jumped right off the bed. "Maggots in the sugar!" he said, as he made one leap across the room to have a look. But as he leapt, so did I—right onto the bed.

"Thanks very much, Gerry. Sleeping were you?"

"Maggots in the sugar" is one of Steve's favourite stories and he never fails to tell it when we get talking about old times.

*Tommy Connors, three years old,
wearing soldier suit in 1939.*

*Tom (right), eleven years old, with some kids
at Skinners Pond, PEI in 1947.*

At fourteen, with my half-brothers,
Bobby and Tommy, in 1950/51.

At the age of sixteen or seventeen with my father and half-brother Tommy.

*My mother, Isabel, in Montreal
in the 1960s.*

*My step-father, Russell Aylward,
of Skinners Pond, in the 1970s.*

*My step-mother, Cora Aylward,
in the 1970s.*

My step-sister, Marlene, in the 1970s.

*Cousin Danny Aylward of Waterford, PEI,
circa 1982.*

At about sixteen or seventeen years old.

At seventeen, near Hearst, Ontario.

At seventeen, with Lloyd Wagner
in Rouyn, Quebec.

In Rouyn, circa 1953, when I was playing at the Royal Hotel.

At nineteen.

*Steve pickin' while I provide some
casual rhythm. Late 1950s.*

Playing in a club in Montreal, circa 1955.

With Steve, pickin' up a storm in the early 1960s.

A "friendship photo" of me and Steve crossing guitars.

Reg and Muriel Chapman at home
in Etobicoke, Ontario, circa 1964.

At twenty-eight, playing at the Chapmans' house in early spring, 1964.

With some friends at the Larder Lake Hotel in 1964.

Singing with a local church choir in Timmins, 1965.

*Chatting with Prime Minister Lester B. Pearson
in Timmins, 1965.*

*Going over "the Reesor Crossing Tragedy"
with the Millettes. Kapuskasing, 1966.*

In Wawa, Ontario,
beside the Wawa Goose, 1966.

Gaet Lepine, bartender at
the Maple Leaf Hotel in
Timmins, Ontario, circa 1966.

Bud Roberts, circa 1970.

At thirty-one in 1967, Canada's centennial year.

Ray Goguen, learning to play the fiddle in the 1980s.

Playing at the King George Hotel
in Peterborough, Ontario, in 1967.

Pool-shooting buddy, "Lucky"
Jim Frost, in the 1980s.

Now known as "Stompin' Tom," 1968.

Steve, Tom and Gerry

Leaving Calgary, there were now three of us on the road. We were heading east to Toronto, and while the going was slow with a lot of walking most of the time, we did get two or three very long rides, one from Medicine Hat to Regina, which, at that time, on the road was about three hundred miles.

The guy who gave us this ride was a travelling salesman. And when he let us out in Regina, he told us to go to his house when we got to Winnipeg and tell his wife and other relatives that he sent us. He said he'd probably be home a couple of days after we got there and asked us to wait until he arrived. About three or four days later we were knocking on his door. His wife answered. After hearing our story she invited us in, introduced us to some of the relatives and gave us a bite to eat.

It soon became plain that a part of this family were stage and circus people, and within the next couple of days we had met a magician, a juggler, a little hunchback woman and a comedian. They also did a little bootlegging on the side. Every couple of days some farmer friend of theirs from out of town would drop by to make a delivery of some very fine moonshine. With so many people coming and going, there was a party every night.

With beer and moonshine they kept me singing and playing. And when this motley crew weren't dancing, they themselves were entertaining. When the comedian wasn't telling jokes, the juggler juggled and at one time the magician even made the little hunchback disappear.

Steve, who was already quite good at some minor sleight of hand, was particularly interested in the card and coin wizardry of the magician. He even got the guy to show him some new tricks and soon added them to his own repertoire.

Gerry, who was also a good singer and played the guitar, would often spell me off from time to time. This worked great until one time he started playing and all of

271

a sudden he began to bark like a dog. This apparently was the result of a post-hypnotic suggestion given to him earlier when he was hypnotized by the magician.

All in all, we had one hell of a time for about three days and three nights. The house was going all the time and except for an hour's catnap here and there, nobody was getting any sleep.

On the fourth day, when the salesman hadn't come home yet, we decided to leave. This didn't sit too well with the little hunchback, who had taken quite a shine to the three of us. She was crying some when we left.

About 12 o'clock that night we arrived at the Kenora police station. The two cops there were having their lunch. In exchange for a few songs, they gave us each half a sandwich and a cup of tea. Next morning, we were aroused by a couple of cops who had now come in for the day shift. These guys were none too pleasant. You might say, downright grumpy. As they told us to scram, you'd think they'd just been called in to kick us out of the Royal York Hotel or something. What a difference between them and the guys who were on duty the night before.

The next two or three days were rather uneventful, until finally, in Kakabeka Falls, an elderly fellow picked us up and drove us into Thunder Bay.

He took us home and had his wife cook us up a big feed. After supper we played some music and did a lot of talking. He liked us quite a bit and gave Steve an old banjo he could no longer play because of his arthritis. It wasn't in very good shape. The strings were old and the neck was warped, but Steve accepted it anyway. Next morning we left Thunder Bay, heading east. Three guys, a guitar and a banjo.

Somewhere that day, on the way to Nipigon, we landed back in the doldrums. The rides were no hell. We were walking a lot, and conversation was at a bare minimum. Just as Steve was saying, "It's hardly worth hitchhiking at all," an old panel truck came chugging by and Gerry was the only one who stuck out his thumb. As the truck pulled up in front of us and stopped, we all ran up to open the door and hop in.

Gerry sat in the front with the guy and Steve and I sat in the back seat area. There wasn't really a back seat, just a couple of blocks of wood and a piece of some kind of machinery.

As soon as we got in we looked at each other, and we all had exactly the same thought. This guy looks exactly like Elmer Fudd, the guy that's always after Bugs Bunny, that "waskily wabbit," in the movie cartoons. He even talked like him.

Just as he finished saying it was a "bad woad for wides awound here," I said, "Your name wouldn't happen to be Elmer, would it?"

I'm sort of sitting behind him, and Steve is on the other side. Well, Steve broke up when I asked if he was Elmer. The driver had the very same way of talking and, of course, I was acting dead serious when I asked him if he was Elmer. He said, "No" and asks, "Why?"

I said "Well, you look like a guy that I met somewhere before or some guy I saw." He took us about fifteen miles and he never caught on the whole time to what I was talking about. I supposed maybe he had never seen the cartoon. I now began to get into everything I could think of that might have been said between Elmer and Bugs. "Do you like rabbit stew?"

"Wabbit stew," he says, "Yeah. I weally like wabbit stew."

"You must like hunting rabbits, then," I said, as I thought of Elmer always shooting at Bugs with his big shotgun.

When I saw he was still not catching on, I even started calling Gerry Marks "Bugsy." The driver didn't know our three names, and I was saying how appropriate I thought our buddy's nickname was and asking him if he felt comfortable sitting up there in the front seat with such an exceptional driver. "What do you think, Bugsy?"

Poor Steve, he couldn't breathe. He was lying down in the back of the truck, laughing so much he got himself full of grease. Gerry's face was beet red as I kept on with this until finally he let us out.

As soon as the truck and the driver headed down the road we all broke into wild, hysterical laughter.

I don't think I ever saw Steve laugh so hard in all his life. I think he laughed for a whole day. This "Elmer" guy was answering everything just as straightforward as you could get, and the boys knew exactly what I was up to, but it was all they could do not to laugh. If that guy had only known, he would have killed us. But we were only young fellows having a bit of fun. And besides, it sure cured our doldrums.

There were millions of rides in all those years and you always met somebody different and it wasn't altogether uncommon to frequently have strange and funny things happen.

While it took us more than a week to get to Toronto, the trip was fairly routine. We slept in cabins, boxcars, used cars, empty buses, jails, train stations and often beside the road. When we had a couple of dollars we bought mustard, baloney and a loaf of bread. And when we had no money, we ate just whatever anyone would give us. That might be anything from a good home-cooked meal to a few raw potatoes and turnips taken from a farmer's field.

By the way, the old banjo even came in handy to get us a good meal one day. When there was nothing else to do, Gerry and I, who both played the guitar, began to poke fun at Steve carrying that "stupid old banjo" that he couldn't even play.

He got so mad on several occasions, he threatened to wrap it around a tree if we didn't shut up. We'd cool it for a while and then wink at each other and start again.

One day when we got to either New Liskeard or Haileybury we were glad he hadn't smashed it. We went into a restaurant to offer our services of scrubbing the floor, washing the dishes or doing whatever job there might be in exchange for a meal. Unknown to us, and sitting right beside the cash register, was a pawnbroker having a cup of coffee. When he heard our request, he offered to buy one of our instruments.

Well, with too many potential meal tickets still left in my guitar, I certainly wasn't about to part with it. But the banjo, that was another story. So all eyes fell on Steve. After driving a hard bargain, he finally got $4 for it and we were eating again. While the owner of the restaurant really went out of his way to give us special value for our money, I seem to recall Steve asking me and Gerry, "Well, what do you assholes think of that stupid old banjo now?"

Gerry and I looked at each other as much as to say, "I don't have the foggiest idea of what he's talking about, do you?"

We both then looked at Steve. We all smiled and just kept right on eating.

When we arrived in Toronto we looked up Gerry's brother, Hal. I think he'd been working at a dry cleaner's and had just been laid off. When we found him, we all went with him to collect his final paycheque.

He had one little room with a double bed, and for two or three nights we all shared it. Hal hadn't seen Gerry since he went out west with me two years before, and it seemed like they wanted to spend some private time together.

As Steve and I began to realize this, we both began to make our own plans. The thing was, his plans were not the same as mine. And on the third day when Gerry and I came back to the room with a few groceries, and I asked Hal where Steve was, he said he was gone. "Gone where?" I said.

"I think he said he was heading back to Saint John. That's all I know." With that, Hal went down the hall to go to the bathroom. Gerry looked as puzzled as I was and couldn't figure out why Steve had left on such short notice.

After that I left Hal and Gerry alone to make their

own plans. I hung around Cabbagetown for a couple of weeks, sang and played at two or three jamborees, and then decided to head west again. As the rides are so much more plentiful when you're alone, it only took me one day to go to North Bay, and by the next afternoon I was in Englehart. Though my plan was to go out west, my next ride helped me to decide otherwise.

The driver was going to Kirkland Lake so I decided to go there, too. As I was sitting in the back, singing, he began to tell me about all the bars in Rouyn, Quebec. He said he often went there for a good time on weekends because the town was wide open.

"With the way you sing and play," he said, "you could probably get a job anywhere."

Well, by the time we got to Kirkland Lake, he had me convinced. I stayed the night at his place and in the morning I was movin' on to Rouyn.

Playing in Rouyn, Quebec

By noon that day I was in Virginiatown, and there the pavement stopped. I walked on the dirt road for about four miles till I came to a very small place called Kearns. In a small garage with one old gas pump, there was a guy working on a car. I asked him for a drink of water and how far it was to Rouyn. He said it was about thirty miles, but twenty of it was all twisty and nothing but gravel. "It's all woods," he said. "And very little traffic in the middle of the week. And I wouldn't really chance it if I were you, if you're walkin'." I thanked him for the advice, but proceeded anyway. About a mile down the road I came to the woods, and the guy was right.

It was a small, narrow and bumpy road. I could practically reach up and touch some of the limbs of the trees, and a lot of the corners didn't even have curve signs on them. I walked for about three hours and still no pavement. What was even worse, there was still no traffic. I had walked about fifteen miles from Kearns and not one single car had come through.

I was just beginning to think I'd have to walk all the way when this big stake truck came rolling by. After choking me with dust, he put on the brakes, stopped, and picked me up and drove me to the outskirts of Rouyn.

It took me less than fifteen minutes to walk from the outskirts of Rouyn to the corner of the main drag, which was Perreault Street and Rue Principale. It was now late afternoon, about 5 or 6 o'clock, and not knowing which way to go from there, I walked into the first hotel I came to. It was called the Royal.

The lounge (or more precisely, the drinking room), would hold about two hundred people when packed. The tables were small and round, the floor was of a cheap marble-like finish, and there were booths all along one side. Just inside the front door and to my left was the stage.

At the back of the stage was a heavy curtain that

277

covered the plate glass window, which faced the street. There was a small bar at the far end of the room from which two waiters were carrying drinks. The one bartender was serving everything from bottled beer and draft to hard liquor.

The room was not quite a quarter full, and except for two guys sitting at one table speaking English, everyone else was speaking French. As I walked to the back of the room towards the bar, I noticed the bartender didn't look a day older than myself, though the regulations required him to be at least nineteen or twenty.

"Oui, monsieur?" he said, giving me the once over.

"I'm sorry, but do you speak English?"

"A little bit," he said. "What can I do for you?"

When I told him I was looking for a job playing the guitar and singing, and therefore wanted to see the owner or the manager, he said, "Oh, that would be my father, Mr. Perron." And immediately opening a door to another room, he went to get him. In a moment he came back with his father, who was a greying man of about fifty, and quite tall. He spoke very good English.

"My son tells me you sing and play the guitar, and that you are looking for a job?" he said, eyeballing my rather dusty western shirt and black cowboy hat. When I nodded and said I was, he said, "Well, first I'll have to hear you. Go up on the stage and do your stuff. My son will turn on the mike for you." In another five minutes I was up singing.

After several numbers and lots of good applause from the patrons, Mr. Perron called me in the back and hired me. The pay would be $5 per night for six nights per week, plus a room in the hotel. "We don't have any band playing here at the moment," he said, "but if you know lots of songs and can bring in lots of customers, you may be just the guy I am looking for. Besides, the people are good tippers around here and you should be able to make yourself another $5 or $10 a night. Now go on out to the bar and I'll tell the boys to give you a couple of beers while I find a room for you and figure out your working hours."

Back at the bar I learned that not only was the bartender a son of Mr. Perron, but so was one of the waiters. I seem to remember their names were Roger and Ernie.

They proved to be very nice guys and we soon became friends. One of them loaned me $5 and after I had a couple of beers and a sandwich, they showed me to my room. By the time I dusted off my pants, had a good wash and put on my other western shirt, which I had wrapped around my guitar, it was 8 o'clock and time to play.

As I walked onto the stage I turned on two mikes, one for my guitar and one for singing, and let go with Hank Snow's "I'm Movin' On."

The house, which was still about a quarter full, gave me polite applause. Next I went into "Jambalaya" by Hank Williams and everyone applauded with more enthusiasm. Then I really tore into a Wilf Carter song called "Take Me Back to Old Alberta," which has a lot of difficult yodelling in it, and every face began to turn towards the stage. Everyone stopped talking and began to applaud right in the middle of the song. By the time it was over, I lost any nervousness I might have had before, and I knew I really had them.

At the end of my first set, they gave me a standing ovation and at every table there was a beer waiting for me.

Everyone who came in that night stayed, and the tips were really flying. Along with other yodelling songs, I must have sung "Take Me Back to Old Alberta" about ten times that night. And on the weekend the place was packed with everyone wanting to see and hear "Le Cowboy de l'Alberta."

This made Mr. Perron very happy. He had to hire two or three more waiters and even raised my pay to $40 a week. This enabled me to buy some shirts and a couple of pairs of black jeans, which I sorely needed.

Things were going very well for the next four or five weeks till I began to experience one drawback: over 90 per cent of my audience spoke French, and I couldn't sing any French songs. At this point, Mr. Perron came up with a solution. He brought in a local band from Evain, just outside of Rouyn, to back me up. The leader of this trio, Yvon Auger, knew the words to a lot of French cowboy songs. The other two members were Raymond Pilon and his sister Marguerite. Yvon played flat-top, Ray doubled on lead guitar and fiddle and Marg played the piano.

This arrangement worked out great until the night of the big fight. It all started with a few of the boys who were arm-wrestling at one of the back tables. As most of the talking and yelling was in French, I never did understand how it all got started, but it sure ended in a big free-for-all. Just about everybody was into it, including the women.

Several tables and chairs had been thrown and smashed and glass was flying everywhere. It only lasted for about ten minutes, but you'd think a war had taken place by the time it was over. Six or seven guys were laid out and carried out, and just about everyone had somebody's blood on him if it wasn't his own.

As for the band, one of our main instructions was to keep on playing if and when a fight should break out. And tonight, our ability to follow these orders was being tested to the very limits. Ducking the flying bottles and purses was only the mild part.

At one point, two big guys had hold of another guy right in front of the stage; one had him by the feet and the other had him by the head, and after two or three swings they let him fly towards the stage. As we all ducked down, or stepped out of the way, he went right over our heads and into the curtain behind us. The force broke the plate glass window behind the curtain and out he went, into the street, curtain and all.

As he was struggling to find his way out of the curtain, the police paddy-wagon drove up, and a couple of cops got out. They didn't even bother to try to get the guy out of the curtain. They just tied a big knot in one end of it and threw the whole works in the back of the wagon and took off.

When the fight was finally over, half the waiters kept serving booze to the customers, while the other half began the job of cleaning up. So far the band hadn't missed a note. There were even some people watching and listening to us from the street, through the window that wasn't there.

About an hour later, a couple of carpenters showed up with some plywood and boarded up the window, the boss's son came out and strung up another curtain, and not counting the blonde wig still hanging from one of the chandeliers, the place was almost back to looking "normal."

The band members each got an extra $5 in their pay envelope that week for what the boss called an "extra effort." We called it danger pay, something we would rather do without.

The following Monday the glass in the window was restored and everything was again running smoothly. Almost too smoothly. Our French singer, Yvon Auger was beginning to get a swelled head. This caused a great deal of dissension in the group and we had to split. Marg left the band as soon as the arguments started. A few days later Yvon took off and left me and Ray to finish out the week.

When Mr. Perron found out what was happening, he tried to get us a French singing replacement. When he couldn't find one, he tried to find a band which would incorporate Ray and myself, but again he was unsuccessful. He then had no alternative but to hire another full band and let us go. Incidentally, though Ray Pilon and I never played together again, we've always remained friends, even up to the present time.

While our band was still together we called ourselves the Midnight Train Gang, and besides playing the Royal Hotel through the week, we played for dances in other towns on Sunday nights. It was on one of these nights that we played a town called Duparquet and there I met a lead player who had just lost the singing half of his duo and was looking for another one. His name was "Gene" (Luigi Groulx), from Thurso, Quebec, and he was now stranded in Duparquet playing for a few tips at the Radio Hotel. (By the way, Walter Ostanek, Canada's Grammy-winning polka king, is from Duparquet.)

Another excellent lead guitar player who was floating around Rouyn at the time was Lloyd Wagner. When I lost my job at the Royal, I asked him to form a band with me. When he refused, I thought of Gene Groulx and went to Duparquet. From there, Gene and I teamed up, and as I had a little money, I bought us both a bus ticket to LaSarre.

For the next week we played each night between the sets of a larger band at the LaSarre Hotel, and on one of these nights we spoke with a guy who owned the hotel in Amos, a town about sixty miles east of LaSarre. He said he liked our music, and because his hotel was small and he couldn't afford much more than a duo, he thought we would work out just fine. So he hired us.

We played about two weeks in Amos at $35 each per week, until the owner lost the hotel in a wild poker game and the new owner immediately brought in a new and larger band. Gene and I then loafed around for a week until we picked up a job in Malartic.

While we were playing there, we got a phone call from the guy in Amos who said he had just won his hotel back in another poker game. He asked us if we wanted to come back and play. We told him we would think about it, but by the end of the week when we were finished playing Malartic, we moved on to Val d'Or.

As the reader will remember, I was unable to speak French, so it was my partner, Gene Groulx, who was doing all the negotiations. He also knew a few French songs that he would attempt to sing on stage, but he was not very good. Only his guitar playing was up to par.

In Val d'Or we played for a couple of months, alternating between the Dumont Hotel and the Ritz. After that we both went to Senneterre, and that's where we parted company. Gene ran into a friend of his from Thurso, and after a week or so more of playing he decided to quit the music and go back home with his friend.

With my negotiator now gone, I found it harder to land a job in that part of the country, and because it was now mid-winter, I decided to head back to Toronto where it was a little warmer.

First I went back to Val d'Or to see a travelling salesman I had met a few times while playing in the hotel. And as he was always going back and forth from Val d'Or to Ottawa, I thought I might catch a ride with him instead of paying the money for bus fare. Besides, I had a big suitcase by now as well as my guitar, and to be hitch-hiking away up here in the snapping cold with all this extra baggage didn't make much sense. My salesman friend told me it would be another day or so before he was leaving again. So I booked myself into the hotel and waited.

Two days later we left. By noon that day we had a couple of beers and a meal in Maniwaki, and two or three hours later we arrived in Hull and crossed the bridge to Ottawa. He said he still had a half an hour or so before his designated appointment, so he drove me out to the highway going to Toronto, and there I thanked him and said goodbye.

Because the sun had been shining all that day and the weather was comparatively mild, I had decided to hitch-hike instead of taking the bus. And besides, I wanted to save as much money as I could to get a room in Toronto instead of going to the Sally Ann with all my newly acquired junk.

So far my luck was holding out. It was about 4:30 in the afternoon, and although I stood on the road for another hour or so, I wouldn't find out today just how heavy that damn suitcase really was. That would come tomorrow.

The first lift I got took me right down to Perth, Ontario, a distance of about a hundred miles, There I got a cheap hotel room for the night and a sandwich to eat before going to bed. I think the whole thing cost me less than $5.

As I dozed off to sleep I remember thinking how great it was to be hitch-hiking with enough money in my pocket to buy a hotel room for the night instead of sleeping outside or in jail. But when I thought of working at jobs other than music, I came to the conclusion that maybe jail was better. As I began to wonder why there was so little opportunity in this country for people to pursue a career in music, I dropped off to sleep.

The next day I checked out and went to a restaurant to have a good breakfast (little did I know I was really going to need it). When I walked out on the highway the morning was nice and clear.

I got a ride for about ten miles and the driver let me out. He was going up another road. I didn't get another ride after that for about three hours. The wind came up and it started to snow. And did it ever snow.

It also began to get cold and I had to start walking to keep warm. That's when I began to find out just how heavy that suitcase could get. I couldn't see a thing ahead of me, and with both hands occupied, I couldn't prevent my damned hat from blowing off, especially when a truck went by.

The snow was so thick I couldn't see the cars coming and they couldn't see me, either. Even a bus I tried to flag down didn't see me and just kept on barrelling through. Although the snow was getting deep along the side of the road, I had to walk as close to the ditch as possible, for fear I might get hit.

Several times when my arms just couldn't take the weight of the suitcase any more, I'd stop and just sit down on it. When I got too cold and covered with snow I'd pick it up and start walking again. As the walking distance got shorter and the sitting spells got longer, my desperation brought me to only one conclusion. Throw the damned suitcase away or freeze to death sitting on it.

In a few minutes I had a couple of shirts wrapped around my guitar, an extra pair of socks and shorts and my razor safely tucked away in the pockets of my jacket, and after heaving the suitcase and all the rest of its contents in the ditch, I started walking briskly down the road.

About fifteen minutes later I was feeling warmer; the snow storm was letting up and the sun began to shine. A guy picked me up and drove me as far as Kaladar. From there I got a lift to Marmora and had to walk some more. By the time I arrived in Peterborough late that night I was already slumped over sleeping in the front seat of a guy's car. When I asked him if he would be kind enough to take me to a hotel that wasn't too expensive, he pulled up and let me out at the King George.

When I got inside I don't even remember who gave me the room. I just went upstairs, opened the door and fell on the bed. I must have slept like a log, because it was after 10 o'clock the next morning before I woke up. I had a quick wash, grabbed my guitar and headed down the street looking for a cheap restaurant. Soon I was back on the highway to Toronto, never dreaming how prophetic the last twelve hours had been. For how was I to know that in eleven or twelve years from now I would play at the same King George Hotel in Peterborough, walk in as an entertainer known as Tom Connors and walk back out as "Stompin' Tom."

Blind Charlie in Toronto

In Toronto I got a room on Parliament Street in Cabbagetown. The rent was only $5 a week and they supplied a one-burner hotplate for making tea or heating soup. I went out to a grocery store and brought back some canned goods, a jar of mustard, a pound of baloney and a loaf of bread.

There was no use buying anything that wouldn't keep. I knew, for instance, that I would have to buy a little meat every day. And the loaf of bread I always hung on a nail in the middle of one of the walls, so the mice couldn't jump up and get at it. Now I had to scrounge around town to see what was going on and find out if perhaps I could play my guitar somewhere for a few bucks once in a while.

In the afternoons I began to hang around Fred Roden's music and saddle shop on Queen Street, where a number of country musicians would always sit around and jam.

Some of the boys I met there were King Ganam, Chef Adams, Yodellin' Bob Gillin, Wally Dean, Cliffy Short, Reg Bartley, Brian Baron, Bob Regan, George Pasher, Smokey Powers and a host of others too numerous to mention. As a matter of fact, I soon found out there were a hell of a lot more country musicians in Toronto than there were places for them to play.

There were several jamborees going on every Sunday night which could only hire a limited number for a very small amount of pay, and the night clubs that hired bands on a weekly basis were limited to the Horseshoe, the 300 Club, the Famous Door and Duffy's Tavern.

As winter began to turn into spring, I couldn't afford my room any more. The only jamboree I could get to play in every Sunday night was at the Polish Hall on the southeast corner of Dovercourt and Queen Street. Although I went over very well there, Johnny Elash, the guy who was putting on the show, would not pay me more than $2 per night, and that was if he paid me at all. I think he still owes me $6 or $8. On the nights I didn't get paid it was especially discouraging because after walking from Parliament Street to Dovercourt, a distance of about three miles, just to play the jamboree, I would then have to walk home again empty-handed. This was around the time when I couldn't afford to pay my rent, let alone ride on the streetcar.

It was around this time I began to call myself Hank Spur. And around town, in the music circles, everyone knew me as Hank. I tried to join a band that was being formed by Brian Baron, but I could only make it to one practice, as he and the rest of the group lived a long way out of town, somewhere west of Long Branch.

Another group I actually played a couple jamborees with was the Mullins Brothers. There were Johnny and Ernie, their sister, and a couple of others, most of them from Nova Scotia.

By this time I was staying at the Sally Ann, where the doors were locked by 7 P.M. If you were out rehearsing till after that you just didn't get in.

I did get a job as a single on a couple of weekends, playing at the Famous Door. The owner would pay me $5 at the end of each night, and because it was always too late to get into the Sally Ann I would buy a flop-house bed somewhere for seventy-five cents or $1. These places were usually filthy and if you didn't mind the strong smell of cockroach spray, and a few loud screams in the night, you could get a few hours sleep. One other story which comes to my mind from that time involved a blind guy by the name of Charlie. He played the lap steel guitar and was also staying at the Salvation Army Hostel. I had spoken to him a couple of times when I saw him carrying his steel around, but I had never heard him play.

I was wandering along College Street one Saturday afternoon and passing by the 300 Club, I decided to pop in to see the manager and ask him what my chances were for playing in his bar. He said a couple of guys had just quit on him the night before and he would need another duo for the following week. As he also had no music for that very night, he told me that if I was to show up with another guy by 8 o'clock we could play the whole evening as a sort of audition. The least he would do was to pay each of us $4 for the night and if he felt we were good enough he would hire us for the next week at $5 each per night.

I thought of calling Johnny Mullins, but I didn't have the dime. I then thought of Charlie, the blind guy, and immediately beat my way back to the Sally Ann in hopes of catching him there.

About 6 o'clock Charlie came wandering in from an after-supper stroll and I began working on him. I use the term "working on him" because I knew it might be hard to get him to stay out later than 7 o'clock as that would mean he would lose his bed.

"C'mon, Charlie, do it," I said. "We're gonna make $4 each tonight and I'll get us a bed later with the money. Besides, if we get hired for next week we'll each have $30 by this time next Saturday. And who knows, we may even get hired for another week again after that?"

By about half-past six I had him convinced, and up the street we went with our guitars. The distance we had to walk would be about two miles, and we needed to get there in plenty of time to set up. So at approximately ten minutes to eight we approached the 300 Club, with me walking about three steps ahead, carrying the instruments, and right behind me came blind Charlie, just a white-canin' 'er.

When we got inside we went directly to the stage and began setting up. By the time I got Charlie's steel plugged into the amp and a chair for him to sit on, the manager came out from a little door beside the bar at the other end of the room and shouted out the playing time. "Twenty minutes on and twenty minutes off," he said. "And pay for all your drinks. We don't allow the musicians to run up a tab."

As I tested the mikes, I knew that could only mean one

thing. The quick beer that I was going to split between me and Charlie was going to have to wait. We were both dead broke.

It was about two minutes after 8 when we finally got started. On the songs that Charlie knew, he could play pretty good, but on the ones he didn't know, he was pretty bad.

So after the first twenty minutes we sat down at a table and decided on what to play the next time up. As most of the songs we both knew were slow, I had to tell him to stop playing when I sang some of my fast ones. Charlie was also a bit nervous, so I told him not to worry as there were only a couple of tables with people sitting at them anyhow. There were actually about five or six, but without being able to get us a beer to relax with, I figured he'd be better off not knowing the difference.

As we were talking, the waiter came over to our table and asked us what we wanted to drink. "We'd like a beer," I said, "and I know it's against the rules, but couldn't you just trust us till the end of the night? We have no money now but the boss is going to pay us $4 each later on and we'll pay you then."

"No dice!" he said. As he turned around to leave, I said, "How about a plain old glass of water then?"

"You'll find lots of that at the bar," he said. And he walked away.

As I was coming back from the bar with two glasses of water, one of the customers said, "Where in the hell are you going with that? First time I see the entertainers drinking water."

When I told him the full nature of the problem, he took me back to the bar and said, "Give this guy a couple of beers on me. You don't expect him to sing on water do you? And here's enough for a couple more when he's done with those."

As I thanked the guy, the waiter and the bartender gave me a dirty look, but I just ignored it and headed for my table. We only had time for one quick sip and then we got back on the stage.

A few more people came in, listened for a moment and sat down. By the end of the second set we were getting some mild applause. While we drank our much-appreciated beers I explained to Charlie how I had come by them. This brought on a big smile, the first I'd seen all day. And he played much better when we hit the stage for the third time.

As more people came in, the more applause we got, and while we didn't set the world on fire, I figured we were holding our own. By the end of the night, more people were buying us beer and some of them were inviting us to sit at their tables.

After the last set of the night, some even expressed the hope that we might be back next week, but I soon found out it was no-way written in the cards.

While some of the customers were still drinking up, Charlie and I packed up our guitars. And while he sat down to finish his last beer, I went up to the bar and asked for the boss, as I wanted to get paid. The bartender said, "Just sit down for a while, and when all the people have gone, the boss will be out to pay you."

"Fine," I said. As I finished my beer I told Charlie we would have to wait for a while, and when I saw the last customer go out the door I again headed for the bar. By this time there were several waiters and two bouncers standing at the bar when I asked the bartender if I could see the boss. "The boss has gone home," he said rather abruptly.

"Gone home?" I repeated. "Well, did he leave any money for us?"

"No!" was the unconcerned reply.

"Why?" I said, as I began to feel quite agitated.

"Because he said you were no goddamned good and you didn't deserve to get paid."

Well, he no sooner said that when I bolted for the little door beside the bar. I figured the boss was in there because I had seen him go in not more than five minutes before.

When I struck the door to open it I found it was locked, and immediately the two bouncers had hold of me. As they pulled me away from the door, it opened and out came the boss. "Throw the prick out," he was shouting. "He's no f——— good anyway." As I squirmed and wrenched to get free enough to hit the son of a bitch, a couple of waiters joined the bouncers and before I knew it I was given the bum's rush. They carried me the full length of the room and while the extra waiter opened the door, they tossed me right through it. As I picked myself up off the sidewalk with the intention of bashing my way back inside, the door quickly opened again and Blind Charlie came flying out on top of me.

With both of us now all tangled up on the sidewalk, they threw our guitars out behind us. And with a final "Get the f——— out and stay out!" they slammed the door.

While poor Charlie began to whimper, "What are we going to do now, Tom?" I hammered on the door a few times, but it was no use. As I checked the guitars and found they were all right, except for the tuning, I reassured Charlie that I would try my best to coax the night man to let us in when we got back to the Sally Ann.

I couldn't bring myself to tell him that our only other alternative was to sleep in jail.

It was nearly 2 A.M. when we arrived at the hostel and I could see through the glass of the front door that the night man was dozing inside his little wicket. When he woke up at the sound of my pounding he just waved me off and tried to ignore me. I kept pounding and he kept waving and shaking his head.

Finally, when he saw I wasn't going to take no for an answer, he came to the door and without opening it he demanded that I tell him what I wanted through the glass. But as I tried to tell him the story he just shrugged, went back inside and disappeared from view.

I just kept on pounding and pounding until the night man came back. He gave me one more wave to stop as he picked up the telephone to show it to me. I knew it meant he was going to call the police, but I just kept on pounding. Pretty soon a cruiser pulled up and out jumped two cops. "What's going on here?" one of them wanted to know.

When I told him what had happened at the 300 Club and he saw that Charlie was blind and really shook up, the cop made a sign to the night man to open the door.

"I don't have any beds left for them," the night man said, after the cop indicated that he should take us in. "Well, let them sleep on a bench or on the floor some-where. They've been through quite an ordeal already tonight. And besides, I have no intention of locking a blind man up for doing nothing but asking to come in out of the cold. And as for this other fellow, he didn't leave him stranded out there somewhere on the street, so why should you?"

With that, the night man let us in and took us to a room where we slept on a couple of benches. In the morning we were awakened by one of the Salvation Army officers and given a meal ticket for breakfast. He said he was sorry about what had happened the previous night, and that he wanted to have a talk with us in his office after we ate.

During breakfast I told Charlie how sorry I was about the way things turned out. And even though he still appeared somewhat shaken up over the whole thing, he smiled again and said he understood.

After breakfast I walked him upstairs and took him down the hall to the office door. There I shook his hand and said goodbye. "Aren't you coming in?" he said.

"No," I said. "It's time again for me to get rollin' down the road." As I walked down the hall and looked back he was just going into the office. And that's the last time I ever saw Blind Charlie.

From Gaspé to the Maritimes

About a week after leaving Toronto I was in Mont-Joli, Quebec, on my way to Matane, on the south side of the St. Lawrence River. Three guys who had been drinking picked me up on their way to a party. They couldn't speak English and I couldn't speak French, but they sure liked country and western music.

I had been singing in the back seat and when we arrived in Matane, they each gave me $5 and made me understand they were paying me to go with them.

Right away, I said, "*Oui*. Okay." And I figured to myself, if these guys are that free with their money, I should be in for a good time. And I was.

We soon pulled up to a house on the outskirts of town. And we no sooner got inside when they were getting me a beer and asking me to take out my guitar and start singing. Then they were on the telephone and holding it near me so the people on the other end could hear. Within an hour the house was full and everybody was ready for a good time.

As I sang, everybody smiled and listened intently, even though I was sure they didn't understand most of the words I was saying. By the time I drank half of each beer several guys were vying for the honour of opening me another one. About 10 o'clock, just when everyone was getting really happy, the door opened and in walked a guy carrying a fiddle case and a little bag which contained several mouth-organs. The whole gang now let out a roar and made it very plain that they were glad to see him. They gave him a beer and brought him over to meet me. I recall his name was Jacques.

After listening to me play for a few minutes while he finished his first beer, he took his fiddle out and indicated he was ready to tune up. I gave him an E! A! D! G! And after a few short twists on the keys he put the bow to 'er, and did he ever play.

Some of the tunes he played I hadn't heard since I was

a kid back in Skinners Pond. As I kept the rhythm with the guitar, and he kept smiling approval, the crowd were clapping and banging their feet and two or three couples were swinging around the kitchen.

By this time I was really getting into it all. The enjoyment was really contagious. I hadn't seen so many people having such a good time in a long while.

Another thing I found so great about playing with Jacques was that he could accompany my singing so well. It didn't matter whether he was playing the fiddle or the mouth-organ he was equally adept at both.

Between 12 o'clock and 1 A.M. that night they began to run out of beer. But it wasn't long before they had a fresh supply brought in by a friend of theirs who owned a hotel. He stayed and had a couple of beers himself and before he left he came over to me and shook my hand. "You're a good singer," he said to me in English, "and the people here like you very much. They have secretly taken up a small collection for you and they have asked me to present you with it." With that he took a small bowl from one of the guys who had brought me there and gave it to me.

I stood up and thanked everybody very much with my best "*Merci beaucoup*" and all hands applauded.

As I sat down and put the money in my pocket without counting it, a couple of girls began passing around sandwiches. But the party was by no means over. After the guy who owned the hotel left, a couple of the others began to tell some jokes. When one good-natured fellow tried to explain a couple of them to me in broken English, I laughed like hell to make him feel good, but I didn't understand a word he was saying.

Everybody was having so much fun by that time I guess it didn't really matter anyhow.

As soon as the dishes were put away, out came the fiddle and away we went again. One woman asked me to sing "You Chicken Eye." When she saw the blank look on my face she began to hum a line or two of the melody.

We both laughed when I finally caught on and started to sing it. The song she wanted to hear, but couldn't pronounce the title, was "Your Cheating Heart."

Then there were more fast numbers and lots of yodelling. I indicated to Jacques that the "Saint Anne's Reel" was my favourite old-time tune and he not only played it on the fiddle but did every bit as good a job of it on the mouth-organ. By 4 o'clock that morning everyone was still swinging and dancing although some were now bumping into chairs and tables as well as into each other.

When everybody finally staggered out the door to go home it was after 5 o'clock. The last guy remaining was one of the guys who had brought me there in the first place. He was still smiling and asking me to sing some more songs as he opened us up one last beer before going to bed. About half an hour later he showed me to a little room at the top of the stairs, shook my hand again, and said goodnight.

I closed the door and immediately dug into my pockets to count my money. I had $51 altogether. The collection had been $36 and the rest was the $15 the boys had given me in the car. I felt like a millionaire as I crawled into one of the most comfortable beds I had ever slept in, and before going to sleep I knew I had enjoyed myself to the fullest, and that this had been one of the greatest parties ever.

Nobody bothered to wake me the next day and I didn't come downstairs until about 3 o'clock in the afternoon. At the kitchen table were three or four guys drinking beer and they offered me one. As I was drinking it the wife of the guy who owned the house made me some bacon and eggs and toast. After I ate and sang another half-dozen songs a couple of the boys drove me out of town to another little place about seven or eight miles east of Matane. There they thanked me for coming home with them the night before and let me out.

About two or three days later I was looking through

the hole of Percé Rock on the far east coast of the Gaspé Peninsula.

A day later I was in New Carlisle and was invited to another party almost identical to the one in Matane. There were fewer people, but they also had a fiddle player and took up another collection by passing the hat. This time I made about $22 and the following day, one of the guys who had been at the party drove me down to Campbellton, New Brunswick.

It was almost a week later when a French couple picked me up just outside of Shediac. They had relatives they were going to see in Cheticamp, Cape Breton Island, and that's where we arrived about 10 o'clock that night.

It took me almost three days to get to Sydney by way of the old Cabot Trail and then another day to get to Port Hawkesbury and back to the mainland, Nova Scotia. For most of the next month I hitch-hiked just about everywhere in Nova Scotia from Ecum Secum to Halifax and Lunenburg, and from Liverpool, Shelburne and Yarmouth around to Digby, Annapolis Valley and back to Truro, Springhill and Amherst.

By the first of July that year, 1954, I was back in New Brunswick, hitch-hiking from Moncton to Saint John. I was thinking about going out west again, and I thought I'd stop by and see if Steve was home and find out if he wanted to go with me. I knew he hadn't been to British Columbia yet and he might still have the desire to go.

Jeremy and the Pies

When I got to Saint John, Steve was nowhere to be found, but a mutual friend told me he had gone to Montreal. He left a message that, in case I came around looking for him, I should go to Moe's Lunch on Dorchester Street in Montreal and they would be able to tell me where he was.

Meantime, I ran into an Irish fellow in Saint John by the name of Jeremy. He hadn't been over from Ireland very long before he wound up broke. He said he had some relatives in Montreal, but had no way of getting there. I told him I would be hitch-hiking there and he was welcome to join me if he wanted to. He had never hitch-hiked before, but because he was desperate he decided to give it a try.

As I was also broke at that time, I decided to go up to King's Square and take out my guitar and do some singing. Once we had a crowd around, I got Jeremy to pass the hat and then hightail it out of there.

In those days, doing this sort of thing was against the law. And if the police caught you doing it they could lock you up for panhandling. So one had to be very careful.

By the time we had about a dozen people standing around, Jeremy passed my cowboy hat and collected about $2 in change. Just about then I spotted a cop coming towards us and we took off on the double.

By the time we were out of the park the cop gave up the pursuit. That night we stayed at the Sally Ann and the next morning we left town.

During the next couple of days, I was explaining to him some of the dos and don'ts as I often did with guys who were on the road for the first time. For example, when you are begging for food, it's better for one guy to go by himself. Whether it's a remote farmhouse or a bungalow on the main road, the last thing the person opening the door wants to see is a delegation of bums.

Even if there are only two of you hitch-hiking, best you take turns to knock on doors.

Anyway, me and Jeremy were going down the road one very hot day when we came up to a farmhouse to ask for a drink of water. It was his turn to ask and we both got water without any problem. He didn't mind asking for water but he didn't like asking for food. A little later when we came to another farmhouse and he knew it was my turn to ask, he kept nagging about how hungry he was. As was the plan, Jeremy was going to wait at the road, and if they invited me in, I'd signal to him, and we'd both enjoy the banquet.

If the lady of the house happened to say, "Oh, I didn't know you had a buddy," or "I didn't know there were two of you," then I would come back with "Oh, yeah, I forgot to tell you he was out at the road." Which usually brought a response of "Oh, well, sit down anyway and we'll give you both a sandwich." After agreeing to feed one person, it was hard to refuse two. So that's the way we got in.

But on this particular day, it was one of those farmhouses where the big end of the house is in front and then there's a kitchen built on the back. So you walked around the big part of the house and then there was maybe about three feet in to the outside wall of the kitchen.

So as I came around the edge of the house by the side of the kitchen, I had to pass by a pantry window before I got to the door.

Just as I was about to knock I saw this hand come out and place two lemon meringue pies on the windowsill. They were just hot out of the oven. The woman was setting them in the window to cool off.

I took a look at the pies, took a look at the door, and another look at the pies, and wondered whether I was going to knock and ask for a sandwich or not. The pies looked awfully good. The temptation was too great. I thought I might not get a piece of pie at all if I asked.

So I reached up, took the two plates off the windowsill and hit for the road. The pies were warm and smelled really good. I said to Jeremy, "C'mon, let's go, I hit the jackpot. Here's yours, here's mine." And we jumped over a fence where there was a hill down into a gully with a brook running through at the bottom.

We went down over the hill and sat there on a rock eating the pie. I can still hear Jeremy saying, "Beautiful —I think this is the greatest pie I ever ate."

We were sitting there lickin' our lips and lickin' the plates when Jeremy said, "See that rock across the river? I bet you I can hit that with this plate."

He was just about ready to throw it when my light bulb went on. I had an idea. "Just a minute," I said. "I don't think you should do that. This woman was good enough to give us these pies and because I went and asked, the least you could do is wash the plates in the brook over there and take them back and thank the lady."

Jeremy agreed that would be a good idea. So he started washing the plates and making them nice and clean while I did everything I could to not look at him so I wouldn't burst out laughing. On the way back up the hill, he said, "Geez, that sure was a kind lady, and those pies were some good, weren't they?" "Just absolutely delicious," I said.

Now, there was a bit of a woods in front of the house so they couldn't see us coming or going from the house. When we got up to the gate he said, "Are you coming in?"

"No, I'll wait here. You just run the plates in and thank her and then we'll get going."

"Okay," he said. And in he went, plates all nice and clean. He had them in one hand and went up to the door. I was just getting over far enough to see around the corner of the building so I could watch him knocking on the door. Big, big knock on the door and a big smile on his face as he's getting ready.

A great big strapping farm woman opened the door. She was mopping the floor with one of those great big mops with real long stringy hairs on it. Without saying a word, she took the mop and gave it a swing and wrapped it right around his head until it came around and tied itself in a knot on the other side.

Jeremy dropped the plates and was trying to run, but didn't know what direction to go. He couldn't see. The mop was covering his face and she was kicking him in the arse as she pulled back and forth on the mop. He was all arms and legs and he didn't know where in the hell he was going.

Finally, the mop came off his face and now he could see. But he was still wondering where the road was. He got the legs going, but still she continued to chase him, hitting him over the head with the mop.

When he got out to the gate I was lying down in the ditch, laughing. I was just out of it altogether. He came out and looked at me and said, "You SOB, I never want to see you again." He was all wet and full of soap suds and you could see the marks of the mop all over him.

He went up the road, but I was too weak and I couldn't get up. I must have stayed there about twenty minutes laughing. Finally, I thought I had better go and apologize to him. He had turned the corner in the road and kept on walking. I couldn't see him until I turned the corner. There he was sitting on the milk stand at the next farmer's gate. I thought, well at least he's waiting for me. So as I got up to him, I was thinking to myself, "Geez, I've got to say I'm sorry and that I didn't mean it. It was kind of a dirty trick, and above all, I'd better not laugh."

So I was trying to get my face straightened out and trying not to think about it. He was sitting there staring right across the road with his feet dangling down as I approached. When I got up to him I had my face straightened up and everything was under control, that is, until he looked at me. And when I saw that glare and thought of what caused it, I fell into the ditch again.

That was it. He took off up the road and for another fifteen minutes I just couldn't get over laughing. It had to be the funniest thing I ever saw. When I finally got out of there and caught up to him, he was walking really slowly. I started hollering at him for about a quarter of a mile, "I'm sorry, I'm sorry."

Every time I said I was sorry he walked a little faster. But, eventually, he forgave me for it. So we carried on. I said I thought he would have done the same thing to me had he thought of it first. After calling me all the names under the sun, he not only agreed he would have done the same thing to me, but he promised he would cook up one of the damnedest tricks to pull on me sometime when I least expected it.

Fortunately for me the rest of the trip was uneventful, and Jeremy never did get to play his trick.

When we got to Montreal we went to Moe's Lunch to enquire about Steve. The waiter said he had been there and gone again, but that he would be back in about a week. He then let Jeremy use the phone to call his relatives and in no time they were there to pick him up.

As he was leaving the restaurant, he came over and shook my hand and said with a wink, "I don't think I'll bother to tell my friends all the details of my first hitchhiking trip with a Canadian." We both laughed and wished each other luck, and that's the last I ever saw of him. But from that day till this, I always have a good chuckle every time I think of Jeremy and the pies.

To Ville Marie with Maurice

While all this was going on, the waiter from behind the counter had been talking in French to a fellow named Maurice who was sitting on one of the stools. Maurice had apparently lost his job sometime before, and not having any money to get back home to Ville Marie, Quebec, he found himself in dire straits. His room had run out the previous night and without a place to stay he didn't know what he was going to do.

Just then the waiter called me over and told me the situation. As I had just come in off the road from hitch-hiking, he wondered if I might have a solution or at least some advice for the guy. It seemed that although he had never hitch-hiked before, he was considering it.

When I found out the guy could hardly speak one word of English and most of his four-hundred-mile trip to Ville Marie would have to be through the province of Ontario, I told him I'd take him there. I also told the waiter to tell Steve where I was when he got back, and that it would probably take me a week or two before I returned, as the total distance was about eight hundred miles. The waiter then gave us a couple of streetcar tickets and we rode the tram out to the west end of the line. From there we started to hitch-hike.

The first ride we got was by another French guy who couldn't speak English, and the two of them were now talking up a blue streak. From the gist of the conversation I knew they were talking about me and everything was very complimentary. The tone of Maurice's voice indicated how grateful he was that I would go so far out of my way to see that he would get home. They both seemed to be surprised that an English guy would do this. And when we got out of the car the driver gave Maurice a $5 bill and wished us well on our trip.

Though we walked for the next hour, Maurice appeared quite happy. He had $5 in his pocket and I guess he figured this hitch-hiking business was a real snap. We must have been having a real stroke of beginner's luck because we only got two more rides and we were in Ottawa. And during each ride we were given two more dollars.

It was around 10 P.M. when we hit Ottawa and Maurice began to make signs that we should spend our money on a cheap room for the night. This was going to be a real test of our new-found friendship. I knew the money we had left would come in handy for eating in the next few days in the event there was no more forthcoming, so I made him understand that he should follow me and keep his money in his pocket. As long as he thought I was going to perform some kind of miracle, he remained quite content. But when I marched him up to the police station I had one devil of a time to get him to go in. He thought I was trying to get us both arrested.

He started walking back down the street in the opposite direction with me behind him trying to explain that I had done this sort of thing many times before and that the police would let us out first thing in the morning.

He still wouldn't believe me until I assured him that there would be a French-speaking officer inside and if there wasn't, we wouldn't stay. He finally came in with me and I asked for a policeman who could speak French to my buddy so that he would understand the nature of our request and to explain to him that we would not be locked up permanently.

The first officer we came to was bilingual and before long he was smiling and talking to Maurice, who by now was telling the whole story.

When we were finally shown to a cell, we were also given a couple of blankets, which in my experiences was very rare. When we finally settled down to go to sleep, Maurice was still shaking his head. I guess he just couldn't believe he was really in jail.

When they let us out in the morning, he let out a big sigh of relief and he began to smile again, at least once in a while. When we went to a little restaurant, he seemed quite disturbed at how little I'd ordered us to eat. After a fried egg sandwich and a cup of coffee, he was again looking at the menu when I indicated it was time to go. He wasn't at all pleased. I also had a hard time making him understand that any money he had in his pocket belonged to both of us and that the same thing applied to me.

Up until he finally got my point, he believed he could spend "his" money on whatever he chose. It didn't seem to occur to him how unfair it would be for him to stuff himself at every lunch counter along the road with the money he considered to be his own, and then expect me to buy him something with the money I had left after his was gone. At first, all this was a little strange to him. But after a couple of days he began to see the logic of it all.

He didn't seem to mind sharing the food and sandwiches I would beg from the farm people along the way. But one time after I sang in the back seat of a car and the guy passed him a dollar, I had a hard time convincing him it was meant for the both of us.

On the morning of the fifth day out from Montreal, we were just leaving North Bay. We had spent the night in jail again and just had enough money in our pockets for toast and coffee. We then headed out for Temiscaming and were facing what was about to be our hardest day yet. The distance would be no more than fifty miles, but we had to walk more than half of it.

We slept on the side of the road that night and finally, at the crack of dawn, an old jeep picked us up in the middle of nowhere and took us into Temiscaming. The driver then told us if we wanted to wait around for a couple of hours, he would take us right on up to Ville Marie. When we considered it was still another forty or fifty miles through the wilderness, we had no problem making the decision to wait.

We didn't meet one car on the whole trip, and if we hadn't got a ride in the jeep we might not have made it at all. We went through potholes, mudholes and washboards and by the time we got out I felt like I'd been operating a jackhammer all day. The one good thing about it, though, was the fact that our driver was bilingual and Maurice was beginning to feel at home at last.

When we got to Ville Marie we walked about a mile out of town till we came to his parents' farmhouse. I can't describe how happy they were to see him. He had two younger sisters who were about fourteen and sixteen. And everybody was hugging everybody and even I eventually got in on the act when they began to understand why I was there. It was plain to see this was one very tightly knit, happy family.

Although they weren't too prosperous, they were very kind. And each time Maurice would recount some part of his recent journey, his mother would get up and hug me again. She stuffed me full of food and hardly let me get away from the table. I sang some songs for them and when I suggested the next day that I would have to leave and go back to Montreal to see my buddy Steve, they wouldn't hear of it. They had invited some close friends to come to their house that night for a welcoming home of their son, and they wanted everybody to meet me.

Attending the party was a guy who spoke some English and in between songs everybody had a number of questions they wanted to ask me. I don't think there was ever another interpreter who was kept quite so busy as this one.

The following day when I insisted on leaving, Maurice's mother gave me a big bag of sandwiches, and with a tear in her eye, she gave me another big hug and a kiss on the cheek. She must have thanked me about ten times as I got into a pick-up truck with Maurice and his father, and she was still waving as we drove down the road and out of sight.

Maurice's father had advised me not to take the road back from which I came and drove me north around Lake Timiscaming to New Liskeard, Ontario, a distance of about thirty miles. With a few more thank-you's and a couple of handshakes, I said goodbye and headed back to Montreal.

In less than two weeks from the time Maurice and I started out, I arrived back at Moe's Lunch, where Steve was waiting for me.

That night we were put up by a couple of Steve's friends, and the next day we were heading out west again. Only this time we were resolved to go right to Vancouver.

El Toro in Thurso, Quebec

It **was around** the first or second week of August when Steve and I left Montreal. Within the last two weeks I had hitch-hiked the road from North Bay to Montreal twice on the south side of the Ottawa River, and I now suggested we take the highway on the north side, through Quebec, as far as Hull, and then cross over into Ontario.

Besides, the Quebec highway would take us through the town of Thurso where my old friend Gene Groulx was from. You will remember he was the guy I played in hotels with up around Val d'Or the previous winter.

The first night out of Montreal, after a lot of walking, we managed to get as far as Lachute. On the second night we arrived in Thurso. As it was very late we decided to go to the police station first. And then on the following day we would try and find out where Gene Groulx lived.

When we got to the police station, the cop informed us that the jail was across the street attached to the fire hall and proceeded to take us over and put us in. Well, when we got there and the cop left, we had a pretty good laugh. The cells were made of wood. Yes, just good old-fashioned two-by-fours. And the doors were practically falling off their hinges. While the cell doors couldn't be locked, the cop locked the fire hall doors before he left and said he'd be back around 7 o'clock in the morning to let us out.

After we were there about half an hour we decided we were hungry. And as we still had a dollar between us, we decided to "break out of jail" and spend it. In no time we were out one of the windows and up town having a hamburger and a coffee. As soon as that was over we returned and "broke back into jail." After having another great laugh about this, we finally went to sleep on our wooden bunks. When the cop came back to let us out in the morning, he was none the wiser. He was smiling and we were smiling, though obviously for different reasons.

That day we found Gene Groulx's house, but Gene wasn't there. His dad said he was now in Montreal, but because he had often spoken of me, we were certainly welcome to spend the night. They gave us a good meal and afterwards, I played and sang.

By early evening Gene's older brother and one of his friends dropped in and after a little while they decided to take me and Steve up to one of the hotels for a few draughts. Well, we hadn't even finished our first one when a French guy who obviously wanted to start some trouble tapped me on the shoulder and in broken English wanted to know why I was wearing a stupid cowboy hat. He suggested it must be because I thought I was tough. When I told him it wasn't because I thought I was tough, but that I was wearing it because I liked it, he went back to his table. The only trouble was, the table he went back to had about twenty guys or more sitting around it. They were all his friends, and they were egging him on.

At that point I would have preferred to leave, but the waiter had just dropped us each another draught and Gene's brother had already paid for it. I no sooner got the first sip of the second draught into me when the guy was back. This time he punched my shoulder rather roughly and said, "If you don't tink you tough guy, why you don't take off you stupid f——— hat?"

I said, "I'll take off my hat if the waiter tells me I have to take it off. So why don't you go and ask him about it?" With that, the guy left again and went back to talk it over with his friends.

I was now becoming quite disturbed that Gene's brother and his friend had not said one word to this intruder. They had obviously drunk here before because they knew the waiter on a first-name basis, so I was beginning to wonder if they were chicken or something.

At any rate, I said to them, "If that guy comes back here again and bothers me one more time, I'm going to nail him." I also told them that we'd better drink up and go somewhere else. I hardly got the words out of my mouth when the guy was back for the third time. With even more confidence than he had before, he gave my shoulder another jostle and said, "I tink you'd better take off dat f——— hat now. Because I tell you."

Well, this time he got the surprise of his life. I came off the chair with a backwards haymaker that caught him right in the throat and knocked him back to his own table. By the time he got there, I was right behind him and gave him a couple more dandies right in the chops. I upset the big table on some of his friends who still hadn't had time to get up off their seats, and when two guys made for me from this side of the table, I hit one of them with a chair and knocked him into his buddy.

At this point one big fellow picked me up off my feet, but before he could do anything I got my thumb in his eye and gave it a gouge. When he let me go, I jumped over the bar and started throwing bottles. Just then the bartender and one of the waiters rushed me from behind and got a hammerlock on me and dragged me down a back hall and threw me outside. Somehow my hat got jammed in between my neck and the bartender's arm, and as I landed outside, the hat fell out the door with me. As the side door of the hotel had now opened, and a bunch of the guys started pouring out, I was going over a fence and running like hell down an alley. I then made my way back to Gene Groulx's place and hid outside until Steve and the others came back and everything had blown over.

When we finally got in the house and Gene's father heard the story, he opened up a bottle of Cointreau he had been saving and gave me a big shot. As we all had a few drinks and the excitement of the evening began to fade, I asked the boys where they were while the fight was going on. They told me that when I made my move, there were so many tables and chairs upset that they all got pinned against the wall and therefore isolated from the action. Besides, everything had happened so fast that everybody was stunned. And by the time they had a chance to do anything, it was all over and I had disappeared.

At this we all had a great laugh and polished off the bottle of Cointreau.

Next morning Steve and I left Thurso and headed for Ottawa.

Steve and the Meat Cleaver

At Hull, Quebec, we crossed over the Ottawa River into Ontario and headed west to North Bay. Instead of hopping a freight west this time though, we headed straight north to Cochrane and west to Kapuskasing and Hearst.

On a late August afternoon we entered Hearst in the back of an old station wagon with two guys who worked in the bush. The first place we landed was in the hotel. After they bought us a couple of draughts, they wanted to hear some more singing. I told the guys to go and check with the management to see if it was all right and when they came back with the okay I started.

There was hardly anyone but us in the hotel. And after drinking for a few hours, I began hinting around about getting the boys to buy Steve and me a sandwich or something. We hadn't eaten all day and the beers were starting to take a hold, especially on Steve. I noticed he was beginning to get giddy and starting to slur his words. At this point, one of the guys got up and said he was going next door to the Chinese restaurant to get us a couple of cheap rooms for the night, as they also rented rooms upstairs over the restaurant.

The plan was that he and his buddy would sleep in the one room and they'd let me and Steve sleep in the other. After the rooms were secured, we were going to have a few more draughts and then go to the Chinese restaurant and have a good meal before going to bed. The guy then decided to take Steve with him to show him which room was going to be ours.

The plan sounded great, but it didn't work out very good in the end. As a matter of fact, it turned out to be a real mixup. In the first place, it was a Chinese woman who showed them to their rooms, and when the guy paid for them, he signed his own name for both of them and decided to leave the keys at the cash in the restaurant. When Steve and the guy came back, we were having a

311

few more draughts when who walks in the hotel but their boss. He was mad as hell that they hadn't checked in with him when they arrived in town and he'd been looking all over for them.

He now insisted they drop whatever they were doing and head out with him to the camp so they would be there first thing in the morning. One of the guys whimpered something about having a room next door, but the boss said, "To hell with it. Get off your ass and move it. We're leaving right now."

As they got up from the table, they left their draught and a couple of dollars sitting there and took off, pronto.

Steve and I finished our draught and went next door. With the couple of bucks we grabbed off the table, we decided we'd have something to eat and then go up to bed. After a couple of hot hamburgers, I was finishing my coffee, when Steve decided to go up to the cash, pay for the meal and get the key for our room. That's when all hell broke loose.

There was a Chinese man now on duty instead of a woman and he wanted to know where Steve's name appeared on the register. Of course, it didn't. And the argument started. Steve tried to explain that another guy had paid for him, but the little old Chinese guy not only rejected the explanation, but he wouldn't give an inch.

As I figured myself to be a little more sober than Steve at this time, I thought I would be able to go up and eventually explain all this. But for now I was finding the whole thing rather amusing and decided to wait a little longer to see what was going to happen.

"The room's paid for," Steve was saying, "and I want the key." But when he was asked, "What numba yo' loom?" he didn't know. "So-o-o?" the Chinese guy said, "how come you pay fo' loom an' you doh know la numba?" Steve said, "I didn't pay for the room. Another guy did."

"Well, when ulla guy come, I give ulla guy loom.

Because you no pay, I no give you klee fo' loom. Zat's all, now you go."

With that remark, Steve lost his cool. He reached over the counter and grabbed a handful of the Chinese guy's shirt and shouted, "Are you gonna give me that god-damned key or not?" At this the Chinese guy broke loose with about half a shirt and started running for the kitchen with Steve right behind him.

Now the setup of this restaurant had a single row of booths along each side wall and a double row of booths down the middle. This allowed for an aisle on each side of the room. The kitchen door was through the middle of the back wall and the doors swung back and forth.

In the kitchen itself there were a couple of big wooden tables in the centre with lots of room to walk around them. So this was the scene when the "chase" began.

Steve chased him in the kitchen. They ran around the tables a couple of times and back out through the swing-ing doors and up the other side of the restaurant towards the cash. They both grabbed the cash register in making the turn and spun it around a couple of times. They then headed down the other side of the restaurant and back into the kitchen. Around the tables they went again and back out through the doors for another trip around the restaurant.

The Chinese guy's determination to stay several steps ahead of Steve was making his face white, and Steve's determination to catch him was making his face red. There were a couple of guys in a booth on the other side of the restaurant who were just killing themselves laugh-ing, and so was I.

All of a sudden there was a change in the situation. After going around the tables in the kitchen a couple of times, the Chinese guy got his hands on a big meat cleaver. He then turned around and headed for Steve, who now decided he better start running the other way. Out through the swinging doors they came again and up the other side of the restaurant. It was obvious that Steve had forgotten where the front door was, for as he got to the cash register, he just grabbed it and spun it around the other way again and headed back for the kitchen.

The Chinese guy by this time was beginning to look an awful lot like the "Old Maid" wielding her dust-mop on the jar of Old Dutch Cleanser. His face was now turning red and Steve's was now turning white. By the time they came back out of the kitchen and around the cash register once more, I threw out an arm as Steve was going by and wrestled him down into the booth and then turned to face the Chinese guy who was hollering, "Lemme hit him, lemme hit him, Cheezes Klice, he luin my lestaulant, I kill la plick."

"Take it easy," I said, "you go and call the police and I'll hold him here until you get back." I was only trying to buy some time, and when he ran in the back to make the phone call, I grabbed my guitar, and Steve and I got the hell out of there.

It didn't take him too long to realize that he had been tricked. But by the time he got back out to the front of his restaurant with the meat cleaver, we were turning down an alley. When we got about three blocks away, we found an old woodshed in someone's backyard and stayed in there on a couple of old broken-down chairs for the night.

It occurred to us that we might have stood some kind of a chance by staying around the next morning and explaining our situation to the police. But given that this was only a one-cop town and that he would probably remember us as the two bums he told to get out of town a couple of years ago when we came walking in on the railroad tracks, we decided we'd better be on the highway before daybreak.

We were, and by noon that day we were in Geraldton.

From there on it took us about a month to get to Calgary. We had decided in Portage la Prairie, Manitoba, to take a more northern route than we had taken on our last trip, and this brought us into Yorkton, Saskatchewan.

From there we took a lot of minor highways to Prince Albert and back to Saskatoon. Then on to Rosetown, Alsask, and into Drumheller, Alberta. We were still bent on spending the winter in Vancouver, but as it was only the first of October when we arrived in Calgary, we figured we still had plenty of time on our hands. This assumption, however, was wrong. Once again fate stepped in, and Steve was not going to get to see British Columbia.

I remember saying as we rolled into Calgary that afternoon, "What do you think, Steve, it's only early in the day yet. Why don't we just walk to the other side of town and head for B.C?" Had we done that, everything would have worked out according to plan.

But Steve said, "Naw, what the hell, Tom, let's go to the Sally Ann. We'll try to get a meal ticket and a bed for the night, and after a good rest we'll strike out tomorrow."

"Okay," I said. And off we went to the Salvation Army. We got our meal ticket and a bed all right, and we were just ready to settle down for the night when our plans began to change.

The Woodpecker's Watch

A s Steve was coming from the washroom, I noticed his attention was drawn to a guy on the other side of the dormitory. Soon he was sitting on the guy's bed and listening to his hard-luck story. The guy had apparently driven a car from Toronto out to Calgary and for some reason, the deal went sour. The owners didn't pay him the amount of money they were supposed to pay him and now he was just about broke and trying to figure how the hell he was going to get home. Finally, Steve brought him over to talk to me with a promise that "we'll see if we can't do something about this."

He said his name was Eddie Van Overbecker, but I just couldn't resist calling him "Eddie Woodpecker." He was about three or four years older than we were, kind of lanky and a bit wimpy. As he sat on my bed and started telling me the story, I said to Steve, "Well, it's up to you. If we don't need to get to Vancouver this week, or this month, let's take him back to Toronto."

"Oh, will you? Will you take me back to Toronto? Oh, that's great. What are you driving?"

"We're not driving anything," I said.

"You got money?"

"No."

"Well, how are you going to take me back to Toronto?"

"We're going to hitch-hike back."

"Hitch-hike?"

He wouldn't hear of it. "Well, you want to get back to Toronto, don't you?" I said. "I mean, we just left Montreal a few weeks ago and we're hitch-hiking to Vancouver, but we'll take you back to Toronto and then we'll come back and finish our trip. So do you want to come, or don't you?"

"Hitch-hiking?" he said.

"Yes, hitch-hiking."

Well, we finally talked him into it.

But by the time we got him to Winnipeg I was starting to wish we had never taken him in the first place.

With this guy everything was a problem. He incessantly complained about the weather, and when his feet weren't sore it was his head or something else that was hurting. He was either tired, thirsty or hungry and never stopped crying about no rides and that we'd never make it back to Toronto. And on top of all this, everything was our fault.

He was also wearing this very expensive watch his wife had bought him. At that time it was around eighty or eighty-five bucks I think he said, which in those days was a lot of money. So once when he was crying about food, I suggested, "Why don't you hock your watch and then when you get home maybe you can send back the pawn ticket with the money and get the guy in the hock shop to send it down to you?"

"Oh, God," he said, "if I ever reach Toronto without this watch my wife would kill me."

I said, "Well, don't be yapping about your empty stomach then."

We finally got him down as far as Dryden, Ontario, where we went to the cop shop and got them to put us up for the night. It was back in the basement where we had often slept before. But they didn't want to put us in the cell, as they were expecting they might have to bring somebody in that night. Instead, they gave us some newspapers and cardboard and told us we could sleep on the floor over near the furnace.

About an hour later a little plan began to form in my mind, one that might teach "Woodpecker" a lesson and give us a few laughs besides.

At any rate it was a plan that was too good to resist. Now as Van Overbecker was always the first one to go to sleep, I got looking at his watch. Steve said, "Tom. I don't like that look in your eye—you're up to no good. What have you got on your mind now?"

I slipped the watch off his arm, took his shoe off, put the watch on his ankle and pulled the sock up over the watch. Then I put the shoe back on again and laced it up and tied it. After about an hour of snickering together,

Steve and I finally went to sleep.

The next morning the "Woodpecker" woke the both of us. You could hear the goings-on and the crying and the bellyachin'. He wanted to know who stole his watch. I told him a couple of bums had come in earlier in the night and as they had gotten up and left before we woke up, they probably had his watch half-way to Vancouver by now. Not taking my word for it he searched the place high and low, thinking he might have taken it off before going to sleep. When he still couldn't find it, he said, "Are you guys sure you didn't steal my watch?"

"Come on, we're your buddies," I said. "Search us—we haven't got your watch." After searching us thoroughly, upside down and inside out, he was satisfied we didn't have his watch. And, of course, how could we have it when he had it himself?

Going down the road, all he talked about was that watch. He was cryin' and moanin' the blues and he'd sit down on the side of the road and tell us how mad his wife was going to be when she found out he'd lost it. Between snickers, Steve was nudging me once in a while, asking me when I was going to tell him where the watch was. I said, "I'm not telling him anything. While his mind is on his watch, he's not yapping about everything else."

Anyway, I let that go for about twenty-four hours and he still didn't know that he had his watch on his ankle. Finally, during the afternoon of the following day, when I couldn't stand his whining any longer, I asked him what he would do if he didn't have his watch to complain about. "What would you cry about then?"

"Nothing," he said. "Absolutely nothing."

"Well, what would you say if I told you I know where your watch is?"

"You got my watch!" he started to shout. "I knew you had it all the time."

"I haven't got your goddamned watch," I said firmly. "I told you before, I haven't got your watch. And neither has Steve."

"Well where is it then?" he asked. I said, "Look, you stupid suck, nobody's got your watch but you, and you've had it all the time. It's on your goddamned ankle."

When he finally discovered it, he got this happy, stunned look on his face and without a thank-you or anything else, he said, "Gee! That's funny, I can't remember putting it on there."

With that, Steve started laughing his ass off, and I just shook my head and walked down the road.

Sometime the next day it was suggested we split up. The rides were no good with the three of us and the going had become unbearably slow. Some cold October weather had set in and we had only gone sixty miles in the last two days and, of course, the Woodpecker was back to his whining.

As Steve and I knew that Van Overbecker would have to go with one of us, we decided that Steve would take him as far as Thunder Bay, where we would all meet at the train station (whoever arrived first would wait for the other party to get there), and then I would take him as far as Nipigon. And there we would change again, etc., until we got him back to Toronto.

Well, to this day, I don't know exactly what happened, but the last time I saw them together was in Ignace, Ontario. I got to the train station in Thunder Bay and hung around for three days waiting for them, but they never showed up. I didn't even go to see my Italian friend or try to play on the radio for fear of missing them. Finally figuring they must have gotten a ride right through and took it, I proceeded on my easterly trek.

The next time I saw Steve I asked him what had happened, but he also couldn't explain it. He said he and Van Overbecker arrived in Thunder Bay and also waited for a couple of days and then left for Toronto. It's odd that we didn't see each other somewhere on the road as we passed in a car, but I guess that will always remain one of the mysteries of my hitch-hiking days.

At any rate, Steve finally got the Woodpecker back to his wife in Toronto and our mission was accomplished.

Visiting My Mother

As I still wondered if Steve wanted to spend the winter in Vancouver, I thought the best way to make contact with him again would be to go back to Moe's Lunch in Montreal and just hang out for a while until he showed up.

By the time I got to Montreal, it was about the first week in November and nobody around Moe's had heard anything from Steve. So I told the waiter there that I would call in from time to time as I would be either at the Salvation Army or just looking for a place to hang my hat. And if Steve showed up in the meantime, tell him that I'm around.

Now, since I last saw my mother in Saint John when I was fourteen, each of the first couple of times I came through Montreal I tried to contact the woman for whom she had given me a phone number.

The woman had said she didn't know where my mother was, and later on, with all my drifting around, I lost the number. Consequently, during my last few trips to Montreal, I had no idea where I might find her. But on this trip, it was going to be different.

I was looking through the phone book one day, and as I was just browsing I came across the name "Ezekius." It occurred to me that this was the name of the people who lived on a farm north of Montreal where my mother took me when I was only five or six years old. And because this name was so uncommon that there were only one or two of them in the whole book, I decided to play my hunches.

At the first number I called they didn't know what I was talking about. But at the second number a very grouchy old lady with a northeastern European accent answered and said she didn't know where Isabel was living, and then quickly added the correction that she didn't know anyone by the name of Isabel anyway. She then hung up the phone very abruptly. I was now certain that this was the woman I had met many years ago as a child and I made up my mind to go and see her. I wrote down the address and started asking people how to get there. When I found it was going to be a very long walk, I waited till the next day before starting out.

It was about 3 P.M. next afternoon when I arrived and knocked at the door. When Mrs. Ezekius answered, I knew right away we had met before. While at first she wanted to close the door on me, she soon relented when I told her I was once that little boy who ran away with her husband's horse and wagon when they lived on the farm. She now believed I was Isabel's lost son and invited me in.

We sat and talked for about two hours, and in this time she was able to give me enough leads to find out where my mother was living. She wanted me to stay to meet her husband when he came home. But as I had a long walk back, I told her I would try to come and see them sometime when I found my mother. I then thanked her for all her help and left.

Within another two days, I was knocking on my mother's door.

I had found out she was living in the top storey of a rooming house on Park Avenue. Outside her door was a little mailbox with a card in it which read: Mrs. I. Connors. When I knocked there was no answer, so I sat on the top step and waited. After about half an hour I heard her voice as she spoke to someone down on the second landing, so I went down to meet her.

"Can I help you with your groceries?" I said, as she started up the second flight of stairs. When she looked up and saw who it was, she shouted, "Oh, my God! Tommy! How did you get here? How are you? Where have you been?"

"Here, let me have your bags, Mom," I said, "and I'll tell you all about it when we get inside."

As she opened the door we entered a fairly large multi-purpose room, with a small kitchenette off to one side and a door which led to a small bedroom. As I sat the groceries down on the table, she was talking a blue streak and asking a million-and-one questions.

She made some tea and we talked. Then she made some supper and we talked some more. In the early evening she sent me down to the little grocery store, which was only next door, to get us three or four quarts of beer, and then we talked till way on into the wee hours of the night.

With so many years of catching up to do, we just kept jumping from one subject to the other. Neither one of us had a chance to answer one question when several more were already on the table.

It was about 4 o'clock in the morning when Isabel finally got a couple of blankets and made a bed for me on the couch. She said she was working in the kitchen of a restaurant about three or four blocks away and wouldn't have to be in until Monday. As the following day was only Saturday, we wound up talking for that whole weekend. She then insisted that I stay around for a while. Which I did. And I didn't leave again until the following March.

To summarize what had happened to her over the years since the Children's Aid took my sister and me away from her, it seems the first thing they did was incarcerate her in some rehabilitation centre in New Brunswick. After a few months she escaped from there, found out what orphanage they had put me in and came to visit me before running away to Montreal, where she figured she had a better chance to hide. (The reader will be reminded of the day she met me in the woods at St. Patrick's Orphanage in Silver Falls and told me to remember her thumb and the small birthmark on my neck.)

She then had two more little girls, which the authorities took away from her shortly after I discovered her walking with them in Saint John. She was again institutionalized and finally released. She then came back to Montreal and vowed never to go back to New Brunswick again, although in later years she did go back for a few brief visits.

(As I reflect on my mother's life today, in 1994, I see her doing only what any other natural woman would do in her circumstances. She merely became a victim of the times and the narrow-mindedness of a society devoid of understanding. As far as I am concerned, it was the rehabilitators who needed the rehabilitation.)

After I was at my mom's place for a week or two, I started to get some singing jobs down along "the strip" on Main Street (St. Laurent Blvd.). There was the Saint John's Club, the Rodeo Tavern and a number of others. They didn't pay very much, but it provided something to help out with the groceries. Then I was able to get on to a CHCH Radio jamboree, emceed by a guy who called himself "Tall-in-the-Saddle Destry." This also didn't pay a hell of a lot, but it got me known enough to be able to land a job at the Diana Sweets "candlelight room" restaurant.

This is where the famous Hachey Brothers and Mary Lou always played when they came to Montreal at the time. The pay was really good (more than I had ever made playing anywhere else up to then), and they brought me back for an additional week on several more occasions during that winter of 1954–55. The Blue Angel night club was also on the go at that time and although I appeared once on stage as a guest, I never could land a job there.

While all this was going on, I half expected Steve to come knocking on the door one of those days, but it never happened. I had left my address at Moe's Lunch a couple of times, but either they lost it or Steve just never bothered to call in on his way through.

My mother had a boyfriend around this time, as well, but as his job kept him travelling a lot, they didn't get to see each other too often. When he was in town he'd come to see her mostly on the weekends, and when he wasn't, Mom and I would go and visit some of her old friends on Sunday nights.

On several occasions we went to see Mr. and Mrs. Ezekius, and I was able to renew my old friendship with their son, Tony, and their daughter, Mary. We also went to see another of my mother's friends by the name of Mary, who lived in Montreal North. She had a fairly large family and a son who was around my age; his name was Sonny, and we both got along pretty well. It was at Mary's house that we spent Christmas that year. And as I always took my guitar everywhere I went, we always had lots of singing and parties. And as I said before, my mother knew lots of old cowboy songs and everybody always got her singing them. Just give her a couple of beers and she could sure liven the place up.

On February 9, 1955, I turned nineteen at my mother's place and she bought me a wristwatch. It wasn't all that expensive, but it was the best watch I had ever owned. I was very proud of it, and especially for the thought behind it. Even after it stopped running, I wore it for a long time as a keepsake.

I wrote quite a few songs that winter, and once or twice I even tried to get my mother's boyfriend interested in putting up some money for me to make a recording. He had a good job and could have afforded it. But he just didn't believe that the music business was a viable place to be investing money. I told him I understood and I didn't say anything more about it.

About a month later, I got those itchy feet again, and though my mother didn't want me to leave, I packed up one day, gave her a big hug and headed out for the east coast.

Working on a Tugboat

About the only memorable thing that happened on this particular trip occurred when I was walking late one night somewhere between Rivière-du-Loup and Cabano, Quebec. When I came up to a little house about forty yards off the road I decided, because it was so cold outside, to ask the people of the house if they might let me stay in a small barn they had on the property.

When I knocked on the front door, there were people talking. But when they heard the knock, they immediately turned out the lights and all was silent. Pretending not to notice, I knocked again and said, "Hello, is anybody home?" I wasn't even finished my sentence when the window to my right was quickly raised and out came a gun barrel. A very rough male voice shouted something to me in French and then the gun went off only two feet from where I was standing. It thundered like a .303 calibre rifle and I thought I was dead.

When I realized I wasn't, it didn't take me very long to turn around and hightail it back to the road, while several more shots came whizzing by my ears.

After the run and the very brisk walk I had for the next half hour, the cold didn't bother me at all. I finally got a ride from a guy going as far as Cabano, and when I told him about the incident, he said it would be very wise not to try that again around these parts as there were some very wild characters living around there. From that time on, I always avoided that spot whenever I came travelling through.

It was somewhere around the first of April when I arrived in Saint John, and because I had a little money on me I rented myself a cheap room for a week on Coburg Street. This didn't leave me much to eat with, but I figured I'd get by till I found out if Steve was in town or at least what was going on before I decided to leave again.

The room I rented was away up on the fourth floor of

a very old building, and as I was walking along the landing on my way to the last flight of stairs, a door opened up to a room where there was a party going on. One of the people spotted my guitar, and they asked me if I'd come in and give them a few tunes. I told them I'd think about it, but first I wanted to check out my new room.

About five or ten minutes later, I answered a knock on my door and when I opened it a guy from the party was standing there with a beer for me and asked me again if I would like to join them. My watch said 8 o'clock and as I thought to myself it would be too late now to go and look for Steve, I took my guitar out of the case and followed this fellow downstairs.

For the next couple of hours the beer was flowing pretty good and everybody was enjoying the songs and having a good time. All except for one guy, that is.

This one sort of a burly fellow was getting a little more obnoxious with every beer he drank. He was told a couple of times to watch his foul tongue by the wife of the guy who rented the room, but he just ignored it.

A little later when I stood my guitar beside the wall, to go and get a beer, he staggered against it and knocked it down. When I said, "Hey! watch it, will ya?" he just glared at me for a moment and said, "If you could fight as good as you can play, you wouldn't need that f———— thing anyway."

As I grinned a little, as if to shrug it off, he took a swing at me and missed. So I up and clocked him in the chops and sent him backwards against the wall. In a second I was there to give him some more, but a couple of the other guys grabbed him and pushed him out the door and told him not to come back.

Everybody apologized and asked me not to be too upset about that "asshole," as he was always known to be a trouble-maker and they should have told him to go home before all this happened anyway.

I accepted their apology and agreed to stay and sing for a little while longer, but as I went to pick my guitar up off the floor I found that an electric clothes iron had fallen on it during the scuffle. It apparently fell when the little table it was sitting on got jarred. There was a dent and a small crack in the box of the guitar up near the neck, and, of course, it was out of tune. After a little time, and with considerable difficulty, I got it tuned up enough to sing a few more songs and have a few more beers before calling it a night.

The following day, when I was sober and my ear was a little sharper, I realized the intonation of my guitar was shot. When no amount of tuning or friggin' with it would bring it back, I decided it was time to look for another one. About an hour later I walked out of Joe Gilbert's pawn shop with $5 I didn't have before, and minus my old guitar.

I then went over to Steve's house to see if he'd been home yet. His mother said he'd been home now for a while, but he wasn't in town at the moment. He was working with his father and they had just left town for a few days to do some job out in the country.

After I left there I went down to the unemployment office to see what I could pick up in the line of work. After all, I had no guitar now, and I couldn't think of a better way, at the moment, to get one.

As I walked in the UIC door, who was walking out but an old friend of mine from Rustico, Prince Edward Island. He was just in collecting his last pogey cheque before signing on to a new job. I asked him where it was, and he told me it was on a tugboat called the *Alice Porter*, owned by the Porter Dredging Company who had just got the contract to dredge out the Saint John harbour. He also said he thought they needed more men, and if I was interested, he would take me down to their office.

The following day I walked aboard the *Alice Porter* with my few belongings tucked into an old shopping bag and went up to meet "the old man" (otherwise known as "the skipper") and introduced myself as his new deckhand. After I told him about my sailing experience and found out the watches were eight hours on and sixteen off, I asked him how many mates he had. When he told me one, I asked him if he had a bo's'n yet. And if he didn't, "who was in charge of the night watch or midnight shift?"

"Well," he said, with a bit of a smile, "I guess it will have to be you, until someone better comes along."

"Thank you, sir," I said. "And who's in charge below, on my watch?"

"I don't know," he said, "the company hasn't sent me a man yet. Do you know of anyone who could handle an oil-fired steam boiler?" When I told him I thought I could get him a good man for the job in a day or so, he said, "Okay, I'll see that he gets hired providing you can get him here before the company sends me someone else." With that, I was dismissed and went to meet the rest of the crew. In the back of my mind I was hoping that Steve would take the job when he got back to town. Although I knew he didn't have any experience, I thought that, with my help, he might be able to fake it for a while until he was able to catch on.

For the next four or five days we didn't do too much but run up and down the harbour a few times. The company still didn't have a full crew for the tugboat, let alone the dredge. It was only on the fifth or sixth day that we even pulled the dredge out to do any work, and then it was only for the day shift. I really didn't mind this at all, because all I had to do on night watch, so far, was to tighten or slacken the lines once in a while and keep my eye out for intruders. And I could always go ashore during the day if I liked.

On the fifth day Steve was back in town and I told him about the job and what questions they would probably ask if he came to apply for it. So far they hadn't got anybody. At first he was a little hesitant, but when I told him I could get the four-to-twelve man who had to do the same job to teach him the ropes, he came aboard the following day and got hired.

On the same day, another guy, known simply as "Piece

o' Meat," was also hired. He acquired the name because he was always bragging about how strong and tough he was.

Now, as one of the main functions of a tugboat is to haul the dredge from place to place, all the men on deck are required to familiarize themselves with the use of lines and winches. They must learn how to splice cables and ropes, tie all kinds of special knots and develop a good accuracy when it comes to throwing a "heaving line."

Well, the first Sunday afternoon that I was aboard, we were tied up to the wharf in west Saint John, and I was supposed to be showing some of the inexperienced guys how to make a "monkey fist" at the end of their heaving lines.

Along came Piece o' Meat, and while bragging as usual, he started telling the boys about his expertise in all facets of seamanship. "Can you throw a heavin' line?" asked one of the boys who was doing a little practising.

"Heaving line?" he said, as he flexed the over-abundance of muscle exuding from his T-shirt. "Here, let me see that thing. I'll show you something you have never seen done with a heaving line before in your life."

With that, he grabbed the heaving line, stood up on the side of the tug and gave her one hell of a swing. Just as he let 'er go, the rope got tangled and the monkey fist hit him on the side of the head, causing him to lose his balance.

As everyone began to laugh at the surprised look on his face and his unusual acrobatics, he was…going…gone.

SPLASH!

He fell overboard into the sludge-covered water between the tug and the wharf.

As he came to the surface with oil and grime running down his face and what looked like a condom stuck to his forehead, he was all tangled up in a mixture of seaweed and soggy toilet paper. And as if everybody wasn't laughing enough by now, someone suggested we "throw him a heavin' line."

As we dragged him aboard there were lots more comments like "Geez, Piece o' Meat, that was really great! You'll have to show us how to throw a heaving line like that again sometime."

And someone else said, "Aw, shut up you guys. After all, Piece o' Meat really showed us something we never seen done before in our lives, didn't he?"

But all we heard from Piece o' Meat himself was a bunch of cursing and swearing as he went below to change his clothes.

The next Sunday as Steve and I appeared on deck, everybody's attention was centred on the six- or seven-hundred-pound anchor, which was destined to go aboard the dredge. With bottles of beer in hand, they were all wondering if it was possible for a "good man" to lift it. Then someone said, "It would take a 'good man' to even move it." This last comment, of course, brought Piece o' Meat right to his feet.

"If anyone can move it, even one inch from where it's sitting, he's the best man aboard the tug," he said, and immediately dropped his beer and straddled himself over the anchor.

As everyone took a sip and watched anxiously, he bent over with both hands and grabbed it fore an' aft rather firmly. He then buckled his knees and began to strain. Soon one end of the anchor raised about a quarter of an inch above the deck. And with sweat now pouring down his red face, he dragged it over about an inch, with one end still touching the deck, and dropped it. "Now, gimme a goddamned beer," he said, "and I'll bet you five dollars there's not another man aboard who can move that son-of-a-bitch further than I did."

As each guy in turn tried to move it and failed, I was thinking of some of the extraordinary feats of strength I had seen Steve perform in the last two or three years. I had seen him not only move but actually pick up and carry some logs in the woods that any two other seasoned lumberjacks would not even bother to tackle. As these thoughts ran through my mind, I nudged Steve, who was standing beside me, and whispered "Take a crack at it, Steve. Nice and slow. I know you can do it."

He hesitated for a moment, then looked me in the eye. I gave him one of those special winks of reassurance and a friendly little tap on the shoulder. Then in a voice just loud enough for everyone to hear, I said, "Don't put your five dollars away yet, Piece o' Meat, there's still one more guy here who wants to give it a try."

As Steve bent over the anchor, took his grip and braced his feet, he just paused for a moment to focus his concentration. In that moment Piece o' Meat began to laugh. And thinking Steve had already tried and failed, he said, "Well, it's plain to see who the best man on this tug is." He then kissed his $5 bill and began to laugh some more.

Well, the one thing Piece o' Meat didn't know was that laughing or making fun of Steve Foote was the biggest mistake he could ever have possibly made.

This made Steve mad and more determined than he might otherwise have been. As the smile began to quickly fade on the face of Piece o' Meat, Steve with a slow and steady pull had now lifted the entire anchor about an inch off the deck, and with tiny, shuffling steps he carried it for a distance of about eighteen inches. He then let a great big fart and dropped the anchor.

With a big grin on my face, I said, "A fartin' horse will never tire, and a fartin' man is the man to hire." While everyone was laughing, I went over and snatched the $5 bill out of the hand of a surprised-looking Piece o' Meat and gave it to Steve, with one additional remark. "Here, Steve, you'd better take real good care of her; I've just seen Piece o' Meat kiss her goodbye."

The day after I received my third paycheque, I came aboard the tug with a brand-new guitar. I think it cost me around $60 and from that time on I was playing it every chance I got. Some of the boys didn't even know I played until I started rhymin' off the songs. This came as somewhat of a pleasant surprise to them, and all hands drank a toast to their new celebrity, "Tugboat Tommy."

But, alas! The career of Tugboat Tommy, like that of Hank Spur, was soon to come to a dramatic end. It was only two nights later when the tug was tied up to the dredge, which in turn was tied up to the wharf, that all hell broke loose.

I was over on the dredge, tending to the lines around 4 o'clock in the morning when I heard one hell of an explosion. The tugboat bounced up against the dredge and the dredge in turn slammed up against the wharf, nearly knocking me overboard.

I ran across the dredge, hopped on the tug and darted for the door of the engine room where big puffs of smoke and steam were puffing out in the early morning air. I poked my head in the door and hollered, "Steve! What in the hell is going on?" I couldn't see a damn thing in the smoke- and steam-filled room, so I climbed down the ladder and hollered again. This time I heard Steve holler back, "Come down here, quick, Tom, I think she's gonna blow."

As soon as I found him wandering around in the steam, I got him to show me where the main fuel valve was and I shut it off. Then between the two of us, we found all the other valves and shut them off and headed up the ladder to get some air.

There were only two other guys around that night, and they had both been sleeping aboard the dredge. They were now awake and heading for the tug. I told Steve to go back down to the engine room till I talked to them to see if I could get rid of them. But as it turned out, one of them was a dredge foreman whose authority certainly outranked mine, and as I couldn't keep him from going down to the engine room, I had to tell him what happened.

When he came back up from having a look, I spoke with him again. He said the captain and the company would have to be notified and he was certain that Steve would be fired. After no amount of pleading would change his mind, I saw him back to the dredge and went to give Steve the bad news. We both resolved to leave the tugboat there and then and went to pack up our stuff. A day later, we were back on the road again.

Steve and I in Skinners Pond

After a month or so of rambling around New Brunswick and parts of Nova Scotia, we found ourselves in Port Elgin, New Brunswick, only fifteen miles from Cape Tormentine, where the ferry goes over to Prince Edward Island.

As Steve had never been there before, he suggested that we go over and hitch-hike the length of the island to give him an idea of what it was like, then come back by way of the Wood Island's ferry into Nova Scotia.

Throughout our travels, I had often described how picturesque the Island was, and because he had heard the song "My Home Cradled out in the Waves" that I had written about it and sung so many times before, he could only fancy it as some sort of romantic story-book land. And my recounting of my life as the Huckleberry Finn of Skinners Pond no doubt contributed to that sort of fancy.

At any rate, I agreed to go, but on condition that when we got up to the western end of the Island, I would not be going to Skinners Pond. With that agreed, we headed for the boat, and before too long we were approaching the red capes of Prince Edward Island.

Like everyone else who ever sets foot on the Island, Steve couldn't help but remark how red the soil was in contrast to the little white houses beside the many rolling fields of emerald green. And while it may not have been the story-book land that I had built up in his mind, Steve had to admit he had not yet seen anything in Canada to compare with the exquisite beauty of a landscape with so many quaint settings.

After three or four days of hitch-hiking around the eastern end of the Island, we headed for West Prince and North Cape. The closer we got to Tignish and Skinners Pond, the more I began to wonder how Russell, Marlene and the old folks were doing, and if Cora had changed any over the last five years since I'd been home. I also wondered if her attitude towards me would be different if

I showed up with a personal friend. After all, I thought, hadn't she always been on her sweetest behaviour whenever there were strangers around?

As we arrived at North Cape and looked out over the water, I stood a little distance away from Steve so he couldn't see the tears in my eyes as I tried to deal with the surge of gnawing hunger that only comes from a deep need for a place to call home and a sense of belonging to someone who cares.

I also thought of my mother in Montreal and realized that, even after I stayed with her a few months and got to know her a little better, the ties that normally bind a mother and son, which had been forcibly severed so long ago, must now, sadly, remain forever broken. The long years of separation and grief had taught us both to live and think independently. And now we were two different people from two different worlds.

As I took my eyes off the far horizon for a moment, I looked at Steve. He was now throwing a few stones over the cape. I walked up to him, threw my arm around his shoulder and said, "Come on, buddy, let's go down to Skinners Pond."

When we got to the house, I knocked on the door with my fingers crossed and waited for somebody to say "Come in." Upon hearing the words, we entered, and of course everyone was surprised. Russell and his father shook both our hands and Russell's mother gave me a great big hug. As Cora continued to stand at the far end of the kitchen, I walked over with a big smile. I had the intention of hugging her for the first time, but she just extended her hand, and I shook it.

After explaining to everyone who Steve was, where he was from and what great friends we were, I enquired as to the whereabouts of Marlene. When told she was spending the night at a neighbour's house with one of her school chums, I couldn't help thinking, Boy! That must be great! It certainly wasn't allowed back when I was her age.

About half an hour after the old folks went upstairs, Cora asked us if we were hungry and gave us a sandwich. We discussed our travels and I asked Russell if he could use a little help for a few days. When he said he could, I noticed that Cora made no comment one way or the other. And after a short time, she hinted that it was now time for "everyone" to be going to bed. "You and your friend," she said, "can sleep in your old bed at the head of the stairs. It's still there where you left it."

The next day Russell got us to hitch the old mare and haul in some wood. Later on, I got to meet Marlene when she came home from school and showed me some of her drawings. They were actually quite good for her age and I told her so. I also noticed something I had never seen before. Believe it or not, Cora was also capable of lending lots of encouragement to someone.

Another surprise came right out of the clear blue sky when Marlene asked me if I still stuttered and still said, "Yeah but; yeah but" all the time (all a part of the idiot act I used to have to play to please Cora).

With everyone in the kitchen listening for my answer, I thought fast and said, "Well, I still do once in a while, but I'm gradually getting over it." I'd have given anything to know what Cora was thinking at that moment, but Marlene just accepted it and went on to tell me more about how she was getting along in school. I could certainly see her enthusiasm for it, which was something I never had. (In not too many years after that she became a school teacher).

At suppertime that evening, it was also very noticeable that nobody ever said much. That is, with the exception of Marlene, who talked all the time. And it soon became obvious that Cora was in no way interested in any conversation that might be initiated by anyone else. If Marlene didn't say it, it wasn't worth saying.

With the same thing occurring after supper, I could see that Steve was getting a little bored with all these "remarkable achievements" of an eleven-year-old, so I suggested we go outside for a little walk.

This move, of course, didn't escape the watchful eye of Cora, who, within the next couple of days, slowly began to resume her position of maintaining complete control over all the adults in the house. Whenever Steve and I would come in from work, for instance, she'd make sure there were only two chairs in one end of the kitchen. The one for Steve was always placed on the opposite side of the room from the one in which I was expected to sit.

Then on the evening of the fourth day, as Steve entered the kitchen first, he unthinkingly walked over and sat in "my" chair. The response came very quickly. "That's not your chair, Steve. That's Tom's. Yours is over there."

"Oh, sorry! Mrs. Aylward," he said. "I guess I just wasn't thinking." As he was about to get up I said, "That's okay, Steve. I'll sit over here for a change." And that seemed to be just what Cora was waiting for.

"Well, you never sat in any other chair but that one while you lived here, so why should you do it now?" Without waiting for an answer, she walked into the pantry while Steve and I changed places and just looked at each other. A few minutes later, as Steve tried to make up for the so-called mistake he made, he wound up making a bigger one. As it was always Cora's custom to tell everybody when it was time to "bring your chair up to the table" instead of saying "supper's ready," Steve thought he'd be helpful by putting his chair up to the table now, and then stand around for a minute until he was called.

Just as he brought his chair up to the table, Cora came out of the pantry. "You'll just put that chair back over there, please, until you are told to come to supper." Just then, Russell's mother came out of the living room, and seeing that Steve was in such a dither, she grabbed the chair from him, took it back to the table and said, "If you're hungry, son, just sit down. You've worked hard all day, and you've earned it."

Well, that was one of the worst things she could have done. With an old spark of determination, and a fearless look of silent knowing, she had defied Cora. And somehow I sensed she was rather enjoying it. She purposely avoided looking at Cora, who was now throwing darts at everyone around the table. You could see she was just seething, and she had no intention of letting the matter drop.

While you couldn't hear a fork touching a plate during the meal, I was reminded of the great anxiety I often felt as a kid each time I found myself in her "bad books." It didn't matter how long it took; she always waited till you least expected it, then she'd always get even.

And where was Marlene at this time? Just when some chatter was needed the most? She was up the road again at a neighbour's house.

When supper was finally forced down, and Steve left something on his plate for the first time in his life, we all got up from the table. As the old folks walked into the living room, they were immediately followed by Cora. It wasn't hard to hear how she lit into the old lady with things like "That just better not happen around here again." And "Until you start making the meals around here, I'll be the one who tells people when they can come and eat, and when they can't. So just lay off from now on and mind your own business."

As she raved on, the old folks just sat there and took it. When she came back to the kitchen and sauntered into the pantry, Russell put on his cap and went to the barn. With heavy hearts, Steve and I went outside to talk things over. The next morning, we left. And as we walked down the road together, I vowed I'd never go back to Skinners Pond again.

Analyzing the Problem

Now **that Steve** had met Cora, we spent all that day trying to analyze her motives for being the way she was. She always seemed to set up a system of rules that were impossible for any average person to follow, rules that would be recognized by any outsider as being completely absurd. If you were a chance visitor and happened to break one of these rules that you didn't know anything about, it was easily overlooked. And you therefore walked away with the impression that everything was normal.

If, however, your circumstances caused you to become more than just a visitor, and you wound up within her sphere of control, the "rules" would be pointed out to you in direct proportion to the degree of respect she held for you. In other words, if she really liked you, you enjoyed total freedom from the rules, due to the fact you were never told about them. If, on the other hand, she didn't like you, she soon made you aware of the rules and also how agitated she would be if you broke one.

You were always alone when she told you the rules. And later on in the presence of company, when it was almost impossible not to break one of these absurdities, she seemed to take pleasure in making you squirm with one of her looks that always meant "I'll get you later for that."

This was her way of always putting you on the defensive and making you feel totally uncomfortable. You were always afraid of making a mistake whenever she was around. It therefore followed that this was her way of getting rid of people she didn't like. You were put into a no-win situation without even knowing why you were there. And because you were never told you were disliked, you could never ask why, how or even in what way you could help to improve the situation. She was your accuser, judge, jury and executioner, in a kangaroo court where you had no defence because no one even read the charge.

In a nutshell then, her system seems to have been one

of making the life of her unsuspecting victim both mentally and emotionally as miserable as possible, and then claiming absolutely "no fault" when the person left because they couldn't stand it any longer.

This was also extremely effective when the victim tried to explain to others that he left because he felt disliked or unwanted. The would-be sympathizer, basing his judgement on a few friendly house visits, as a consequence, would then naturally have to conclude that Cora's so-called victim was either mentally unstable, suffered from delusions, or at the very least, was a damn poor liar.

Reflecting upon these thoughts today, I believe the foregoing to be an accurate assessment of Cora's so-called method. But as to her motive, I'm still in the dark. Why, for instance, with the exception of Marlene, would she seek to entrap, control and intimidate another person in varying degrees, with no apparent reason? And why, in particular, would she seek to do it to a defence-less orphan boy of nine or ten years old, whose only crimes were an amazing appetite, an inventive mind and a spirit like that of the wind?

Indeed, there were times when I felt like a caged animal whose only purpose in life was to be teased, taunted and toyed with, in much the same way as a cat might play with a mouse. My road to promised rewards was always booby-trapped. And if I succeeded in spite of the odds, the reward was always pulled away, or an excuse was made for why it was undeserved. On the other hand, certain reprimand for all mistakes was a promise never broken.

So why make mistakes? Because it was impossible not to. In Cora's eyes, everything I did from morning till night was a mistake. It was set up that way. It wasn't always what you were supposed to do, but how you were supposed to do it.

If you didn't sit, stand, walk, eat, wash and work in the prescribed manner, you were making a mistake and deserved the penalty. Most jobs, in and of themselves, could have been accomplished without trouble or mishap, but under the constant and watchful eye of a resolute fault-finder you were soon discovered to be a "stumble-bum" or a "nincompoop."

The dos and don'ts of every activity were regulated in such a way that all the facets of daily life had become one continuous cycle of never-ending mistakes. While being busy all the time was considered to be a virtue, no action could be accomplished without making a mistake. And you couldn't avoid making mistakes by doing nothing, because doing nothing itself was a mistake. It therefore follows, at least in the mind of a child, that striving to be virtuous and living your whole life in error is really one and the same thing.

At this point, I hope the reader will now understand at least part of the greater dilemma from which I tried to extricate myself. Between the ages of nine and thirteen there were times when Cora had my mind so mixed up that I hated the sight of her. I didn't know whether to kill, run or go crazy. And while the option to attack was ever-present, my better sense of judgement always told me to run away.

This would only release the pressure valve for a short while, however, and every time the Mounties brought me back, I was again left to deal with the realities of the third option: find a way to keep from going crazy.

This was accomplished by leading Cora to believe that I was partially crazy. Each time I acted nervous, fidgety and supplicant, she always showed a kinder side. And when I stuttered and stammered like an idiot, she'd quickly honour my smallest request with a smile of delight and approval. The more I learned to babble, it seemed, the less of a slave driver she became. I really think she was trying to drive me nuts. For as the so-called act became more pitiful, the more pleased she became with the progress.

Is it any wonder then why Marlene, so many years later, would still remember the highlight which impressed her the most about her "brother Tom"—the

STOMPIN' TOM: Before the Fame

one highlight that prompted her to ask in front of everybody if I "still stuttered," and if I "still said 'yeah but,
yeah but,' all the time."

Like I said before, I have no idea what the motive for
all this was. I only know that, with the exception of
Marlene, she sought to control everyone within her
sphere to a certain required extent. I also know that
after each time I ran away, she never appeared happy or
relieved upon my safe return. On the contrary, she
always looked disappointed.

So, while bearing all these facts in mind, and without
having consulted the expertise of a psychiatrist, I will
now venture to speculate upon Cora's "motive" for the
indignities to which I alone was subjected. I believe
when Russell took over his father's farm, he realized he
would soon need help to manage it. He sent Cora to
New Brunswick to bring back an orphan boy for that
purpose. Cora, not wanting a boy, came back with an
infant girl. This was Marlene. Russell may have been
slightly disturbed about this, and the following year he
sent her back again for a boy. In complying with
Russell's wishes, and still not wanting a boy, she devised a
plan to take a boy for a while and then find some reason
for sending him back later. Unfortunately, the deal she
made, for some unknown reason, could not be renegoti-
ated, and she therefore had to keep the boy.

Instead of trying to make the best of things and learn
to live with the boy, she was still determined to get her
own way and so she made a plan to either drive him
away in such a manner that his departure would appear
as if he had left on his own, or barring that, she would
put him through such a mentally taxing program that he
would snap in the face of the pressure and therefore
would have to be put away or institutionalized. Either
way didn't matter as long as the result was the same. She
just didn't want a boy around and that was that.

Now, until this guess is verified with documentation,
which is extremely unlikely, its accuracy will have to

stand on gut feeling alone. Those with any first-hand knowledge about this affair have never bothered to come forward, so I've never had the opportunity to discuss it with anyone.

This guess also doesn't answer why Cora would have such an extreme aversion to boys, why she couldn't seem to distinguish between a "real enemy" and an innocent person for whom she may only have had a personal dislike, and why she had to seek and maintain this odd form of control over those who came to dwell within her sphere.

When you are walking along the road with your buddy and you have nothing much better to do than talk, it should come as no surprise that topics such as the foregoing were often discussed. You might say we often became each other's sounding board on subjects we might not otherwise wish to discuss with just anyone else.

So on that day in 1955 when Steve and I left Skinners Pond, it's not hard to imagine why the actions of Cora became the number one subject. And it stayed with us till long after we left the Island. We may not have analyzed it quite as deeply as I have here, but as a recurring topic it always received a great deal of attention.

New England to Montreal

Once we got back to New Brunswick, we decided we'd take a trip down through the States. By the time we arrived in Saint John, however, Steve decided not to go, so I went alone. I crossed the border at Calais, Maine, hitchhiked for a couple of weeks through the New England states and crossed the border again at Cornwall, Ontario.

About the only thing that sticks in my mind about the trip, other than just viewing the scenery, happened on a day when I got a ride with a very religious guy, who was extremely zealous and tried to convert me.

Unfortunately, for him, I wasn't too easily converted. After listening to his spiel for about the length of time it took me to realize he was never going to stop, I told him to "take your wonderful 'light' and shove it up your wonderful arse with all that wonderful 'power' you got there, buddy. Because good things won't hurt ya. And further more, I'm not your goddamned 'brother'. So you can just stop this f—— chatter and let me out at the next telephone pole."

As he quickly stopped in the middle of nowhere, I got out and slammed the door. I was far less tolerant with the religious types back in those days than I am now.

When I left Cornwall I went back to Montreal to see my mother for a few days and was very surprised to find out that she had become a new mother again to a bouncing baby boy. She said she called him Stephen in honour of the high regard which I always held for my buddy Steve. I told her how delighted I was and that I'd be sure to tell him about it at the very next opportunity.

As the baby's father was out of town for the few days that I was there I didn't get to see him, but my mother assured me that he was very proud of his son and that everything was going along just fine. As I gave her a hug on the day I left, I had no way of knowing it would be another eighteen or nineteen years before I'd see either one of them again.

Lombardo's Grill

I spent that fall and winter of 1955–56 odd-jobbin'
around Toronto, doing everything from delivering
handbills and shovelling snow to loading trucks or mopping floors. When I had a job, I had a cheap room. The
rest of the time I went from the bed-lines to the bread-
lines, from the Salvation Army to the Scotts Mission.
Once in a while I got to play my guitar for a few bucks at a
jamboree, but that was seldom. I wrote a few songs, but
they didn't pay any money; and when I tried to get someone to record them, there were no takers.

And to top things off, just when the weather started to
warm up and I was preparing to leave town, someone
stole my guitar. I was out helping a guy move some furniture, and when I came back to my room that evening the
lock on the door had been jimmied and the guitar was
gone. My other belongings were still there, and for some
strange reason, so was the guitar case. "Well," I thought,
"at least he left me something to carry my shirt and
socks in. Nice guy. Very thoughtful. If I ever meet him
with my guitar, I'll be sure to tell him that…before I kill
him!"

That evening, I couldn't think of a better thing to do
than go down to the hotel and get sloshed. By closing
time I was carrying a pretty good jag, and on my way
home I dropped into Lombardo's Grill to get a sandwich
and a coffee.

I knew the restaurant quite well because it was right
across the street from the Sally Ann on the corner of
Sherbourne and Queen. On the afternoons when I was-
n't doing anything, I'd often take my guitar in and play a
few songs. Pretty soon I got to know the staff quite well,
and once or twice when I was singing, Mr. Lombardo
himself popped in and even requested a couple of num-
bers. (It was here that I also wrote the song "Benny the
Bum" a number of years earlier.)

Anyway, on this night, as I walked in, Rusty was behind

the counter. As he was usually on the afternoon shift I didn't think anything about it. But when 12 o'clock came and he just kept right on working, I asked him what was going on. "Are you working a double shift or something?"

"Yeah," he said. "The guy that usually works the grave-yard shift just quit, and I gotta work double till the boss gets a replacement."

"Well, I don't know a hell of a lot about cookin'," I said, "but if you think you could teach me, I sure as hell need a job bad."

When he heard that, he said, "Well, get yourself around the counter here and I'll teach you all you need to know and when the boss comes in in the morning, I'll recommend that he hire you."

As I went around through the kitchen door he handed me an apron and showed me where everything could be found. I told him he'd better have lots of hot coffee around, 'cause "I'm gonna need a good bit to get 'unsnapped'." He laughed and said, "You won't have to worry about that around here. Ninety per cent of your customers will be 'half-snapped' anyway. Especially on the midnight shift."

I soon found out he was right, and before an hour was up, I was cookin' for most of them. And as beginner's luck would have it, I didn't get one complaint.

Everything was cooked on the grill and there wasn't anything harder to do than serve up a small steak. The rest was mainly hot sandwiches, hamburgers and hot-dogs, and a lot of stuff with eggs, such as western sand-wiches and omelettes. Making cold sandwiches was a snap because everything was previously laid out, and all one had to do was put them together.

When 8 o'clock came and Mr. Lombardo walked in, he recognized me right away. "How do you like your new job?" he said. "You'll start at 12 o'clock tonight." With a look of surprise on my face, I soon realized that Rusty must have winked at him and nodded his approval of me the minute he walked in the door.

Though I never liked asking for an advance on my wages on the first day of getting a job, I had to, because I only had one more night before my room ran out. And if I was going to be working all that night, I wouldn't have any place to stay tomorrow. After explaining this to Mr. Lombardo he gave me the amount I needed, plus a little more, and said that Rusty would stay behind the counter a couple of hours with me after his own shift tonight, to get me started. After that, I was on my own.

I rented a new room that day on Shuter Street, about a block away from Lombardo's Grill. It was the last room on the top floor of a four-storey building that was run by Chinese people. And though the last flight of stairs was rickety, the room had a good lock on it. So I took it.

After a good long sleep that day, I went into work early that evening to get a few more tips from Rusty. It was going to be a long night, and after 2 o'clock in the morning I was going to be alone. About 11 o'clock that night Mr. Lombardo showed up and gave me some last-minute tips and advice. "If in doubt about getting paid for a meal, don't serve anybody until you get the money up-front. And if anyone gives you trouble, don't call the cops because they just don't want to be bothered. You can give a guy one warning, and if he doesn't leave, then just throw him out."

After giving me a couple more minor rules, the last thing he said before he left was, "Whatever you do, don't take any shit."

A couple of hours after that, Rusty left, and that's when the trouble started. Although it wasn't very busy that night, it seemed that everyone who came in wanted to test the "new boy." And test me they did. When they found out I wasn't going to bend the rules for anyone, they began to make all kinds of threats. Some guys said they were personal friends of the boss, and he was going to be terribly disappointed with me when he found out in the morning that I hadn't served them for some reason. Other guys were going to do everything from "sue the boss" and "kick the shit" out of me, to threats of "wrecking the goddamned place," and catching me "on the way home, later." I wound up throwing about three or four guys right out through the door that night and the rest of the trouble-makers had sense enough to leave after the first warning. One guy even pulled out a switchblade, but he ran like hell when I jumped over the counter with a butcher knife in my hand.

I was surprised to find out the next day that Mr. Lombardo knew practically everything that went on that night. He had apparently sent in two or three friends at different intervals to check out my performance. He not only said he was pleased, but he laughed like hell when he said that I had even kicked out one of his friends who refused to pay up-front for a sandwich.

After the first few nights of establishing a reputation of being a no-nonsense type of guy, it was only the odd stranger who gave me any trouble. The rest were all pretty good. Most of the customers were drifters, ex-cons, guys who got kicked out of their rooms and the odd drunk. Among the regulars there was everything from pimps and prostitutes to bums, winos and petty thieves.

And, of course, there was also a good number of common everyday working people who just happened to be out late at night for one reason or another.

It also wasn't very long before I was giving the odd free meal to those who genuinely needed it. And it really didn't matter whether I particularly liked them or not. As long as they didn't come across as phoney and arrogant, and their hard-luck story was sincere, I didn't have any problem giving them something to eat. After all, hadn't I been in the same position myself? And might there not come a day when I would be again?

There were also some working people to whom I had to extend credit. These were people who mostly came in early in the morning for breakfast before going to work. And their custom was to always settle up on pay-day. Ninety-five per cent of these people could always be trusted, but if I felt leery about someone, I could always refuse and tell them to speak to Mr. Lombardo when he came in.

So this was the setting when several weeks later I received a couple of unexpected customers. It was just after my 6 A.M. to 7 o'clock rush hour. I turned around from cleaning some of the grease off the grill, and immediately did a double take. Right there in front of me, getting ready to sit down on a couple of stools, were my buddy Steve and another good friend from Saint John, my old pal "Lucky" Jim Frost.

You could have knocked me over with a feather. "Well, whadayaknow," Jim said, giving Steve a friendly push on the shoulder. "We hitch-hike half-way across Canada to search for the weather-bitten, rough-and-tumble Tom Connors, and what do we find? A dish-pan flunky training to be a soda-jerk."

We all laughed and shook hands. "If you bums think you're gonna fast-talk me into a free meal, you're probably right. So what'll it be?" I said.

After they named everything they could find on the chalkboard menu, I finally dished them up a couple of plates with lots of ham and three or four eggs and topped them off with a healthy scoop of freshly fried potatoes. Between comments like "These eggs taste like rubber, these potatoes are way too greasy, and this ham is tougher than shoe leather," they both ate like a couple of pigs.

When 8 o'clock came I took them back to my room and said, "Well, whadaya think, guys? This is where we live." Both of them pounced on the bed at the same time, leaving no room for me. "Not bad," Steve said. "I think me and Jim are going to enjoy ourselves around here. What do you think, Jim?"

"I dunno," Jim said. "Maybe if the meals improve a little, I might stick it out for a while."

Spraying the "Crab Apples"

As I let them have their fun, I had to make a quick exit. I went down to the ground floor and borrowed a big fly sprayer from the landlord. It was an old hand-pump model, with a big can on the end of it. Unknown to the guys, I had caught the crabs over the last few days and they were beginning to itch. Thinking I'd better deal with them before they got too bad, I went out to the drugstore the day before and asked to buy some "blue ointment." But as the druggist sold me on some new liquid stuff, which he said was a lot milder and easier to apply, I brought home a couple of bottles and a special kind of soap to wash it off with.

I now went back up the stairs to the first landing, walked along the hall till I came to the only washroom in the house which had a bathtub and turned the water on slowly for the bath I would soon have to take. Then I went up to the next landing, walked along the hall to the last flight of stairs and up to my room.

As soon as I walked in with the fly sprayer the guys, of course, wanted to know what was going on. "I got the goddamn crabs. That's what's going on," I said, "and I'm gonna need your help to get rid of them."

Well, you should have heard the laughing. I think they came up with every outlandish crab remedy that was ever heard of and even a few that weren't. "Rub your bag with sand and whisky, and when they get drunk they'll pick up rocks and 'stone' each other to death," said one, and "Why don't you let them get big enough till you can pick them off with boxing gloves?" said another.

Meanwhile, I just kept pouring the liquid into the sprayer can and getting undressed in preparation for the big ordeal.

The directions on the bottle said to rub the liquid on "generously" and then wait for fifteen minutes before taking a bath and washing thoroughly with the special soap. But always being one to find a quicker way to a solution, and not wanting to spend all that time rubbing the stuff on, I figured the spray-can method was the fastest way to solve the problem. That's why I bought the two bottles. I had to allow for waste.

When I finally got undressed and passed the sprayer to the guys, they had to flip a coin to see which one of them got to do the spraying first. By the time they each had a turn I was pretty well saturated. And while the stuff was dripping from me everywhere, it also began to sting. As I still had to wait for fifteen minutes before taking a bath, I began to think there was something wrong.

The druggist said this stuff was milder than blue ointment and here it was stinging already. And each second I stood there, it only got worse. When five minutes went by and I couldn't stand it any longer, it occurred to me to open the sprayer can and have a look. When I poured a little bit out, instead of the clear-looking liquid that I had poured in, it looked just as white as milk. In a flash of stinging panic, I realized what must have happened when I poured the anti-crab solution into the sprayer.

"Jesus Christ," I said, "the Chinaman left some cockroach spray in the bottom of the goddamned can."

Well, you talk about two assholes laughin'? I couldn't even get one of them to find me a towel. As my bag shrivelled up, I darted around the room till I grabbed a pillowcase off one of the pillows and headed for the door. The last thing I heard before bounding down the hall was, "What's your hurry, Tom? You're supposed to wait another ten minutes before that stuff begins to work."

I almost took the banister off the stairs to reach the next landing, and just as I was running through the hall to get to the next staircase, a door opened and two old ladies stepped out. When they saw me running towards them, they weren't sure whether I was trying to get the pillowcase quickly wrapped around me or trying to take it off.

With a scream and a flutter they pushed each other back in the room and slammed the door. With a couple more leaps I was down the stairs to the next landing, but I had to quickly put on the brakes. The landlord had just come out of the bathroom and was headed towards the stairs at the other end of the hall. As soon as he was out of sight I made my final dash. In the bathroom I locked the door and jumped into the tub. And wouldn't you know it, the landlord had let all the water out.

I put the plug back in the hole and quickly turned the water on again, but both taps were cold. As the pain was getting worse and the water was rising too slowly, I began to splash it up on me. When that seemed only to aggravate the problem, I remembered I'd forgotten to bring the special soap.

"What the hell am I gonna do now," I thought. "I'll have to go back and get it."

Just as I was about to open the bathroom door, I heard the landlord coming down the hall again.

He was complaining to one of his tenants. "Ploblems, ploblems, ploblems," he was saying. "All you wanna gimme is ploblems." As he stood outside the bathroom door, I couldn't help but think to myself, "Problems? And you think you've got problems. If you were standing on the other side of this door in my place you'd really have a problem. And if you don't get your ass downstairs pretty quick, this whole goddamn house is gonna have a problem."

As soon as he took off, so did I. Two halls and two flights of stairs later, I was back in my room where the guys were pretending to be overly helpful and sympathetic. But I could tell by the flushed look on their faces, they couldn't wait for me to leave so they could get back to their laughing jag. With no time to spare, I grabbed the soap, told them to bring some clothes down to the bathroom for me, and disappeared.

When I hit the bottom of the first stairs, the same two old ladies were again stepping into the hall. This time one of them was carrying a large paper bag full of odds and ends. When she saw me coming, she dropped the bag and ran back into the room, causing several balls of yarn to escape and roll wherever they may.

In my effort to get past all this junk, I kicked one of the balls. As it flew down the hall ahead of me, with a string of yarn trailing behind, it bounced against the wall and rolled down the stairs. When I got to the bottom I didn't bother to look and see where it went. I just darted for the bathroom and into the tub.

By now, I was stinging so bad all over I thought, If those crabs can survive all this, I'm going to be scratching for a long time, 'cause there's no way I'm going through this ordeal again. I was still stinging after I got the stuff washed off and Steve came to the door with some clean clothes. I asked him if he happened to see the landlord around anywhere, and he said, "No. The only thing I saw was a couple of old ladies up on the next landing, rolling up a few balls of yarn."

I didn't bother to tell him just then what had happened because I knew he'd only bust out laughing again. So I just got my clothes on and we headed up the stairs.

As we reached the top, I felt like turning around and going back. 'Cause here were the two old ladies with their bag of yarn walking down the hall and coming towards us. As we got close up, one of them was looking at me very strangely, as if she knew me from somewhere. For a moment it almost looked as if she was going to stop me and ask me where we had met, but I just avoided her gaze and quickly walked by. After a few steps, I turned slightly to glance back, and when I saw her still looking at me, I quickly got my ass up the stairs.

When we finally got back into the room and I quickly locked the door, Steve asked me if I was nervous or something When I told them all about the old ladies and what happened to the yarn, they both went into a fit of hysteria and there was no sense even talking to them again for the rest of the day.

Later on that evening I eventually got a few hours' sleep while the boys went out for a few draughts. When the hotel closed they came back to wake me up, and as they were now pretty hungry, we all went back to Lombardo's.

When Steve and Jim had left Saint John, their plan had been to hitch-hike to Mexico. Upon hearing of their plans, I decided to go with them. However, this was only Wednesday, and I would have to wait till Saturday night before I could get paid. By then I would have over $100, counting my cheque and what I had already saved up. And with this I could buy another guitar.

Between Wednesday and Sunday the boys slept in the room at night and I slept in it by day. During that time I was able to give them a meal before going to bed and once again in the mornings if they were able to arrive before my shift was over. When Sunday came I had my cheque, but I had to wait till Monday to get it cashed. I then packed my clothes in my guitar case and we were off to Mexico. I didn't bother to buy another guitar right away. I knew they were cheaper in the States, so I decided to wait.

Bridge over Niagara

A couple of days later we were in Fort Erie, Ontario. We tried to walk across the car bridge, but the customs officers wouldn't let us through. We then came back and went to a pool room. There we learned of a railroad bridge that spanned the Niagara River just a mile or two down the road. We also found out the best time to attempt to cross it would be at 11:30 that night when the tower guards were changing shifts.

When we arrived at the bridge, we found the entrance to be well lit up with spotlights from the tower. There was also a five- or six-foot fence with a strand of barbed wire along the top which would have to be scaled. Looking the situation over, we decided on the route that had the most shadows and waited in the bushes till about twenty-five minutes past eleven.

Just then a car drove up to the building below the tower. Someone got out and began to go up the stairs. We gave him a few seconds to get to the top and then we made our move. Within a minute we were over the fence and running to the shadows provided by the bridge itself. As it was always our custom to dress totally in black whenever we hitch-hiked, our clothes proved to be a great asset on this particular night.

As there were lights at intervals all the way across the bridge, and the watchmen could see the full length of the tracks from their towers on both ends, we climbed up only as far as one of the wide beams that ran along under the railroad itself. And from there we walked when we could, and sometimes crawled to the other end.

There wasn't one of us who dared to comment about what we were thinking. Should anyone happen to miss a step, the Niagara River was churning below us, and somewhere, not too far downstream, was Niagara Falls. (Not a very nice place to be floating around at night without a barrel.)

Each time the wind blew and the bridge shook, we'd

latch on to one of the upright braces and hope like hell there wasn't a train coming through.

As we jumped off the bridge on the American side and scurried across a small patch of light, it became obvious that someone in the tower thought he saw something. As if they didn't have enough spotlights already, they turned on some more, and one of the guards came out with his gun drawn.

A huge searchlight was now darting around as we dove into a small thicket and rolled part-way down the river's embankment.

There we lay quietly for three or four minutes till the guards turned out the lights and went back in the tower, probably thinking they had made a mistake. We then crawled back up the embankment, walked about half a mile through the woods and finally came up on the road.

At the first light we came to, we dusted off each other's clothes, and walked into Buffalo, New York. As I figured now, we'd be a lot better off by putting as much quick distance as possible between us and that railroad bridge, I went into a bus terminal and bought three tickets to Erie, Pennsylvania. This would be about a hundred miles away. And after catching a couple of hours' sleep on the bus, we arrived at about 4 or 5 A.M. and immediately headed out to the highway.

On the Way to Nashville

Two days later, while going through a small town in Ohio, we were walking by a pool room, and, of course, we had to go in. Lucky Jim was practically born in a pool room, and I don't think I ever saw him pass one without going in for at least one game.

He was somewhat of a pool shark, and because he never wanted to discourage a "mark" when he found one, he'd always set the game up in such a way that he would only beat his opponent by one ball, that being the black one. And as it appeared he always won the game merely by the skin of his teeth, everyone soon began to call him "Lucky Jim." The consensus always seemed to be that, without his "luck," they would be a sure winner. The trouble was, the luck was always still there long after their money was gone.

So whenever we were on the road with Jim, no matter how broke or hungry we got, we always saved at least a quarter in case we came to a pool room. A quarter was the ante in those days, and every time Jim found his man, the quarter would turn into at least enough to get us all a square meal.

On this particular day, even though I was trying to save as much money as I could to buy a guitar, I gave Jim a couple of dollars and said, "Go to work." After watching a few guys play, it was no time till he found his man. He'd always win two games out of every three and never lose one when the bets were doubled.

After he relieved one guy of about $20 I suggested we leave. But just then, another guy who thought he was pretty good insisted that Jim had just been "lucky" and he was all fired up to take him on. Well, to cut a long story short: three hours after we walked in, Jim walked out with almost $45. Not bad, when you consider that $50 a week at the time was a pretty damn good wage.

After winning that kind of money, instead of eating in the local restaurant, we beat it out to the highway. And after getting a ride, we ate further down the line. You can never tell how sore a guy might get when he loses that kind of money. He may decide to get some of his friends together and try to get his money back by force. At any rate, this was not one of those times. Three days later, we found ourselves in Nashville, Tennessee.

Upon deciding to take a bus to the downtown area, we paid our fare and plunked ourselves down in the very last seat at the back of the bus. This action soon became not only a learning experience, but also an out-and-out embarrassment to three very unobservant Canadians.

As the reader is now probably aware, at that time there were many cities in the United States, especially in the south, where they didn't allow black people to sit in the front of the bus. In fact, black people were not allowed to precede white people anywhere down there. They were expected to eat in their own restaurants, drink in their own bars and segregate themselves from whites at all functions attended by both races.

As we sat down, it didn't even occur to us that there was anything wrong when every single black person stood up. I guess we just figured they were all getting off at the next stop. When the stop came and only two or three people got off, we still wondered why some people with heavy parcels just kept on standing with so many empty seats available.

At the next stop, after one of the black guys got off, he came around to the back of the bus, knocked on the window and shook his fist at us. This told us that somehow we had offended the blacks. And realizing we were the only whites in the section we immediately got up and went to the front of the bus. As soon as we did this most of the black people sat down. A couple of stops later, as we were getting off the bus, we would have liked to apologize, but with all the dirty looks we were getting from everybody, we figured we'd be better off by just remaining silent.

Buying an "Old Guitar"

It was now about noon and almost half an hour after we got off the bus, when we came across a little furniture store that also displayed a few belt buckles and other such paraphernalia in one of their windows. Some of the new buckle designs caught our eye, and we decided to go in and have a better look.

While standing around browsing, I happened to notice what looked like a guitar case with a couple of lamps sitting on it away up on the very highest shelf. When I asked the guy if it was a guitar, he said it couldn't be. They had been in the furniture business for several years now, and it would be extremely odd to have a guitar in the store that would not have been noticed for such a long time.

He also explained, however, that the previous owner had been a pawnbroker, and while he remained skeptical, his curiosity prompted him to get a big ladder and check it out. To his amazement, it was a guitar case all right, and when he brought it down and set it on the counter it was found to contain a Gibson "Southern Jumbo" guitar.

I ran my fingers across the rusty strings, they were totally out of tune, but the intrinsic quality of the instrument was undeniable. As I thought what a beautiful sound this guitar would have with a new set of strings, I knew I just had to have it.

Hiding my enthusiasm, I immediately began to find as many things wrong with it as possible. After pointing out its age and the fact that it hadn't been looked after for so long, I suggested the glue was probably dried out by now, and if subjected to any kind of use, it might fall apart. "Still," I said, trying to show no more than a passing curiosity, "how much would you want for it anyway—forty dollars?"

Admitting he knew nothing about musical instruments, he said he'd have to go in the back and show it to his partner before he could come up with a price. Upon his return he said he'd have to have $100 in order to part with it.

Though $100 would have been a steal, I knew we only had about $85 or $90 left now between the three of us. So I resolved to dicker with him till I got the price reduced. "Well, it's not worth more than fifty," I said, "but I'll give you sixty and no more."

He then came down to $90 and I went up to $70. That was all I had in my pocket. But I felt quite sure I could get the rest from the boys, providing I got him down low enough and we had a few dollars left to eat with.

"Eighty-five dollars," he said, "and that is that. Take it or leave it." When I came up to $75 he wouldn't budge.

"Well, I don't know how you're ever going to sell it for that," I said, "and besides, who's going to come into a furniture store looking to buy a guitar, anyway?" With that, I turned and said to the boys, "Let's go."

Once out on the street, we stopped around the corner to talk it over. Steve and Jim agreed the guitar was worth a lot more than $100, but if we bought it for $85 it would still need strings, and that would leave us absolutely broke. I just had to go back and get him down to at least $80.

When I went back into the store, he was just getting ready to put the guitar away. "Look," I said, "I'd like to try and be reasonable with you. You want eighty-five dollars for the guitar and I want to give you seventy-five. If I go and buy an eighty-five-dollar guitar somewhere else, it's going to have brand-new strings on it. Furthermore, you're trying to sell me a guitar case which I don't need, but the value of it is included in the eighty-five. So why don't you sell me the guitar for seventy-five dollars, I'll buy the strings for it, and you can keep the guitar case."

Well, after he thought it over for a little while, he went back to talk to his partner. When he returned he said, "The best I can do is eighty dollars. You buy the strings and I'll keep the guitar case."

"Okay," I said, "it's a deal. But since you've been nickel and diming me, the least you could do is throw in a couple of those buckles for good measure."

I paid him the $80 and we left the store with the guitar un-cased, two bolo ties and a buckle. As soon as I got to an alley I threw enough clothes out of my old guitar case to allow the guitar to fit in, and away we went to look for a music store to buy some strings.

In less than an hour we were sitting in a small park and I was playing on one of the finest flat-top guitars that any of us had ever heard. From then on I couldn't keep my hands off it. I was playing it all the time.

That was the guitar I had the last time I ever hitch-hiked, and that was in October of 1964 when I arrived in Timmins, Ontario, and got a job playing at the Maple Leaf Hotel. Four years later that was the guitar I used when I wrote "Bud, the Spud" and a great many other songs that I now have recorded.

Over the years that guitar has gone through four or five different cases, and many times when it didn't have a case I just covered it with a garbage bag, or nothing at all. It was always slung over my shoulder, in all kinds of weather, in all seasons. From the snow and the rain to back alleys and freight trains, that old guitar has been through a lot.

By the time I retired it in 1972 the frets were worn down so far my fingers had even made holes in the finger-board. The box was cracked in two or three places, the pick-guard was worn through, and it was covered with stains, gouges, and scars. Though it was in really bad shape, it had stood me in good stead for sixteen years. Whether I was lonesome, broke or hungry, it was always my friend and will always be my favourite guitar.

Twenty years after it had gone into retirement, on Christmas Day of 1992, I got up in the morning to find it standing by the Christmas tree. Only this time, it wasn't the shabby old weather-beaten guitar I had once put away. It looked even newer and shinier than it did on that day in 1956 when I bought it in Nashville. It was completely reconditioned. And to say that I was delighted would be the understatement of the century. I was actually dumbfounded. And when I picked it up and strummed it, I knew it hadn't lost a thing. Whenever anyone spoke to me for the rest of the day, they must have noticed a faraway look in my eyes. I was probably listening to an old freight train whistle from days of youth and lost sunshine. Days when me and that old guitar had no other home but the highway.

When I finally came back to reality, my wife Lena told me the whole story of how she sneaked it out of its case in the closet and replaced it with a log of firewood and a couple of pillows, so I wouldn't notice the weight difference, in case I moved it. She then had one of my friends in the music business take it away to have it repaired. The whole job cost her between $800 and $900, a far cry from the $80 I originally paid for it. But it was certainly worth it.

The guitar is estimated to be around sixty-five or seventy years old, which means it must have been made sometime between 1924 and 1929. I can only guess at its dollar value, but to me it's priceless. I'm still writing songs with it, and I hope to be for many years to come. It no longer has to be subjected to the hardships that both of us once had to go through, but if it could only talk, I don't believe there's another guitar in the world that could tell a more fascinating story.

And if and when it ever does talk, I am pretty sure I know what the words will be: "Dear Lena: On behalf of me and Tom, I'd like to say how grateful I am for this wonderful transformation that has taken place. In spite of the impossible odds, we thank you very much, for being able to 'recondition' the both of us. Sincerely, Tom's Old Guitar."

With a Song for Hank

So here we were in Nashville with about $7 between the three of us. But armed with a new guitar, we now had the potential to pick up another couple of dollars here and there, or at the very least I could sing for our supper once in a while.

When me and the boys started out from Toronto with the intention of hitch-hiking to Mexico, I took them by way of Nashville for a specific reason. As I've said, somewhere around 1951 I had written a song called "I'll Be Gone with the Wind," and just this previous winter I had finally been able to put it on a small reel-to-reel tape. It contained no other music except me singing with my old guitar.

Everyone who ever heard this song always said it was tailor-made for Hank Snow, so the reason for going to Nashville was to find Hank and try to get him to listen to it.

From pictures in an old songbook I knew that he lived at his Rainbow Ranch in Madison, which was just outside of Nashville, and that's where we were now headed.

We got there about three o'clock in the afternoon when there was nobody at home. A little way from the house there was an old pole fence leading up to the corner of a small barn, and this is where we decided to sit and wait till someone came home.

About an hour later a big limousine drove in the yard followed by two or three other cars. As seven or eight people got out and walked towards the house, we could see that one of them was Hank. As he paused for a second and pointed in our direction, we could hear him say to one of the musicians, "Get rid of that riff-raff over there."

As everyone went in the house, a lone musician walked over to us and tried to put a nice face on what had happened. With a friendly smile, he said, "Hello," and asked us how we were, where we were from and

363

what we were doing there. We introduced ourselves, and he told us his name was McDaniels and that he was Hank's bass player.

When he heard that we had hitch-hiked all the way down from Canada with a song we wanted Hank to listen to, he said he'd take the tape in to Hank and see what he could do. But as Hank was not in a very good mood today, he suggested we leave and go back to Nashville where he would meet us about an hour later in a certain restaurant.

When we got to the restaurant, we each had a hamburger and were just finishing up when in he walked with the tape and placed it on the table. After asking us what we had and offering to pay the bill, he sat down for about five minutes and told us what had happened.

He said that Hank had liked the song but was only prepared to pay me some small amount. I'm not sure now exactly, but I think it was around $75. Anyway, it was an insult. I had expected that if Hank liked the song, he would have offered to record it. And in that event, I would have been prepared to wait as long as it took to receive some royalties.

As I immediately turned down the offer, I'm sure he could feel my displeasure. "Well," I said, "I might be broke now, but I'd rather starve before selling a song outright to Hank Snow or anyone else."

I didn't say anything more because I knew it wasn't the fault of Mr. McDaniels that things turned out the way they did. And as far as Hank's "moods" are concerned, I've met him more than half a dozen times since that day at Rainbow Ranch, and even shared the same stage with him on several occasions, but I've never known the man to be in any other mood except the one I've just described. In fact, it would come as a big surprise to me if I heard someone say otherwise.

After leaving the restaurant we started walking in a westerly direction and about twenty minutes later we came to the Ryman Auditorium, the Home of the Grand

Ole Opry. As the front steps were just around the corner from the main drag, we decided to sit down and have a little rest. I guess we weren't sitting there two minutes, when a guy comes out from inside and says, "Hey, you guys, get the hell off the steps. What do you think this is, a park or something?" Well, ordinarily I would have just got up and left, but with my mind still on the events of the last couple of hours, I said, "Look! There's no pedestrians on this street, your steps are full of old banana peels and newspapers, and all we want to do is sit down for five minutes and have a rest. So if you can't find a reason why we're bothering you, we're staying right here. What the hell is the matter with this town anyway?"

With that, the guy said, "Okay with me. If you guys don't want to move, I'll damn soon get someone to move you." After he went inside, I had a small argument with the guys. I wanted to stay right there to see what was going to happen, but they wanted to go, so we all got up and made our way to the west end of Nashville. When we finally got to the outskirts near the countryside, we came to a place where there were lots of big trees by the side of the road. There we stepped across the ditch and decided to sit down for another rest.

Insects, Duffel Bags and Watermelons

The day had been very hot and we had practically walked all over Nashville twice, not to mention walking all the way to Madison and back. By the time Steve, Jim and I found a rock or something to sit on, I again had my guitar out and was just lazily picking some old song under a big tree while the boys took their turns going to the road to thumb cars whenever we saw some coming.

While I just sat there amusing myself with my sleeves rolled up, something fell out of the tree and landed on my left arm. It was about three inches long and appeared to be just a twig. Without missing any chords, or interrupting the melody I was humming, I gave my forearm a couple of shakes, but the twig just seemed to stay there. After a couple of more harder shakes, when the twig still didn't fall off, I figured it was somehow stuck to one of the hairs, so I just decided to ignore it till I was finished my song.

A couple of seconds later, when I thought I felt it move, I glanced towards it just in time to see a big, long, slender tongue dart out to a distance of about five or six inches, or approximately twice the length of its body.

As it snapped out and in again, I wasn't long brushing it off, dropping the guitar and flying up the road on the dead run. I didn't stop till I was about thirty yards away, and when I did, my skin was all covered with goose bumps. Here it was a hot day, and I was feeling cold all over.

Steve and Jim were laughing and wondering what the hell had happened. "I don't know," I said, "but I'm not going back there. I saw something that looked like a twig off one of those trees, but it wasn't. It was some kind of a bug with a six-inch tongue, and I'm not going back for another look. So just bring my guitar up here and let's get going."

As Steve got my guitar and case together, Jim went looking in the grass and finally found the bug that created all the stir. As he started walking up the road with it in his hand, he said, "For Christ's sake, Tom. It's only a 'stick insect,' that'll never hurt you. They're absolutely harmless." Apparently, he'd read up on these things and seemed to know all about it.

Once he put it down on the road and explained that it was beneficial to man because it ate other harmful insects, I got brave enough to take another look. Its long tongue, he said, was coated with a substance that other small insects stick to, and because it doesn't move very fast its camouflage of looking like a twig fools other insects into thinking it's harmless. And before they know it, *zap!*, the long tongue comes out and the stick insect has got them.

"Yeah, well, that's all well and good," I said, "but I still don't like the look of the damn thing. So let's get out of here before it decides to zap us." As the boys had another chuckle or two we all headed down the road.

Normally, I'm not scared of bugs, but that thing just got to me. I had never even heard of a stick insect before, let alone seen one on me. And to my knowledge, we don't have such things in Canada because our weather is too cool.

Later on, the further south we went we encountered other unusual life forms. Everything from snakes, lizards and armadillos to giant cockroaches and tarantulas. But, thank heavens, none of us had the misfortune of being startled by having one of them crawling on our body.

Another thing we noticed in the States was that the people living in houses along the roads were a lot less likely to give you a handout than they were in Canada. Because of this, we ate a lot more raw vegetables from farmers' fields.

About four days out of Nashville we crossed the Mississippi River at Memphis. It was a sweltering afternoon, the rides were very slow, and we had walked an awful lot that day.

As we approached the bridge, Steve was doing a lot of

grumbling about how heavy his duffel bag was getting. He always kept all kinds of junk in it, and because he was pretty rugged, you hardly ever heard him complain about the extra weight. As I watched him shift the bag from shoulder to shoulder, I could see he wasn't very comfortable. And the more he perspired the more he grumbled.

So after winking at Jim a couple of times, I said, "You know, Steve, if I were you, I'd ditch that heavy duffel bag. Any man who would hitch-hike with a bag like that deserves to be tired in the heat like this. All I have is my shirts tied around my guitar inside the guitar case and my razor. That's all I need."

I was riding him pretty good and making him feel touchy. "If you've got to carry all that weight around, what the hell's the good of it, plus it's getting you down."

As we neared the middle of the bridge he was getting upset because I wasn't letting up. I said, "Any man that would carry that thing across the United States in this heat must be crazy. Look at me, all I've got is a guitar and no problem at all."

He eventually got so mad, he said, "Okay, then, Tom, okay, all right, you've been after me enough, so here it goes." Though I really didn't think he'd do it, he grabbed the duffel bag and tossed it over the bridge. Jim and I took to laughing as we watched it float down the Mississippi River. "There goes your belongings, Steve, now you are a real bum. Now you're initiated," I said. As Jim and I laughed, Steve just stood there without a grin on his face looking longingly at his big duffel bag as it went bobbing out of sight. I guess he was thinking about all the little things he must have had in it, wondering if he could do without them.

By the time we got to the other side of the bridge he started on me. He said, "Geez, Tom, that guitar looks heavy." I said, "No, no, it's not heavy at all, Steve. As a matter of fact it's as light as a feather. And if you think I'm going to go back and throw it over the bridge, you're crazy. And besides, when you're not carrying anything, people might start to think you're nothing but a bum."

Just then a guy stopped and gave us our first ride into Arkansas. Now down there in a lot of places they have roadside tables where you can go in and get cold watermelon. Well, on this evening, a guy was just about to close up so we went in and told him we were hungry and asked if he could give us a bite to eat, or could we help him clean up to earn a couple of watermelons.

"No you can't help," he says, "me and the wife have it all pretty well cleaned up. Just a couple more tables to wipe. But if you guys are hungry, there's a bunch of watermelons there, so just help yourselves."

Well, as we hadn't had much to eat in the last couple of days, I wish you could have seen the watermelons that we put away. He just left us there to eat them. Before long we were feeling much better and started telling jokes and pitching seeds at one another.

We arrived there about 9 o'clock and the guy finally told us to leave about 12. That was after we had each consumed about six watermelons. Steve probably had about eight as he was always a much bigger eater than the rest of us.

Death Valley and the Devil

Isoon began to notice that the further south we travelled day by day, the more lethargic we became. Instead of keeping our focus on going to Mexico, we began to just wander around Arkansas, Louisiana and the eastern part of Texas.

The weather was so hot down there that everybody just closed up shop for two or three hours in the afternoons to have a sleep or just lie around. As the three of us began to feel like everybody else, we found ourselves hanging around the little towns a lot, just trying to put up with the heat. There were many times each day when our thoughts flew back to "nice and cool Canada," and the boys were talking a lot more about home, in good ol' Saint John, New Brunswick.

Anyway, with all this slow movement around the south, there were many occasions for each of us to apply our trades. Steve was very adept at sleight of hand, and when I wasn't playing the guitar or Jim wasn't conning some guy into a game of pool, Steve would be there with his tricks. He could bring a quarter out of nowhere, make it vanish in the air, and later find it in somebody's ear. Magic was always an attraction. And he always had a patter to go with it.

He'd make little bets with guys our own age. Not a lot of money, just nickel, dime and quarter stuff. At first he'd do things rather slowly until they were absolutely sure they knew where the coin was. But after a quick shuffle, the coin disappeared and wound up in the least expected place. And everyone was wrong again.

Steve also used to like to tell a lot of tall tales and really embellish them. He could tell a story that was so outlandish, so exaggerated that you wouldn't think people would believe it. But he had a knack for drawing everybody in and having them believe that every story was true. When Steve got wound up with one of his stories, nobody wanted to listen to me playing the guitar any more. So when he'd start on some of his stories, it would give me a break from singing.

Once he got everyone's attention I'd usually walk over to the other end of the room because I always kept thinking that sometime somebody might say, "Well, look, you bullshitter, you're just lying through your hat," and maybe cause some tempers to flare.

I always liked to be a little on the sidelines to secure an advantage in case a fight started. None ever did, but I just wanted to be prepared.

One of the most outlandish stories Steve would frequently tell was about Lucky Jim and the big scar he had on his back. Now the truth of the matter was that Jim had had tuberculosis (TB) when he was younger and he spent a number of months in the sanatorium where he was treated and healed, but not before losing the biggest part of one of his lungs. It was the removal of this lung which left Jim with an ugly scar that started from a spot between his shoulder blades and went all the way down practically to his kidneys. Anyway, Steve would get telling this story how he and Lucky Jim and I were hitch-hiking across Death Valley.

He said the desert sun was pouring down so hot you could fry an egg on the rocks or on the hood of any car. But we could never get a ride because no one was ever brave enough to drive a car that far down the road. Besides, the road was so littered with skulls, a car couldn't drive down it anyway.

So we came to this gulch that was dried up, and we bedded down for the night where it was as cool as it could get in that God-forsaken part of the world. We were supposed to be quite close to the Mexican border and we could see a town off in the distance, but we didn't know if it was just a mirage, or not. This was during the day. We could always see it there in the distance and it looked like a bunch of Mexicans with sombreros walking around.

This was all just plain old bullshit, of course, and we

never even hitch-hiked across Death Valley in the first place.

Now he gets telling about this one night on the desert when it was so black and dark you couldn't even see your hand in front of you. And because we always dressed in black we couldn't even see each other, never mind seeing anything else out there in the desert night.

Jim wandered away a couple of feet to have a leak. Then it happened. Somebody, or something, attacked him. He didn't know whether it was some kind of an animal with sharp claws, or whether it was a guy with a knife. We could hear Jim hollering, but it was just so dark we couldn't find him.

Finally, he says, we ran over in the dark to where we heard a loud blood-curdling screech and a skirmish with a lot of running around going on. When we got there Jim was dying. He had a hell of a big gash in his back and fought all he could to get rid of this thing. We don't know if it was the devil himself, or not, but we could hear strange whisperings and the odd sound of a hollow laugh now and then not too far away through the intense darkness.

"Today, Jim's got a great big gash on his back. Show them Jim." At this point, Jim would have to lift up his shirt—everybody would have a good look and gasp, "Holy geezes, what a scar he's got."

Steve would now continue his story by telling everyone that the two of us had to carry Jim on our back. We headed in the direction of this Mexican town. We walked for four days while Jim was bleeding to death, but we finally got him to a Mexican hospital and got him to a doctor who sewed him up.

That was the kind of stories Steve would tell which would have these guys standing open-mouthed with eyes as big as saucers. And they'd ask us, how did you do this, and how did you do that, or how did you get out of this scrape and how did you get out of that one? He always had the answers and I don't know to this day how everybody believed him, but he just had that way about him.

There was even a night when he had four or five young fellas believing that an old relative of his, who once was a pirate, had a grandfather clock that was so old the shadow from the pendulum had worn a hole through one of the boards in the back.

So we were quite an interesting crew—one guy sang all these cowboy songs, another guy would tell stories and do magic tricks and the other was a pool shark who once had a fight with the devil.

Detained in Southern Texas

Around the first week of September that year, while roaming around through Texas, we came to a little town called Carthage. It was here that Steve, Lucky Jim and I all fell in love with the same girl. We ended up arguing with each other and eventually decided to split up. I left town first, and where they went from there I didn't know. I drifted around for a while alone, until I wound up in San Antonio, where I landed a singing job for a number of nights at a place called Guy's Dude Ranch out near the Alamo. After that I ran into this other guy from Alabama who was also a drifter who liked to sing and play the guitar.

He and I were born on the same day—February the ninth, 1936. I forget his name now, but he looked a lot like Hank Williams. We both played and sang in a few bars together, doing guest shots around town. We also did a lot of talking and drinking and just seemed to have a lot in common. What he didn't tell me, though, was that he had stolen a bunch of speakers, hi-fi's, radios and record players.

One morning at daybreak we were on our way to his place to get some sleep. We had had a few beers and were just walking along minding our own business, when two cops in a squad car pulled up and told us to get in the car. Although I had had nothing to do with the theft they took me along because I didn't have any identification on me.

After separating us at the police station they locked him up and put me in a detention centre. A couple of days later I wound up in a "wetback camp" way down in Brownsville, at the southernmost tip of Texas right near the Mexican border.

A lot of Mexicans who try to enter the States illegally do so by swimming across the Rio Grande, which forms the border between Mexico and Texas. As fast as the authorities can pick them up and deport them, they are in the river again swimming back. Hence the name "wetback."

When I told the police my name was Tom Connors, they said they were looking for a U.S. draft dodger by the same name and wondered if I was him. When I told them I couldn't be because I was Canadian, they decided to hold me till they checked everything—to find out who I really was. This wound up taking nearly a month.

I wanted to take my guitar in to the camp with me, but they wouldn't let me have it. The Mexicans couldn't speak English and I couldn't speak Spanish, but because I had a pretty good idea they liked music, I figured my best ticket to getting along with them was to have my guitar in there with me. So by hook or by crook, I was going to get it. I started my own little campaign going. I refused to eat. Every time they lined everybody up to go out through the fence of the compound to another building where they had the mess hall, I didn't line up with them. So they'd come and get me and ask me what was the matter with me.

"Aw, I'm not hungry—I miss my guitar."

This went on meal after meal. Then there were other things I would do. The compound was square with a very high fence all around, with each side being about an eighth of a mile long. There was a high turret on each corner with an armed guard keeping watch, and you weren't supposed to walk around the fence, or even go near it.

I now took up the habit of continually walking along the fence from one corner to the other, looking up at each guard in turn and staring at him until he ordered me to move on. Corner to corner I'd go in a continuous circuit, guard after guard after guard. I'd do this sometimes for hours and hours on end, day and night. When I was tired of walking I'd sit near the Mexicans and catch a large beetle or cockroach and break its wing so it couldn't move very fast, and watch the ants tear it apart piece by piece. I'd sit there with a big grin on my face and look around at the Mexicans with wild eyes, as much as to say isn't this great, isn't this delightful?

I wasn't eating and I was doing this fence routine and

when the guards weren't looking at me I was playing these games with the Mexicans and finding out that they were very superstitious and were slowly becoming afraid of me.

I wasn't speaking to anyone and every time a guard asked me a question, I wouldn't answer, except to say I missed my guitar. They soon got to the point where they said you're not getting your guitar in here, so there's no point in you playing these games. So this went on and the Mexicans began to steer clear of me.

When I went in the building, they'd all go outside. Soon they all began sleeping outside and I was the only one sleeping inside. Then, without warning, I'd reverse it. At 3 o'clock in the morning I'd move outside and they'd move in. That's how bad it was getting. They didn't know what was wrong with me, and I wasn't telling them. Soon they got so restless they were all complaining and demanding that I should be taken out of there; otherwise there might be a riot. Everyone was edgy and beginning to think I was bewitched. My movements became their only preoccupation as they watched me continuously.

After almost three weeks of this, the guards finally brought in my guitar. When I immediately started playing it and singing, the Mexicans were delighted. They all began to dance around. I started to eat and everybody got happy all of a sudden. For the next week or so we were all singing and having parties every night and the camp finally became a very bearable place to live. Even the guards' attitudes changed and they'd let us stay up and party an extra hour each night, just so they too could enjoy the happy times and the music. Before I left, one of the head guards apologized and said if he had only known from the start he would have let me have my guitar right from the first day.

After I'd been there about a month they put me on a plane to Oklahoma City where two immigration officers kept me overnight in some kind of a lock-up. And then from Oklahoma City they flew me to Chicago, then on to Toronto.

A Doctor with Heart

When I got off the plane it was a real cold day in November, and what a contrast from the heat of southern Texas. All I was wearing was a thin white shirt and I was freezing. I walked out of the airport in Malton and all the way down to Cabbagetown, Toronto. The distance might be fifteen or twenty miles. I didn't get there until close to midnight, and I was blue from the cold.

I asked Rusty, who was still working at Lombardo's Grill, if he would give me a meal and put me up in his room. He took one look at me and immediately got somebody else to look after his duties behind the counter and he took me home and put me to bed in his room. I wound up with a bad cold for a while, but I finally got over it. Many years later, the speculation in some circles has been that "a possible reason why Stompin' Tom has not bothered to pursue a career in the States is because he may have been deported from there." Well, the speculation is wrong. I have never been deported from anywhere. I have no problem getting in or out of the United States whenever I wish. And the true reasons for my wanting to pursue a musical career in Canada will become more apparent as this story unfolds.

After hanging around Lombardo's for a few days, I got wind of a restaurant about to open up in Alderwood, a distance of about ten or fifteen miles west of Toronto. At present, the name of the place was Harry's Grill, but the Chinese owner was hoping to get his liquor licence and soon open up a small night club. As he also intended to have entertainment, featuring small groups and singles, I figured I'd better go out and hang around the area for a while. This way I might get to meet the owner, present my talents and get in on the ground floor, so to speak.

On my way there, I was picked up on the road by a guy named Jack, who, by sheer coincidence, was working at a TV repair shop right next door to Harry's Grill. As Jack also played the guitar, we found a lot in common, and before I knew it, we were singing songs together after having supper at his place.

It also just so happened that Jack was leaving his job at Empire Television for a better job elsewhere, and because one of the owners of Empire was related to him, he said he could probably get me in there.

While I wasn't too eager to work, I recognized this as a great opportunity to be handy when the proposed night club finally opened. So after putting me up for the night, Jack took me over to Empire Television the next day, and got me hired. My job was to be installing TV antennas with a guy named Stan, and I'd be able to start the following Monday.

Jack also got Art, who was one of the bosses, to advance me some money, and then he drove me to a place where he knew I could get a room.

The next day being Saturday, I went down to Harry's Grill and met the owner. I told him I played the guitar and sang and because I worked right next door, he could contact me at any time after his licence came through. He extended me a line of credit for meals whenever I wanted them and asked me to bring my guitar in some evening and sing a few songs.

For the rest of the winter that's all I did. I worked at Empire Television through the day and hung around Harry's Grill at night. Some evenings I'd just sit and chat with people my own age, and other evenings I would bring in my guitar and sing songs. I made a lot of friends there, but a paying job for singing was still as far away as ever.

I turned twenty-one that winter, and when the warm weather came and people weren't watching TV as much, the demand for antennas dropped right off, and Empire Television found they no longer needed my services. Then, as I was trying to find another job to tide me over until that damn night-club licence came through, I developed pneumonia.

I stayed in my room for several days not knowing what

was wrong. Finally, I realized I'd better go to the out-patient department of the hospital to see what the hell was going on. The Queensway Hospital was about a mile and a half from where I lived, and I'd have to walk across the Queen Elizabeth Highway to get there. Well, to this day, I don't remember crossing it. I must have been delirious. I know I tried to get over a fence when I saw the hospital on the other side of a large field, but I just fell over in the tall grass and passed out.

Some time later, I got up and walked some more. The next thing I remember is being in some kind of stupor while asking the nurse at the desk if I could see a doctor. She was asking me for a card of some kind, and when I told her I didn't have one, she said there was nothing she could do for me. When I just stood there for a few minutes, she told me to leave. I then went outside and sat on the steps, and I guess I must have fallen asleep, because the next thing I recall is a man waking me up and asking me what I was doing there.

When I told him I didn't know what was wrong with me, he said I should go inside and see the nurse. When I told him I had already been in there and that the nurse turned me away because I had no card, he said, "You come with me then, and I'll make sure you get in." As I tried to get up, I fell down and passed out. I woke up again briefly, to realize that two men were carrying me past the desk, and the nurse was catching proper hell. I believe it was from the same man who had spoken to me outside.

As I tried to gain control of my feet to assist those who were holding my arms, someone must have given me a needle to put me out, because I didn't come to again for several days. When I finally came around, I asked about the circumstances surrounding my admittance to the hospital, but everything seemed to be hush-hush.

The only thing I could find out was that the man who spoke to me on the steps that day was a doctor and that he worked in some other department of the hospital. (If he ever reads this book sometime and remembers the day, I want him to know I think he's one hell of a great man, and that I was truly grateful for what he did. But the bureaucracy that demands such heartlessness, and the people who acquiescently allow themselves to become slaves of it, I have little or no respect for.)

On about the sixth day, I was sitting up in my bed when the word came that I had some visitors wanting to see me. And, before I knew it, a whole gang of young people from Harry's Grill came traipsing in. This made me feel just wonderful. I hadn't expected to see anybody because I really didn't know anybody. When I asked them how they found out I was here, they said they missed me at the restaurant, and when my landlady said my guitar was still in my room, though she hadn't seen me for several days, they began to check around.

Just on a hunch, someone phoned the hospital, and sure enough, they found me. And it proved to be a great dose of medicine as well. I started feeling better already, and in two more days I was back on the street.

That same night I walked down to Harry's with my guitar to let everybody know I was all right. I thanked them all for their thoughtfulness, and after singing them three or four songs, I went back to my room and went to bed. I didn't feel much like going anywhere the next day, and when my landlady, Mrs. McFarland, heard what had happened to me, she brought me some soup and later on invited me to sit in with her and her family for supper.

In and Out of New Toronto

In another few days I was off and running. I landed another job driving a catering truck to construction sites. The kind where you open the doors and everybody gathers around to buy kaiser-roll sandwiches, tea, coffee, pop, soup, chocolate bars and cigarettes. I didn't mind the job, but I wouldn't have taken it had I known that the liquor licence for Harry's was going to be rejected. A couple of months later when I found out the licence was turned down for sure, I put in my two weeks' notice.

I still had about one more week to go on the job when who should show up at Harry's Grill but Lucky Jim, and as I hadn't seen him since we separated at Carthage, Texas, we had a lot to talk about. He and Steve had left Carthage shortly after I did, and then they'd gone their separate ways. He said he didn't know where Steve went, but he had made his own way back to Canada without getting picked up by the police, and then went to Lombardo's, where Rusty told him I might be out around Harry's Grill, in Alderwood.

The first thing I did now, while I still had the use of the catering truck, was to get ourselves a bigger room. Mine only had a single bed. (As I was also allowed to bring the truck home after work, I got to use it in the evenings as long as I replaced the gas I used.)

The first room we got was at Eddy and Donna Culnan's place in New Toronto. And as Eddy was a real party maker back then, and a big country music enthusiast, we certainly had some great times. Soon I was out of a job again and that suited me just fine. I had saved up enough money to be able to afford a room with Jim for a while, and with him bringing in a few bucks here and there from the pool room, we weren't going to starve.

Between Jim's pool-room money and the money I could pick up from the many parties I played, it kept us going for the rest of the summer and right up into December. And because the best pool room to make money in at that time was Benny's, in Long Branch, we soon moved to Long Branch and conveniently got ourselves a room not more than half a block away.

Around Christmas time, when we started to get behind in our rent, and the weather became very unfavourable for hitch-hiking, we flipped a coin to see whether we should get jobs or not. Heads meant we should, and tails meant we shouldn't. When the coin came up heads we decided to go for the best out of three. We flipped again and came up with another head. After going again for the best out of five and coming up with another head, we decided to get a job. (Only till the weather got milder, or till we got our back rent paid up, of course. Whichever came first.)

Jim got a job at a sheet-metal place and I landed one driving a delivery van for a drugstore. When I think back on it now, the weather must have been terribly severe that winter, or we must have been a lot further behind in our rent than we thought, because I was still driving that damn van over three months later.

Anyway, about the first of April, 1958, when the bad weather disappeared, so did our jobs. Jim had some people in Toronto he wanted to visit for a while, and after I kicked around Long Branch for another month or so, I also hit the road.

This time I looked at the map of southwestern Ontario and drew a line along every highway that followed the entire perimeter. Any road that went along the shores of any body of water was the road I was going to take. First I went north to Barrie and Orillia, along the coast of Lake Simcoe. Then I cut across to Midland, on the south shore of Severn Sound. From there I went to Penetang, crossed over to Nottawasaga Beach and travelled along the southern shores of Georgian Bay to Collingwood, Meaford and Owen Sound.

Then from Southampton, I followed the eastern coast of Lake Huron down to Sarnia, and along the St. Clair River to Wallaceburg, Chatham and over to Belle River, on the south shores of Lake St. Clair. From Windsor to Amherstburg, I followed the Detroit River till it emptied into Lake Erie, and from there I came east through Kingsville, Leamington, Blenheim and Port Stanley. By the time I went through Ports Burwell, Dover and Colborne, and then to Crystal Beach and Fort Erie, I had seen the entire north coast of Lake Erie.

After passing the old railway bridge that Steve and Jim and I had crossed a couple of years earlier, I followed the Niagara River to Niagara Falls, and eventually wound up at Niagara-on-the-Lake. Once back on the shores of Lake Ontario, it was no time before I passed St. Catharines, Grimsby and Hamilton. And the next day I arrived back in Long Branch.

The whole trip had taken about two months, and the distance travelled was about nine hundred miles. One must also bear in mind that, at that time, over half these roads were only secondary, and sometimes even third class.

The rest of the summer I spent hanging out at different friends' houses from Alderwood to New Toronto. And whenever anyone was going north to cottage country, I was usually invited to tag along. This always got me free lodging and booze and sometimes a few bucks in exchange for the entertainment. I enjoyed the fishing, camping and boating as well, of course. I even got to go to the race-track a few times, and once when I put a couple of dollars on a long shot, it came in and paid me $120. This paid a lot of rent on a room that was only $7 a week.

It was around this time that I ran into a fellow by the name of Ted Lithgow. I met him in the pool room, of all places. I say this because, while he could hold his own at the snooker table with some of the best of them, he only had one arm. His technique was to rest his cue on the hair side of the brush normally used for cleaning tables, and shoot with his one good arm. And, like I say, it always took an above-average player to beat him.

Ted and I became great friends, and whenever I was around town after that, we always got together for a good chat or a couple of hours of pool. There was even one time that I had him playing the guitar. At first, he didn't think it was possible, of course, but after I converted his brother's old Spanish guitar into a dobro, his skepticism soon gave way to belief. With a clothes-hanger wire attached to the handle of an ordinary table-knife, and the loop of the wire firmly wrapped around his left leg, he could now slide his home-made bar back and forth along the full length of the guitar neck merely by moving his leg from side to side.

After learning the positions of only two chords, the hand started strumming and the leg started swaying, and by the time I got my cowboy hat on his head, he was playing and singing "Jambalaya" with a grin on his face a mile wide. To say he was delighted would be an understatement. He was acting like an orphan kid with a new toy.

(If any of my readers happen to be physically challenged in the same way Ted was, and you'd like to play the dobro guitar, just get someone to rig up the apparatus I've described; buy yourself a little book on how to chord the dobro, and in no time you'll be singing and playing for all your friends. It will be even better if you can find somebody who can weld an appropriate piece of metal to a real bar for playing the dobro, and once you get it to fit your leg properly, you're away. Try it, it works. And it is possible for a one-armed person to enjoy playing the guitar.)

Another guy who used to hang around the pool room at that time was Terry Roberts. Although he didn't play the guitar very well, he was a good singer. Well, it just so happened that on the night that Terry and I and a bunch of the boys had planned to go down to Palace Pier to catch one of the country shows that were frequently brought in, I couldn't go. It may have been due to a lack of funds, I forget now. But, anyway, while they were there, one of the Toronto radio station announcers, who was emceeing the show, called for volunteers to come up on stage and sing a song.

As a result of Terry going up to sing, he was selected by the radio station to make a recording of a song called "Oh, Lonesome Me." The song was already out by Don Gibson, but for some reason, the station wouldn't play Don's version, and this is how Terry received his big break.

Although Terry didn't know the song, he was told to go home and learn it and have it ready to record in a few days. He was also given a substantial advance of money to go and buy himself some good clothes because they were going to book him into the Brass Rail, a night club on Yonge Street in Toronto, the week after the recording.

It was only about the second afternoon after the Palace Pier incident. As I walked out of the pool room, who should I bump into but Terry Roberts. He was just coming out of Jack's Men's Wear with his arms full of boxes and parcels and loading them into a car that he said now belonged to him. While I stood there dumbfounded, he said, "You're just the guy I want to see. Wait here till I go in and get the rest of my parcels, and I'll buy you a coffee somewhere, so we can talk."

When he came out of the store again he was loaded down in much the same way as before. When the back seat of the car was finally loaded with parcels, we jumped in and he drove me to a restaurant. In a few minutes, he was telling me the details of how he came into his quick fortune.

Only two days before, he'd been just another pool room bum like the rest of us. Today, he had a recording contract, a car with a back seat full of new clothes, lots of spending money, and a job entertaining in a big night club downtown. "Wow!" I said. "This is great! I'm really happy for you. Congratulations! Now, what was it you wanted to see me about?"

"Well, it's like this," he says, "I've heard you sing 'Oh,

Lonesome Me,' and I really like the way you play the guitar to it. So I was wondering if you could show me how to chord it. I have the words here and I'm trying to learn it."

"No problem at all," I said. "If you got some time, I'll show you everything you need to know." A few minutes later he was sitting in my room and getting the chords down pretty good, and all he was going to need was a lot more practice. He was also having a little problem getting the right beat.

Soon he noticed a ring binder I had sitting on my little table. "What's this?" he said. When I told him it was a book of some of the songs I had written, he said, "What! Over five hundred of them?" I said, "Yeah, I've been writing them since I was eleven years old. I have a lot more than those memorized, and they're just the ones I haven't committed to memory yet."

As he paused to read a couple of songs all the way through, he said, "Hell, this is great stuff. And you mean to tell me you also got melodies for all of these? How come you haven't got any of them recorded yet?" I laughed and said, "I guess opportunity just hasn't knocked yet. Maybe it's a case of just not being in the right place at the right time." I then asked him if he had written any songs.

"I started on a couple one time," he said, "and I got half of one written down somewhere, but I never got around to finishing it." When I told him he should finish it because he'd probably need a lot of new songs now that he had a recording contract, he asked me if any of the songs he was looking at were available, either to buy, or could they in some other way be placed at his disposal.

After thinking for a moment, I said, "Well, ordinarily, they are not for sale. But maybe we can make a deal." I told him how long I'd been writing and singing and that I'd been looking to get a break in music ever since I was fourteen.

"That's eight years ago," I said, "and the prospects don't look any brighter today than they did back then.

So I'll tell you what I'll do. I feel confident that I can make it in the music business, but I need to be heard by someone who has the power to put me on records. You, on the other hand, have a recording contract, but you don't have any material to sustain it. So I'll pick six songs out of this book that are particularly suited to me, and sign all the rest over to you in front of a lawyer. This means that 494 of these songs will be yours, lock, stock and barrel on one condition. And that is that you ask the people who are responsible for giving you this opportunity to also give me an audition at their earliest convenience. And whether I'm accepted or not, after a genuine audition, the songs are yours."

I have no idea what ran through his mind as he thought for a moment, then looked at his brand-new watch and said it was time he had to be going. Less than a week after that, it seemed that all you could hear on the radio was Terry Roberts "with his brand-new smash hit, 'Oh, Lonesome Me.'"

Without exaggeration, there was one station in Toronto that had to be playing Terry's record every twenty minutes, all day long and every night. As a matter of fact, there are still people in the Toronto area who will not believe that it was Don Gibson who wrote "Oh, Lonesome Me" and had the world-wide hit for singing it. Although Don's record was the only version played everywhere else, Terry's version was the only one played in Toronto.

Over the next two or three months I saw Terry come into the pool room a number of times, all dressed up in his fancy duds. And although I spoke to him on several occasions, he never let on he heard me. There was also one time later that I met him on the street with three or four girls hanging on his arm, and again he never spoke. I guess he was having too much fun.

There's one more footnote to this story, and it happened in Sudbury about nine years later in 1967. After seventeen long years of trying, my first album was finally out. It was called "Northland's Own" and was sort of a compilation of most of the songs I had written about the north and songs that I myself had recorded on a number of small singles.

One night, while passing through Sudbury, I stopped to have a couple of beers in a place I think they called the Horseshoe Club. It was around 10 P.M. when I entered the room and the only people there were sitting at two tables. As I sat down to have a beer the band was just going on stage. And wouldn't you know it, the lead singer was Terry Roberts.

I thought it was very odd that he was able to recognize me right away, even though the lights in the place were dim. Before he came down from the stage, he sent the waiter to my table with beer and soon he was down talking to me. When the formalities were over, I asked him how things were and why I hadn't heard too much about him for so long, especially as far as his records were concerned.

"Oh," he said, "I recorded a couple more after I saw you last, but the songs weren't all that strong, I guess. By the way, do you still have all those songs you wrote? I could certainly use some of them."

"Yeah, I've still got lots of songs, Terry, and I'm still writing lots more every day," I said, "but I finally got the chance to record some of them after all these years, and as I have a pretty good idea that I'll be recording a hell of a lot more of them, the songs are just no longer available. But why didn't you take me up on my offer a long time ago when you could have had them for nothing?"

As he thought for a moment, and didn't seem to have anything to say, I looked at my brand-new watch and said, "Well, I guess I'd better be going." And that's the last time I ever saw Terry Roberts. Come to think of it, it's also the last time I ever heard of him.

For the next two and a half years, from the fall of 1958 to the spring of 1961, the life of Tom Connors the drifter had become very tumultuous. For one thing there was a girl who wanted me to settle down. But try as

I might, I didn't do a very good job of making myself over.

In my efforts to be just a regular guy like everyone else, in order to fit the regular mould, you might say I failed miserably. I worked in a machine shop, a tire manufacturing plant and a dry cleaner's. I painted buildings, drove trucks, cleaned offices, delivered handbills, erected scaffolding, and did just about everything except what I wanted to do. And that, of course, was to play music. My whole life was wrapped around it.

I remember one job I had, where I got a little ahead in my work and was standing by a pole humming a new melody that had just come to my mind, when the foreman walked up behind me and asked, "What the hell do you think you're doing?" Without thinking about lying, I immediately replied, "I'm writing a song. I just got this great idea for…" And before I got to finish the line, he said, "Oh, 'great idea' eh? You're 'writing a song'? Well, I'm going to write you a song. It's called, 'You're fired,' and it's the best goddamn idea I've had all day."

The longest job I held was at the Goodyear plant in New Toronto. Although I hated it, I gave it my best efforts till I got hurt pretty bad one day. Soon after, they laid me off and never called me back. It took me more than six months after that to be able to bend over and pick up as little as ten pounds.

In the midst of all this turmoil, one question always kept surfacing. How can I ever be any good to anybody if I can't be true to myself? And the answer was always the same: it's impossible to give what you don't have to give. If you don't have peace of mind, you can't impart it to anyone else. If you're not pleased with what you're doing, then you can't please anyone else by doing it. In a nutshell, it all seemed to boil down to one thing: the reason I was given the talent to sing and write songs was because somewhere, somehow, sometime, it was all going to mean something to someone. So by the spring of 1961 I emerged with a resolve and a philosophy that nobody else seemed to understand.

I figured the only worth I had was to make others happy, and the only time I seemed to be able to impart happiness to others was when I was singing. Therefore, the only time I had worth was when I was singing. Without worth and without singing I might as well be dead. So from now on I was just going to live to sing and sing to live or die as I lived, unwanted.

Vancouver Job Offer

In the early spring of 1961 I decided to go to Vancouver. And upon hearing about a car dealer who was looking for people to drive cars out west, I took the job, to "kill two birds with one stone," so to speak. I'd get paid for driving to where I wanted to go and they'd get their car delivered.

Unfortunately, I hit a small patch of ice in northern Ontario, which resulted in a number of scratches on the side of the car as I temporarily left the road and scraped along one of the guard-rails. When I reached Vancouver and turned the car in, they deducted the cost of repairs from the money they owed me, and there I was again, virtually broke. I had just enough money to get a room and a few groceries, and from there it was back to scraping the bottom of the barrel.

One day, around the middle of June, just after I'd bummed enough money on the street to pay for my bed that night in the Sally Ann, I was walking down Hastings Street with another guy I'll just call Jack, because I forget his name now. Anyway, a nice-looking car pulled up to the curb and a well-dressed guy at the wheel called out to us, "Hey, you guys. You looking for a real good job? Come here." As we walked over to the car, Jack said, "Yeah, maybe. What have you got?"

"Jump in," the guy said, "and we'll drive around a bit while I tell you about it."

As we drove down the street he was asking questions like "How would you guys like to own your own car in less than a week?" and "How would you like to have a lot of nice clothes to wear for a change?" And before we knew it we were driving out of town. Pretty soon we arrived at the top of a twisty mountain road and came to a swanky-looking house. Stopping the car at the front door, he said, "Come on in and have a cool drink and I'll give you all the details of what the job is all about."

Soon we were walking into one of the largest living

rooms I had ever seen. The furniture was very expensive and the large bay windows overlooked the whole city of Vancouver from a distance. As he showed us to our seats on one side of the big glass coffee table, he walked over to a huge liquor cabinet and poured us a couple of good shots of whisky with ice and brought them over to us. Then he went back and returned with his own drink and a carafe containing ginger ale for mix.

Just before he sat down on the sofa on the other side of the coffee table, he opened his coat to reveal a holster containing a hand-gun attached to a shoulder strap. Detaching the gun and holster from the strap and laying them down on his side of the coffee table, he said, "Ahh! That's more comfortable." And after he sat down and had a drink, he said, "And now let's get down to business."

The essence of his proposition was: We were each to be given a fairly new car in our own name, three suits of clothes and an apartment each downtown, with everything paid for up front. We were also to get $500 a week for spending money and a personal expense account to look after things like rent, car repairs, keeping our clothes cleaned and other "little necessities."

"In exchange for all this, the job is very simple," he said. "Both of you will be on call. Then, every once in a while, one of you will be selected to take a trip across the border to Seattle or some other town in the United States. You will be told where to lodge for a couple of nights and exactly where to park your car. You will then take taxis to and fro, get some women and have a good time. Then you will get into your car and come back to Vancouver, and once again you will park in a pre-arranged place. After a day or so, when you are notified, you can then drive your car anywhere you choose, until you're called to make another trip."

After giving us another drink, he explained that we would be smuggling dope. It would be planted on or in the car we were driving, and the less we knew about it, the better off we'd be. If we got caught at the border or anywhere else, we were to act completely innocent. And if we had to, we would have to take the rap, which would probably be light because of it being our first offence.

"Now there's only one more detail," he said, as he took the hand-gun from its holster. "The people I'm associated with don't fool around with anybody who has a big mouth. It doesn't matter whether you're in jail, out of jail or where you are. We'll track you down to the other side of the earth, if we have to. And when we find you, you'll either have a nice fatal accident or you'll have so many holes in your head you'll feel like a piece of Swiss cheese. Now, here's a copy of a phone number, and you've both got forty-eight hours to make up your minds. If you want the job, call the number for further instructions. If you don't, just remember one thing. We never had this conversation, we never met before in our lives, and you're both still breathing."

About fifteen minutes later, he let us out where he picked us up, and as he drove away down the street, I said, "Whew, what do you think of that job? Let's go in and have a beer. I think I'm gonna need one."

In the course of the conversation, I really couldn't tell whether Jack was going to take the job or not. But I assured him that I wasn't. "There's no amount of clothes, cars or money that'll get me involved with drugs," I said, "and besides, I may not have anything, but it's better than rotting in prison and still not having anything."

After we finished our beer, we agreed to meet at a certain restaurant the following morning and talk about it some more. The next morning I arrived with my guitar and suitcase, planning to tell Jack I was going to put some distance between me and that asshole with the gun, but Jack never showed up. I waited for about an hour and a half and then struck out for the highway. About two weeks later I pulled into Edmonton, Alberta.

For the next three months I hung around the Flamingo Restaurant and played every day for nickels and dimes while trying to draw as many people as I could to come in and eat. The restaurant was owned by a Mrs. Cline whom everybody called "Ma." She let me sleep in the back once in a while, when I couldn't get enough money to pay for a room, and I'd also get the odd meal when there was something around to do that I could help out with.

A couple of weeks before I left town, I got to sing a song on television, but it didn't pay much and it didn't open any doors. The song was one I wrote, called "My Little Eskimo," and was one I sang around the Flamingo quite often.

I think it was on a Monday, October 2, 1961, when one of the regulars came into the restaurant for breakfast and happened to mention that he was on his way to North Battleford, Saskatchewan, and that he was driving alone. "Well, if you'd like some company," I said, "and maybe like to listen to a few songs along the way, I'd like to go with you."

"Okay," he said, "but can you be ready in five minutes?"

"I'm all packed and ready to go now," I said. And with a look of surprise on his face, he said, "That's my car across the street. Jump in, and we're off." About two o'clock that afternoon, in North Battleford, I thanked him, said goodbye and headed for the east coast. After hanging around for a day or two here and there in a few towns along the way, about a month later I crossed the New Brunswick border.

Heading for India

Once inside the border, the first ride I got was a long slow one. The driver's name was Roy Bairns and he was coming from Alberta and heading for Shelburne, Nova Scotia. Besides his wife and three kids, his old dilapidated car was packed with all their belongings, and they were going back to Shelburne to live.

When he stopped the car to pick me up, it was like getting in with the Beverly Hillbillies. By the time I got my suitcase jammed in between the roof and the big rolls of bedclothes, they were asking me to play my guitar already. And I wasn't even in yet. "Are you sure you've got room in there for me?" I said. "You've sure got a lot of stuff."

After coaxing me to get in, I first took my guitar out and passed the case to Roy's wife, and she held it there in the front seat till I managed to squeeze in the back with my guitar. After several attempts at banging the door against my leg, I finally got it closed. And away we rumbled.

I don't know how I managed to sing and play with one kid's leg resting on my left arm and another's feet on my shoulders, but they all thought it was great anyhow. They were real friendly people, and even offered me a sandwich as we drove along. Roy's wife was making them in the front seat, and it was my guess that that's all they were eating all the way down from Alberta.

Roy said he was expecting to get a good job when he got to Shelburne and gave me his address to come and see him at any time, if I was ever in the area. When we got to Fredericton a number of hours later, they let me out. I was going to Saint John and they were going on to Nova Scotia, by way of Moncton.

I really enjoyed their company, but when Roy came around to open my door, I damn near fell out. We both laughed and shook hands, and as I tried to get a kink out of my leg, I watched them disappear down the road.

It was late that night when I arrived in Saint John, and

even later by the time I found out where Steve was living. But when I finally knocked on the door of his basement apartment, and Steve opened it, it was just like old times. He had been getting quite a bit of work stevedoring around the docks, and it just so happened that he had a case of beer on hand. It didn't take us long to get into it.

When we finally brought each other up to date on what we both had been doing, the subject took on a very strange twist. Out of the clear blue sky, Steve got up and went into another room to bring out a couple of books. Thinking he had gone to the bathroom, I opened my suitcase to show him some of the books that I, myself, had been reading. I had brought them all the way from Vancouver with me, in case he might find them interesting. It was a little chilling, to say the least, when we found out that we had not only been reading up on the same subjects, but almost half our books were identical.

The subject matter of the books mainly covered such things as yoga, psychic phenomena, reincarnation, the occult, flying saucers, mysticism, astrology, comparative religion, faith healing and everything from lost continents to the building of the Great Pyramid. It seems that, coincidentally, we both began to ponder these great mysteries at the same time. We found them very intriguing. And for the next couple of months, we discussed them almost every day.

Around the last of November, we hit upon a very unusual plan. Had it worked, we probably both would have been a couple of monks in a Tibetan monastery by now. We decided that, in order to pursue our studies, the best place to do it would be somewhere in the mysterious East, probably around northern India, where we might find a guru and become his disciples for a while.

The first part of the plan was to go to Halifax and get aboard a tramp ship heading to the Far East. We would work for our passage if we had to, and sooner or later, even if it took a year, we would eventually arrive at our destination.

Two days later, we left Saint John, hitch-hiking, and on December 1 we were in Halifax. Then we ran into a snag. Checking at several marine offices and other places where merchant seamen hang out, we found that, due to immigration laws, we couldn't board a tramp ship without a passport. As this might take a couple of weeks of waiting, and then we might be faced with some other kinds of red tape, we abandoned our plans and decided that we probably wouldn't have made very good monks anyway.

What Happened in Nova Scotia

So here we were in Halifax, and what to do now? While digging through one of my pockets, I came up with an address. It was the address that Roy Bairns had given me, when he invited me to come and see him if I was ever in the Shelburne area. Well, we were now only 150 miles away, so why not pay him a visit?

The first night out from Halifax, a big snowstorm blew up, and when we got a ride it was from a nice couple who took us right up to their house and gave us a bed for the night, and a good breakfast to tackle the road with in the morning. The storm, however, had no intentions of letting up, and it just kept on snowing all that day. That night we came to a little variety store, and when we let it be known that we were hitch-hiking and didn't have a place to stay, the owner put us up in one of his cabins that he had just across the road. He also gave us some canned goods and showed us where to get some dry wood. Pretty soon we had a good fire going, we cooked ourselves up a nice meal, and the place was really comfortable.

As if all this wasn't enough, the next morning when a big sleet storm set in, he came across the road with some more food and told us to stay for another night. Talk about your hospitality. Kindness like that is hard to top. That night, the weather turned really mild for some reason, and the sleet turned into a warm rain. By the time we got up the next morning it felt strange to look outside. After all the snow that had come down in the last couple of days, there was hardly any left. Everywhere you looked you could see puddles of water. When we thanked the guy for his great help and finally hit the road, the highway was bare.

That evening, as we were walking past the road going down to Lockeport, off the main highway, a number of coincidences began to occur. As we came walking towards a railway crossing, we could see all the lights of town shining just to our left. We were talking about our common interest in the books, and also how strange it was that we were both wearing heavy grey coats that were identical. Steve had bought his in Saint John and I had mine given to me by a French guy who picked me up in Quebec on an especially cold day. Just as we stepped into the railway crossing area, we both heard a high-pitched sound which startled us, and as we looked towards Lockeport, all the town lights went out. It was as if someone had thrown the main switch and not a light could be seen anywhere. As soon as we came out of the crossing, all the lights came back on.

At this point I jokingly said to Steve, "Maybe we just walked on the button that controls all the lights around here. Let's go back and see if we can do it again." As we walked back across the tracks nothing happened, but as we came back again from the other side, the lights again went out and stayed out. This gave us a little bit of a chill. But as soon as we began to reason it out, we put it down to just being a coincidence and kept on walking along the highway. About a mile farther down the road, when the view of town was just about to go out of sight due to the woods and trees, we looked back, but the lights were still out.

Assuming they just had a power failure, our attention moved on to other things. The night was not cold, but what you might call brisk, and with not a wisp of clouds anywhere, you could see the entire expanse of the clear night sky, especially each time we came into a clearing after passing a bit of woods. I don't know why, but for some reason, I can't seem to recall whether there was a moon that night or not.

At any rate, as we walked along a straight stretch of road, Steve and I both happened to be looking at the same section of the star-studded sky, when we both stopped at the same time. As I could have sworn I saw a bright star move from its spot and travel in a straight line to another spot, and then, all in the same motion, at a 45-degree angle, move to another spot and stop. I was flabbergasted, to say the least. The star had actually drawn a perfect "V" and was now still shining from its last position.

As Steve began to say in a loud voice, "Tom! Did you see...?" I interrupted him and said, "Just a minute. Let me describe to you exactly what I think I saw, and you can tell me if you saw the very same thing as I did."

While the two of us kept our eyes still glued to the same star, Steve agreed to having seen what I just saw, in every detail. We didn't know what the hell to make of it. As we kept on watching the star for another fifteen minutes, and it didn't move again, we began to doubt our senses. We'd both been out on the road observing the night sky for years now, and this was the first time we'd ever encountered something like this. After going through every possible explanation to account for what we just saw, we finally laughed and said we must have been reading too many of those damn flying saucer books. We still kept our eye on the star though, from time to time, just to make sure it was still there.

About twenty minutes later, just as we were coming out of another wooded area and were approaching a very large clearing, we could see what looked like a bridge about a quarter of a mile ahead, and to our left we were beginning to see glimpses of some flats where there was water leading to the ocean.

Now, as I said before, there wasn't a wisp of clouds anywhere in the sky. But as we came out from around the woods that had been obstructing our view to the left of us, we were amazed at seeing a perfect bow and arrow in the southern sky. And this bow and arrow was formed by some kind of cloud formation that looked exactly like the streams one might see trailing behind a jet plane. Only thing was, no jet or any amount of jets could have drawn this bow and arrow in the sky. It was perfect to the last detail. And besides, the night was so clear and silent in that part of the country that we could have heard a jet plane for miles.

The bow itself was perfectly curved with the thickest cloud stream, and the wispier stream which formed the bow-string came straight down from end to end as if it was undrawn. Then an arrow with a perfect flight and arrowhead was sitting exactly where it should be, as if waiting for a giant hand to pull on the string. The arrow was pointing east. The whole thing looked as if someone had taken a giant piece of chalk and drawn it perfectly on the blackboard of the sky. And again I have to emphasize that nowhere in the sky, either inside this great bow or outside, was there even the smallest trace of a cloud to be seen. It was eerie.

As we started to walk again, we kept looking over our left shoulder. We couldn't keep our eyes off it. It didn't even lose its shape as any normal cloud would do as it moves with the wind. It only stayed where it was until it began to fade. And by the time we got up to the bridge, it was all but gone. By the time we got over the bridge, it had completely disappeared. And as we turned around and started walking backwards to see if there was any evidence left that it had actually been there, our eyes fell on a sign attached to the bridge. It read: "Jordan River." There was no sign facing us when we approached from the other side, and had we not turned to look back, we would never have seen it.

What did it all mean? I don't know. But if the reader wants to ponder it, as I have done for many years, the date was December 6, 1961. And as those who are interested in astrology will know, on December 6, Sagittarius the Archer is at his strongest point on the Zodiac.

To those who love to pass these things off as just coincidence I can only say, maybe you're right, but you might be wrong. I personally believe there's some kind of a sign or a message in all this, but I don't as yet know what it is. At first, I too was willing to pass these events off quickly as coincidence. But how many coincidences does one need to experience within the span of a couple of hours to know that too many coincidences are no coincidence at all?

The identical coats, the lights of Lockeport, the moving star, the Bow and Arrow, the river called Jordan, and the significance of the date. Add them all up and what do you get? Too many coincidences to be a coincidence. Were we both hallucinating? Well, I won't speak for Steve, but if I was, it was the first time in my life, and it hasn't happened again since. It happened for two hours, and I certainly wasn't "on anything."

We walked along and discussed each event in a logical manner, much the same as we did before and after the occurrences, and all other occurrences for that matter. The road, the trees, the tracks, the bridge and everything else during that two hours was experienced as real. So there's no way I will ever be convinced that the phenomena I have just explained did not occur. But as to the meaning? Like I say, I don't know. What do you think?

While still discussing these strange events, a car stopped and gave us a ride into Shelburne. The driver knew the address we were looking for and dropped us off right in front of the door. Roy and his wife were glad to see us, but poor Roy had some bad news. The job he was expecting to get hadn't come through yet, and with Christmas just around the corner, he was scrounging around town looking to do anything that might bring him in a few dollars. Although we played music and sang for them that night, it didn't seem to cheer them up very much, and you could see they were both wishing they had never left Alberta.

Not wanting to be more of a burden on them than they already had, Steve and I decided to pull out again the next day. First we went all around town and picked up enough butts to make up a package of tobacco, and then walked up to a few people on the street and bummed enough silver to make up two or three dollars. After dropping the tobacco and money off at the house, we headed back towards Halifax. From there we went to Truro and Pictou, and then over to Prince Edward Island.

In the Charlottetown Jail

On the night we arrived in Charlottetown, we got the cops to put us up in the local jail. As we arrived quite late and were kind of tired we just lay down on our bunks in the cell and planned on going right to sleep. The cells were down in the basement and one guy was already locked up for some reason, and after the cop went upstairs, he asked us if we had a cigarette. We told him we had some tobacco that we picked up off the street and if he didn't mind that, we had some papers so he could roll his own. He said he didn't mind, and after Steve took him some tobacco and a couple of papers, we turned in.

Just as we were about to doze off, there was a hell of a commotion upstairs. It sounded like there was a war on. Doors were banging like they were being opened and slammed shut, there was a great deal of whooping and hollering going on. And by the sounds of things, the cops were having trouble with some kind of a large mob.

Just as we figured the cops must be getting some kind of a working over, the door at the top of the stairs opened and down came three or four of them carrying this little pip-squeak of a guy in a very light blue suit. When he finally stopped kicking and screaming for a second to catch his breath, they stood him down on a Coke case. And as we sized him up, he didn't look to be any taller than five-foot-nothin', countin' the Coke case and all.

He looked like he was Lebanese, and what he wasn't telling those cops, there wasn't any words to describe. He was calling them everything he could lay his tongue to. "I'm gonna sue you bastards, and I'll sue the whole city of Charlottetown. There's no way you're gonna put me in here and get away with it. I'll get you sons-of-bitches if it takes me till the day I die."

As the cops were trying to get up the stairs, he was grabbing them by their uniforms. They carried him back once or twice and started to run up the stairs with this little guy running right behind them. Finally, they raced him up the stairs, pushed him back through the door and slammed it shut.

He then stood up there hammering on the door for five or ten minutes telling them what he was and what he wasn't going to do.

Steve and I were wondering what in hell was going on, anyway. Why didn't they put him in a cell or something. He wasn't drunk, so he must have been in for something else. The least they could have done, we thought, was lock him up for causing a riot at the police station. It was getting pretty bad when a couple of decent, law-abiding bums couldn't even get some sleep in a jail house.

Pretty soon he came down the stairs and came over to talk to us. Then he went over and talked to the other guy, and then came back over to talk to us again. Me and Steve decided to keep our cell door closed so he'd think it was locked. By the mood he was in, there was no telling what he might do if he ever got in the cell with us.

"Them rotten bastards," he kept saying, as he walked up and down swinging and waving his arms around. "They can't do this to me. I'll get them for this. They don't know who they're dealing with. They're gonna get one hell of a surprise when I sue them bastards, I'll tell you that." He just went on and on and on.

When I thought I might get him on another subject, I asked him if he wanted a cigarette. He paused for a second, looked at me and said, "No, I don't smoke," and immediately went back to how he was going to sue the city.

Every five minutes he'd go back up and bang on the door half a dozen times, and the last time they just opened the door and out he went. There was more hollering and screaming and thumping for a short while, then all of a sudden there was silence. Everything was so quiet you could hear a pin drop. Where he went or whatever happened, we didn't know. All we knew was, now, at last we could get some sleep. (I'll get to explain later how this same little runt not only got to be a future boss of mine, but he also wound up being the best man at my wedding. His name was Johnny Reid.)

After leaving Charlottetown we headed for the Borden–Cape Tormentine Ferry. Although there was some discussion about Skinners Pond, and the fact that Christmas would be here in a few days, I had no desire to go there. I felt the last time I was there with Steve was enough. So on that final hitch-hiking trip to Prince Edward Island, I didn't even go near Prince County. We just got on the boat and went back to New Brunswick.

A Chat with God

For the next two days I tried to convince Steve to stay on the road with me, and just keep on drifting, but the best answer he could give me was a rather doubtful one. He suggested we first go back to Saint John where he would take a few days to think it over and then let me know for sure.

By Christmas Day we were back in Saint John and by New Year's Day, 1962, Steve still didn't know whether he wanted to go or not. I then said, "Well, I'll tell you what. I'm going to leave tomorrow at noon, and if you decide to come by then, okay, and if you don't want to come, that's okay, too. No hard feelings one way or the other."

I did a lot of hard thinking that night and the next day about 11 o'clock in the morning, I said, "Well, what do you think, Steve? Are you coming or not?"

"No, I guess not, Tom," he said. "I think I'll just stay put for a while, maybe do some work longshore, and think about it again in the spring. Where do you think you'll be headed, anyway?"

"Well, you know me, Steve. I never know where I'm going till I get there, and I never know whether I'm ever going to be back or not. And this trip is going to be different than any other. In the first place, I'm not going to be needing this any more." I then pointed to my old guitar, the one I'd bought in Nashville, and pushed it over to where he was sitting.

"I'm giving you my old guitar to keep. It's not a loan or anything, and I don't just want you to keep it for me till I get back from somewhere. From now on, it's yours. It belongs to you, and you can do with it whatever you wish. You can keep it and play it, or you can pawn it, sell it, or trade it. You can give it away if you want to, or you can do whatever you like with it. It's now officially your property. And remember one more thing. Even if I was ever to ask you to give it back to me, providing you still had it, of course, you are under absolutely no obligation to do so. What is yours is yours to dispose of in any way you see fit."

As I got up and walked to the door, with only the clothes I had on my back, Steve said, "What's the matter with you, Tom? I've never seen you like this before. You can't possibly mean what you just said about your guitar. Are you not feeling well, or something? Where the hell are you going, anyway?"

As I opened the door and turned to leave I looked at him. "Have you ever known me to say anything I didn't mean? Of course I mean it," I said, "and, yes, I'm feeling okay, but as to where I'm going, I can't be sure. I only know one thing; that wherever it is, I'll be having a good long chat with God. And I won't be needing my guitar to do that." As I closed the door and walked down the hall it occurred to me that tomorrow would be Steve's birthday. As I chuckled over the coincidence and hoped he'd enjoy his unexpected present, he opened the door again and called my name, but I just turned around with a smile, waved and kept on going.

When I hit the street, it was a nice bright sun-shiny day for that time of year, but the sun was no match for the frost in the air which was turning my breath into steam. After walking briskly for about twenty minutes or so, I came to the bottom of Fort Howe Hill. And, as this is one of the highest points overlooking the city and the harbour, I decided to go up to the top for one last look at the town in which I was born.

When I reached the top and began to survey the landscape I was feeling very despondent. With tears in my eyes I felt sad for myself and sad for the city that spawned me. As I looked at the buildings, the church steeples, the streets, the alleys and the hovels, I somehow knew I was saying goodbye for the last time. Not so much goodbye to physical structures, but goodbye to all my previous attachments.

The city of Saint John would no longer have a hold on me. For that matter, I was now completely unattached from everything in the world—Skinners Pond, Saint John, my mother in Montreal—and even at this very moment, I was reappraising the strength of the bond between me and Steve.

From where I was standing on Fort Howe Hill, I could see all approaches to Main Street and Chesley Street, which both led to the Reversing Falls bridge, and this was the only way out of town if one were heading west. I somehow still hadn't given up hope that Steve might change his mind at the last minute and decide to catch up with me before I got to the highway.

Had this been his decision, I would have been able to pick him out as he came walking along any of the streets below me, and I could then have scrambled down from the hill to meet him.

I must have stood there for over an hour, just waiting and half hoping to see him coming. As I painstakingly studied the few people walking along the frosty streets, the wind on the hill was getting colder and colder, and so were the embers from the fire of my youth.

As I looked in the direction of Brook Street, where my father was born, I wondered why God never allowed him and my mother to provide a normal home for me. Why, I wondered, couldn't I have been like everyone else, instead of being a misfit who never seemed to be able to fit into any mould? From being an outcast at three years old with my mother, to the orphanage, and then to Skinners Pond and beyond, I'd never known the feeling of ever being wanted by anybody.

Why had they worked me so hard in the orphanage, and then in Skinners Pond? And was this why I could find absolutely no reason for working anywhere for anybody now? And why had God let all this happen anyway? Would it always be my destiny to walk alone, live alone and die alone? And what about the songs I'd written? They must be all for nought, as well. Just like my life, I thought, it all seemed to be such a terrible waste.

At this point in time, only Steve knew more than

anyone else just how much singing and playing and writing songs had meant to me all my life. He also knew that I'd give anything to become a country music entertainer and recording artist. But it didn't seem to matter where I travelled or how willing I was to sing and play for people, I just never met anyone who was in a position to help me achieve my goals, nor did I meet anyone who had the wherewithal and the financial capability to help me, who had ever been in the least bit interested in doing so.

It also seemed mighty strange to me that God would give someone a talent that practically borders on an obsession to write songs about the people and the places he's been, and to sing and play them, and yet provide no opportunity or outlet for them to be heard. Nothing whatever seemed to make any sense.

For the last little while now, I had been doing a lot of thinking. What if God really didn't want me to become an entertainer at all? And what if my attachment to my guitar was really preventing me from seeing what God really had planned for me?

Well, I thought, that's exactly why I am standing here today without it. Though it had always been the only thing between me and starvation, the only thing left that gave me any reason to even bother to go on living, if there was any chance at all that it might possibly be the only thing left in the way, as an obstacle, preventing me from knowing and pursuing my true destiny, then, no matter how much it meant to me, it had to go.

And now I was wondering if God would send Steve and the guitar to find me. I guess you could say I was waiting and hoping for a sign that would prove that, because I was willing to give up the only thing I had to live for in life, God would restore it to me as a verification that a life in music had been meant for me after all.

When the hope that Steve would show finally had to give way to the biting cold that now threatened to turn me into a frozen monument, I said goodbye to the city, goodbye to my youth and goodbye to Steve and my old guitar. The door to my past was now officially closed, and all I had left was the memory.

As I came down from Fort Howe Hill, the future looked even blacker than the past, and my heart was completely devoid of hope. For the next several days and a couple of hundred miles, I must have gone through many towns and got many rides, but I don't remember any of them. I guess I was just too deep in thought.

I somehow felt like a leaf that had just fallen off a tree and was now being blown to wherever the wind would take me. I once thought I knew how the wind felt, but now I knew I was only just beginning to know how the wind felt. The wind and I were one. We didn't know where we came from, why we were here, or where we were going. Many years later, it was the memory of these thoughts that prompted me to write the song called "I Am the Wind."

It was somewhere on a stretch of lonely highway, up around Rivière-du-Loup, Quebec, that I came wandering along and decided to sit down for a while near the side of the road. As I climbed up on top of one of the banks of snow and looked around, there wasn't a house in sight. All I could see for miles was snow. Walking down a few steps, on the other side of the snowbank and well out of sight of the highway, I sat down to roll a cigarette. And there I had my serious talk with God.

"What do you want me to do?" I asked. "And where do you want me to go? Shall I go north, east, south, or west? Or stay right here and die? Why won't you give me some direction? Or just send somebody or something to let me know in some way that you even care? Nobody in this world has ever wanted me, and the only way I was able to go on, up until now, is because I figured you did. But if you don't, then I'm worthless. And if I'm of no use to you, and no use to the world or the people in it, then take me away now."

I then dug a hole in the snowbank and crawled in with

the intention of staying there till the snowplough came and covered me up, or until I just fell asleep and froze to death. After I was in the hole for a while, I began to ask more questions. Why must I wait till I go to sleep or until the snowplough comes? Why prolong the agony? Why not pull the snow down over myself now and smother myself to death?

"Well, I can't do it myself," I was now saying out loud. "Why can't I do it myself? Because that's God's prerogative, not mine. I didn't give myself life, God did. And if I didn't give myself life, then by whose right or authority should it be taken away? Mine or God's? And if I take away my own life, would this not be the highest insult I could give to God? And did I not just say a few minutes ago that I was worthless and useless? And if so, then how could such a no-account as myself have the audacity to take the divine right of God upon himself to throw the gift of life back in the face of the giver just because I don't want it, and because I have judged it to be worthless?

"Who in the hell do I think I am, anyway, to set myself up as a judge of whether or not a life has value or worth? Whether it is my own, or that of another person or creature? Is it not up to God to judge the worth of each life God has created?

"Just because others have shunned me because they have judged me to be worthless, doesn't mean that I have to judge myself by their same rules or standards. I may have worth in the eyes of God even though I have no worth in the eyes of men. It is not God telling me that I'm worthless, it's men. For if God had judged me to be worthless, He would have taken my life away long before this.

"This also means that because I have life, I have worth. And if I'm judged to have worth by God, then why should I care about the judgement of men. Who the hell does man think he is, anyway, to set himself up as a judge of the worth of his fellow man?"

As soon as I realized that to God, all life has worth, no

matter how insignificant it may be in the eyes of men, I wasn't long wiping the tears off my face and scrambling the hell out of that snowbank. As I straightened myself out and got back on the road, I didn't care any more what people were going to think of me. I just knew that when God was ready, in His own time, He would deal with me as He saw fit. And those who condemned me would have to take it up with the God that made me.

If I made it in the music business, or any other business, it would be all right, because it would be God's doing. And if I didn't make it in the music business or any other business, that would be all right, too, because that would also be God's doing. And if everything I did from that time on was God's doing, then God was on my side. And, if God was on my side, what fear should I have of those who were against me?

For the next three days, on my way to Montreal, I was resolved to walk the daily path that God set out before me, without feeling ashamed any more. I somehow felt like a lost lamb who had finally found his way back to the shepherd. At the feet of God, I threw what I came to believe was a worthless carcass, and instead of Him throwing it on the trash heap, He injected it with new life and new meaning and gave it back to me.

In the eyes of others, there was absolutely no change, for that had all taken place on the inside. The old Tom had been captain of a ship where God had been merely a passenger. The ship got lost at sea and battered by the storms of life, till at last, she appeared to be sinking. In a final and desperate move, Tom enlisted the help of his Passenger, and God took over the helm.

When I arrived in Montreal, it was back to waiting in the long lines, at either the churches, Sally Anns or the missions. There were no great miracles, nor did I expect any. The only transformation that took place was the way I began to see everything in a new light. I began to see God's involvement in everything, everywhere, while everyone else didn't seem to have this consciousness.

It was like I had entered into the Kingdom of God where all the inhabitants looked identical to those in the previous world, but were now, in reality, the people of God, both holy and divine. The only problem was, they had not, as yet, awakened to the fact.

After five or six weeks of bumming and begging on the streets of Montreal, I started to get the urge to write songs again. I don't know why, but I took it as a sign that maybe God had decided it was time I had my old guitar back again. "But I gave it to Steve," I said to myself, "and it wouldn't be right to ask him for it back. Besides, he may have run into hard times and sold it, or for any one of a number of reasons he may not have it any more."

After wrestling with this problem for a couple of days, and trying to determine whether this urge was really from God or just the re-emerging of an old desire, I decided I would have to find out.

"I'll go back to Saint John," I thought, "and if Steve still has the guitar, that will be one indication that maybe it's meant that I should have it back." Because I knew Steve well enough to be able to detect even the slightest sign of unwillingness, I figured if I asked for the guitar and found absolutely no hesitation in his wanting to give it back, I could then feel I was meant to have it for sure. On the other hand, if this scenario did not play out exactly, I would merely inform Steve about recent happenings, and then leave without asking for the guitar at all.

During the next several days, nothing much happened till I arrived back in New Brunswick. I had stayed overnight in the Fredericton jail, and when they let me out the next morning, it was in the middle of a blizzard. The snow and freezing rain were blowing everywhere. There wasn't a single person on the streets anywhere, not even a dog.

After walking with a crouch against the force of the wind for about half an hour, I came to a nuns' convent and decided I'd go around to the side door and ask for something to eat. After knocking and waiting for a couple of minutes, the door opened a bit and a small nun peeked through the crack and asked me what I wanted. When I told her I was cold and hungry, she said she couldn't let me in, but if I wanted to wait for a few minutes, she'd see what she could do about getting me a sandwich.

After waiting for only about ten minutes, but what seemed like an eternity under the circumstances, the door once again opened and the same nun passed me out a little brown paper bag which contained a ham sandwich and a small paper cup full of hot tea. After apologizing for not letting me in and explaining that even what she was doing was against the rules, she said something that sounded like "May God be with you," and closed the door.

As I headed down the street with the wet snow freezing to my clothes, I wondered where or how I was going to get the chance to get a drink of that tea while it was still hot enough to do me any good. Between the gusts of driving wind, I was able to catch a glimpse of a Catholic church on the other side of the street, and decided to make my way over there to see if I could get in. To my great relief the door was open, so I stepped inside and closed it behind me. After brushing as much snow off me as I could, I then made my way to the very back pew where I sat down and took my tea and sandwich out of the bag.

As I took my first drink of tea and a bite of the sandwich, a priest came out from behind the altar to light some candles. When he spotted me sitting there, he came to the back of the church and asked me what I thought I was doing. When I told him my circumstances and how the nuns had given me the tea and sandwich, and that because of the extreme weather conditions I had no other place but the church in which to take refuge, he ordered me out.

"This is a house of worship," he said, "not a place for lazy derelicts to come and eat their lunch. Look at the crumbs you're leaving on the bench, and the water you're dripping on the floor. Don't you have any sense of respect at all? Now pack up the rest of that mess and be on your way."

"I'm sorry for the trouble I've given you, Father," I said, "and I'll gladly clean up the mess and mop your floor, if you can only let me stay inside for another minute or two till I finish my sandwich and tea."

"We have proper maintenance people who are very capable of cleaning the House of God," he said, "and they did a very good job until you came in and messed it all up. And if you have any shame for your intrusion, you'll leave immediately."

"But, Father," I said, "did Jesus not say that we should help the homeless and hungry?" With that he grabbed me by the shoulder and pushed me towards the door, saying, "How dare the likes of you tell me what our Lord Jesus said or didn't say? You are very fortunate that I am a priest, or I would throw you out the door myself for your insolence. Now get yourself out of here at once."

By now he had pushed me out the door and slammed it shut behind me.

As I once again stepped into the howling wind, I couldn't believe what had just happened. I stuffed what was left of my sandwich into my mouth, poured as much tea as I could in with it, put my hands in my pockets to try to keep them warm, and headed down the deserted street.

"God sure works in mysterious ways, sometimes," I said to myself, "and I sure have one hell of a lot more to learn."

Sometime in the late afternoon of the following day, I was back in Saint John, at Steve's place. I wasn't in the door long enough to say "Hello" when he had the guitar out, passing it to me even before I asked. "I knew you were coming back for it, Tom," he said. "I dreamed I saw you come to get it about a week ago, and I've had this strong feeling you were on your way back for it ever since, especially in the last two days."

What could I say? He even had it all shined up for me, and ready to go. I asked him if he was absolutely sure that he wanted to part with it, because after all, it was really his, and he immediately answered, "Yeah, I know it's mine. But now it's yours, because I just gave it to you." And as an afterthought, he said, "And though I may be a month late for your birthday, happy birthday, anyway." Now we were both laughing, and soon I was relating everything that had happened to me since I saw him last. He was very impressed, and said he felt strongly that somehow the old guitar was surely meant to fit into all this in some way. After a couple of days, and many hours of speculation upon the meaning of all that had happened, I again said goodbye and was back on the road.

Learning to Be Patient

As I slowly made my way to Ontario, I couldn't help but think that getting my guitar back must have meant that somewhere, somehow I was going to get a break in the music business. All I had to do now was wait till God provided the opportunity and then pounce on it like a lion.

Little did I know that the opportunity was still two and a half years away.

I must have let my enthusiasm get the best of me. I guess I thought my opportunity was just behind the next door I knocked on. Or maybe the next. Or the next, maybe? Not realizing God was going to accomplish things in His own sweet time, I began rushing things. For most of that year it was just push, push, push; and between pushes I always wound up in the doldrums. I still hadn't learned the full lesson of my experience. I still found it was hard to remember that I wasn't steering the ship anymore. With my new-found confidence that God was on my side, I thought things were going to happen overnight. I was expecting a miracle in a month, but found myself being taught a few more years of patience instead.

I must have gone to every record company and music publisher there was that year, and every door I knocked on it was the same old answer. "Don't call us, we'll call you." Out of dozens of bars I visited, I landed only a week's work in two of them. Every time I heard there was a jamboree in some town, I would hitch-hike there to see if I could get on, but there were very few takers. Even the amateur shows I got on always seemed to give the prize to the cute little two-year-old girl with the prettiest dress.

I now began to hear Gary Buck and Gordon Lightfoot being played on Canadian radio in many places, and as the deejays would say, "Here's another one of their national hits," I would wonder when it was going to be my turn. But, alas! It was never to be. It seems the lesson

417

that I was supposed to learn was: "Whatever will be, will be," and I would never know what God's plan for me was to be until He was damn well ready to tell me. And that would probably be on the day it happened.

I may have been given a glimpse of what and how things really were at the present moment, in order to give me a justification for life and a reason for wanting to live it, but as for the future, I would just have to wait and see like everyone else.

When the next winter came, I was just as much in the dark as ever. Was I meant to make it in the music business or not? And did it matter? No, it really didn't. After a year of stupidity, I was finally coming back to the original truth. God is the Captain of the Ship, and I am merely one of the passengers. As the ship pulls into each port, all the passengers will be given their separate instructions. But not one minute before. So what must I do for the present? Just sit by, be patient, and let things happen as they will. And when action is required, I shall be notified. But I must not go to sleep. I must stay on watchful alert, and always be ready when the Captain calls.

Another thing I had been doing all this time was trying to explain to people what it was that I had come to know. I wanted to share this grain of truth with everybody. But, needless to say, I was often being thought of as an idiot for holding such far-fetched ideas. The attitude seemed to be, "We don't mind listening to your songs, but when it comes to your ideas, you can keep them to yourself."

And that's just another thing I had to learn. If you know something about a higher truth, keep it to yourself. If you try to force it upon those who are not ready for it, they will only use it against you, and make you look like a fool. Again, one must learn to be patient. The only time a person can pass on a truth is when God decides to send you a receptive listener, who will then ask the appropriate question, because he is now ready to receive the appropriate answer.

The Bootlegger's Entertainer

In 1963, sometime after I turned twenty-seven, I was sitting in a bootlegging joint in New Toronto. This was something I enjoyed doing because I could sing and play for people, drink a few beers and try to grab the odd free sandwich that might be floating around. I also found the atmosphere conducive to the inspiration of writing a song. It wasn't the beer so much as it was the people and their topics of conversation.

One of the customers that night was a French guy by the name of Ray Goguen from New Brunswick. I could see he was really enjoying the songs, and it wasn't long before he introduced himself and invited me to come to his house sometime. I accepted his offer, and soon after that I was walking down Fourth Street and decided to knock on his door.

Once inside, it was no time before a full-fledged party was under way. Ray had made a couple of phone calls to some buddies he worked with at the Continental Can Company, and while they were on their way down, Ray introduced me to his wife, Grace, who was from P.E.I., and then showed me his guitar.

It was a hell of a great bunch of guys that arrived that night, and Ray and I sang and played till away on into the wee hours of the morning. The next day was Sunday, and while we had a few beers and talked for most of the day, we learned a great deal about each other's background. Ray was from a very large family and had a couple of brothers and sisters now living in the New Toronto area. Grace, who was also from a large family, had a brother who was now a tobacco farmer in the Port Elgin area of Ontario.

As soon as Ray and Grace learned of my financial status, they invited me to stay at their place for a while and meet some of their friends and relatives. I was quick to agree to this proposal, and it wasn't long before we were having a party every second or third night. When the crowd didn't gather at Ray's, we could be found at a variety of locations from New Toronto to Brampton, and from Oakville to Southampton. And wherever we were, a good time was always had by all.

It must have been June before Ray and his friends were all partied out, and even though it was time for me to move on, I still went back from time to time to see them. Ray and Grace have always been good friends and great supporters of mine over the years, and we still, to this day, get together for a few sing-songs whenever we can.

After leaving Ray's, I spent a week or so up in Bala, Ontario, just partying around with a guy named Lenny Brown and a few of his friends, and even got to water ski for the very first time. I naturally fell on my head a few times (the guys driving the boat were having a few laughs and were not too easy on me), but I eventually got the hang of it.

As soon as we got back, I heard that an old friend of mine was now running a bootleg joint somewhere in Long Branch. It was in the afternoon when I found the place, and as I walked in the yard the place was lined with motorcycles. After looking at the crest of some guy's jacket, which he had left draped over his bike, and reading, "Black Diamond Riders," I walk up and knocked at the door. When one of the B.D.R. boys answered, I asked for Eddie. When he said Eddie wasn't here right now, I asked him if anyone would mind if I just came in to wait for him, because he was a friend of mine.

Once inside, the guy serving the beer asked me if I wanted one. "It's a hot enough day for a cold beer," I said, "but I can't afford one right now." I knew I had spoken just loud enough for most of the guys to hear me, and it didn't take long for someone to come up with the expected response. "Play us a few tunes on your 'git-box' there, buddy, and we'll buy you a couple of beers."

By the time Eddie walked in, I had a house full of brand-new fans, and I could hardly hear him holler over the noise of the gang. "I knew goddamned well it was you, Connors, the minute I pulled into the driveway and heard the music. How in the hell are you doing, anyway?" As I pointed to a half-dozen beers sitting in front of me, he didn't need an interpreter to tell him I was doing fine. "I'm pretty busy right now, Tom," he said, "but I'll talk to you a little later." I gave him a bit of a nod and started singing another one of a long list of song requests.

Later on that night, when the Black Diamond Riders left and the rest of the crowd began to thin out a bit, I got to talk to Eddie for a while. He said I could sleep on an old cot in the basement as long as I played a few songs every day. He also thought I might pick up a few tips once in a while, to help keep me going. As it turned out, the free beer always flowed pretty heavy, but the tips were hardly anything at all. As a result, the meals were very scarce.

Two or three weeks after I was there, the B.D.R.s made me an honorary member of the motorcycle club. From that time on, even though I didn't have a bike, I got to ride on the back with many of the guys when they all went camping or just touring around. My guitar, of course, always enjoyed the same privilege, riding on the back of some other guy's bike.

One night, around the last of September, the place was really hoppin', when a guy walked in with a marked bill, bought a beer and left. Five minutes later, the place was crawling with about twenty-five or thirty cops. The place was being raided. As soon as they found the marked bill, they loaded us all into paddy-wagons and took us all off to jail. Before the night was over, everyone got bailed out, except me. Sometime the next afternoon, one of the cops on the desk asked me why I was still there and why I didn't get bailed out along with the rest.

When I told him my circumstances, why I was living at the bootlegger's in the first place, and that I didn't have anybody to bail me out, he left. About half an hour later, he came back with a piece of paper. "Sign this," he said, "and we'll let you go." I forget what kind of paper they said it was, but I signed it anyway, and soon I was on my way back to Eddie's to get my guitar.

Eddie wasn't there, but some people who were cleaning up the house let me in. I was glad to see my guitar still in one piece. And after thanking the people, I was back on the street.

By now, it was evening, and although I was pretty hungry, I was even more tired. There was no bunk in the cell the cops had put me in the night before, and I didn't get very much sleep by sitting down nodding my head in the corner. So now I just wearily made my way down to Marie Curtis Park and went to sleep under some bushes.

The next morning I left my guitar where it was for about an hour, till I went up around the Lakeshore to bum enough money for something to eat. I then went back for the guitar and found a little restaurant where I had a couple of hamburgers and a coffee.

The next three weeks were spent sleeping a night here and two or three nights there at the houses of a few friends and acquaintances, guys I would happen to bump into around the Eastwood Hotel. One of the guys even let me stay at his place for almost a week. I think his name was Wanamaker. He liked my singing and playing a lot and said he had some friend that might be able to help me get into the music business. After he had a talk with him, the deal unfortunately fizzled out.

The next house I went to was only for one night, and while I was singing and playing, we ran out of beer. It just so happened that the bootlegger he called was the same guy I had met several times before, when he delivered beer at Ray Goguen's house. After we got talking for a few minutes, he asked me if I'd like to go to his place for a while and sing for his "in-house customers," much the same as I was doing at Eddie's.

The fact of the matter was, I had planned to leave town the following day, but I said to myself, "What the hell, I'll go and give it one more try. At least I'll be singing for people again." When I told him I'd go, I also asked him if there was anything in it for me. "Just bed and board and whatever you can make in tips," he said. Well, I knew all about the tips and how much that was going to be, but the board? That would be an improvement, even if it was only one meal a day.

The guy's name was Ron, and the next day around suppertime I arrived at his door in Alderwood. The first thing he did was take me down to the basement, where he gave me a beer, and explained the conditions to which I would have to agree. Other than going up to use the bathroom at the head of the stairs, all the rest of the upstairs was off-limits to me. Twice a day, once in the morning and once in the evening, he would bring a sandwich down and put it on one of the tables in the drinking room, and I could eat it whenever I was hungry. And then he showed me to my sleeping quarters.

He walked over to one of the corners of the drinking room and opened a narrow door. Then, as he passed me a very old worn-out blanket, he said, "You can sleep in there." As I looked inside, I found it to be a room about the size of a walk-in closet, approximately six feet long by four feet wide. There was an old narrow couch in there, with a handmade straw mattress lying on the top, and that was all.

There was also a very strong musky smell coming from the room, and when I asked him what it was, he explained that it had been caused by two German shepherd police dogs he used to keep in there. And when I asked him where the light switch was, he said there wasn't any. He said he used to have an old blind man staying with him and he always slept in there with the two dogs, so there was never any need to install a light. When I inquired as to the old man's present whereabouts, he told me, "The poor fella just died there in bed one night."

Just then a knock came on the door, and as he went up to let in some "clients," he quickly explained the last regulation. "Free beers 'on the house' are limited to six bottles in every twenty-four-hour period, and all the rest you might drink will have to be bought for you by the customers."

There might have been ten or twelve people who came in that first night, and each of them was a bit surprised to see me sitting there singing and also to learn that the price of their usual beer had gone up by five cents a bottle, due to the "entertainment."

Everyone seemed to enjoy themselves, though, and in a very short while the word got around, and the place soon became packed every night. It got so that I didn't have to dip into my quota of six free beers a day at all. The customers were buying me a lot more than I could drink. And while this pleased Ron very much, he didn't find any reason to pass on the extra dividends. I think, at the time, he believed it was quite enough that he was providing me with my "first big break."

By the second week of November, a lot of guys who worked at the Continental Can Company that I had previously met through Ray Goguen, started coming in. And on a couple of occasions, so did Ray himself. I was always glad to see Ray, because he usually seemed to find a way to liven up the party, and sometimes I could even get him to spell me off by taking my guitar and singing a few songs.

By the end of the next week, on Friday, November 22, to be exact, while the whole world was deeply concerned with the assassination of U.S. President John Fitzgerald Kennedy, I was deeply concerned with a problem of my own. With all due respect to Mr. Kennedy, I had just worn an irreparable hole in the arse of my pants. And because they were the only pair I owned, I had to stuff black cloth down there so nobody could see my underwear. Every time I turned around I could only hope the cloth had not moved out of place.

One afternoon shortly after that, a fella by the name of Ray Chapman stopped in for a couple of beers on his way home from work. As he was quite taken by the music, he said he just had to bring his brother Reg in to hear this. When Reg arrived on the following day, he had a few beers, and before he left he invited me to come to his house for an evening on the following weekend.

At first I was a little reluctant to go, citing the fact that Ron, the bootlegger, might not be too pleased if I left him for a night without his entertainment, and besides, I wanted to keep him in a good mood because I planned to ask him for enough money to buy myself a cheap pair of pants.

Pretty soon Reg was saying, "Aw! Come on, Tom. Come on up to the house. I got an awful lot of friends who would love to hear you. And for all you know, there may be a few bucks in it for you."

Well, as soon as he mentioned the word bucks, I thought of the pants I so badly needed, and the possibility that I might not have to ask Ron for the money to buy them after all. "Okay, Reg," I said, "where do you live? Is it a long walk from here?"

"Don't worry about that," he said. "Somebody will be down to pick you up. So we'll see you on Saturday evening."

Though Ron didn't say much when I informed him of my plans, he remained a little sullen for the rest of the week. I didn't know whether this would mean there might not be a place for me when I returned or whether it was just one of his moods. He was one of those guys who rarely changed facial expressions, so it was hard to tell. At any rate, I had said I would go, and whether I lost my little cubby-hole apartment or not, when the car came, I went.

The Chapmans lived in a fairly new subdivision in northern Etobicoke, about a ten- or fifteen-minute car drive from Ron's place, and when I got there everybody seemed to be dressed like they were ready to meet someone important. As I walked in and everybody stood up to say "Hi! How are you," I kept wanting to look back to make certain the focus of all this attention wasn't really meant for someone standing behind me.

As Reg gave me a beer and his wife, Muriel, asked me to sit down and feel relaxed, I couldn't help but feel a little uneasy. Nobody had ever made me feel quite this welcome before, and frankly, I wasn't quite sure how to handle it. Muriel, in her efforts to make me feel right at home, had even asked me if I would like something to eat before anyone asked me to play. "Wow!" I thought. "In the world I'm from, they ask you to play first, and you're only lucky if they ever offer you something to eat at all." (I could remember exceptions to the rule, of course, and this night would certainly become one of them.)

It was also a joy to play for these people. Though the living room was full, everyone gave me their undivided attention. While this had also happened a few times before, in most cases you'd have to try to sing over top of a few loud-mouths who were trying their best to talk over top of you. (I remember a couple of occasions when I had to actually put the guitar back in its case, excuse myself to those who really would have preferred to listen and just walk out.)

There may have been eight or ten people there that night, and everyone had a great time, including me. The only discomfort I felt was when I had to walk sideways each time I went to the washroom. As I didn't want all these nice people to see my underwear, I tried not to leave my seat too often.

(Years later, when I got to be great friends with the Chapmans, they told me that on the following day, everyone was saying how remarkable it was that I could just sit there drinking for so long without ever having to go to the washroom. When I told them, "The real reason I was able to hold it for so long was because I didn't want anybody to see me with the arse out of my pants," they all had quite a chuckle.)

Someone also picked up a collection for me that night, while lunch was being served, and after everyone left I was shown to a nice bed in the basement. The next morning, after breakfast, they told me to be sure to come back sometime. And after thanking them very much, I was on my way back to the bootlegger's. As Ron didn't seem to be in a very good mood when I got there, I just sat around and didn't say too much. I assumed that he may have been a little unhappy about the night before, when some of his customers arrived to find he had no entertainment.

That evening, only a few stragglers came in and left early, which didn't help the situation too much. After they left, and I went to the fridge to get another beer, he made some remark that intimated he wasn't selling enough to pay for the beers I was drinking. When I asked him to explain himself, he went off on some tangent about the last time "my friend" Ray Goguen was in. He said that a whole twenty-four of beer had somehow got stolen from the fridge that night.

When I asked him if he was suggesting that Ray stole it, or even that I might have helped him to steal it, he didn't fully answer the question. He just started up the stairs, mumbling something about how the loss of the beer would have to be made up for, somehow.

For some reason, my stinky little cubby-hole was smelling a little stinkier that night. And I didn't care for the idea that Ron might be thinking that I had anything to do with a missing case of beer. When I got up the next morning to find there was no sandwich on the drinking-room table, I was off to buy a new pair of pants and hit the friendlier highway.

From Scarborough to Port Elgin

When I got to New Toronto, I bought a new pair of black jeans at the Army and Navy and went to a washroom in a restaurant to put them on. I then went to see Ray and Grace Goguen. I stayed there overnight and the next day I hitch-hiked into Toronto.

Once in the city, I went to Vernon Acorn's place to see if he'd heard anything of Lucky Jim lately. Vernon was married to Jim's sister, Betty. A day or two later, we found out that Jim was working at a glass-making company in Scarborough and living on Greenwood Avenue. When he found out where I was, he took a streetcar up to get me, and for the next three months I lived at his place.

The glass company was a good paying job, and Jim was renting the whole house we were living in. His mother was now separated from his father, and she was also living in the house with Jim's two younger brothers, Chris and Randy.

Jim also had a brand-new Gibson Hummingbird guitar, at that time, and along with several of his friends who played instruments, we wound up having a lot of parties and jam sessions. I also got to write quite a few songs that winter, mainly when Jim was working and the two younger boys were at school. I even taught Chris, the oldest of the boys, how to chord and strum the guitar, but I don't know whether he ever pursued it or not.

The glass company also provided Jim with a very inexpensive way to obtain glass. And as a result of the many pieces he brought home from time to time, he had built himself nine or ten large fishtanks in the basement. As each tank now contained several varieties of exotic fish, and for just an average guy who started out with a small hobby, his aquarium soon turned into a very elaborate setup. From all the books he was reading, he soon became very knowledgeable about the food, breeding, habitats, etc., of practically every kind of fish, and for a while there, he had even become a supplier for one or two of the stores.

Every couple of weeks or so, I would also go back to see the Goguens and the Chapmans, and on one occasion, I stayed with the Chapmans for about ten days. On a weekend with the Goguens, we also took another trip up to Port Elgin and Southampton to see Grace's brother, Ira, and his friends, Pete Ens and Jimmy Fordham. We always had such a good time up there, that it always seemed like a weekend was never enough. They kept asking me to come back and stay for a while sometime, and I told them I would. But just when, I didn't know.

Not too long after the Port Elgin visit, we were all sitting around at Lucky Jim's, having a party, when another one of Jim's brothers, Alan, came in with a guy who mentioned that someone he knew had been to a party "at a Steve Foote's place" not more than a week before. Upon hearing the name Steve Foote, both Jim and I were all ears. We wanted to know if it was the same Steve Foote that we knew. When the guy said he'd try to find out more from his friend, we soon dropped the subject and went on playing music.

A day or two later the guy called up and said his friend had remembered that while he was at the party at Steve Foote's place, the names of Tom Connors and Lucky Jim Frost had both come up several times. He also had an address for an apartment building in Scarborough.

Now, it just so happened that Steve was having another party that coming weekend and had invited a bunch of the boys to bring their instruments. Well, it was priceless to see the look on Steve's face when Jim and I walked in with the others. He looked like he was going to crap his drawers. "How in the name of geezes did you guys know I was even in Toronto, never mind knowing where to find me?" he asked. "I've only been here for a little over three weeks." After everything was explained, we really settled into a hoedown that night.

The landlord had to eventually come to the door two or three times before we finally got everything shut down. (I must add that Steve was also playing guitar and singing and writing some damn good songs by this time.) After everyone else left, Steve and I and Jim sat around and talked for another couple of hours. And when Jim finally had to go home, I wound up staying and sleeping on the sofa.

As Steve now had a job and a few bucks to keep the rent paid, I spent the next while going back and forth from Steve's place to Jim's. Then, sometime in April or May, Steve went back to Saint John, and I went to Port Elgin again with Raymond and Grace Goguen.

Grace's brother, Ira Osborne, and his wife, Liz, were, of course, glad to see me. And when they asked me again if I would like to stay around for a while, I told them, "I'd be delighted."

Ira's tobacco had already been planted, but there were always other things to be done between now and the harvest. There was weeding and hoeing, kilns and greenhouses had to be cleaned out, the roof of the house had to be shingled, and there were many other odd jobs. There was also a lot of partying to do, and that took place everywhere.

When the party wasn't at Ira's, it was over at Pete and Irene's. When it wasn't there, it could be at Jimmy Fordham's, or any number of places within a radius of five or ten miles. On a couple of occasions, we even travelled as far as Aylmer, Ontario, where Liz's brother, Joe Zimmer, had a dozen kids and a dairy farm.

Another guy I met around Port Elgin was Junior Grass. There were a lot of tourists around at that time of year, and a lot of parties going on in all the cabins along the beach. At one stretch there, I think Junior and I attended them all.

There was also a friend of Ira's from Prince Edward Island who was up to work with him for the summer. I used to call him "Meeshore," but his name was Roy Lecoe. It was Roy and I who shingled Ira's roof that year.

I also spent a lot of time around Jimmy Fordham's

place in Southampton. Jimmy was the fish-bait dealer around those parts, and I guess he and his wife, Olive, met more people in their day than Carter's got little liver pills. When we used to have parties there, it was always fun to see Jimmy play the harmonica with his nose.

Another guy that was a lot of fun was old Jim Claisie, who played the fiddle. He may not have been in the same league with Don Messer, but once he got a couple of drinks into him, he was a lot more lively. Jim always seemed to show up more when the party was at Pete Ens's place. I guess Pete just had a way of getting him going more than anyone else. It was Pete, by the way, who first got me interested in the story about the Black Donnelly Clan from Lucan, Ontario. He told me about a book he once read, and two or three years later, when I finally got around to doing some research on the subject, I wrote a couple of songs which I eventually recorded. The titles are "The Black Donnelly Massacre" and "Jenny Donnelly."

I guess I hung around Port Elgin and Southampton for about three months that summer, and then one day it was time to leave. Ira and Liz drove me out on the highway for a distance of about ten or twelve miles and dropped me off near a little town called Allenford. There we said goodbye and I started hitch-hiking towards Owen Sound.

About a week before that I had had some kind of an attack of severe pains at the top of my stomach, just where it meets the rib-cage, and I had to go to bed for a couple of days. The damn thing was hurting day and night and I had no idea what was wrong with me. In the last couple of days the pain had been subsiding and today I wasn't feeling too bad at all. But as time went by, it began to recur every now and then, depending on how and what I ate. For the next little while, although it bothered me, it never got quite as bad as it did that first time.

In a Drifter's Opinion

Anyway, the first day out from Southampton, I got as far as Collingwood. After spending the night in the local jail, I decided to head north and maybe go to Quebec or just continue on out west. Once again, it really didn't matter, as long as I was going somewhere. And only God and fate could know where that somewhere was.

And there's those words again. God and fate. What do they mean? Here it was August of 1964, there's a twenty-eight-year-old man sitting under a tree by a road somewhere in Ontario, and every experience he's had up until now has only brought him to one simple conclusion: That God and fate are essentially the same thing.

This conclusion didn't come as a result of thinking about it for an hour or so during a lunch break, while a million other problems were running through my mind. It also didn't come in a day, or in a month, or even in a year. This conclusion came from inspiration, observation and contemplation, which began on the day I started to think. And God knows I had plenty of time to do that. By the time I was twenty-eight there had already been thousands of days and nights, thousands of roads, and thousands of trees under which to sit, with nothing else to do but continually think, without interruption. And the final conclusion of all this thinking? God and fate are one.

Now, I'm not trying to convince anyone, or convert anyone to this way of thinking. For everyone who thinks, thinks differently. And everyone who thinks will come to his own appropriate conclusion. I only state my own conclusions here, because this is my autobiography. And if the reader ever hopes to gain an insight into who Stompin' Tom really is, he will have to know how Stompin' Tom thinks, and what makes him tick.

And that's what I'll try to do before this book is finished: Provide an insight into Stompin' Tom that was heretofore unknown. So in order for this to happen, the reader should remember that the "truths" in this book, which I declare to be "self-evident," are only presented here as a foundation upon which to build an understanding of one individual. And whether or not these, or any other "truths," should be accepted or rejected by other individuals, is really beyond my concern.

Being a drifter not only provides an opportunity to meet many different people, but you often get to see their bad side as well as the good. When people see you coming as a drifter, they don't have to smile when they meet you, like they're inclined to do when you drive up to their service station looking to buy gas for your car. When they think you have money they look at you favourably. And because you're a potential customer, they're certainly not going to put the run to you.

But with the drifter coming down the road hitch-hiking, it's different. They've seen you a mile away, with your thumb out, and when you walk into their service station they often suspect you may be up to no good, so they're always on their guard.

After spending so many years on the road, I've often wondered why so many people think in this particular way. In my mind, I've always felt their suspicions were misplaced. For instance, if a young guy were to steal or rob a substantial amount of money, the first thing he would probably do is buy some of the things he doesn't already have, such as a new car and some nice clothes. (This was probably the motive for stealing in the first place.) Then, to maintain his dapper appearance and new-found "status," he will probably be on the alert, looking for some nice, smiling and trusting person he can hoodwink and steal from again.

On the other hand, the drifter has no car and his clothes are plain at best. He has no place in which to conceal a weapon (the cops are stopping the drifter and checking him out almost daily) and if he was stupid enough to steal from somebody, how far would he get with no transportation, no change of clothes, and no place to hide the stolen goods?

Everybody has had a good look at him by now, and for purposes of identification, he's dead meat. Anyway, if he's already robbed somebody by now, he sure as hell picked a slow and stupid way of making his escape from the scene of the crime.

It seems to me that while everyone is watching the hitch-hiker, the dude with the fancy car is running away with the till. And that's the guy they always bend over backwards to impress. If there's one thing I learned on the road, it was if you're going to be a drifter you'd better learn to keep your nose clean, because if anything untoward should happen, you'll be the first one to get the blame.

While heading north, in August of '64, I just took my good old time. The weather was warm, and my thoughts were many. Some days I wouldn't make more than twenty or thirty miles. Each time I came to a nice out-of-the-way spot, I'd just sit down and relax and try to answer not only some of the many perplexing questions that other people asked me, but a whole lot more that I'd often asked myself.

Some people I met were beginning to ask me if I was a hippie. I'd say, "What in the hell is a hippie?" and they'd have to tell me, because I didn't know. I thought that some of those weird-looking characters I was beginning to see on the road were just some poor unfortunates trying to get from one place to another. It never occurred to me that a lot of them were actually the sons and daughters of quite wealthy people. At any rate, whoever they were and whatever they were doing, it was their own business. At first, I used to wonder how they survived, but as they didn't ask me, I didn't figure it was my business to ask them.

Throughout the '50s and early '60s, before they began to open up hostels for the hippies, you just went from hand to mouth, as they say, depending on the kindness and goodness of people's hearts. Sometimes you might get a beer for singing a song, or if you did a little work somebody might put you up and give you a sandwich. That's pretty well how you survived.

If you saw someone working around a house, or in the yard, or maybe some guy painting a shed, you just walked over and asked him if you could give him a hand. "Do you suppose if I helped you with some painting, you might see that I get something to eat?" Other times, helping a farmer split some wood or take in some hay might get you a buck or two, or a place to hang your hat for a couple of days.

In all my years on the road, I don't think I made $5,000 in total, and with that kind of income, you don't even bother to fill out an income tax form.

I also don't think the way I was brought up had anything much to do with the fact that I was always on the road. It wasn't my childhood or disruptive family life that was to blame for my not wanting to settle down. It had more to do with fate and predestination. I always figured that someday I'd settle down, but in the meantime there was always this thing that I never wanted to take on an ordinary job. It was just too boring. I had to see things, meet new people and learn about life. I used to tell any friends that I met, "If I don't become a country entertainer some day, I'll just die somewhere under a park bench." I still meet some of them today who often remind me of that old statement. They say, "Well, Tom, we haven't found you under a park bench yet."

Other than singing, playing and writing songs, I could never find a job that ever really caught my interest. I couldn't see myself working in a factory, standing at a conveyor belt or assembly line, and doing the same thing over and over again forever. Turning this nut and oiling that machine each and every day for the next forty years was not my idea of living an interesting life. While I certainly respect those who are capable of buckling down to those kinds of jobs, the everyday grind was not for me. I just wasn't cut out for it.

I would only work if I needed a meal or a new item of

clothing, when the holes got so big that I couldn't patch them any more. When I could afford it, I'd always carry a needle and thread so I could do a lot of my own repairs. My days in Skinners Pond had taught me a great deal when it came to the use of hooks and needles. I was pretty good one time in the arts of patching, sewing, knitting, darning, crocheting, hooking rugs, etc.

Whenever I had a bit of change in my pocket, I'd buy my usual bread, mustard and baloney. Then I'd walk out of town, stop at the first bridge or stream that I came to and settle down for a while. Here I might have a bath, go for a swim, wash some clothes, sew a button on a shirt, or just have a sandwich and watch the river run by.

Playing my guitar and writing a song was always one of my favourite pastimes when the spot was just right. The subject of the song was usually about something I saw or did in the last few days, or a story that someone told me while giving me a lift from one place to another.

A small amount of string and a fish-hook was something else I always tried to have handy. You could always find a worm or two under a rock, and before you knew it, you had a fish roasting at the end of a stick over a small fire. When the weather was good, I might decide to stay right there for the night. But if it looked like rain, I just packed my few belongings back in the case with my guitar and rambled down the road.

Although I was a drifter and considered wild in that sense, I was fairly honest 99 per cent of the time. I might have played the odd prank on someone once in a while, or stole the occasional pie when I was hungry, but I never did anything untoward or injurious to anyone.

Often, when I was on the road with some other guys, the first day they got a hungry feeling in their stomachs they'd start suggesting that we hit someone over the head, or break a window and steal something from a store. But on these occasions, I was always able to talk them out of it. I wasn't shy when it came to telling them that if they didn't get those ideas out of their heads we might as well part company right now. Even though this had been a way of life with me and my mother when I was a child, something changed all that in me over the years. Maybe it was the fact that I knew that both my mother and my father had been in jail several times for committing similar offences.

I could never buy all the stories you hear about these guys who go out and beat, rob, rape or kill somebody, and say it was because they had a poor childhood, or because they were abused by someone. I have a hard time buying that line, and I think it's a cop-out or a poor excuse at best. As far as I'm concerned, two wrongs don't make a right. Just because someone was hard done by at a certain time in their past is no justification for setting out to harm somebody else. If this were the case, then I'm sure a whole lot more of us should be out there killing somebody.

It sure didn't work that way for me. It worked the opposite. Because I knew what hurt was, I always felt sorry and sympathetic for the hurt being felt by others. And while I certainly believe in self-defence, I can't see going out and laying extra burdens on people who already have a load that's heavy enough now for them to carry. Instead of adding to other people's troubles, we should be doing our best to help alleviate them.

I think my own hard times and hard knocks have made me more understanding of the plight of others. I think the adversity has given me a greater appreciation of the few good things one may come to expect in life. I don't believe a person can fully appreciate a nice sunshiny day unless he's been through a few rain storms. As I thought, for instance, of the modern psychology that all parents were now adopting towards their children, I did nothing but sit and wonder. It seemed that every parent I came in contact with was of the opinion that because they had experienced more storms in life than sun-shiny days, they were bound and determined that their children were never going to feel the discomfort that they had to go through in their earlier years. "As far as I'm concerned," they would say, "the wants and needs that I once knew will never be experienced by my kids, as long as I've got two hands and a good back to provide for them the opportunity in this life that I never had."

As I thought of how commendable the motive was, I often wondered how wise or realistic it was to fill a world full of children unfamiliar with adversity. How would children, born in the sunshine, cope with their first rainy day? Would they, as young birds, be able to fly away from their home nest with confidence, and face all the challenges of life on their own? Or would they be terrified and desperately flap their wings back home at the first sight of an eagle?

As most of my life up to this point in time had been spent meeting and dealing with people on the ground level of society, I was beginning to see a much higher degree of insensitivity developing as the years went on. The prevalence of this insensitivity was seeming to grow in direct proportion to the amount of ease and affluence now progressively being enjoyed.

In other words, what I was seeing was the less pain or suffering one came to know in his life, the more apt he was to inflict pain or suffering on others. He didn't seem to know what he was doing or to realize the consequence of his actions. There is no way to understand or sympathize with the pain or suffering of another if one has never personally endured a similar experience. One may go on hurting others, and never stop, until he himself has been hurt.

Had I done many of the things on the road that other guys had wanted me to do, I would have spent a lot of time running from the law, or spending most of my life behind steel bars. I knew what it was like to have nothing, and it sure didn't feel very good. So why should I deprive someone else of what they worked hard to get, and make them feel the same discomfort? All those who work for something deserve what they have, and no one should take it away from them.

As it was often very hard to explain this kind of reasoning to some of my road pals, I would often discuss the deterrent of going to prison to bring them back to their senses instead. I'd often say how much "I'd rather be a hungry 'free bird' than a well-fed 'jail bird.'"

It would then quite often happen, after the tough time was over and we had gotten something to eat somewhere, that the guys would be more contented for the next day or two. They would then frequently say how glad they were that we hadn't broken into some place, or done some of the things they had previously suggested. Sometimes, they'd even thank me for encouraging them to stay away from crime. There have even been a few that I met later on in life, who came up to me and told me how they still follow the "no-breaking-the-law" rule that I always maintained.

I'll never forget the time Steve Foote said to me, "You know, Tom, you made a man out of me. Had I stayed in the direction I was going, I would have been in jail for the rest of my life. Those were the circles I was moving in." Well, when somebody says that to you in later life, it somehow really makes it all worth while. It tells you that even a bum can be worth something after all, even though you may not have been aware of it at the time.

I remember on a couple of occasions I had to get pretty mad at a couple of guys who wanted to do something crooked. I had to tell them, "Look, you foolish bastard, there's no way I'll take any part in your stupid scheme. If you can't listen to reason, then go ahead and do whatever the hell you want, but don't friggin' well include me in it. If you're a friend of mine, you'll come with me, and we'll get by somehow. But if you're not, you can f———— off right now." I remember one guy who did take off, and a number of years later, I heard he wound up in the pen.

At twenty-eight years old, these were some of my thoughts and opinions during those last few days of August, in 1964, as I whiled away the hours on the side of the road. There were many other thoughts and reflections too numerous to include in the pages of this first book. Perhaps I will get to recount more of them at a later time.

Timmins, Ontario

It was late morning when I pulled myself out of the back seat of a wrecked car in a remote junkyard in northern Ontario. I had slept there for the night and was feeling kind of cramped. Along the road came a fancy convertible, and when I stuck out my thumb the driver pulled over. Seeing my guitar he told me he was an entertainer playing rock music in Kirkland Lake, and he was just out for a drive through the countryside for the afternoon.

When I told him how much I'd like to have a job singing somewhere, he told me there was a hotel in Larder Lake which had no entertainment at present and that maybe I should give it a try. As he let me out in front of the Larder Lake Hotel, he gave me a buck for a couple of beers, wished me luck and headed out for Kirkland Lake. His professional name, he said, was "Big John Little."

As I walked in the hotel the place was empty, so I just took a stool at the bar. A girl named Ann served me a beer and when I asked for the boss she said, "Oh, that would be Jerry" and she went to get him.

After talking for a few minutes he said he'd try me out for a night and give me five bucks. If I was any good he would hire me by the week to sing every night for $25, plus my room. That night the people really liked me and I wound up playing the Larder Lake Hotel for five or six weeks.

One day I asked Jerry for a $5 raise and he said, "What do you mean a five-dollar raise? You never had it so good."

I said, "Well, if that's your answer I'm moving on." I had quite a few people coming in to the Larder every night to see me play. At least it was entertainment they didn't have before, and $25 a week was a steal for the owner.

I knew people liked what I was doing because they

would come in and request songs, one of them being my newly penned "Movin' on to Rouyn." And I knew so many songs that it was a rare occasion when someone made a request for a favourite that I didn't know. That impressed people. I could sing around 2,300 songs at that time, and all of them by heart. I didn't need a book and I didn't need sheet music—I couldn't read music anyway!

So I pulled out of there without much money. I took a bus to Kirkland Lake, about twelve miles away, to see if I could get a singing job at Tony Poloni's place, the Queen's Hotel. When that was no go, I tried a couple of other places, but they all gave me the same answer.

Then I started hitch-hiking. I headed out towards Highway 11 and a guy named Culker picked me up and said he was going into Timmins. Little did I know when I got into his car that this would be my last lift. This would be the ride of rides, the one that took me to the end of my hitch-hiking career.

When the driver said he was going to Timmins, I said, "That's where I'm going." If he'd said he was going north to Cochrane or south to North Bay, I would have gone to either place with him. As long as I was moving I didn't care where I went. So here I was going west on Highway 101 without the faintest idea of what was in store. We arrived in Timmins on an evening in the middle of October, just as the rain was letting up. My driver dropped me off at the corner of Spruce Street and Third Avenue, near the Golden Arrow Chinese restaurant.

I'd been into Timmins a number of years before and I remembered going to CKGB radio station and asking if I could sing a couple of songs on the radio. The answer at that time was no. I don't remember what the reasoning was because I used to do that every time I'd go to a town that had a radio station.

After walking down Third Avenue for three or four blocks, I came to a lounge called Leone's and walked in. I parked my guitar alongside of the chair and I asked the waiter if there was any chance I could see the boss.

The boss told me he had a three-piece band playing there, and when I asked if I could get up on the stage and sing some songs with them, he said, "Yeah. No problem."

When musicians want to, they can make you sound good or they can make you sound terrible. As it turned out, these guys just weren't in my camp. When I was singing they were poking fun and snickering behind me, and so the customers were laughing, too. After I sang a couple of songs, the boss called me over and said he didn't want me singing any more. There was no work at Leone's for me.

About 9 or 10 o'clock I left Leone's feeling pretty dejected so I just headed back up the street. I didn't know where the jail was, so I thought I'd wander along and see what I ran into first, the jail or a cop who could tell me where it was.

As I came along Third Avenue to Balsam Street, I looked over to my right and saw a hotel that looked pretty quiet. There didn't seem to be much going on, so I thought I'd wander in and see if I could get a waiter to give me a beer, or just direct me to the town lock-up.

Little did I know the decision to go up to that forlorn-looking place was to change my life entirely. The neon sign over the door read: The Maple Leaf Hotel.

As I walked into the lounge there was a French-Canadian guy by the name of Gaetan Lepine behind the bar and the rest of the room was empty. Going up to the bar, I spoke with Lepine and told him my story and asked how much for a beer. "Forty cents," was his reply. After looking in my pocket, the most I could come up with was thirty-five cents. "This is all I have to my name," I said. "You don't suppose you could give me the extra nickel to put with it, do you? I could sure use a beer." Unknown to me Gaet was an avid country and western fan and pointing to my guitar case he said, "Do you play the guitar, or is that just where you carry your clothes?"

"Yeah, I play it."

"Well," he said, "sing us a couple of songs and I'll give

you a beer."

So I took out the guitar and unwrapped the shirt and all the other stuff I had packed around it. I had spent most of the money that I had earned over in Larder Lake on a couple of half-decent shirts (one was on my back and the other was wrapped around my guitar) and an electric shaver that I had always wanted. (I could very seldom afford razor blades and the ones I always carried were usually rusty and dull from excessive use.) I also bought an extra pair of shorts and a couple of pairs of socks and I even had a little bag to carry them in. Hell, I was good for a trip around the world now.

The first song I played was "Pick Me up on Your Way Down" and the second was "I've Been Everywhere."

By the time I'd played two or three songs I could see in Gaet's eyes that he liked what he heard. As he dropped me a beer, I asked him, "Do you have anybody playing here? I was just down to Leone's." I told him the story about what happened down there.

"Nobody's playing here," he said. "How many songs do you know?"

"About twenty-three hundred."

"What?"

"Yeah, twenty-three hundred."

He said, "You know 'em all off by heart?"

I told him I did and that I'd been playing over in Larder Lake; but when I'd asked the guy for a $5 raise he wouldn't give it to me, and that was why I was back on the bum again.

He went into the back to get the Maple Leaf's owner, Pete Kotze, and then got me to sing a couple more songs. The boss now told Gaet to give me another beer, and the two of them went back inside for a little more conversation. Then Gaet came out with a half grin on his face and said, "How would you like to play here for Friday night and Saturday night? And if people come in, if they like you, maybe we'll hire you for next week."

"We'll give you a room," he said, as he took me

upstairs and showed it to me, "and the boss says we'll give you a meal a day, so you can come down to the dining room in the morning and get something to eat. But for tonight you can just hang around until closing time and if anyone comes in you can sing them a few songs. And when tomorrow night comes, and Saturday night, you'll just have to work for tips."

I said, "Fair enough."

So they pulled a table out from the corner of the lounge by the women's washroom and told me that was where I'd be playing. There was no stage. I stood on the floor. Pretty soon a couple of Indian guys and a girl came in for a drink and I asked if they would like to hear some songs. They requested a lot of Hank Williams stuff, mostly tear-jerkers, and, of course, I knew them all.

I just stood there and sang to them and they stayed for the rest of the night. A couple more people came in later and they also hung around. When they closed the place up, Gaet came up the stairs with me and told me how much he enjoyed the songs and said, "Goodnight."

Well, when I crawled in between those bedsheets it was a good night. I slept like a log and didn't even stir until noon the following day. I went down to the dining room and got my one meal (I made sure it was a big one), and began to psych myself up for the show I would be doing that night.

When 8 o'clock came, I took my place over in the corner and began to sing. As it was Friday night a few people came in, ordered a drink or a couple of beers and began requesting some songs. Soon the tips started coming, and best of all, nobody was leaving. At the end of the night Gaet told me that was a good sign. "Normally, most people just come in for one or two drinks and leave." On Saturday night, signs that it was all going to work got even better. About three-quarters of the people who had been there the night before came in again and brought a few friends with them, and they all stayed until closing time, and so did the ones who had come in for the first time that night. The boss was delighted: the lounge was almost half-full and nobody had left.

At the end of the night he hired me for the next week. And after I had been there for about two or three weeks, he decided to build me a little stage.

I remember the whole thing—the building of the stage, the sign for the window, the microphone, the PA system, the speakers—everything came to $45. Not much for a guy who now had the place packed on weekends and three-quarters full every other night of the week, with people complaining that they couldn't hear me.

The two little six-inch speakers that he installed—one at each end of the room—weren't very much. But they were a start. My hours were from 8 P.M. until 1 A.M. six nights a week, with a ten-minute break every hour. We mutually agreed on a work termination notice of fifteen days and the pay was $30 a week. It was plain to see that Pete was a cheap old bugger, but I did manage to get a $10 to $15 raise out of him every couple of months or so.

The pay may not have been very much considering I soon began packing the place every night for him, but I was enjoying the work, and besides, there were always a few tips to consider. By the time he let me go, I had been there about fourteen months and was making about $130 per week. While this was still not an awful lot of money, I was a good saver and was able to buy some good clothes for a change, and even a new guitar. (I kept my old one, of course, for writing songs, but its appearance had become a little too shabby for stage work.)

Pretty soon Gaet and I became very close friends. Every second night after last call at the Maple Leaf, he used to take me out to a couple of bootleggers, and there was one place especially where we used to have some pretty crazy times.

Gaet had his favourite room at the bootlegger's. We called it the "blue room" because everything in it, from the walls to the ceiling, and every stick of furniture, was painted blue. Every time we went there I would order a case of twenty-four beer and he'd have a twenty-sixer and we wouldn't leave until the beer was gone and the bottle was drained. We had lots of fun doing all kinds of crazy things in that room, just the two of us, each with a guitar, and we'd be laughing and singing and telling jokes and coming up with all kinds of ideas for writing songs. Most of it was a lot of crazy stuff, but we had a good time doing it. If nothing else, it was a great way to wind down after serving the public all night.

Early one morning we were walking home past a bank on one of the streets. In front of the bank there was a bulldozer sitting there where they were doing some new construction. There was lots of mud and puddles of water on the site. Gaet said, "I can drive a bulldozer, can you?" Thinking there was no key in the bulldozer in front of us, I said, "No, but I'd like to see you drive that one."

Gaet said, "I bet I can, even if I have to hot-wire it." Then we both jumped up on the bulldozer. He took the seat and I was standing on the lugs. I was sipping away on my beer and laughing at his efforts when, all of a sudden, the bulldozer started and took a leap with a chug, chug, chug. I immediately fell off in the large puddle of muddy water. Without spilling my beer, of course.

The bulldozer again gave a chug and a big leap and stalled. I swear the blade had stopped about two inches from the plate glass window of the bank. Had it made one more leap Gaet would have been inside the bank. With his face as white as a sheet, he immediately jumped off the bulldozer and we headed up the street and through a series of alleys, me leaving a trail of mud wherever I went. There were no repercussions for us, but we often wondered later whether the guy who operated the bulldozer caught hell from his boss the following day for parking it so close to the bank.

On Christmas Day that year Gaet was the only person who came around to visit me in my room. It was in the evening and he brought around a forty-ouncer of Canadian Club whisky. As always, I had a case of beer under my bed, and Gaet said, "This is Christmas, and for once you are going to celebrate it in style. Put away your beer and have a shot of this." He poured me half a tumbler of CC and in no time I was flying. It wasn't long before the two of us were sitting in a corner of the room drinking CC out of one of my overshoes.

About this time, we decided we should write a song. As it was supposed to be a bum song, I suggested we should write it out in an alley somewhere to get the real bum atmosphere, as the hotel room was in no way appropriate. We took our guitars and lots of writing paper and headed out to find an alley. Although the snow was falling lightly, we went out around the back of the Maple Leaf Hotel and sat down against the wall and tried to come up with some ideas to write our bum song.

The next thing I remember, I was being awakened by a couple of policemen who were checking the alley. I was lightly covered with snow and by chance they had stumbled over me. "What the hell are you doing there?" asked one of the cops.

"Oh," I said, "I'm just writing a song with my buddy here," but when I reached over to find Gaet, he was gone. He had apparently got up, taken his guitar and gone home, leaving me there.

"Well, there's nobody around here," the cop said. "By the way, aren't you the guy that plays at the Maple Leaf?"

"Yes, I am," I said. "Where is it?"

He said, "You're sleeping against it. Now get the hell in there to your room before we lock you up."

I wasn't long grabbing my guitar, scooting around to the front door and up the stairs.

To this day, I don't know if we wrote a song that night or not: the papers were covered with snow and I left them in the alley.

Lots of different people started coming to the Maple Leaf, including the local radio guys from CKGB and the reporters and ad salesmen from the *Timmins Daily Press*. From businessmen to miners, lumberjacks, prospectors and diamond drillers, you name it, I made friends with them all. Even the mayor of Timmins had become a great fan.

But it was my association with the radio people at CKGB that put me onto the idea of how to get my own songs on records. And just as soon as I had enough money saved, I made a stab at it.

It was the announcer, Nick Harris, who first invited me to sing on the radio, which I will speak more about later, and it was Dan Kelly who offered to get some information for me on how to get some records made. He put me in touch with Quality Records in Toronto and I wrote a letter to them enquiring about prices for getting some custom records done. "Demos" is the word for them today, although back then people felt it was similar to a vanity press; you know, where someone can't get a book published, and they decide to publish it themselves.

Quality sent me a brochure explaining how much it would cost and how many copies I would get, etc.

I went to the radio station and, with my guitar as the only accompaniment, recorded "Carolyne" ("T-I-M-M-I-N-S, that's the town I love the best...") and "Movin' on to Rouyn" ("From Kirkland to Larder, through V-Town and farther..."). We used a regular reel-to-reel tape and sent it down to Quality Records. I had to send them their money up front—the whole thing. And they sent me back a hundred 45 RPM singles with "Carolyne" on the A side and "Movin' on to Rouyn" on the B.

When the records arrived by train a few weeks later, I carried the parcel down to the Maple Leaf Hotel and couldn't wait to get the box open and see my first record. I was just like a little kid at Christmas. I don't usually get excited, but on that day I was all fingers and thumbs trying to get the wrappings off.

All it said on each side of the record was CKGB and the song title, sung by Tom Connors. But that was good enough for me. I had dreamed of cutting a record all my life, and now my dream had come true. I sat on my bed

and looked at one of the disks for the longest time.
Then I wanted to know what it sounded like. I ran up
the street and bought the cheapest record player I could
find and just sat and listened to it for the rest of the
afternoon. A little later, as Gaet was on his way to start
his shift, he dropped by my room to see what was going
on. I autographed one of the records and gave it to him,
saying, "Whether or not I ever get to make another
record, you can always say you got the first one." Thirty
years later, in January 1995, he still had it.

That night when I went into the bar I brought a box of
the records with me. They came twenty or twenty-five to a
box. I think I sold two boxes of them the first night. The
rest of them went before the end of the week.

Then I thought, "Holy shit, this is okay." Now I had my
money back plus a little more. I probably made—taking
into account studio time and freight—maybe twenty or
twenty-five bucks off the whole works.

So I sent down for another order and got three hundred the next time. After that I thought, "There's a buck
to be made here," but my number one consideration was
not so much the money I was going to make, but the fact
that if I could get enough of these records into enough
people's homes, they'd listen to the songs and my name
would get better known.

That was number one with me.

One thing led to another and after I started to make
enough money to keep the thing going, I began putting
other songs on record.

Altogether, there were eight or nine records made in
Timmins, one in Wawa, and another one after that down
in Owen Sound.

This last song was about the opening of the Hepworth
Country Music Auditorium. I got to be the first guy to
sing on the stage, but the thing didn't last any more
than one summer and they had to close it down because
somebody ran away with the receipts.

But today those records are collectors' items. Even I

don't have copies of them all. I'm told the whole set could be worth up to $1000 today—that's for eleven singles in mint condition. I wouldn't mind having a mint set of them myself. There is a lot of sentimentality attached to them.

In Timmins, jukeboxes were still very big back then and record players were not in every home as they are today—and no one had even heard of cassette tapes.

I would take my records around to those who had jukeboxes and find out who owned them and who placed them in the restaurants and bars. Usually, the guy's address was inside the jukebox, so I would go to his house and ask him to put my records on his machines.

First I would give two or three records to the guy at the bar or the restaurant, just in case I didn't get a chance to see the jukebox owner before he came in to change the records. Before long, my songs were being played on about a hundred jukeboxes throughout the Timmins area.

As I mentioned before, it was Nick Harris, at CKGB, who helped me to launch my own radio program. Nick would come in to the Maple Leaf a couple of times a week and we'd have a few beers together. He said he liked my singing a lot and as he began to come in more regularly he said to me one day, "Come on up to the radio station and we'll put you on the air."

He promised me five minutes to sing a couple of songs. They weren't going to pay me, but didn't mind if I put in a plug for the hotel where I was playing. I put a couple of songs on tape and they ran it that Saturday evening right after the news. Then Nick asked me if I wanted to do the same thing three days a week—a couple of songs on three different days. Then it became six days a week for five minutes. And then it got extended to fifteen minutes a night. Then to twenty-five minutes six days a week. I'd sing seven or eight songs, plug the hotel and advertise the availability of my records by mail. That was quite a boost. The program lasted for about a year and a half. Even after I left Timmins I would come in from Ansonville, Kirkland Lake or Kapuskasing on Sundays to tape enough programs for the following week. All this time I was getting lots of mail orders for my records and had become a real busy man.

I looked after everything myself, from taking the orders to packing, addressing and mailing the records. I even had to create the packages.

I used to go over to Mike's Supermarket and get cardboard boxes and tote them into my room. I bought a stapler and utility knife and cut the boxes into the right sizes to fit the records so I could put two or three of them into one package at the same time. I'd then staple and address them and put them into the mail.

I had people send me in twenty-five cents for postage and a dollar for each record, and there were quite a few of those $1.25s coming in. After a while I was making as much money at that as I was singing at the hotel. People would come into the Maple Leaf now and request my own songs, which they were hearing on the radio, and best of all they usually wanted to buy my latest record. It felt great.

During the year of 1965 I sold twenty times more records in the town of Timmins than did the Beatles. I had them all over the place. I was like a travelling salesman—I had to have a schedule every day to keep all the places well stocked.

My three biggest outlets were Drouin's music store, Eddy's Office Supply and Kresge's. In these places the records were going like hot cakes. I'd come in and they'd always need some more. I'd drop off three or four more boxes and go back in another week and they'd all be gone, or there might be only one or two records left. For a while there, I was having a hard time to keep up. DJs were spinning my records daily and I was mailing them to communities throughout the listening area, as far away as 250 miles from Timmins.

I used to keep a record of all my figures so I could

prove to all the skeptics when I came down to Toronto that my phenomenal sales in Timmins should at least warrant their giving me a chance to cut an album to see what I could do in a larger market. This, of course, was my ultimate goal. I also wrote several letters to Quality who were supplying me with all these records, but for some unknown reason they chose to ignore the fact. Their answers always included phrases like "the material is not commercial" and other such irrelevancies.

The Real Stompin' Begins

In less than three months from the time I started play-ing in Timmins, the word around town was that the Maple Leaf was really the hot spot to go. If people didn't get there by 7 P.M. each evening, their chances of ever getting a seat were very slim.

My usual time to come in and start the show was 8 o'clock. And one evening, as I did so, there were two old ladies sitting at a small table right in front of the stage.

I always had a habit of tapping my left heel on the ply-wood stage each time I sang a song that was up-tempo, and I began to do this during my first couple of num-bers. No sooner had I started when the two old gals became extremely annoyed.

One of them shouted, "Will you please stop banging your foot when you sing? It's very rude of you to do that when someone is trying to hold a conversation." I stopped for a few seconds, but as it was an unconscious habit, it wasn't very long before I started again.

"If you don't stop that infernal banging," said the other woman, "I'm going up to see Mr. Kotze and he'll make you stop, or we won't be coming here again. We are friends of Mr. and Mrs. Kotze, and we've been com-ing here for a good many years before you arrived."

Well, I hadn't seen them in the hotel for the length of time that I had been singing there, but just in case they had the kind of influence on my boss they said they did, I thought I'd better try my best to cool it, at least until they left.

As I started out the next fast song, a couple of guys who were sitting at a table of eight began to shout, "What the hell is the matter, Tom, you got a sore foot tonight? Let's have a little rhythm there." Seeing myself between a rock and a hard place, I decided to tap my heel a little bit, and hope like hell the old ladies didn't notice.

Well, that was only wishful thinking. Without saying another word, up to the bar they went to ask for Mr.

Kotze to file their complaint. Soon, one of the waiters came up to the stage to inform me that Pete wanted to see me as soon as my set was over. When I saw Pete, he said I was going to have to stop banging my foot because it was bothering the customers. When I told him there were other customers who were spending a lot more money because they wanted to hear the banging, he told me to "keep it a little more quiet then." I said, "I tried to do that, but these two old biddies didn't want me to make any noise at all. So what was I supposed to do? Sometimes I do it without being aware of it, and I can't seem to stop."

"Well," he said, "you're just going to have to cut it out then while they are here. And those two 'old biddies' you're talking about just so happen to be very good friends of mine."

"Well, in that case," I said, "you're giving me no other alternative. If the business they bring here is more important to you than the business I bring here, you'll have to choose between me or them. Because if they get their way, there's no way I can do the job you hired me to do."

With that, he grunted a couple of times and finally said, "Okay then. Go and do whatever you have to." And that's exactly what I did. I couldn't wait to get to the stage, strap on my guitar and let 'er go.

When I got to the mike the two old gals were looking so satisfied with what they thought they had accomplished, you could have cut the air of their smugness with a knife. As soon as I looked at them, they looked at me. Then I gave them a great big smile and came down with the goddamnedest banging they ever heard in their lives. There was dust and sawdust flying everywhere, and chips of plywood the size of quarters landing in people's drinks half-way across the room. I think I scared the livin' geezes right out of them. I never saw two old hags move faster in all my life. As the glasses began bouncing on the table right in front of them, and me acting like a wild man from Borneo, they weren't long getting their asses the hell out the door.

Practically everybody in the room was laughing and hollering, "Attaboy, Tom, pound the shit out of 'er." And that's what I did for the rest of the night. I would say, without a doubt, that was the night the stompin' really began. The word soon got around town about what was happening and that only drew more people into the club. And while Mrs. Kotze never spoke to me much after that, business was booming. Some people were even collecting sawdust and chips of wood off the stage as souvenirs, or just to show their friends what was actually going on. My buddy Gaet still has a matchbox full to this very day.

It's strange that I didn't get the name "Stompin' Tom" right then and there, because I certainly did a lot of it after that. And there wasn't much left of that old plywood stage by the time I got through with it either.

I was also being bothered a great deal by those pains in my stomach that winter. Since I had left Ira Osborne's place in Southampton the summer before, they had gotten progressively worse. Then one morning, as I awoke with what I thought was a knife going through me, I had a hard time getting out of bed. As I got to my feet, I immediately fell to my knees and stayed there for about twenty minutes. I knew I had to see a doctor, but I couldn't get to a phone. There was no use hollering for anyone, as there was nobody in the upstairs halls at that time of day.

When the pain finally eased enough that I was able to get to my feet, I managed to dress myself and make my way down to the lobby, where someone told me the closest doctor's office was just across the street and down a couple of doors towards Third Avenue.

As I got half-way across the street, I fell to my knees again, and a guy stopped his car and helped me up. He then walked me along to the door of the doctor's office and went back to his car. When I got inside, I could hardly talk, so the nurse got me in to see the doctor right away.

After an examination, a shot of something, and an X-ray, the pain began to lessen, and I was told to come back the following day to find out the final results. In the meantime, the doctor said he thought I'd had an ulcer attack, and he put me on a strict milk diet until further notice.

When I went back, the ulcer was confirmed and the doctor said he would have to make an appointment for me to have an operation. He then gave me a paper with a starvation diet on it, and I mean starvation. I could have as much milk as I wanted, but the rest of my meals were to consist of one boiled egg-white and a small piece of toast. And I was to stay away from everything else, especially alcoholic beverages, till I came back to see him in a couple of days. That's when he would know the date of my operation.

I was sure looking some stupid at the Maple Leaf Hotel every night, telling everybody who wanted to buy me a drink that I would be having milk. But as the pain was still bothering me every day, I figured I'd better stick to the doctor's orders.

A couple of days later the doctor told me the operation was set for a date about three weeks away; in the meantime I would have to stay on my strict diet. After working like hell every night and not eating, I was getting weaker and weaker. I was getting to the point where I didn't know whether I was going to be able to continue or not. Then, one day while I was reading the *Timmins Press*, my eyes fell upon an unusual article. Written in a rather derisive vein, it was comparing the healing methods employed by the "enlightened" medical profession of the western world with those of the "superstitious" countries of the Orient.

The article was pooh-poohing some doctor from India who had recently made the claim that he had cured seventy-four out of seventy-six ulcer patients by allowing them to eat whatever they wanted, including fried foods, as long as they adhered to a 100 per cent salt-free diet. One of the two patients who had not received a full cure had gone back on salt when he wasn't supposed to.

After reading the article over several times, I asked myself, "What if the guy is telling the truth and the salt-free diet really works? It might be a long shot, but if it helps me to avoid getting the knife, why not?" But just to be on the safe side, I decided to talk it over with the doctor.

"Are you crazy?" he said. "Another attack like the one you had a couple of weeks ago, and you may not be around any more. You better make sure you keep that operation appointment if you want to go on living, and never mind listening to those quacks over in India."

As I walked out of his office, I thought, "What the hell. Maybe I'll just try it for a week or so, and if it starts to work I can always cancel the operation then. Besides, if I don't get a good meal into me soon I'll be dead from starvation before the operation date anyway."

As I walked into the restaurant where I always ate, I went into the back and had a talk with the cook. "From now on," I said, "I don't want you to put any salt of any kind in any of the food I order, whether it's in the morning, at noon, or at night. Please follow the instruction meticulously. I've got to get rid of this ulcer somehow. Now give me a good-sized steak with lots of fried onions."

Looking rather surprised, he said, "But what about your milk and toast?"

"My milk and toast?" I repeated. "You can just take that and shove it."

A week later, I went back to the doctor and cancelled my appointment with the knife. When I told him I was feeling great, he said it was psychosomatic and had nothing to do with the salt. When I told him I was back on the beer and eating foods that I hadn't been able to eat in months, he only shrugged and told me to watch out because I might be sorry. I then left his office and never went back. For the next ten or fifteen years I stayed completely away from salt, and since then I might take just the smallest bit about once a week. I've never been bothered by an ulcer again, and that was thirty years ago. Was it psychosomatic? Was it the lack of salt? All I really know is that it kept me away from the surgeon's knife. So let the reader judge for himself.

Another very important incident that seemed rather insignificant at the time happened one night when a group of eight or ten teachers came into the Maple Leaf for a drink. They no sooner sat down when they began to display an unusually high degree of interest in some of the songs I was singing.

Before long they asked the waiter if he would extend their invitation for me to come and have a beer with them after my set was over. About thirty minutes later they were telling me how they had just come back from a teachers' exchange program in Germany, and how well they were all treated while they were there. After briefly recounting the pluses of their recent experience, they began to tell me about what they considered to be the big minus of the whole trip. At the many parties they were invited to attend, they would often be asked to sing some of the songs they knew from home. But unlike the teachers from all other countries, these Canadians didn't know any. The German teachers had no problem singing songs about their country, and the Americans had no problem; neither did the Irish, English, French, Swedish and all the rest. Only the Canadians couldn't come up with one identifiably Canadian song. They felt like real oddballs at these parties because the perception was that they had no pride in their homeland.

When pressed to "at least sing something" they had to resort to either "O Canada," which they learned in school as a child, or some American song they had become familiar with due to the predominance of American music on Canadian radio.

When they walked into the Maple Leaf Hotel that night and saw one solitary performer singing so many songs about Canada, they were flabbergasted, to say the least. They wanted to know where I learned all these songs. When they found out I wrote most of them, they couldn't get over it.

Why, they wanted to know, hadn't somebody like me made a success out of singing these types of songs about Canada long before now? And why hadn't the Canadian population at large even noticed how few songs there were about their own country?

These questions, and many more, which I couldn't answer back then, were put to me that night as the teachers stayed till closing time. They had only dropped in for one drink to celebrate their safe return home, but upon hearing so many songs about different parts of Canada, they not only stayed till the end of the night, but they all came back periodically to get what they called "another earful of Canadiana."

Today, I believe it was the concerns of those teachers that set me to thinking for the first time how really important it was for me, and other Canadians, to write and sing about this country of ours. Before that night, I guess I had always written songs because they held a personal interest for me. But from then on, I began to see how my songs could have special meaning for the people of the whole nation.

While there were so many little stories about the things that happened while I was in Timmins, due to the need of space for other things, I won't be able to tell them all here. But I should make mention of the first suit I ever bought. While I had no desire to ever wear a suit, and no intention of ever buying one, you might say I got talked into it by my good old buddy, Gaet Lepine.

After telling me how nice and sharp a suit would look on stage, and how people would respect me more, and a dozen other reasons why I should have one, he finally coaxed me into a men's clothing store one afternoon, and before I knew it, we were headed back to the Maple Leaf with five or six big boxes. Gaet had gone around that store buying everything he could think of, as long as I was paying for it, and by the time we got it all back to the room, he was going to show me how to put it all on.

As we opened each box, I was finding stuff I didn't even know I bought. Not only that, I didn't even know what they were for. As I stood in front of the cloudy mirror on my dresser, he kept passing me stuff and saying, "Here, put this on," and I was saying, "What the hell is it, anyway? How do you expect me to put it on when I don't know what the hell it is?" Everything was a charcoal black, except for the shirt, which was white. When I came to put that on, I said, "What the hell did you buy this for? The goddamn sleeves are a mile too long."

"No," he says, "you roll the sleeves up and you put one of these in the holes." And after I started calling them "fancy buttons" he told me they were cuff-links.

By the time he got me all duked out with shiny flat shoes, garters on my socks, fancy buttons on my shirt, a dinky little stick-on bow-tie and a stupid looking hat that didn't even have a brim, I felt like a real f——— arse-hole. With me trying my best to get it off, and him trying his best to keep it on, we goddamn near got into a wrestling match. "If you think I'm gonna wear this sucky lookin' outfit on stage tonight, you're crazy," I said.

"Tom!" he was saying. "It looks great on you. That's what you've always needed. Just wear it once, and you'll see the great reaction from the people. After you play just one set the people will just love you. They'll no longer think of you as a bum any more. They're gonna be stunned."

Well, I don't know why, but I let him talk me into it. And he was right. The people were stunned all right. They were so goddamned stunned, they thought I was somebody else trying to sing like Tom Connors. Nobody bothered to listen, clap, drink, shout or do anything. They just kept staring at me like I was some kind of monkey in the zoo. When I finally caught a glimpse of Lepine ducking down behind the bar for a good laugh every once in a while, I soon caught on. And it didn't take me too long to get the hell off the stage, get my ass upstairs, and change back into my regular clothes.

When I finally came back down and went up on stage, everybody gave me a standing ovation. "Glad to see you're back, Tom," everybody was saying. "That asshole that tried to replace you couldn't sing worth a shit. Not only that, but you should have seen the stupid lookin' suit he was wearing."

Well, that was it. I threw a few darts at Lepine and a few more beers into myself, and made a firm resolution to mothball the suit forever.

I had a gentleman's agreement with the owner of the Maple Leaf Hotel, that when he wanted to get rid of me he would give me two weeks' notice. And I agreed to give two weeks' notice if I intended to leave. As it turned out, Mr. Kotze had no intention of honouring the agreement.

On Saturday night, December 12, 1965, I played my last shift at the Maple Leaf, and the following morning at half past 6 or 7 o'clock, to my total surprise I not only didn't have a job any more, I didn't even have a room. I was kicked out.

Coincidentally, my old buddy Jim Frost had arrived in town. We talked most of the night and didn't get to sleep until 5 o'clock on Sunday morning. An hour and a half later, the cleaning lady came banging on the door. "I've got to do your room now," she said.

"My room?" I said. "What's going on? You know I don't get up before 11 or 12 o'clock, and besides, I just got to bed."

"Well, I'm sorry, Tom," she said, "but that's my orders, and Pete says that you're done."

"Pete says I'm done? That's the first I know about it." So I got my clothes on and went down to talk to Pete. And although he was in the building, he wouldn't see me or talk to me.

I went into the bar and I tried to find him. No luck. I went down to the kitchen and asked Mrs. Kotze what was going on. She said, "You're done, you're finished—that's it. Goodbye."

"Is that the word from Pete?"

"That's the word. Goodbye." And she walked into the kitchen. I said, "Well, geez, that's a nice how-do-you-do." She didn't stick around to even hear me. I went back upstairs, still not knowing what had happened or even why.

As Jim helped me pack my stuff I apologized, but I had no explanation to give him. With everything I owned jammed into a taxi, we went over to the Goldfields Hotel, two blocks away, where I got a room for a week until I found out what was going on.

When Jim left on Monday, I went back to the Maple Leaf to see Pete. He didn't want to talk to me, and when I finally cornered him he simply said, "You're gone."

I asked him why. He said, "I got a new band coming in tonight. Had to give your room to the new band."

"The new band?" I said. "What new band? And why didn't you tell me what was going on?"

"Haven't got time to talk now—too busy."

I said, "What about my two weeks' notice?"

"I haven't got time to talk about that."

"Well, that's a nice dirty trick," I said.

But Pete was gone. I then tried to talk to Gaet.

"I don't know what's going on," Gaet said.

I went to Vince MacAlinden, who always boasted he knew everything that was going on around there, but he didn't want to talk to me, either. Gaet was the only one who would talk to me, and I believed him when he said he didn't know what was happening.

I told Gaet I was going to the Ministry of Labour about this. I knew that because I wasn't there under a musician's contract at the time, I also wasn't considered self-employed, but an employee of Mr. Kotze.

When I told the labour board my story, they said I was

entitled to vacation pay, and that they'd get in touch with Mr. Kotze about the matter. They also said they would get at least one week's pay in lieu of notice from Kotze. I waited for a couple of days and then I went into the Maple Leaf and sat at the bar and had a beer. When Pete heard I was there he came out with a cheque for a week's wages in his hand, plus vacation pay for fourteen months earned. He grunted, put down the cheque and said, "Here's your money." That was it.

I said, "Thank you very much, Mr. Kotze—and thanks for keeping your word—thanks for everything."

He turned on his heel and walked away.

Several years later Gaet told me how Pete cried the blues when I appeared on national television billed as Canada's number one country entertainer and complained to people for days how terrible and ungrateful it was of me to not even mention his name. After all, wasn't it his great "kindness and generosity" that gave me my start? (It was also observed at the same time, however, that he never once acknowledged that the value of his hotel on the real estate market had tripled during the time I was there.) Gaet tells me he was also let go under similar circumstances. And the same thing happened to poor old Andy, who never missed a day working for Pete since the day the doors were opened. Pete just walked over to Andy one day and said, "You're too old to work here now. Goodbye."

Andy cried.

And the talk was all over town. I heard later that Pete sold the Maple Leaf and, due to very poor health, died a few years later.

In the fourteen months I was there the hotel was renovated three times. It had changed from a simple ladies' and escorts' room and a men's beverage room to an excellent night-club-sized lounge area, with a big stage. It now really looked like something and I thought I had everything to do with that transition. In less than a year and a half from the day I walked in the door, the Maple

Leaf Hotel had gone from a little-known bar for rubby-dubs to the foremost country music night club of the North. And while it's true that I owed my start to the Maple Leaf, I felt that, for the most part, the Maple Leaf owed its rapid climb and good reputation to the hard work of Tom Connors. And I certainly wasn't ready for the shock of getting kicked out on my ear just when everything was going so well.

Even today, I can't figure out what was going on in Pete Kotze's head when he let me go. Not only was I performing to full houses every night, but the free publicity I was generating for him through the press, records and radio was enormous. The thousands of people who were buying my records obviously liked me and every time they would play them in their homes it was a constant reminder of the Maple Leaf Hotel and the guy who was singing there. Two or three times a day for six days every week the hotel was getting free plugs on my radio program and the DJs were playing my records besides. Was it the money he was paying me? In fourteen months he paid me a grand total of just under $4,800. The last Saturday night I was there I played to two hundred people who sat there and drank for six hours. You don't have to be a rocket scientist to figure out that if each person only spent $2 per hour, it would only take the receipts of two nights for Mr. Kotze to pay me for my entire fourteen months of entertainment. Where can you get better value for the buck?

Even the *Daily Press* was carrying favourable articles. I had a good reputation around town and was always sociable and cordial with all the patrons. So what was the problem? Well, the fact that he wouldn't (or couldn't) speak to me when he so contemptuously threw me out only seems to point to one word—greed, greed of a special kind.

The word had already been around Timmins for a long time about the unsavoury way in which he dealt with his original partner in order to gain full possession of the hotel in the first place. This would also seem to indicate that he wasn't a man who could share anything. And now with the word around town that the Maple Leaf's rise in worth and popularity was more due to the efforts of Tom Connors (to whom he was paying peanuts) than it was to Peter Kotze, he once again had to make his move.

As he couldn't bring himself to pay me what he knew I was worth, he figured that by firing me and hiring another band he could regain the glory and perception that the good name and success of the Maple Leaf was entirely due to his own efforts. Today, I believe he began to see me as a threat, and therefore had to get rid of me. I believe this because the band he got to replace me was costing him at least $600 per week.

So I was feeling pretty down and dejected when I was let go without even rhyme or reason. I had always needed an opportunity to prove my worth, and when I got it I worked my ass off. And now this. Even my naïveté at the time could not stand in the way of my one burning question. "How was it possible after consistently packing a place six nights a week for fourteen months and all of a sudden in one night, bingo, you're fired? There must really be something about this music business I don't understand."

Just having a maid wake me up and tell me I was finished was a coward's way of doing things. It was chickenshit. It was lousy. And at the time it sure hurt me inside.

Even the last moment or two that I saw Mrs. Kotze was something I'll never forget. When her husband hired me, he placed a little sign in the lobby window. It was just a piece of bristol board about eighteen inches high by twelve inches wide, and there were only four words on it: APPEARING NIGHTLY, TOM CONNORS. Over the last fourteen months the condensation from the window in the wintertime had soaked it so often that the lettering was all stained and blurred, and the sunshine in the summertime had caused it to be warped, yellowed and curled.

On the morning I was leaving, I went to the window and raised the venetian blind to get the dilapidated sign for a little souvenir. Right over my shoulder came the stern voice of Mrs. Kotze. "Where do you think you are going with that? That doesn't belong to you. My Pete paid good money for that sign, and you can leave it right where it is. Now go." As I looked at her to say "I'm sorry," she had such a disdainful scowl on her face I just couldn't form the words, so I left without saying anything.

With no time to make any plans, I found myself thrown out on the street. All I could do was wonder if God had once again set me up to be knocked down. Had this really been the beginning, or was it the end?

If I was ever going to build on the foundation I had started, I'd have to find out right away if the ink I got from the *Timmins Daily Press* and the air time on CKGB radio was important enough to get me jobs outside Timmins. Within a few weeks I found out that it was.

When I started getting hired in communities around Timmins—like Ansonville, Kirkland Lake and Kapuskasing—I realized it was working, and that getting fired from the Maple Leaf may have really been a blessing in disguise.

At least, I now had two choices: I could return to hitch-hiking or carry on with my dream of being a country music singer. And as long as I could see that the dream still had a chance, the hitch-hiking could be put on the back burner and I could be content just to sing about it.

Timmins showed me that the songs of a drifter had value, and though the dream was temporarily shattered, I became determined to prove in other communities that the people of Timmins were right.

Another one of the things I learned in Timmins was how to deal with the media. I met a lot of great guys from the press including Bill McIntyre, Brian Gannon, John Farrington and a host of others. These guys would come in to hear me sing, buy me a beer once in a while and discuss the news of the day. They kept me posted, for instance, on all the latest developments taking place during the fire at the McIntyre mine in February of 1965. This helped me considerably in the writing of my song "Fire in the Mine," which I immediately recorded and began to sing in the Maple Leaf. They also gave me some tips on how to get some ink in the newspaper and how to determine whether a story might be newsworthy or not. Although I was a little naïve back then, I soon realized how significant this could be for my career.

I knew that a federal election was coming up and that Prime Minister Lester B. Pearson was coming to Timmins. Now if I could get to meet the prime minister and present him with a few of my records, that would be newsworthy.

It was one of the reporters from the *Daily Press*, Bill McIntyre, who got me in to see the PM. He seemed to have a good handle on everything, because when I got into the room it was he who introduced me to Mr. Pearson. Bill told me beforehand that he would also have a photographer ready to snap a good picture, and he'd take it from there.

Besides giving the prime minister a number of my records, I presented him with a membership in the newly formed Tom Connors fan club. It was pulled off well and the story was put right on the front page of the *Timmins Daily Press*. Under the picture of me and Pearson was the caption: "Tom Connors makes PM fan club member." Now that was news.

Whenever I sum up my thoughts about Timmins today, they hardly ever include the raw deal I got from Mr. Kotze. Instead, I always think of the friends I made, the great people I met and the wonderful times I had during my stay at the good old Maple Leaf Hotel. Timmins was the real springboard of my career. And to all those who bought a record from me or helped me in any way, and to those who just shook my hand and wished me well, I want to say thank you, I am grateful, and yes, I do remember.

Controversy in Kapuskasing

I soon found my temporary room at the Goldfields Hotel was too expensive, so a couple of days before Christmas I rented a two-room apartment in Mountjoy, a suburb of Timmins, on the other side of the Mattagami River.

It was here that my girlfriend at the time moved in with me for a while and proved to be a great help in keeping all the doom and gloom off my mind during the so-called festive season. But as soon as January 1966 rolled in, I was busy making plans for a future in music while I still had some money to do so.

If I was going to travel around looking for other jobs, I would definitely need a car. And as my driver's licence had lapsed over the years, due to the lack of money to renew it, I would have to get a new one right away. Besides, I had two guitars now, and a big suitcase full of clothes to carry around, to say nothing of the four or five hundred records I still had left to sell.

The car I bought was a 1958 Ford for $850. It was grey in colour and in real good shape. With that I went to get my licence. Soon after, I bought a small PA system, which consisted of one small column speaker, one amplifier and one mike stand with two microphones. All I needed now was a couple of window posters with my name on them, and I was ready to hit the road. When all was said and done, the total cost to me was under $1,200, counting the price of the car. This left me with about $100 for gas. And if I didn't leave Timmins right away, I wouldn't have that. So the girl and the housekeeping had to come to an abrupt end. I had also recently joined the Musicians Union and obtained a number of blank contracts and a guide book on how to fill them out.

The first place I tried to get a job was in Kirkland Lake, but all the hotels were booked up. I then went to Ansonville, where a new club in a small motel was just opening up. Here they would hire me for two weeks, providing I had another guy with me. I immediately contacted my friend Hubert Cook in Timmins, who I knew was not working at the moment, and upon hearing that he would take the job with me, I wrote up the contract and we started the following Monday.

Hubert played the stand-up bass and the snare drum at the same time, while I played my guitar and did all the singing. The first night we went over really well, and by the time we started the second evening, I had a new song written for the town. It was called "May, the Millwright's Daughter," and it immediately assured us of a contract renewal.

Altogether, we played in Ansonville for about four weeks. Then Hubert had to play somewhere else, due to a previous commitment, and I couldn't keep the job because I had no one with whom to form a duo. I then tried Cochrane, with no success, and then moved on to Kapuskasing.

I was able to secure a three-week contract at the Radio Hotel in Kap, but I would have to wait for another two weeks before the opening came up. In the meantime, I went to Hearst and played there for a week while I was waiting.

While all this was going on, I would race back to Timmins every Sunday to tape another six programs on CKGB Radio for the following week. The roads were often very hazardous in the wintertime, especially that far north. From Kapuskas-ing to Timmins was 140 miles and from Hearst it was 200. Quite often it was all I could do to get to Timmins on Sunday, tape my shows, get some sleep and head back the first thing on Monday morning. If I ran into a storm, I'd make it back just in time to play on Monday night.

During my second week at the Radio Hotel in Kap, I was doing a lot of research about a shooting incident that arose out of a labour dispute that had taken place exactly three years before I began playing there. It occurred in February of 1963. It was my custom to write a song about practically every town I stayed in for any length of time, but this song was taking me longer to write than usual. I was having a hard time finding anyone who wanted to talk about it.

The incident had taken place about thirty miles west of Kapuskasing at a little siding called Reesor Crossing, during a strike at the Spruce Falls Pulp and Paper mill in Kap. As a subsidy to the farmers around Reesor, they were often given licence to cut pulpwood in the winter and haul it out to stockpile it beside the railway tracks. The hauling had to be done while the muskeg was still frozen or else, in the event of an early thaw, they wouldn't be able to stockpile at all. And if they didn't, they wouldn't receive the subsidy.

Now, in order to respect the union strike against the mill, the farmers agreed to stockpile their pulp and not load any on the mill-bound train. This arrangement was going fine until one night some instigator decided to stir up some shit. A phone call was made by someone to the union hall where four or five hundred workers were having a meeting as well as a few drinks. The false message was that twenty or more farmers were loading pulp on the train at Reesor. This angered the union workers, who decided to jump into their cars and head for Reesor to put a stop to the alleged infraction.

Meanwhile, the farmers also received a phone call which said that a cavalcade of a hundred cars full of "armed" union men were on their way to Reesor to stop the farmers from stockpiling. The farmers, who wished to protect their stockpiling rights and knowing nothing about the accusation that they were loading, immediately rushed home to get their moose-hunting rifles. Upon returning, they no sooner took up their positions behind their stockpiles, when the huge cavalcade began its approach.

It's not known how many of the union men were armed, but when they got out of their cars and started heading for the piles of pulpwood, a shot or two was fired in the air by the farmers, as a warning to stay away. This caused shots to be fired from the union side, and pretty soon a full-fledged battle was on.

By the time they arrived at a cease-fire, three men lay dead and eight more were seriously wounded. From beginning to end, the whole thing took place within about two hours, but the results would go down in Canadian history as the "bloodiest labour dispute ever" up until that time. Strangely, the newspapers of the day didn't give it very much coverage. For what reason, I still don't know.

A number of people got together at the time and demanded that a monument be erected on the spot in honour of those who fell and as a reminder of what can happen when cooler heads are not allowed to prevail. The moment the monument was erected there were a number of warnings received by the authorities which said that if any names were carved on the monument plaques, which had been installed for that purpose, the monument would be blown up.

For a good number of years, while I was still in the north, the plaques remained blank and the monument remained standing. Today, I believe, it is still there, but whether or not the names have finally been inscribed, I couldn't tell you. But I've noticed that the road maps of Ontario are no longer marked with the name of Reesor between Hearst and Kapuskasing.

Now, on Monday of what would have been my third and last week at the Radio Hotel, the boss called me into the office and told me to write up a contract for an additional three weeks, if I wanted to stay. He said he was very pleased with the number of people I was drawing to his lounge, and even though my stompin' had worn a couple of holes in his stage carpet, he didn't care, because it was an old one anyway and needed to be replaced.

Soon I had the contract written up, and after we both

signed it, I told him I was working on a song about Kapuskasing. When he heard this he was delighted and asked me what it was about. I told him it wasn't written yet, but I'd show him the lyrics in a day or so, and I intended to sing it on Saturday night.

The next day I wrote the "Reesor Crossing Tragedy," but when I began telling people about it, I didn't get the response I'd expected. Even some of the people who had helped me with the research were now a bit leery about my singing such a song. Some expressed fears that the words might get me into a lot of trouble. So I decided to go to a little stationery shop on Wednesday, and get a hundred copies of the lyrics made. I then passed them around to people all that day and later on that night, just so they could see the song was factual and that I had not taken any sides in the matter. Also, on each sheet was the short announcement that I would have it memorized and be ready to sing it on the coming Saturday night.

By Thursday afternoon the word was all over Kapuskasing and the message wasn't good. It went something like this: "They might have let that asshole sing and write songs about Timmins, but he better not try it around here, and especially about what happened at Reesor." I somehow knew these messages were coming from people who hadn't read the lyrics, but there wasn't a thing I could do about it. Their minds were made up.

That night on stage, instead of getting the normal song requests, the pieces of paper sent up to me contained the warning: "Sing of Reesor and die" or "Sing your new song at your peril."

Even the boss started getting notes, and after the show that night he said he wanted to see me. "You'd better forget about singing that Reesor song," he said. "Most of the people around here want to leave dead dogs lie, and some things are better left unsaid. You're doing well enough as it is now, and we'll all be a lot better off if you just leave well enough alone."

As he also had the waiters and the bartender on his side, I just shrugged and said I couldn't believe how a simple song could bring so much fear in the minds of so many people who hadn't even heard it yet. "I'll be singing it on Saturday night," I said. And with that I went to my room to put my guitar away. I then grabbed my coat and headed up the street to the all-night restaurant for a bite to eat.

As it was quite late when I entered the restaurant, there was only one table occupied. The five or six guys at it immediately gave me the once-over. As I sat down in one of the side booths to wait for the waitress, one of the guys got up from where he was sitting and came over and accused me of sitting in his booth. Although I sensed something was up, I said I was sorry and moved to another booth. Immediately, another guy came over and said that booth had been his, and he was just sitting with his friend while he was waiting for his order. This time I sat at a table away down at the far end of the room. In no time, another guy was asserting that that had been his table.

I then went up to find the waitress to ask her if it was possible for there to be one table left in this deserted restaurant that wasn't taken up by any of the guys all sitting in the same place. After looking past me to the guys who were now snickering, then boldly looking back at me, she said that all the seats in the restaurant were spoken for. When I asked if I could take something out, she said the grill was down and that I'd have to wait a long while before I could get anything.

With that, I walked to the door and opened it, and left in the middle of a big cheer, with the waitress's voice, over the top of the rest, saying, "Goodnight, singer."

I went to bed without anything to eat that night and resolved that tomorrow I would go to a grocery store and stock up with canned goods for just such an emergency, should the same thing ever happen again.

On Friday I went to my favourite day-time restaurant,

which was run by the Goldsboroughs, and told them about the incident on the previous night. Before I knew it, Mrs. Goldsborough had made a bag of sandwiches for me "on the house," that I could eat after my show that night, but she also warned me that maybe I shouldn't sing my new song because of the talk she'd been hearing. I'll have to admit that by now I was beginning to get a little scared myself, but I had no intention of letting anybody know it.

Later on that afternoon, I was walking down the street on my way back to the hotel, when I had to pass by a number of guys who were standing in my pathway on the sidewalk. As I approached, they just stood side by side with no room to get by without having to walk into the street to get around them. Little by little the message was becoming very clear; they didn't want me singing the "Reesor Crossing Tragedy."

That night, the word around the lounge was that I was going to get myself killed. Every time I went to someone's table for a beer, they told me of another threat they had heard somewhere, and if I knew what was good for me, I'd get the hell out of town.

It was starting not to matter if I sang the song or not. Someone was going to get me anyway. Again, when the night was over, the boss told me if I sang the Reesor song on the following night he was going to fire me. I let on it wasn't bothering me and told him I'd let him know for sure when I got up tomorrow.

I then went upstairs to my room and stayed there. I ate my sandwiches that Mrs. Goldsborough gave me and started to think, What in the hell is going on around here? Is this Canada, or isn't it? Do Canadians have free speech, or don't they? You'd almost think that I had been responsible for the tragedy that happened at Reesor. And why in hell do I have to wind up in the middle of a problem I didn't have anything to do with?

It would be so easy, I thought, to just not sing the song at all. At least, that would make everybody happy again.

All I'd have to do is say that it had all been just a big joke, come out smiling, and everything would be back to normal. Or would it?

What would the war veterans say? What would those people who died to give me the right of free expression say if I turned out to be too much of a coward to exercise it? If I let those who were afraid to face up to their own mistakes intimidate me and cause me to be silent, was I not worse than they were? Should brave men have died so that I could live to be a coward? Who were these people who were trying to keep others from telling the truth? Who were these people who didn't want to hear a song because it spoke of reality?

By the time I finished talking to myself, I wanted to go on the stage right away and sing the hell out of my new song, but I still had to wait till tomorrow night.

When I got up on Saturday morning, I got into my car and drove around aimlessly. I didn't want to be around the hotel where I might run into the boss and have to argue with him about my intentions.

When I came back, just after supper, I went right to my room and waited for the final hour. Fifteen minutes before show time I went down to the lounge and was surprised to find the place was jam-packed. But the strange thing was nobody even bothered to say hello to me. There seemed to be a tension throughout the whole room, as if everybody was just waiting for something to happen.

After downing a beer at the bar, I went to the washroom. While I was inside, three big lumberjack types came in, and one of them shoved me up against the wall. Just the look of him was scary. He had a long knife scar that ran from his right temple, down his right cheek and across his upper lip to his lower left jaw, and when he spoke, it made his whole face twist right out of shape.

With a knife in his hand he told me if I didn't want to look like him, I'd better keep my mouth shut about Reesor. He then let me go and the three of them walked out.

As I straightened myself up and looked in the mirror, I was as pale as a ghost. A couple of minutes later I walked on the stage, strapped on my guitar, took a deep breath and turned on the mike.

The crowded room was absolutely silent. Even the boss, the waiters and the bartender had stopped doing what they were doing and just looked. "Ladies and gentlemen," I said, "by now you've probably already heard that I wrote a song about Reesor Crossing. It's a song that takes no sides, but only states the facts the way they happened."

I then started to sing:

> *Just a little bit west of Kapuskasing;*
> *Reesor Crossing, that's the name.*
> *Farmers hauled from out of the bushland,*
> *pulpwood for, the mill-bound train.*
> *Twenty farmers met that night*
> *to guard their pulp from a union strike,*
> *unaware this night would see*
> *The Reesor Crossing Tragedy.*

Before I was finished the first verse, half of the room, which seated about two hundred people, got up and left. And before the whole song was finished, the house had emptied out, with the exception of two tables in front of the stage who had been stalwart supporters right from the start.

By the time I started into my second song, the boss was waving his arms for me to stop and was signalling for me to come over to the bar where he wanted to talk to me. The first thing he said when I got there was, "That's it. I told you not to sing that song, and now look what's happened. The whole goddamned place is empty, and it's all your fault. So you can pack your junk and don't bother coming back. You're fired."

"Well," I said, "it's not going to be quite that easy. I have your signature on a new three-week contract, starting Monday, and I'm going to be here on Monday night ready to play according to my obligation. If you prevent me from doing so, I'll have to go to a lawyer and sue you for breach of contract.

"However, if you want to pay me now for the full three weeks in advance, I'll rip up the contract and be on my way. Furthermore, unless you prevent me, I intend to honour my present contract by playing for the rest of the night, even if I have to sing to the walls."

With that, I grabbed a beer and went to sit with the people at the front tables.

When I told them the boss had fired me, they felt pretty bad. We bought rounds of beer for each other for the rest of the night and tried to figure a way out of the dilemma. I made sure I played all my sets on schedule, and by closing time, my friends were resolved to start a petition going over the weekend and get as many signatures on it as they could. They said it just wasn't right that I should have to take the brunt of all this for the sake of a few hundred ignorant people. I had sung the song several more times that night, and not one of them could see anything wrong with it.

As the lounge closed and we said goodnight, I noticed a small gang of guys hanging around outside. Not wanting to take any chances, I went up to my room, changed my clothes, and left the hotel by way of the back fire-escape. I then got into my car and headed for Timmins.

The next day, while taping my advance radio programs, someone handed me a copy of the previous day's *Daily Press.* There on the inside of the front page was a long article about an interview I'd had the previous Wednesday with John Farrington, while he was in Kapuskasing to cover another story. He had asked me how I was making out, and I told him about the problems I was having in getting the local people to accept my new song.

I had no idea I was going to make the papers, but there it was. I still have a copy of the article today. It was dated Saturday, April 16, 1966. Knowing what I know

now, I only wish he had waited for the final outcome of the story. But although it wasn't printed at the time, the unexpected outcome now follows.

On Monday, April 18, about 7 o'clock in the evening, I arrived back in Kapuskasing. There must have been 150 people milling around outside the hotel, and I wondered what in hell was going on. Not wanting to go in by the front door, I drove around to the back, parked my car and again returned to my room by way of the fire-escape.

About fifteen minutes before playing time, I took my guitar and headed down the hall towards the steps that led to the lobby. By the sound of all the noise and the shuffling that was going on, I knew there must have been one hell of a crowd downstairs.

As I approached the top of the stairs, I saw the lobby was full of people. Some of them were sitting nearly all the way up the steps, and all hands were drinking beer. As soon as they spotted me, someone shouted, "There he is," and about six big guys rushed up to meet me.

Before I could say, "What the hell is going on?" one guy took my guitar from me and the rest lifted me up shoulder high and carried me down through the lobby and into the lounge. After a struggle to make their way through the huge crowd, they finally dumped me on the stage and passed me my guitar. The only time I'd seen such a motley looking crowd as this before was in the movies, when they were getting ready for a hanging. But not to worry.

The whole damn house began to sing, "For he's a jolly good fellow" and ended up with everybody shouting, "Reesor, Reesor! Sing about Reesor!" I couldn't believe what I was hearing. I immediately turned on the mike and began:

> *Just a little bit west of Kapuskasing;*
> *Reesor Crossing, that's the name...*

The house went absolutely wild. Five waiters, with trays

full of beer, all came over at once and placed every bottle in a line around the edge of the stage. I was soon so choked up I could hardly sing, but still the people were shouting, "Sing 'er, Tom, by the geezes, sing 'er."

As soon as I finished the last verse, those who were not already standing immediately did so, and the whole room rang out with a deafening applause.

"Sing 'er again, Tom, sing 'er again," they kept shouting. The pandemonium was so great I don't think anybody heard me when I thanked everybody and told them how happy I was that things had turned out the way they did. I guess I was half laughing and half crying at the same time. I must have sung the song at least five times in a row before everybody simmered down, and then I decided I'd better pause and have a beer. As I did so, I began to pass around some of the many bottles that lined the stage, and then went to sit with a couple of the customers who had stayed in the lounge on the previous Saturday night after everyone else had walked out.

It was here that a Mr. and Mrs. Millette showed me a petition they had gotten up over the weekend. It read, in part:

> *To the manager of the Radio Hotel. This petition is*
> *to keep "Tommy" singing here at the Hotel Radio.*
> [I still have a copy of it.]

It was signed by several dozen people, and they had planned to show it to my boss who had wanted to fire me. As it turned out, it wasn't needed after all. It seems that just the word that there was a petition going around brought a lot of people to their senses, and the overwhelming results were happening right now on this very special Monday night.

While I was talking at the table, some guy who was apparently quite well known by the crowd went up on stage and said a few words on my behalf.

"I can see now why this guy was so well liked in

Timmins," he said. "And it's for the very same reason that so many people are here to see him tonight. We've seen lots of entertainers come through this town before, but this guy's got guts. This guy's got what we in the north have always prided ourselves for having. But because of the shock of what happened to us at Reesor, we've all been burying our heads in the sand for the last three years.

"It's been hard for some of us to realize that life must go on, and that Reesor must now become part of our past history and not something we should let bother us throughout our daily lives. I think Tom Connors and the song he has written, and the events of the last few days, should serve as a reminder that just because one grave mistake was made at Reesor doesn't mean we have to go on making others.

"I think everyone here tonight knows what I mean. And on behalf of all of you, I'd like to thank Tom for the great song and I look forward to the day when I can buy a copy of the future recording. While we all may be just a little shy to say we're sorry for what happened in this room last Saturday, I don't think there's one person here tonight who doesn't hope that, wherever you go from now on, Tom, that you'll always be every bit as welcome there as you are here tonight in Kapuskasing. Ladies and gentlemen, let's hear it again for Tom."

In the middle of another uproar, and while trying to brush away a couple of tears, two or three people were prodding me to stand up and take a bow. When they weren't satisfied with that, they made me stand up on my chair and take another one. Then on the table. By this time they had me laughing again, and soon I felt like I owned the world.

The next set, and all the other sets that night, I sang like there was no tomorrow. The beer was going down like it was water, and I wasn't feeling a thing. In between all the times I had to sing the "Reesor Crossing Tragedy," I had everybody singing along with me on all the old favourites that I knew, and when closing time came, I sang about forty-five minutes overtime.

After everyone left, the waiters and the bartender shook my hand and wanted me to stay for a while longer so they, too, could have a beer with me. They kept saying how unbelievable the whole night was, and that they had never seen anything like it before. They just couldn't seem to get over it.

The boss, of course, was in his glory. He had never had such a good money-making night in the history of the hotel. He was all apologetic for wanting to fire me, and said I'd really saved his butt by coming back when I did, because a lot of people were telling him, in no uncertain terms, that if I didn't, they'd never drink there again. He then brought out some sandwiches on the house for the first time, and even had a drink with us.

When I got to my room, I went straight to bed. As I thought about all that had happened, I just rolled over, said, "Wow," to myself and went right to sleep.

Every night for the next three weeks, the Radio Hotel was packed. The boss said he would have liked to keep me there, but because of prior bookings, he was committed to bring in some other bands. When I left, he told me to keep in touch, and whenever he had an opening for a few weeks he'd have me back. As fate would have it, I would be back some day, but not to play the Radio Hotel. It would be to play a one-night stand in one of the local theatres on my first concert tour across Canada.

On May 8, I was back in Timmins. For the next couple of weeks I played at the Grand Hotel for a Mr. Carotte and then two weeks more at the Russell Hotel. Things were going very well at the Russell till about Thursday of the second week. Then I developed laryngitis, the dread of all singers, especially if you're a single act with nobody to spell you off. I somehow made it through the night, but on Friday night it got worse. About half-way through my second set, my voice began to crack in the middle of some lines and no words would come out at all. When this would happen, I would blame it on a short somewhere in the PA system and immediately start looking for the problem that wasn't there.

This would give my throat a little rest, and after a few minutes I'd start singing till it happened again. Pretty soon some people started to get fed up with me running back and forth. They said they were leaving and that they might be back sometime when I got a new amplifier.

When the same thing began to happen Saturday night, the boss began to catch on to what I was doing and asked me if I was losing my voice or something. He wouldn't buy my story about having laryngitis and figured my days as a singer were over. After another bunch of people walked out, complaining, he told me he didn't want me any longer and paid me off. It was just as well, in the long run. I needed a few days' rest anyway.

The following day I wasn't able to go in to the radio station, so for the next few days my program was off the air. This was the first time that happened since the program started. When I finally got my voice back, I went in and explained what happened. I also told them I had made up my mind to leave the area and see what my singing prospects might be like further down south. I then went to work and taped another two weeks of programs and told them that would be the last. Late that very same night, I booked into a motel in North Bay.

Learning the Ropes

I was now well out of range of the Timmins radio station and would have to rely solely on getting a job and selling a few records in order to build up my reputation.

I also realized my habit of stompin' could sometimes prove to be a liability so I began to carry a couple of pieces of three-quarter-inch plywood around with me in case I ran into arguments from hotel owners who might not want to see their stage carpets destroyed.

One hotel owner in North Bay said he would like to audition me for one night, and if he liked what he saw, he'd hire me the following day. When the following day came he told me I made too much noise with my feet, and he didn't even pay me. In another place, near Sturgeon Falls, the guy told me he'd hire me for the weekend and I could start on Thursday night. When I asked him to sign a contract, he said he would, but only after hearing me do a couple of sets.

When I started on Thursday, he left word with the bartender that he'd been called out of town on an emergency. I was to go ahead and play, and he would sign a contract when he returned Saturday. I could have sworn I saw him a couple of times over the next day or so, but the bartender kept assuring me that he was nowhere around. When I was all done on Saturday night he showed up, and instead of signing my contract, he threw me $15 and told me to take off.

Had it not been for the bartender and a couple of waiters, and also for the fear of getting my guitar smashed, I would have cracked him one. But, anyway, I was quickly beginning to realize that these and many other dirty tricks would probably have to be experienced along the way if I was ever going to make it in the music business.

I guess they call it paying your dues. But one good thing about it, once a trick was played on me, nobody else ever got to play the same trick again—although some tried.

By the beginning of the next week I landed in Sudbury. After trying a number of places, including the Nickel Range, and finding nothing, I finally struck it lucky at the Towne House. The guy had heard about me from a friend of his in Timmins, and without hesitation he signed a three-week contract. Only thing was, I couldn't start till the following Monday, and by now, my funds were getting dangerously low. I would have to get something between now and then to tide me over. Always staying in hotel rooms was a big drain on the pocket-book, and meal times were back to eating baloney sandwiches.

After checking a few small towns north of Sudbury, without success, I finally got to play the Hanmer Hotel for the weekend. This didn't pay very much, but it gave me a free place to stay till the following Sunday. Then I came back to Sudbury and moved into my new room at the Towne House.

For the first week I had a hard time drawing anybody as I wasn't known in Sudbury, and all the hotel's advertisements were going towards the big country dance band they had playing in their much larger room downstairs. However, as the second week rolled around, a lot of my previous week's audience were returning and bringing more people with them.

It wasn't until the end of the third week that I wrote "Sudbury Saturday Night," but by then it was too late for it to draw any people in, and the best I could hope for was to be able to re-introduce it sometime in the future, providing I got to come back for a return engagement. When I spoke to the boss about this, he just said I hadn't done too well, but if I called him in a few months, he'd see what he could do.

One thing I was able to do at the Towne House, though, was sell a few of my little records. This always helped to supplement the meagre wages I was making, and it also helped to spread my name around. And though I didn't fully realize it at the time, the stompin' was also becoming an asset. I only became aware of this as time went by, and people would ask their local hotel owners to bring back "the guy that always stomps his foot." In a lot of cases, they wouldn't remember my name, but they sure remembered the foot stompin'.

There was one hotel owner, in Chelmsford, who especially had good reason to remember the foot stompin'. He had just finished renovating his lounge at the Welcome Motor Hotel as I pulled up on a Monday afternoon. I think he had just recently bought the place and had just fixed it up in anticipation of hiring his first band. And as fate would have it, there I was.

When I told him I was a single act, he was delighted and wanted to hire me right away. He saw this as his golden opportunity to ease his way into having entertainment without it costing him a bundle while he was learning the ropes. After he hired me and showed me to my room, he invited me down to have a beer with him in the new lounge. You could see he was very proud of the place, and especially the new stage. As we walked up the set of five or six steps to get to the top, I asked him why he had built it so high. He said something about it reminding him of the stages they had back home in the old country, so I thought no more of it.

I also took note of the nice, brand-new shag carpet he had just laid, and I immediately thought of my board. As I couldn't foresee any problem, I didn't bother to mention it.

He then showed me how to work the nice panel of lights he had installed at floor level, all along the front of the stage. As we came back down the steps to the lounge, it occurred to me that he wasn't very tall. He might have been five-foot-two and no more. He certainly wasn't tall enough to see the floor of the stage, especially over top of the long panel of lights. And one more thing about the guy, he was a real motor-mouth, especially when he was excited. I mention these incidentals here, because they have a great bearing on the story I'm about to relate.

While I was setting up my equipment, he kept telling me what a large crowd he was going to have for opening night. Although it was very short notice, he had phoned everyone in town, and by the time the word got around, he figured he'd have a packed house. By the way they started to come in at show time, I could see he sure wasn't wrong. It looked like everyone in town had been just sitting around with nothing to do, but wait for the grand opening. About half-way through my first set, the audience seemed to enjoy themselves, but for good reason, Mr. Owner felt otherwise. He came up to the front of the stage, stood on his tiptoes and asked me what it was I had under my feet that was causing me to make all "that banging noise." Realizing he couldn't see the floor of the stage, I raised up the piece of plywood board and showed it to him.

With great finality, he simply told me to "get rid of it." As I started to explain, he just talked over me without listening and repeated several times that he wanted me to "get rid of it." I only sang one more song and purposely cut my set short so I could go down and have a talk with him.

As the place was full and he was very busy, I didn't like to bother him, but I felt it was absolutely necessary. As I approached him, I said, "I'd like to talk to you about my board." He said something about his wife being the cook and we could talk about that tomorrow. When I said, "You don't understand," he got all excited, and told me to "go away, can't you see I'm busy?"

At this point, one of the customers was tugging at me and indicating he would like me to sit at his table and have a beer. As I sat there, I tried to explain to everybody about the board, and what might happen to the carpet if I didn't use it. Everybody agreed with me, and said, "Besides, we like the sound of it, so go ahead and bang on it. And when the owner comes around, we'll tell him so. After all, we're his bread and butter, ain't we?"

They didn't sound too convincing, but for the time

being, it was all I had to go on. I went up to the stage again, put down the board, and let 'er go. By the end of the first song, Mr. Owner was over again. This time, he was talking a hundred miles an hour and wasn't listening to one word I was saying. "I told you to stop that terrible noise," he said. "I will not have that awful banging in my new lounge. If you keep that up, the place will be full of riff-raff by the end of the week."

At some point here, I tried to force an interjection. "Some of the people I was just talking to like the banging," I said, "and not only that, but if I can't bang my foot on the board, I'll have to bang it on the carpet, and…" It was no use. He just kept talking and didn't hear a thing.

"Bang your foot wherever you like," he was saying, "but don't be making that terrible racket. If I hear that noise just one more time, you won't be working here tomorrow night. Now, I don't want to hear one more word about the subject, ever."

As he turned on his heel and marched away, I said to myself, "All right, you little asshole, you won't hear another word about it. Leastwise, not from me. And just like you say, I will bang my foot wherever I like. I tried to warn you, but your goddamn motor-mouth got in the way."

For the rest of the week I became the "Thumper" instead of the "Stomper." The crowds were pretty good every night, and everybody seemed to have a great time. Not one person noticed that I was changing the position of the mike stand during every set. As soon as I was almost through the carpet in one spot, I'd move the mike a little further downstage to another spot, and thump away again.

By Saturday night, there were no spots left. You could see the floorboards in seven or eight places, and where you couldn't, the carpet was ripped and torn into rat-shit, anyway. Had I stayed there one more week, you could have cleaned up the whole stage floor with a lint brush.

As soon as my last set was over, I started taking my equipment out to the car. And when I had everything packed, including the stuff from my room, I went back in the lounge to get another beer and see if my luck was still holding.

Each night through the week, as the carpet got worse, I'd go and get another advance on my pay, just in case somebody made the big discovery. By now, I had the advances up to $75 with $45 still owing. So I thought, with any luck, I might get the rest. But on the other hand, if I ran into any trouble, I'd be a lot better off if I had everything in the car and ready to roll.

When I asked for the rest of my pay and the boss told me he'd settle up with me in the morning, I thought I'd better just jump into my car and go. But when I saw him turn off all the lights, I knew he wouldn't be going near the stage, so I thought I'd take my chances and stay around long enough to sleep in my free room for one more night.

Next morning, bright and early, I started the motor of my car and took a little stroll towards the lounge to see if the boss was ready to pay me. As I looked in the door, I could see at the far end of the room that the lights over the stage were lit. Both the boss and the cleaning lady were standing on the stage, and by the sound of things, they were having a very nasty discussion about some "goddamn no-good entertainer."

As they spotted me in the doorway, the boss hollered, "Hey, you! You son-of-a-bitch. Come here. I want to talk to you." As he ran down off the stage with arms, legs and mouth all going at the same time, I closed the door and hopped into my car. As I flipped it in gear and rolled down the window, he opened the lounge door and shouted something about his carpet. The last thing I remember, he was heading towards me with his fists in the air. I just gave him a little wave and headed down the road for Sault Ste. Marie.

Though I made a lot of enquiries in a lot of little

towns on the way, I wasn't able to pick up any work, and the same thing was true of the Soo itself. A few days later, I arrived in Wawa, the town that takes its name from an Ojibway word which means "wild goose."

Here I played at the Wawa Motor Hotel for two weeks between the sets of Smiley Bates and an additional two weeks alone after Smiley left. It was here I learned about the Ojibway legend surrounding the mating habits of the Canada goose, and incorporated it into a song entitled "Little Wawa."

I had the song written before my first week was over and convinced my boss to pay for half the price of getting a single record made. About two weeks later, we received the records at the motel and immediately put them on sale in the lobby and in the gift shop for tourists. With me also selling the record on stage and singing the song three or four times each evening, we were able to sell two or three hundred before my time ran out and I had to be replaced by another band who had already been booked.

Before I left town, however, I was able to get the boss to sign a return engagement for three or four weeks the following spring. Also, because the motel did a lot of advertising with various media, I was able to get a couple of local newspaper write-ups which dealt with the new song, and the small satellite radio station in Wawa found some time to play it occasionally.

As soon as I left Wawa, I went back to Sault Ste. Marie and hung around town for about a week. By doing this I was able to land a job that Friday and Saturday night at the Royal Hotel. This led to my getting hired for one more week and a contract to return around the same time that following spring when I was due to go back to Wawa. It was also during this time that I met the famous country music personality, Don Ramsay. He had me up to the radio station for an interview and was more than willing to give my little records a spin, especially "Little Wawa."

He also asked me if I was going to write a song about Sault Ste. Marie. I told him I'd give it a try. And before my week at the Royal was over, I had written "Algoma Central No. 69," and was singing it on stage.

When Don came in one evening, he took a tape of it, and while I was off to other places, he played it once in a while over the radio. To a guy getting started in the business, this sort of thing is a great help. Don helped a lot of newcomers this way, and I'm sure they're all grateful. I know I am.

By now, it was around the middle of September 1966, and I was heading back towards Sudbury. Although I knew it had only been a couple of months since I played the Towne House, I thought I'd drop in and pay the boss a visit. I hit it lucky. A band that was booked for two weeks had failed to show up, and I found myself hired again.

This time was quite a bit different than the last time, however. I was only there a few days when the word got around that the guy who demolished the stage up in Chelmsford was back in town. The boss of the Welcome Motor Hotel had apparently talked about me so much that everybody north of Sudbury had heard about the guy who "kicked hotels apart" everywhere he played. While this, of course, was an exaggeration, it sure didn't hurt my drawing power any. The place was soon packed by people expecting me to tear the Towne House down. The song "Sudbury Saturday Night" was also very well received and a lot of people were disappointed that I didn't have a record of it yet.

By the end of two weeks, the boss was delighted with my performance and signed a return contract. Unfortunately, before the date came due, the hotel changed hands and the new owner, for some reason, chose not to honour it.

On the Sunday that I left the Towne House I decided to try my luck down south. I was just a few miles out of town, on Highway 69, when I stopped into a restaurant on the side of the road. The big sign outside told me the place was called the Brockdan. Realizing the restaurant was part of a larger night-club operation, I asked if the boss was around. Soon I was talking to him, and upon learning he currently had no entertainment, I offered my services. He immediately hired me for two weeks. This engagement would prove to be my most successful one since leaving Timmins and Kapuskasing, and would lead to my returning to Sudbury many times thereafter.

It was in the Brockdan that the Laurentian University students got wind of me. After I agreed to go and play for them at the university cafeteria one afternoon, they immediately became fans. In order to make a stage for me, they put a large sheet of half-inch plywood on top of a couple of tables, and when I started to stomp, it took four guys to hold everything steady. The young audience really loved the shenanigans, and by the time I had sung about a dozen songs, I had made a hole right through the plywood and wound up gouging the hell out of the top of one of the tables.

From that time on, the Brockdan was jammed every night with students from Laurentian as well as people who came from everywhere else. Week-nights were every bit as good as Saturdays, and this happened every time I went back.

That first stint at the Brockdan took me to about the middle of October, and then I decided to go south and look for some more gigs. I also wanted to see a few of my friends and tell them all the good news about what had happened to me since they saw me last.

I knew they'd have a hard time believing the events of the last two years or so. I now had a car and two guitars. I also had some records and was finally establishing a name for myself. Maybe this thirty-year-old bum might amount to something after all. But though my hopes were high, I knew there was one hell of a lot of work to be done yet.

Somehow I was going to have to land a recording

contract. How, I didn't know. But without it, I wouldn't be able to go very far in the business. My single recordings were fine in the smaller places, but if I was going to land any big jobs, I'd have to have an album or two on the go. This would look a lot more impressive to prospective employers who hadn't heard of me.

I also figured I'd need an agent right away. This was another reason I was heading south. Most of the agents had their offices in Toronto, and as my friends the Chapmans lived in Etobicoke, which was a suburb at that time, I thought they might let me hang my hat around their place for a while till I could make some contacts.

On my way down to Toronto, however, I decided to make a little detour and visit my friends over in Port Elgin and Southampton. When I got there, Ira and Pete and all the gang were very impressed at the progress I had made, and on the following day, my pal Jimmy Fordham took me for a drive up to Hepworth to see if I could get a job there at a hotel called Duffy's.

I remember telling the owner I would work real cheap, just to establish my name in that part of the country, but he looked at me rather disdainfully and said he could probably get better entertainment locally, and more cheaply as well.

One thing we found out, though, while we were in Hepworth, was that a new building was going up to house the Hepworth Country Music Auditorium. We learned that a John Koker was building it, and the person to see about eventually getting to play there was Clare Adlam, a well-known fiddle player who owned the music store in Owen Sound. After getting his address and resolving to go and see Mr. Adlam in a few days, Jimmy and I went back to Southampton.

On the day I left, Jimmy told me he'd like to have a few dozen of my singles to sell to the people who came to his little shop to buy bait from him. While this was a wonderful gesture, and nobody had ever offered to actually help me sell records before, there was even more to it. He wanted to buy the records from me outright, and at the full price, as well. I was really taken aback, to say the least. He was a good friend and I didn't want to see him get stuck, so I said I'd sell them to him only on the condition that I could buy back the records he couldn't sell.

Although he agreed, it never came to that. He eventually sold them all and wound up buying more. This turned out to be a great help to me, and I've never forgotten the favour.

I also wrote a song about the Hepworth Country Music Auditorium, and on the day I arrived at Clare Adlam's music store I sat down and played it for him. He liked the song very much and wanted to put it on tape. He also thought he might be able to talk Mr. Koker into using some of the auditorium funds to finance making a 45 RPM single that they could sell in Hepworth as a souvenir. I agreed to tape it, but when I went out to the car and got my board, I could see he didn't know what to think.

He set the mikes up and I put the board down right in the middle of the music store floor and proceeded to kick the shit out of it. He started to laugh and said he'd seen a lot of things in his life, but this really took the cake. (Clare is a very good friend of mine today, and he still gets a great chuckle every time we happen to speak of the day we first met. He says he didn't know whether I was a musician or some kind of a new-fangled chainsaw.)

At any rate, we finally got the record made, and it went on sale at the auditorium on opening night. I was also invited to come up from Toronto at the time and open the show with the song. The place was packed solid, and as soon as they cut the ribbon that ran across the front of the stage, I came out with my board and let 'er go. They gave me a standing ovation. Unfortunately, due to internal problems, the auditorium closed after the first season.

After leaving Clare's music store in Owen Sound, I

headed out for the Chapmans, in Toronto. Reg and Muriel were very happy to see me and treated me like a long-lost son. They were surprised to hear about all the records I had sold, all the clubs I had played in, and especially the eighteen-month radio program on CKGB in Timmins. I guess it took me about two days to bring them up to date on everything, and I remember how they laughed when they read the newspaper clipping announcing that Prime Minister Pearson was a member of my fan club. I think Reg asked me if I'd call up and get the PM to lower his income tax.

In the next little while, I went to visit some recording companies, especially Quality Records. But everything was thumbs down. I couldn't understand it. I had saved all my slips that showed how many records I had sold, but still they weren't interested. Even Quality, from whom I had purchased thousands of custom-made records, gave me the run-around, saying my product wasn't "commercial." I wonder if they still feel the same way today, after I've sold over 2 million pieces in Canada alone, with sales still climbing. And all this while I'm still waiting to hear even one of my songs being consistently played on the hit parade of any national radio network.

The booking agents at the time didn't do me any favours either. Although I now knew some 2,400 songs by heart and would always sing them on request, I said I would mainly try to sing and promote my own songs. This they strongly disagreed with; they advised me to be like everyone else, and just sing the current top ten hit parade songs.

This, they assured me, was what all the hotel owners wanted. But I reasoned another way. From talking to the customers in bars, I was finding out that what they wanted was variety. They were getting tired of hearing the same old thing from bar to bar. "Who wants to go out for a night on the town, and every bar you go into, they're playing exactly the same program as the bar you just left?"

That's the way it was getting to be with every band now. They were all concentrating on the latest top ten songs and people were asking them, "Don't you know anything else? Can't you just be a little more original once in a while?"

Who cares what band can perform the same hit parade song better than the rest, if you've already heard the damn thing ten times last night, ten times tonight and ten times tomorrow night; if by then you even care to go out at all? You might as well stay home and listen to the song a few times on the radio.

So with our views diametrically opposed, most of the agents I eventually got to book me did so only when they were in a pinch and had no other band to take the job. Another reason they didn't book me very much was that I was only a single act, and as their commission was always 10 per cent of what the band made, they figured they were wasting their time with me. I could only command a portion of the money the bigger bands were pulling in. So why should the agent tie up the lounge for a week for less money if a larger band was available to take the job? This, of course, was only short-term thinking, on their part, and in the long run, I eventually proved this kind of thinking to be false.

At first, as an incentive to get an agent to book me into a new place, I would pay him 10 per cent of the jobs I had already booked myself. This allowed him to put my jobs on his contracts and thereby gain an introduction to some new hotel owners who had been pleased with me, and then book some new acts into the room as a result. The trouble with this arrangement, however, was that for every job the agents were getting me, I was getting two or three. As long as they were getting me the odd job, they were winding up with the better end of the deal. I soon got wise to the game and eventually returned to booking all my own jobs. The 10 per cent was just as good in my pocket as it was in theirs.

Another thing, as my popularity in each town grew, I

would ask the agent to get me more money. This they were very reluctant to do. They always played "pussyfoot" with the owners for fear they might not get to book the room any more.

I remember the last agent I had. When I asked him to get me a raise from a certain owner, he accused me of having a "star complex." When I asked him what a "star complex" was, he told me, it's when an artist is already making more money than he's worth, and he still comes demanding more. I told him to take his agency and shove it. Little did he know I had just come back from talking to the hotel owner myself, who told me that he would have no trouble paying me $100 more, because I was drawing more business into his club than any other act he had. And that included four- and five-piece bands.

As far as I was concerned, if you were able to draw the crowd, you deserved to make the money. It's the cash register that tells the final story.

Oh, there were some hotel owners at first who couldn't reason why they should have to pay me as much as they were paying a four- or five-piece band. But, as I had played their bars before and they knew what crowds I was capable of drawing, all I had to do was say, "Well, if you don't want to pay me, I'll just take a little walk down the street to the competition, and see if he might be interested in the proposition. After all, he knows even better than you do how his business hurts every time I'm in town. I'm sure he'd welcome the opportunity to see somebody else hurt for a change."

That kind of talk always seemed to bring the odd contrary fellow back to his senses.

Meanwhile, back at the Chapmans', it was the middle of November 1966, and the only new booking I could get from an agent was away up in Swisha, Quebec. That was just across the Ottawa River from Rolphton, Ontario, roughly half-way between Pembroke and Mattawa. The place was so remote that when trouble started it would take the Quebec Provincial Police three hours to get there, and that was by travelling most of the way through Ontario, because there were no Quebec roads going there.

Although the booking was for two weeks I would have to wait until Christmas to get it. I was also told that I was to play between the sets of another band by the name of Bud Roberts and the Bordermen.

Because I had previously met Bud in Timmins, and he gave me his Toronto address, I now went to see him and tell him the news. He was staying with friends, Donnie and Winnie Wortman, who lived out near Port Credit. It was here that Bud informed me that the Bordermen had broken up and he was looking for another band.

When the day finally came to go to Swisha, Bud not only didn't have another band, but he also had no way of getting there. I told him he could come with me.

The agent that booked us also sent another guy with us, and altogether we were to perform as three single acts, each taking our turns on stage. The guy's name was Larry West.

During the trip, Bud got to telling me about the couple of times he played Swisha before, and how he had grown especially fond of the twelve-year-old daughter of a family he was now friends with, the Jennings. As he invited Larry and me to the Jennings' house to meet these people, he remarked how nice it would be if he could write a little song about their daughter some time.

"Why don't we start on it right now?" I said. "Tell me a few more things about her and I'll help you put some words and a tune together, and when it's finished we'll sing it in the club."

That's how Bud Roberts and I came to write "My Swisha Miss" and we were finished with it even before we got to the town. By the second evening we were singing the song on stage. First, I would sing it on my portion of the show and then Bud would sing it on his. Everybody liked it, and the Jennings in particular. They even got permission to bring their daughter in to hear it, during the Saturday matinee. Before our stint was over, even Larry sang it a couple of times.

The hotel was owned by a John Dailey, who was also in the business of grub-staking trappers and prospectors, so the place was always full of some pretty rough characters. Although they could often be a bit obnoxious and unruly, they were good tippers and really enjoyed the kind of music we were putting out.

Although neither of us had the backing of a band, we played continuously, with one guy getting on stage as soon as the other guy got off. We also played on Sunday, as this was now allowed by law in Quebec, and Monday was our night off. If you happened to have another job to go to, where you had to start on Monday, as was the case in Ontario, you didn't have much time to get there, especially if you had to drive any distance.

It was also in Swisha that I came up with the quickest song I ever wrote. We were fooling around with our guitars in Bud's room one afternoon when he decided to go down to the bathroom at the end of the hall and have a shave. He was gone exactly twelve minutes. When he again opened the door of the room, I was singing the "Maritime Waltz."

"Where in hell did you get that song?" he said. "That's good."

"I just wrote it," I said, as I showed him the piece of paper I was scribbling on. "Holy shit," he said, "that was fast. I guess I own half of the song because you wrote it in my room."

"Not a chance," I said. "Maybe the next time you'll stick around when I'm getting hot and help me write, instead of going for a shave. That way you might get a piece of the action."

On the day we all left, the boss said he would contact our agent and have us all back. I eventually returned a number of months later, though not through the same agent, and I know Bud also returned again at a different time, but I don't know about Larry.

As Larry also wrote a number of songs, from time to time, I got him to lend me some of his magazine articles to read. One of the stories was an account of the landslide at Frank, Alberta, just a little distance west of Pincher Creek. The slide took place in the spring of 1903 when half of the mass of Turtle Mountain came down to bury the whole town. A small baby turned out to be the lone survivor and the rescuers named her Frankie Slyde in memory of the town and the disaster. (I understand she died just a few years ago.)

As I had often passed by the spot while hitch-hiking, I told myself that I'd write a song about it some day. Well, here was the whole story in the magazine I got from Larry, and as soon as I got back home to the Chapmans' I wrote the song. I called it "How the Mountain Came Down," and because of the information I was able to get from Larry, I gave him a small percentage and credited him as a co-writer.

Some Tricks of the Trade

It was now January 1967, and also Canada's hundredth birthday. Everybody seemed to be planning a centennial project, and everyone was talking about the "big one" in Montreal, Expo 67. One day I came up out of the Chapmans' basement with a little project of my own. I had written a song called "The World Goes 'Round." It was about all the things I had imagined would be going on at Expo that summer. Although I later managed to get it recorded, it didn't amount to much. But I tried anyway.

As the days and weeks began to roll by, I was beginning to think my agent had forgotten all about me. Then, sometime in late January I called him and he had a job for me in Kirkland Lake at the Franklin Hotel. When I got up there, I got one hell of a surprise. I walked in to ask for the manager, and who should come out of the office but my old bartender pal from Timmins, Gaet Lepine. "What the hell are you doing here?" I said.

"I'm the new manager here," he said, "and from now on you're going to be working for me. I didn't want your agent to tell you I was here, so it could be a surprise."

"Well, it sure was that all right," I said, "and it looks like this gig is going to be fun."

That turned out to be an understatement. Every day we were out to the pool room for a few games, and every night after the show we sat up and either talked or played board-hockey. Sometimes we'd play music or just act the fool. This was especially great for me, as it gave me an opportunity to relax for a change with someone I knew. In a lot of other towns, by the time you got to know somebody whose company you could enjoy, it was time to leave.

Gaet's wife, Jean, was also doing the cooking there. And as the meals were always good, I hardly ever went any place else to eat. We were also having good crowds

501

every night, so everybody was happy all the way around.

While I was there, my agent called me and said he had a week for me to do in Barrie. So late Saturday night, or about 3 o'clock Sunday morning to be exact, I left. It was during one of the biggest snowstorms that winter. There were storm warnings all night and the police were advising everybody to stay off the road. Gaet tried to get me to stay, as we cleaned about a foot of snow off my car, but with another job in a town I never played in before, I wanted to make sure I was there in lots of time.

After shovelling a bit of a track in front of the car, I got Gaet to give me a push to get me off a patch of ice, and away I went. I ploughed through snowbanks and went through just about every hazard imaginable. One good thing about it though, I never met one car till I got almost to North Bay. So there wasn't anything on the road to bother me as I fish-tailed my way along. By the time I got to North Bay the storm had subsided quite a bit, and the roads became a lot better. By that time I would have driven about 150 miles. It took me around six hours to drive 150 miles and I still had another 140 miles to go.

I settled into the Wellington, in Barrie, around 1 or 2 o'clock in the afternoon. And after not having had any sleep yet, I immediately went to bed. Later that evening, I set up my gear and called the Chapmans to let them know where I was. The following Saturday evening, both Reg and Muriel came up to Barrie to see me perform.

It was only about sixty miles from where they lived, so they decided to drive up and surprise me. Besides, they had never seen me perform before, and they wondered what the hell this stompin' was all about anyway. I don't know who was more surprised, me or them. Until they actually got in the lounge and sat down, they couldn't imagine what it was that I was doing to keep the attention of so many people for a whole evening, let alone a week or more. And the fourteen month stand at the Maple Leaf Hotel in Timmins, they couldn't understand at all. But after a few minutes of seeing how everybody was enjoying themselves, they too got in the groove and wound up having a hell of a time. Even when a fight started, I just kept on playing and banging my foot. Everybody was paying so much attention to me and the flying sawdust, they hardly noticed the ruckus at all.

Every time Reg and Muriel got a chance, after that first night, they would drive to wherever I was playing, within reasonable distance, and bring some of their neighbours with them. In this way, they not only had a good night out, but they were also lending a lot of moral support. This was always important, especially if I was playing a place for the first time.

Later on, through the years, a lot more people were beginning to do this. And after a while, it began to be no surprise to see people in my audience who had just taken in the show on the previous week, at a hotel in another town over two hundred miles away. Sometimes there would be so many out-of-town strangers in the lounges that the owners would often joke about how great it was to have an entertainer who always came to town with his own ready-made audience.

A couple of weeks after playing Barrie, I got to play for a weekend at the Village Inn in Bradford, and then it was time for me to go back to Sudbury and honour my three-week contract by returning to the Brockdan. With the house now packed every night, it would have been easy to accept the boss's offer to keep me for another three weeks, but a call came in from the agent who had a two-week job for me down in Leamington. Always on the alert to get myself known in new places, I took it. But not, of course, without getting another return contract signed for the Brockdan. This was becoming standard procedure, now, wherever I played.

I hadn't been in Leamington two days when I wrote "The Ketchup Song." I was playing at the Seacliffe Hotel, and on Wednesday night, when I walked up on the stage, I didn't say a word, but immediately started singing the song. All heads turned and looked at the stage. Not one person took a sip of beer until the song was over. I had to sing it half a dozen more times that night, and the same thing for the rest of the two weeks. With so many people wanting to hear the song, my return engagement was again guaranteed. While I was in Leamington, I put "The Ketchup Song" on tape and went into the Heinz Ketchup factory's head office and played it for the head honcho. He was interested in it, but said he would have to take it higher up. When I went back in a couple of days, I was told that nobody was interested. Strange people, I thought. This song would be great promotion for Heinz, but apparently, nobody could see the forest for the trees. Or was it because the song didn't come to them through some big advertising company from the States?

Anyway, I left Leamington and headed for my return engagement in Sault Ste. Marie. For two weeks I was back at the Royal singing "Algoma Central No. 69." Again, the house was packed every night, and this convinced me all the more that writing songs about every town where they would have me long enough to gather the proper information was paying off. It was good for me and it was good for them, and everybody had something to talk about.

Before I left the Soo for Wawa my old buddy, Lucky Jim, showed up on the scene again. I asked him if he would like to stick around for a while and sell some records for me in the clubs while I was entertaining. It would be great if he just sat at a back table with a bunch of records while I was on stage, and then when I took a break, he could walk through the audience with them once in a while. This would enable me to do more "public relations" by giving me the time to sit with more people. Jim agreed to try it for a while, so we both struck out for Wawa.

As we arrived in town on a Tuesday, and my gig didn't start until the following Monday, we had plenty of time on our hands. We first rented a small apartment, went and bought some groceries, and then went down to the Wawa Motor Hotel to take in the entertainment and see if there were any stray women around.

We no sooner got in and sat down when some guy asked me about a rumour that had been going around town since the first time I played there. In a nutshell, the story seemed to be this: before I arrived in Wawa the first time, some guy had apparently written a song about the Wawa Goose. When I got to town, I heard him sing the song, learned it and then put it on a record. I not only didn't pay the guy for the song, I put my own name on it instead of his. In other words, I didn't write "Little Wawa" at all, I stole it from somebody else.

Well, needless to say, I was more than a little disturbed. After approaching several other people, I found out that they had heard the same story. I said to Jim, "Come on, let's get out of here. I've got to try to get to the bottom of this." We went and had a beer in every bar in town and were told the same story everywhere. "Tom Connors had stolen 'The Wawa Song' from a local resident."

What I wanted to know right now, was, who in hell was this local resident, what song did he write, and who in blazes started this rumour, anyway? But try as I may, no one seemed to know the guy. No one seemed to know where he lived or anything. And if they did, they sure weren't telling me. As a matter of fact, we couldn't even find anyone who had heard the original song, if indeed there was one.

All I was hearing, day after day now, was that I was a song stealer, and I was becoming quite agitated. How could I fight against something I couldn't see? How could I defend my reputation against a rumour when I couldn't find the source? I could deny it all I wanted to, but I could see in the eyes of my accusers that they had come to believe the lies of some local gossip and were not going to take the word of an outsider. So what the hell was I going to do? My good name was at stake. And if I couldn't stop this rumour right here where it started, there was no telling how far it might eventually spread.

Finally, when Sunday rolled around, I hit upon a plan, and I had a hard time waiting till Monday night to put it into effect. When I explained it to Jim a couple of times, we both agreed that it just might work. I would make an announcement from the stage, and if it was worded just right, it might flush out the guy who allegedly wrote the song I was supposed to have stolen.

When I walked up on the stage on Monday night, the first song I sang was "Little Wawa." When it was over, I could tell by the strained applause that most of the audience believed the rumour, and I wasn't going to say anything that would make them believe otherwise. At least not now. No, what I had to say went like this:

> Good evening, ladies and gentlemen. As this is my first night of playing back in Wawa, I would like to pay honour and tribute to one of your own. I would like to announce that I am going to buy a nice steak dinner, with all the trimmings, for the guy who wrote "The Wawa Song." The dinner will be this coming Saturday evening before the entertainment starts. He can bring his wife and another couple if he chooses, and when the dinner is over I will buy them all three rounds of drinks while they listen to the entertainment. I now feel, as you all do, that it is high time the composer of "The Wawa Song" receives his just due and proper recognition.

I then finished off with:

> I just have one little problem, folks, I can't seem to find his present address anywhere. But the first person who will be good enough to write it down and give it to me will receive a free round of drinks to his table.

Everyone applauded. Two minutes later I had the address I was looking for, and the table received a round of drinks.

The first stage of my plan had worked. Without voicing any denial or acceptance of the rumour's claim, I had got the name and address of the guy who wrote "The Wawa Song" (not "Little Wawa"), and everybody went back to treating me as "a nice guy after all."

The following day I went to see the man who wrote the song. His name was Middie. He was a nice guy, and as it turned out, he didn't know anything about the rumour at all. It seems he wasn't the type to frequent the hotels very much. But when I told him about my offer he was delighted and accepted my invitation immediately. I then told him that because his song should receive some recognition by the people of town, he should come prepared to sing it on Saturday night. I would give him a nice build-up and make sure that he and his company felt comfortable.

When Saturday evening came, he showed up with his wife, one member of his family and a couple of friends. When they finished up in the dining room, I had a nice table reserved for them right in front of the stage. By the time they received their first round of drinks, the place was packed, and I headed up to do my first set.

After singing my first song, I announced, "We are honoured this evening to have the composer of 'The Wawa Song' in our midst," adding that indeed "he and his company had received their steak dinner as promised, and as a big surprise-bonus to everybody, he'll be singing 'The Wawa Song' during my second set." To a great round of applause from the audience, he stood up and took a bow of acknowledgement. Everything was working out just fine.

When I finished my first set and came off the stage, I went immediately to Middie's table. After chatting for a few minutes and making sure everybody was enjoying themselves, I assured Middie there was nothing to be nervous about and that I was sure the audience would like his song. I then ordered them another round and excused myself, explaining that I had to do some other public relations throughout the lounge.

As I sat at some other tables, instead of accusing me of stealing Middie's song, people were now asking me when we had written it together. All I would say was that "we didn't write a song together. I wrote my song and Middie wrote his. You'll see that when he gets up to sing it." Then, before leaving the table, I would give them a little knowing smile, and say, "People shouldn't pay a lot of attention to rumours, you know."

When it was time to start playing again, I walked past the back table where Lucky Jim was sitting, and he gave me that crossed-fingers sign which seemed to say, "So far, so good." I smiled a little and headed for the stage.

When my second set was about three-quarters over, I indicated to Middie that I would be calling him up right after the next song. I gave him a reassuring glance and simply stated, "Ladies and gentlemen, here's a little song I wrote called 'Little Wawa,'" and started to sing.

As soon as it was over, I said, "Well, folks, that was `Little Wawa.' And now for the moment you've all been waiting for. Will you please welcome to our stage a man from the very town of Wawa, who is here tonight to sing his own composition, 'The Wawa Song.'"

Middie already had his guitar strapped on and headed for the mike to a thunderous round of applause. I tapped him on the shoulder and said, "Go to 'er, b'y," and went down to join his company at the table.

As this was the first time I had ever heard the song, I realized it wasn't what I would call a real gem, but in fairness to Middie, it wasn't all that bad either. The main thing was, Middie enjoyed singing it, and the crowd enjoyed hearing it. And, of course, I too was delighted with the outcome. The house was packed with people, and every one of them was finally realizing I wasn't a stealer of songs after all. The rumour had been put to sleep forever. Mission accomplished. Everybody had a great time and nobody was hurt. It might have cost me $75, but I felt it was worth it.

When Middie finished "The Wawa Song" I got him to sing a couple more. I then went up to the mike and thanked him, and told him he could come back to sing a couple of songs on my stage any night he wanted. And so ended the second set with another big round of applause.

Later on that night, after Middie left, a number of people came up to me and apologized for thinking the worst of me without giving me the benefit of the doubt. With a smile or two, I just shrugged it off and told them there was no harm done. But I thought to myself, "It might have developed into a hell of a lot worse, had the rumour not been stopped in its tracks." It takes years to build up a good reputation, but a bad one can ruin you overnight.

Sometime during the next week, Jim started to get bored with his job of sitting around waiting for people to buy records and decided to take off. Maybe it was just because there wasn't enough action around the local pool room for him, I don't know.

But anyway, the third week found me back paddling my own canoe again.

On Thursday of my last week in Wawa, I was in the local supermarket buying a few cans of something, when my eyes fell on a large inflatable Heinz Ketchup bottle. It was a bit larger than a six-foot man when inflated, and the store had just recently set it out on display. As I looked at it and thought of "The Ketchup Song" I had just recently written down in Leamington, Ontario, a great publicity idea came running through my head. I immediately went to the man in charge of the store and offered to buy the inflated bottle.

"I can't sell it to you," he said. "It has to remain as a part of the store's new advertising display."

"Well," I said, "it's only new and not very many people have seen it yet. That means that not too many people would miss it. Besides, it could have maybe fallen off a truck on its way here. Anyway, how does $50 sound?"

It wasn't too long before the air plug was out of the bottle, and I was leaving the store with it safely tucked under my arm.

Next day I went to see a guy who used to come into the hotel quite often. He had a light plane, and I had a proposition. After I told him my plan and we worked out a price, he said we could do it, but from that time on I was never to tell who my accomplice was. I had to pretend I didn't even know him.

On Saturday morning, around 11 o'clock, we took off in his plane, ketchup bottle and all. By the time I got the bottle inflated, we were ready to make our swoop. "We'll only have one chance to get this right," he said, "and when I give you the signal, let 'er go."

Just as he flew rather low over the main drag of town, and just a ways beyond, to allow for the wind factor, he said, "Let 'er go." And I did. I couldn't have made a more perfect shot. The big red ketchup bottle acted just like a balloon. She wafted for a minute or two and then came down with a nice soft bounce, right in the middle of the street. Then she went up and came down again with another bounce on the street, and after the second bounce, she landed on a big flat roof and stayed there.

As we wondered what the people on the street were thinking when they saw the bouncing bottle, I thought the guy flying the plane was going to shit himself from laughing. As we landed the plane and headed back for town, he said, "Remember, now, you don't know me." I said, "Don't worry. I don't want anyone to know who did this either."

As it doesn't take long for the word to get around in a small town, I was hardly back in the Wawa Motor Hotel when some of the guys were asking me if I knew anything about the "bouncing ketchup bottle from Mars." "Listen," I said, "I don't get up early enough in the morning to see things falling from the sky. Besides, ain't it just a little bit early in the day to be telling jokes?"

That night the place was packed to the rafters. And as this would be my last night for the present engagement, I sang "The Ketchup Song" twice during every set and three times on the last one. This, of course, only made people suspect me all the more. "We're damn sure you're the culprit," everyone said. "Who else would think up such a prank? And how come you're singing about ketchup so much lately?"

"Oh," I said, "you know me. Every time something new happens in a town, I'm always singing about it." Next day I was heading out for Toronto.

One Heel of a Handle

On the first OF May, I was back in my agent's office looking to see if he had anything new for me, when a guy named Irvin walked in. When I found out he had something to do with the record business, I made his acquaintance. When I told him how many songs I had written and that I had been making a number of 45 RPM singles, an appointment was set up for me to go to his place where he could hear what I had to offer.

A couple of days later, I auditioned for him and a date was set to go into the studio. As the recording session would not be done for another three weeks, and I had no work between now and then, I figured I'd better take a drive around the countryside to see what I could find.

Although the recording date was constantly on my mind, I had been disillusioned a number of times before, so I figured I'd better not get my hopes up too high. That way I wouldn't go too far down in the dumps if it didn't come off at all.

One always had to fortify one's self for the many disappointments one was apt to encounter in this weird and shaky music business. I was also aware that there were a lot of entertainers before me who turned out to be has-beens long before they became somebodies. This business was known for turning out a lot more casualties than it was for turning out successes.

I headed east from Toronto, on the old No. 2 highway, and tried all the bars I could find along the way. From Kingston I headed north to Smith's Falls and over to Perth, and still I had no luck. By Sunday, I hit Peterborough, and recognizing the old King George Hotel as a place I once stayed when I was drifting, I decided to give it a try. And whether or not I was able to land anything, I planned to spend the night.

Once I got settled in, I went back to the desk to find out if I could get to see the boss. Upon learning that he wouldn't be back in town until the following day, I went up to my room, had a couple of beers and turned in early.

The next afternoon, when the boss came back, he wanted me to go up on the stage and audition. Although my PA system was small, I knew it was better than the one he had, so I brought mine in and set it up. I had a small reverb unit by this time, which gave my voice a lot more richness and clarity, and after I sang a half-dozen songs, he hired me for a week.

Though I didn't draw too many people until the weekend, all the staff and the customers kept telling the boss how much they enjoyed my program, so he decided to keep me on for one more week. By this time the word had gotten around town, and the number of customers increased.

By now I was sure I would get a return engagement at a later date, and that was what I always looked for. I also knew I would get much bigger crowds upon returning. At least, that was what usually happened and time would prove that Peterborough was no exception.

I had also written a song called "The Peterborough Postman," and as one of the bartenders was an ex-postman, the song was being requested quite often.

Even at the jamboree, which was held on the hotel stage every Saturday afternoon, some of the local entertainers began to sing it. This, of course, made me feel very proud. It was the first time I'd ever been paid this kind of compliment.

Another thing I found about the King George was that the staff were great people and exceptionally friendly. One of the waiters, Boyd MacDonald, even invited me home a couple of times during that first two weeks. Even though he and his wife, Shirley, had a large family and didn't have too much, they gave me supper and really made me feel welcome. Boyd also played the guitar and wrote some nice songs, and every chance I got, I would get him to come up on the stage and sing a couple.

There were also other families, like the Hills and the

Marshalls, and many others, who always made my visits to Peterborough something to look forward to. I sometimes felt that going to Peterborough was like going home. The city kind of gave me that feeling.

I always did have one drawback, though; something that began to dog me back in those early days and continued throughout my career. And that was that I never could get my records played on the radio. The very popular country DJ in the area at the time was Sean Eyre, and he really didn't think too much of me. He began poking fun at me, even before he ever got to know me or realize what I was all about. I must add, however, that a few years later he personally apologized to me for his lack of understanding at the time, and then began to play me as often as the station would allow. I told him, in my opinion, it takes a pretty big man to admit that he could have been wrong about somebody, and as far as I'm concerned, those are the kinds of people I like to call friends. Although that's a good many years ago now, Sean and I have remained the best of friends ever since.

Upon returning to Toronto, I contacted Mr. Irvin again, and sure enough, the recording session was still on. A couple of days later I was in the studio. I believe it was the fastest album that studio had ever done up till that time. All they had to do was set my levels and away I went. In one three-hour session I had put down sixteen tracks with no mixing required. The only thing I had to put up with was the fact that the engineer laughed all the way through. I guess the songs weren't sophisticated enough for him. But this was something I was going to have to get used to. The engineers on the next two or three albums were going to react the same way. I later learned that it had been said, in some private conversations at the time, that "this album won't sell enough to pay for the ink on the jacket."

(Today, it should be borne in mind that if any country artist sells 5,000 records in Canada it warrants that he or she should be kept on the label, and if sales reach

10,000 or more it's considered to be a hit. Even though this first album is still one of my poorest sellers, its sales are now over the 30,000 mark. So much for the opinion of the experts.)

I was very naïve about the record business back then and I had to make a lot of mistakes before I learned anything. These mistakes were going to be very costly in the end. But when you're young and you hunger to be on record as much as I did, you don't consider the pitfalls until you're in them. For instance, one should never sign a song over to a publisher without a firm commitment that they will try to publish the song within a reasonable length of time. If they don't, then the song should automatically revert back to the writer. In my case, Mr. Irvin got me to sign several dozen songs to his publishing company with a promise of doing nothing. And nothing was what he did. Two years later, when I demanded my songs back because nothing had been done, he quickly sold his catalogue, which contained my songs, to another publisher. It then cost me $3,000 to get them back—a hefty sum of money back then for a struggling entertainer to have to come up with, just to get his own songs back.

To add insult to injury, he borrowed the money from me to pay for the recording session in the first place and never did pay me back. In two months, when the record was finally manufactured, he gave me a dozen free copies. The rest I had to purchase from the distributor at no discount to the artist. And while I was told the record was released and was being distributed, try as I may, I couldn't find it in the record stores anywhere. (The one exception was Sam's, in Toronto.)

The great bulk of the records that were sold were being sold by me. Every two or three weeks I would come in off the road and buy another couple of hundred from the distributor, go away and sell them and return for more. And each time I went back to the warehouse, the pile of my records looked just the same as the last time I'd been there. As far as I could see, the only distribution I was getting was my own.

Here I was writing the songs, singing them, promoting them, paying for the studio, selling the records, and someone else was making the money. You have to want to be on records pretty bad to keep this up. I didn't even learn my lesson with the first album: I went ahead and made another one under the very same deal. By the time two years had rolled around, and I still hadn't received a cent of royalties, I started making enquiries as to how other record companies were operating. After that, I wised up and got the hell away from Mr. Irvin.

By the time I got my masters and my publishing back it cost me a great deal of money. But in the end I was glad to be rid of him. But, like they say, I guess it's all called paying your dues. And believe me, I eventually paid a lot of them. This was only the beginning.

I guess the only real consolation I had out of all this was that I did have an album. And while nobody really knew the shaft I was getting, it appeared on the outside, at least, that I was going places. It looked a lot better to have an album for sale, with a nice big picture on it, than it did to just have a bunch of single 45s packaged in plain paper sleeves.

Along with the look of success, though, also comes the perception that you've got money. From the minute you get your first album out, everybody assumes you're a millionaire. And the first thing they want you to do is give them a free record because they have "always been your best friend." It doesn't seem to occur to them that you have to buy them like everybody else. And if you make a few cents per record, well, even the delivery boy has to get paid something for his work. And besides, for every record I might have given away, I had to sell at least another half-dozen to make the money to pay for it. But, anyway, that's the way it goes. Sometimes you met friends that you just couldn't refuse. (I'm not complaining here, I'm only relating the facts of life.)

While I was still waiting for my first record album to come out, my agent sent me up to Pembroke, Ontario, to play a week at the old Pembroke Hotel. That weekend Gordon Lightfoot would be playing a concert in a theatre just across the street from me. His posters were everywhere and every time you turned on the radio, it was Gordie singing another song. As I watched the people begin to line up for his concert, I remember thinking how nice it must be to be so popular. I knew he had a lot of good songs and deserved his fame, but I still couldn't help wondering why it was taking me so long. Gordie must have had five or six albums out by this time and I was still waiting for my first one.

And mine would only feature me and my guitar—and without the sound of the boot on the board, at that. (I had been advised in the studio that to have incorporated "that noise" into the record would have been ridiculous.)

"Oh well," I thought, "patience. I'll just have to have patience. That's all." That night was Saturday night and all I had was half a house. I guess Gordie had them all across the street. But the boss was understanding anyway and told me he'd have me back sometime. "You work hard," he said, "and you're good with the customers, but you're unknown in this town. And with Gordon Lightfoot playing across the street, it's a wonder we had anybody in at all."

The next day, I packed up and drove to Renfrew, and before the day was out, I had another job for a couple of weeks at the Renfrew Hotel. They had two rooms there, a large one where Mac Beatty and the Melodeers were playing, and a smaller one in the front of the hotel where I was to play.

Again my competition was very stiff. For as everyone knows, Mac and the boys had lots of good records out and were known all through the Ottawa Valley as one of the best bands in the country. They had been on the Don Messer show a lot, and Mac had himself written quite a few songs about Canada. This was something the people could identify with, and I was only too aware of the fact.

Mac and the gang were very friendly towards me, nevertheless, and one evening in between my sets, they even invited me to come in and sing a couple of songs on their stage with them. I later found this kindness to be very typical of all the Ottawa Valley people. Even today, they still have a great reputation for their hospitality.

While I did very well in the hotel, my stay in Renfrew wasn't exactly without mishap. I drove off the road one night and smashed up the body of my '58 Ford. It was just after having something to eat at an all-night truck stop a few miles down the highway. I wasn't hurt, but when I went back the next morning, someone had relieved me of most of my little records I always kept in the car. (As I often joked later, it was probably a big fan interested in helping me with my distribution, no doubt.)

As the motor wasn't damaged, I had it hauled out and put into another '58 Ford body that I found at a wreckers'. This enabled me to at least get back to the Chapmans in Toronto. And there I was able to get Reg to co-sign for me to get another car.

I found a lilac-coloured 1963 Dodge station wagon at a car dealer's that I liked, but I didn't have quite enough money to pay for it. Having always been a rambler and never staying and working for very long in one place, I had absolutely no credit rating, and the dealer wouldn't trust me for the $250 still owing.

That's when I went to Reg. I showed him several contracts I already had signed with some hotel owners to assure him I had the money coming, provided I had a car to get to the jobs, and with very little hesitation, he co-signed for me. I don't know what I would have done, had he not come through and saved my bacon for me. He was really a friend, when I needed one the most. And before another month was up, I made sure I paid him off, even before I paid any of my other bills. One never knows when you might need a friend like that again sometime.

(And we're still the best of friends to this very day.)

Well, now it was Sunday, the twenty-fifth of June, 1967, and I was heading back to the King George Hotel in Peterborough. I always liked to arrive at each hotel on Sunday night, if I could. That way I could set up my equipment with no distractions, get a good night's sleep and have all day Monday to do any new promotion that might come to mind.

Though I went to the radio station on Monday afternoon, nothing came of it, so I thought the day wasn't going to be very eventful. But that night when I came downstairs to do my show, the place was packed. The hotel owner had put an ad in the *Examiner*, the local newspaper (not a common practice at the time), and the results were fantastic. It seemed like everybody who had come to see me the first time I was there not only came to welcome me back to town, but they also brought a number of friends with them.

The rest of the nights that week turned out exactly the same. The only regret I had was that I ran out of records to sell. People wanted to buy them but I had lost over two hundred during my car accident and didn't have any left. I was also waiting for my new album to be released, so I hadn't ordered any more singles. Besides the album would have sixteen songs on it, and most of them were the songs that had been on the singles, anyway.

While it was indeed a great week, something else was about to happen on that first Saturday night. It may not have been earth-shaking, and it may not have changed the lives of the customers, but it turned out to be a big milestone in the career of one Tom Connors. Because that would be the first night anyone would refer to me as "Stompin' Tom" in public.

On a couple of afternoons that week, while I was in the lounge having a casual beer at the bar, there were hardly any customers, and Boyd MacDonald, the waiter and I were having one of our many chats. Pete, the bartender, was washing a few glasses, and Boyd and I were talking about music and laughing about how some people reacted to my stomping.

I think it was on the Friday afternoon, and Boyd said he thought I should have a name change. I agreed the name "Tom Connors" was very plain and said that any name change would probably have to have something to do with the way I stomped on my board. Boyd also mentioned that there was another entertainer by the name of Tom Connors who was on the go at the time, and that he too had played the King George on occasion. This was all news to me. I had never met the other Tom Connors, but I agreed that some sort of a name change was in order, and I'd have to think on it for a while.

Up to that day, Boyd had always called me "Stomper." And as I finished my beer and started to leave, he said, "See you later, Stomper. We'll find some kind of name to call you. Don't worry about that."

Well, Boyd was off that Friday night and wouldn't be back on shift till Saturday night. In the meantime I hadn't thought any more about our little conversation till I was ready to go on stage on Saturday. The house was packed to the rafters, and when Boyd saw me coming through the crowd, he jumped on the stage, turned on the lights and the mike, and with that big friendly grin he always wore, he shouted: "Ladies and gentlemen, it is my distinct pleasure to introduce to you a man who is not only more Canadian than the maple leaf, and more devastating to a piece of plywood than a hungry beaver, but he's even stomped down more streets in this country than a Peterborough Postman. Ladies and gentlemen, make way for the one and only STOMPIN' TOM CONNORS."

He then got the people at one of the front tables to clap and start chanting, "Yay, Stompin' Tom! Yay, Stompin' Tom!" and by the time I got up in front of the mike, the whole house, including the staff, was yelling it.

At first I felt a little stupid and half embarrassed about the whole thing. But when I began to see how readily they all took to the new name, I just threw up my hands and said, "Well, I was looking for a new name anyway. And if that's the one you all want, then that's the name I'll stick with. I guess I'll just have to get used to it. So my first official words as Stompin' Tom are, 'Thank you, Peterborough'."

Then as I started my set with "The Peterborough Postman," the house went into high gear. The applause, the laughter, the friendliness pervaded the whole room for the rest of the night. Every person I talked to between sets was calling me Stompin' Tom and I don't think Boyd MacDonald ever got that grin off his face till the end of the second week.

A record was set that night for the most booze ever sold at the King George—and on my first night as Stompin' Tom. It was a great way to launch a new name. When I went to bed that night, I thought of how ironic it was that, not too many years ago, I had wandered into the King George as a bum, and now I was being named "Stompin' Tom" at the same hotel. (Again, if I had dreamed that night that twenty-five years later, Peterborough would also be the first town in Canada to present Stompin' Tom with the Key to the City, the dream would have come true because it happened.)

During my second week in Peterborough, I was busy getting my new signs and posters made up. Of course, they all had Stompin' Tom on them now. And the old posters? Well, I just threw them away. This was to be the beginning of a new era.

Stompin' Tom was now the Entertainer; and Tom Connors was to be just Mr. Private Citizen from now on. As soon as I had a chance to go back to Toronto, I went to the Provincial Buildings and had the name STOMPIN' TOM registered as my official business name and STOMPIN' TOM LTD. registered as my company.

On Saturday, July 8, it was again my last night at the King George Hotel for a while, and everybody who had been in the audience on the previous Saturday were now there again. It seemed like everyone wanted to say goodbye to the entertainer they all felt they had a hand in naming. And I was beginning to feel almost like a new person. I think the words, "Good luck, Stompin' Tom, we'll see you again when you get back," rang in my ears all the next day as I left Peterborough and drove to my new engagement.

My agent had sent me to Chatsworth, Ontario, just a few miles south of Owen Sound. I had never played there before, and I remember how strangely everybody looked at me when I began to plaster "Stompin' Tom" signs all over their hotel windows. The signs were very colourful, and I guess they thought a small circus had just arrived in town.

Their lounge was kind of small and even though they had no ad in the paper for me, I didn't have any trouble filling it. I was only thirty-five miles away from Port Elgin and Southampton, where I knew a lot of people, and a short visit one afternoon to let them know I was playing in the area soon brought them over in force. Before the week was out, I even had a visit from Irene and Merv Marshall, who had driven all the way from Peterborough. I guess when somebody drives two hundred miles just to take in your show, you can really say you have some good fans. Especially, when they just took in your show a week earlier.

For the next couple of weeks, I was in the Dorchester Hotel in Collingwood. That's where I wrote "Around the Bay and Back Again." It's a song which names most of the major towns around Georgian Bay. And in Collingwood, which is known for ship-building, it really went over well.

It was also here that I wrote a song about a big party that went on one night at the Chapmans' place on Firestone Road in Etobicoke. It named a lot of people who were at the party and was really funny. I never did record it, as I thought it might prove to be a little embarrassing to some of the people who were there. But I did sing it one night when a bunch of them walked into the

Dorchester Hotel to surprise me. It was they who got the surprise. For as I caught a glimpse of them coming in the door, I started singing the song. You can imagine the looks on their faces as I was mentioning all their names. They had no idea in the world that I had the song written, and here I was telling the world what had happened at a private party they had all been to. They took it all with good humour, though, as they knew the audience had no idea the people I was singing about were them.

When I finished up in Collingwood, I went back to the Chapmans to wait for another call from my agent and just sort of rest up. I'd been on the hotel circuit now for quite a while and figured a little pause might do me good. We did have to have a few more parties, though, so everybody they knew could get to hear the "Firestone Road Song."

I wasn't back in Toronto very long when my new record album was finally ready. At first, I was very happy to get the news and I beat my way across town to see Mr. Irvin so I could get my hands on some.

He gave me a dozen "free ones" and then sent me to the distributor to buy some more. In the meantime, he said he was happy to announce that he was setting up another recording session for me, and of course, he got me to sign another bunch of songs over to his publishing company. (As I said before, these were just two more moves I would live to regret.)

Anyway, I was delighted at the time to be able to buy about two hundred copies of my new album and I couldn't wait to get them home to show Reg and Muriel. They were both very happy for me, and one of the first things Reg wanted to do was take me and a copy of my new album to show to a guy he worked with that I really had one. The guy was apparently one of those types who wouldn't believe that some guy that Reg had once met at a bootlegging joint could possibly have the talent to ever put out an album of songs.

When we got to the guy's house, his record player was

in the basement. And shortly after his wife put the record on, he disappeared to some other part of the house and didn't return until his wife invited us upstairs for sandwiches.

When it was time to go, I went down to get the record. And for some reason, I decided to take it out of its jacket and check it. It was cracked three-quarters of the way through and almost fell in two pieces when I handled it. I went back upstairs and asked what happened to it, but no one seemed to know.

I had a very good idea that Reg's so-called friend had been the culprit, but as I didn't actually see him, I had no real proof that he did it. Had I known for sure, I think I would have killed him. Outside of Reg and Muriel, they were the first people to ever have a listen to it.

I've heard of people being jealous before, but to do something so low as to break a guy's first record, especially after he's waited for so many years to get one, is downright despicable.

Researching the Black Donnellys

In a day or two, when most of Reg's friends and relatives had heard the new album, I decided to take it down to Port Credit and play it for Donnie and Winnie Wortman, a couple I'd met through Bud Roberts. After listening to the album and talking about it for a while, our conversation turned to some books we were reading. Donnie knew I liked writing songs about Canadian events, and he asked me if I had ever read about the notorious Black Donnellys of Lucan, Ontario, who were massacred by a group of vigilantes in 1880, and if I had ever considered writing a song about them.

I told him how Pete Ens of Port Elgin had introduced me to the story and after reading a couple of books, I was very interested in writing a song. But before writing it I would like the opportunity to do a little research of my own. Up until now, I just never had the opportunity, nor could I find the time. "Well, what about now?" said Donnie, and that was all it took. In five minutes we were in my station wagon and off for the hundred-mile trip to Lucan.

We arrived about 1 o'clock in the afternoon and by 2 o'clock we had discovered that nobody in town would even give us any directions, let alone stop and talk about the affair. All we had to do was mention the word "Donnellys" and people would just clam up and walk away.

Then it occurred to us that we might be able to kill two birds with one stone. We spotted the Central Hotel, and as it was a very hot day, we decided to go in for a couple of drafts. While we were in there, we thought, surely we could find someone who knew something about the Donnellys and would be willing to tell us where to find the old homestead and the graveyard where they were buried.

No such luck. While we were asking for a beer, we made the mistake of saying something about the

Donnellys. And we just never got the beer, never mind the information we were seeking. After waiting for about ten minutes, and again trying to get the waiter's attention, it soon became obvious that he was ignoring us. When Donnie finally got up and went over to him, all he said was, "Just a minute, I'll be there when I can."

After another ten minutes of watching other people receiving their second beer since we had ordered our first, I got up and went to talk to the bartender. When he saw me coming, he went to the back and stayed there for as long as he could. When he saw that I had no intention of leaving, he came out and asked me what I wanted. When I asked him why there was such a great delay in service, he apologized and said he would send the waiter over right away. Well, from that day till this, we're still waiting. Once we saw people getting served their third beer since we had ordered our first one, we got up and walked out.

Now we decided to just go looking through the countryside to see if we could recognize any landmarks. As we came to a sign which indicated we had found the old Roman Line, where the Donnellys once lived, a guy in a delivery truck was just slowing down to make a turn. When he came to a stop, I jumped out and asked him if he knew anything about the Donnellys and why it was that everybody around these parts didn't want to talk about them.

Well, it so happened that he knew quite a bit, and he didn't mind telling us. But then again, he wasn't from Lucan. He was from another town "just down the road a piece."

After telling us approximately how far down the Roman Line we'd have to go before we came to the old Donnelly place, and explaining how we might recognize it, he then told us that we were standing beside the old church they used to go to "and the graveyard where they were all buried is right over there."

We looked in the direction he was pointing and saw a

small cemetery with a large gate. We could see it had a chain and a padlock hanging from it, and the entire length of the fence was strung with strands of barbed wire.

"That's a strange way to keep a graveyard," I said. "It looks rather sinister."

The delivery man looked at me. "Sinister?" he said. "If you ask me, there's always been a lot of 'sinister' things around here. Seems to me that's why people don't want to talk about the Donnellys. They're superstitious, you know. Every time a barn burns down around here, it's still blamed on the Donnellys, or their descendants. And as far as that graveyard goes, I understand there's been so much vandalism in there they've had to take the Donnelly gravestone out, and nobody's allowed in without some kind of official permission."

Just as he said that, I noticed a little metal sign attached to one of the fence posts. It read, "Keep Out," and a few other smaller words I couldn't decipher.

"Well, I got to be going now," the delivery man said. And when he pulled away, he finished with, "Besides, this isn't the best spot in the world to be hanging around for an afternoon chat."

Before I could ask him what he meant by that, he was gone. When we got back in the station wagon, I said, "Well, what do you think, Donnie? If we can't go into the graveyard, the least we can do is go down and see the old Donnelly place."

By the time we found it and looked over the remains of the old foundations, I began to have some other ideas. As we were driving back towards the church, I said to Donnie, "Let's take another good look at that graveyard on the way by and see if there's not some way we can get in. I hate like hell to drive another hundred miles back home without seeing it."

Donnie agreed. And when we got back and found no good entry spot along the road, we decided to park the station wagon, walk right in the churchyard and jump over the only part of the fence that had no barbed wire.

Once inside, we moved fast, and it didn't take us long to find the Donnelly marker. But the guy in the delivery truck was right. It wasn't the original tall marker that had been described in the books I'd read. Instead, it was a low white-granite stone, which contained the names of the murdered Donnelly family members, but the word "Murdered" had been omitted.

Several other stones nearby bore the names of members of the "vigilantes" who had been responsible for the killings. And as my mind began to wander back to that horrible night of butchery, in February of 1880, a shouting voice quickly brought me back to the present. A police cruiser had pulled up behind my station wagon, and the officer was now demanding what it was we thought we were doing in the cemetery. Explaining that I was a songwriter doing a little research on the Donnellys didn't seem to cut any grass. "Where's your paper of authorization?" he demanded.

"We don't have one," I said, "but we didn't think there was any harm in coming into an ordinary graveyard to look at a few stones."

"The 'harm' is in jumping over a fence that is clearly marked with signs of 'no admittance,'" he said. "Now get off these premises immediately before I decide to run you in."

With that, we were quickly out of there, into the station wagon and gone.

"What a strange place that was," we agreed, as we drove down the highway. "Since when is it a federal offence to enter a graveyard in the middle of a quiet afternoon?" That's all we talked about on the way home. But the whole business didn't hurt my resolve to write a song. As a matter of fact, I wrote two. "The Black Donnelly Massacre" and "Jenny Donnelly," the latter song about old Jim Donnelly's only daughter. She married a man from St. Thomas, Ontario, before the family massacre took place and was therefore spared from becoming one of the victims.

Arriving back at Donnie's that night, we related our daily experiences to Winnie. Then, after we had a couple of beers and a lunch, I headed back home to the Chapmans'. While I was having a beer with Reg, he told me the Old Time Fiddling Contest was starting in Shelburne that weekend and expressed a desire to go. "You can count me in on that one," I said, and before we hit the sack, we had our plans made for Saturday.

The Shelburne Fiddling Contest was a great place to go in those days. Everybody came from miles around. They came in cars, trucks and jeeps and jalopies, and pulled everything from trailers to wigwams on wheels. There were even those who still travelled by horse and wagon. You just pulled into a great big field and squatted your gear in any place you found a spot. First come, first served.

Everywhere you wandered, somebody was playing a fiddle and a host of other instruments. Inside, while the contest was going on, people were step-dancing on the stage, and outside they were step-dancing on sheets of plywood.

When Reg and I arrived, we just parked the station wagon, grabbed my guitar and a case of twenty-four beers and headed for where the music was the loudest. Everywhere there was a gathering, I'd stop and sing a few songs. And when we weren't drinking someone else's beer, they were drinking ours.

Somewhere in the middle of this big fracas, we ran into a guy by the name of Elwood Hill. He was running the big stage shows at Rockhill Park, Ontario, and was due to bring in Hank Snow to play in the very near future. Tonight, he was just roaming around listening to some of the stray talent, and when he heard me sing and play, he asked me if I'd like to appear as a guest on the Hank Snow show.

As I was always leery of guys pretending to be "Music-Biz Big Shots" around small town performers, I said I'd like to play on the show, gave him Reg's phone number and thought no more about it. When the party finally settled down to a dull roar, and we decided to head for home, Reggie happened to mention it again. "Ah! Don't be taken in by those guys," I said. "They're always around at all the jamborees, making themselves look like big-time operators. The guy probably hasn't got two cents to rub together and just wants people to think he's important."

But two days later, this Hill guy called Reg's place and asked for me. He told me I was on the Hank Snow show for sure, and that I should be at Rockhill Park on the afternoon of the nineteenth of August, the night of the show, for further instructions. And what professional name, if any, did I go by when I was performing? He wanted to include it in the newspaper ads.

When I hung up the phone and told everybody what Hill had said, I still didn't believe it. "The guy is some kind of a prankster," I said, "and he's just looking to get more people out to attend the show. In Shelburne, that night, he probably told a hundred guys like me that he'd put them on the show, just to get them and their families to come out and spend their money. The guy that's really running the show is probably paying him a couple of bucks per head for every 'dupe-customer' he brings in."

A few days later, I had to eat my words. An envelope came in the mail with a newspaper clipping in it. Between Reg saying, "I told you, Tom" and Muriel saying, "Oh my God! That's wonderful!" I had a hard time reading the ad.

In big bold letters, it said, "HANK SNOW and the Rainbow Ranch Boys. Appearing August 19th at ROCKHILL PARK."

In smaller letters, just below the words Also Appearing were a number of other names. And at the very bottom of the list, I almost choked up when I read the words, "And Special Guest Star, Stompin' Tom Connors."

Publisher's Note

This is where Tom has chosen to end the account of the first thirty-one years of his life. He is now writing the second half of his autobiography. In it, we expect to learn how Tom was able to capture the big-city audiences of Toronto and other major centres with his songs and stories about rural Canada, how he formed his own record company, starred in his own movie and television series, and won all the Juno awards that he eventually sent back.

We will hear about his various disagreements with the media and the music industry. And Tom will also write about meeting the Queen and other dignitaries, and tell us how he and his wife, Lena, became the first Canadian couple to be married on national television.

So stay tuned for all this and many more insights in the ongoing saga of Stompin' Tom.

Discography

Northland's Zone (1967)

The World Goes Around
Maritime Waltz
Northern Gentlemen
Movin' On To Rouyn
May, The Millwright's Daughter
Algoma Central No. 69
Emily The Maple Leaf
Goin' Back Up North
Streets Of Toronto
My Home Cradled Out In The Waves
The Peterborough Postman
Carolyne
Sudbury Saturday Night
Little Wawa
My Swisha Miss
The Flying C.P.R.

On Tragedy Trail (1968)

Tragedy Trail
How The Mountain Came Down
Shanty Town Sharon
Fire In The Mine
Somewhere There's Sorrow
Don Valley Jail
Benny The Bum
Black Donnelly's Massacre
Battle Of Despair
Reesor Crossing Tragedy
Little Boy's Prayer
Around The Bay And Back Again

Bud The Spud (1969)

Bud The Spud
The Ketchup Song
Ben, In The Pen
Rubberhead
Luke's Guitar (Twang, Twang)
My Brother Paul
The Old Atlantic Shore
My Little Eskimo
Reversing Falls Darling
She Don't Speak English
The Canadian Lumber Jack
Sudbury Saturday Night
T.T.C. Skidaddler
(I'll Be) Gone With The Wind

Merry Christmas Everybody (1970)

Merry Christmas Everybody
Merry Bells
Christmas Angel
Down On Christmas
Jingle Jangled Aeroplane
Kiss Me The New Year In
Mr. Snowflake
Story of Jesus
An Orphan's Christmas
One Blue Light
Gloria
Our Father

Stompin' Tom Connors Meets Big Joe Mufferaw (1970)

Big Joe Mufferaw
Sable Island
Don't Overlove Your Baby
Log Train
Roll On Saskatchewan
Jenny Donnelly
The Coal Boat Song
Algoma Central No. 69
The Night That I Cremated Sam McGee
Poor, Poor Farmer
My Last Farewell
Rocky Mountain Love
Around The Bay And Back Again

Stompin' Tom Connors Live At The Horseshoe (1971)

Happy Rovin' Cowboy
Big Joe Mufferaw
Come Where We're At
The Green, Green Grass Of Home No. 2
Spin, Spin
Muleskinner Blues
Horseshoe Hotel Song
I've Been Everywhere
Sudbury Saturday Night
Bus Tour To Nashville
Luke's Guitar aka Twang, Twang
Bud The Spud

Stompin' Tom And The Hockey Song (1972)

The Consumer
The Last Fatal Duel
The Curse Of The Marc Guylaine
Blue Spell
Singin' Away My Blues
The Hockey Song
The Maritime Waltz
Gaspe Belle Faye
Where Would I Be?
True, True Love
The Piggy Back Race
Your Loving Smile
Mr. Engineer

Stompin' Tom And
The Moon-Man Newfie (1973)

Oh Laura
Isles Of Magdalene
Fire In The Mine
I Can Still Face The Moon
The Bug Song
The Moon-Man Newfie
Roving All Over The Land
Movin' In (From Montreal By Train)
Benny The Bum
Twice As Blue
Little Wawa
Rubber Head

STOMPIN' TOM: Before the Fame

My Stompin' Grounds (1971)

My Stompin' Grounds
The Bridge Came Tumblin' Down
Snowmobile Song
"Wop" May
Cross Canada
Tillsonburg
Tribute To Wilf Carter
Song Of The Irish Moss
Song Of The Peddler
Bonnie Belinda
Name The Capital
Song Of The Cohoe

To It And At It (1973)

Prince Edward Island, Happy Birthday
To It And At It
Keepin' Nora Waitin'
Marten Hartwell Story
New Brunswick And Mary
Moonlight Lady
Muk Luk Shoo
Manitoba
Don Messer Story
Alcan Run
Pizza Pie Love
Golden Gone Bye
Cornflakes

Stompin' Tom Meets Muk Tuk Annie (1974)

Streaker's Dream
My Home By The Fraser
Bibles And Rifles
Paddle Wheeler
Unfaithful Heart
Ballad of Muk Tuk Annie
We're Trading Hearts
Oh Chihuahua
Zakuska Polka
I Saw The Teardrop
Wishful Hummin'
Renfrew Valley
My Old Canadian Home

The North Atlantic Squadron and Other Favourites (1975)

The North Atlantic Squadron
Red River Jane
High, Dry and Blue
Blue Nose
Back Yardin'
Jack Of Many Trades
Unity
Fleur De Lis
I'll Love You All Over Again
(Too Late To Hurry) When The Snow Flurries Fall
Take Me Down The River
Gypsy Chant

STOMPIN' TOM: Before the Fame

The Unpopular Stompin' Tom (1976)
Good Morning, Mr. Sunshine
Where The Chinooks Blow
Zephyrs In The Maple
My Door Is Always Open To You
Blue Misery
The Pole And The Hole
Damn Good Song For A Miner aka Muckin' Slushers
Cowboy Johnny Ware
Ghost of Bras D'Or
Don Valley Jail
Big And Friendly Waiter John
Olympic Song

At the Gumboot Cloggeroo (1977)
Legend of Marty & Joe
Jaqueline
Handy Man Blues
Man From The Land
Farewell To Nova Scotia
Ripped Off Winkle
Gumboot Cloggeroo
Happy Hooker
We Doubt Each Other's Love
Old Forgetful Me
The Singer
Isle Of Newfoundland
Roses In The Snow
Home On The Island

Fiddle and Song (1989)

Lady, k.d. lang
Fiddler's Folly
It's All Over Now, Anyhow
The French Song
I Never Want To See The World Again
Hillside Hayride
Morning & Evening & Always
Return Of The Sea Queen
Canada Day, Up Canada Way
Jolly Joe MacFarland
Skinner's Pond Teapot
Teardrop Waltz
Entry Island Home
I Am The Wind
Wreck Of The Tammy Anne

More of the Stompin' Tom Phenomenon (1991)

Margo's Cargo
Flyin' C.P.R.
Rita MacNeil (A Tribute)
Brown Eyes For The Blues
J.R.'s Bar
Loser's Island
St. Anne's Song And Reel
Made In The Shade
Love's Not The Only Thing
Land Of The Maple Tree
A Real Canadian Girl
Okanagan Okee
No Canadian Dream
(I'll Be) Gone With The Wind

A Proud Canadian—Compilation—(1990)

Bud The Spud
Snowmobile Song
Roll On Saskatchewan
Manitoba
Sudbury Saturday Night
Tillsonburg
Roving All Over The Land
New Brunswick and Mary
Big Joe Mufferaw
Gumboot Cloggeroo
The Old Atlantic Shore
Blue Nose
Fleur De Lis
The Moon-Man Newfie
The Ketchup Song
Lady k.d. lang
The Bridge Came Tumblin' Down
Marten Hartwell Story
I Am The Wind
The Singer (The Voice Of The People)

Once Upon A Stompin' Tom—Compilation—(1991)

Canada Day, Up Canada Way
The Ketchup Song
Zephyrs In The Maple
The Piggy Back Race
The Hockey Song
Cornflakes
Song of the Cohoe
C-A-N-A-D-A (Cross Canada)
Name The Capitals
Little Wawa
Moon-Man Newfie
The Olympic Song
"Wop" May
Unity

Believe In Your Country (1992)
Johnny Maple
My Home Cradled Out In The Waves
Prairie Moon
She Called From Montreal
Lover's Lake
Lena Kathleen
Believe In Your Country
Alberta Rose
Sunshine & Teardrops
My Sleeping Carmello
Lookin' For Someone To Hold
Paper Smile
Smile Away Your Memory
The Ballinafad Ball

Dr. Stompin' Tom...Eh? (1993)
Football Song
Horse Called Farmer
Road To Thunder Bay
Your Someone Lonesome
Just A Blue Moon Away
Old Flat-Top Guitar
Honeymoon Is Over Poochie Pie
Canada Day, Up Canada Way
Blue Berets
Let's Smile Again
Suzanne De Lafayette
Gumboot Cloggeroo
Shakin' The Blues

Kic* Along With Stompin' Tom—Compilation—(1993)

The Hockey Song
To It And At It
The Coal Boat Song
Margo's Cargo
Luke's Guitar (Twang, Twang)
Muckin' Slushers (A Damn Good Song For A Miner)
Handy-Man Blues
Song Of The Irish Moss
Wreck Of The Tammy Anne
Black Donnelly's Massacre
Jenny Donnelly
Tribute To Wilf Carter
Zakuska Polka
Red River Jane
The Consumer
Muk Luk Shoo
Okanagan Okee
Rita MacNeil (A Tribute)
Don Messer Story
Believe In Your Country

Long Gone To The Yukon (1995)

Long Gone To The Yukon
Al Sass and Dee John
Case Closed
How Do You Like It Now?
Country Jack (aka Wino Of Skid Row)
Kitchen Show
Maple Leaf Waltz
Polka Playin' Henry
Broken Wings
I'll Dream You Back
My Home's In Newfoundland
Song Bird Valley
All Night Cafe Blues
No, No, No
Hey, Hey, Loretta
I'll Do It For You
Mrs. Blue Guitar

STOMPIN' TOM: Before the Fame

Sound Tracks Canada—Compilation—(1996)
A Real Canadian Girl
My Home Cradled Out In The Waves
Prairie Moon
She Called From Montreal
The Flyin' C.P.R.
Suzanne De Lafayette
We're Trading Hearts
Shanty Town Sharon
Sable Island
"Wop" May
Canada Day, Up Canada Way
The Bug Song
Football Song
Alberta Rose
Manitoba
Road to Thunder Bay
Fire in the Mine
May, The Millwrights Daughter
Algoma Central No. 69
Maple Leaf Waltz
Where the Chinooks Blow
My Home's In Newfoundland